LIFE IN THE CRACKS

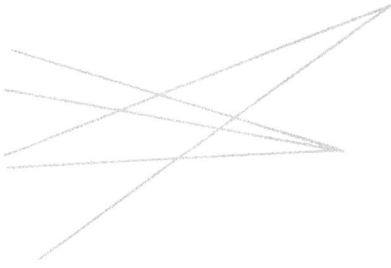

THINKING FROM ELSEWHERE

LIFE IN THE CRACKS

Law, Violence, and Resistance in Haiti

MARCO MOTTA

FORDHAM UNIVERSITY PRESS NEW YORK 2026

Published with the support of the Swiss National Science Foundation.

Visit us online at www.fordhampress.com.

For EU safety / GPSR concerns: Mare Nostrum Group B.V., Mauritskade 21D, 1091 GC Amsterdam, The Netherlands, gpsr@mare-nostrum.co.uk

Library of Congress Cataloging-in-Publication Data available online at https://catalog.loc.gov.

ISBN-13: 978-1531512446 (cloth); 978-1531512453 (paperback)

DOI: https://doi.org/10.5422/SNSF/2316

Printed in the United States of America

28 27 26   5 4 3 2 1

First edition

CONTENTS

Cast of Characters vi

Prologue xi

Introduction 1

1 "We're Holding On!": A Chronicle 39

2 The Silent Wars of the Ordinary 66

3 The Many Faces of Peace 92

4 Theatricalizing the Law 130

5 Inner Forms of Corrosion 156

6 The Murmuring Stream of Life 187

Acknowledgments 225

Acronyms 231

Glossary 235

Notes 237

References 263

Index 287

CAST OF CHARACTERS

All personal names are pseudonyms, as is the name of the main commune (Bouquet-Duvoisin), and the neighborhood (Bwa-Mapou), where the research took place.

Artémis family

Angeline	Frédéric's wife and mother of Anaïca and Marley; born in 1982; accountant, teacher, and housekeeper.
Frédéric	Angeline's husband and father of Anaïca, Marley, Evens, and two other children (adolescents) exiled in Miami; born in 1979; bread merchant, baker, accounting teacher; community activist.
Anaïca	Angeline and Frédéric's daughter; born in 2005; exiled in Boston since 2024.
Marley	Angeline and Frédéric's son; born in 2009.

Close kin

Evens	Frédéric's third son; born from a previous relationship in 1999.
Cherline	Angeline's sister; Artémis family's neighbor; born in 1980; housekeeper.
Robert	Angeline's uncle; born in 1965; head and owner of a private school; ex-mayor; community activist.
Régine	Robert's sister; Angeline's and Cherline's aunt; Sony's wife; *manbo*; born in 1965 and died on February 1, 2020.

Sony	Regine's husband; lived in East New York for twenty years; truck driver; has two grown children in Miami; previously married to a Sicilian woman.
Lovely	Frédéric's sister; in her late thirties.
Jim	One of Frédéric's four younger brothers; in his late thirties.
Danley	Frédéric's cousin; barber; died in his late twenties, shot dead.
Gasner	Danley's elder son; nickname "Bwa Gede."
Melodi	Danley's daughter; Gasner's sister; her left ear was severed in a bus crash; mother of a child born in 2013.
Matant mwen	Frédéric's aunt; Danley's mother and Gasner and Melodi's grandmother; lives alone in the Jacmel Valley.

Friends

Stanley	Friend of the family; unemployed; born in the early 1990s; exiled in Atlanta since 2024.
Alix	Friend of the family; lawyer; theater practitioner; poet; born in the early 1990s.
Mesac	Retailer and photographer; Rosalvo's, Eugene's, and Rodny's cousin; born in the early 1980s; exiled in Boston since 2020.
Rodny	Stationer and retailer; photographer; secret informant for investigative police; ex-convict; Mesac's cousin; Angly's nephew; Lily's son; born in the early 1990s.
Angly	Rodny's and Mesac's uncle; Odlon's son; Brisli's father; born in the mid-1980s.
Brisli	Angly's son; born in the late 2000s.
Judy	Angly's partner; Brisli's adoptive mother.
Rénia	Activist in the Baptist church; worked in an orphanage; radio host; Adny's mother.
Adny	Rénia's son; born in 2007.
Basile	Swiss friend; anthropologist; theater practitioner; lived in Bwa-Mapou.

Active *vodouizan* in the zone

Ariel	*Oungan*; healer; specialized in dealing with conflicts.
Bois d'Eau	*Bòkò*; healer; member of the *sanpwèl* secret society.
Barbara	*Ounsi*; Bois d'Eau's daughter; Stanley's godmother; born in the late 1990s.
Mathias	*Oungan*; manages the cemetery and the Feast of the Dead; travels to Brazil to practice Vodou and invites Brazilians to Haiti.
Odlon	*Oungan*; Angly's father; Rodny's granduncle; died on February 23, 2023.
Mirlanda	Community activist; candidate in the departmental elections; Vodou practitioner.
Wilbert	Neighbor; Vodou apprentice; born in the late 1990s.

Minor characters

Malcolm	Graduate of the Faculty of Ethnology of the University of Port-au-Prince; teacher at secondary level in Robert's school; community activist.
Rosalvo	Director of a vocational school; Mesac's, Eugene's, and Rodny's cousin; exiled to Boston.
Enock Saintil	Judge at Bwa-Mapou's JP court; disbarred for five years.
Yanick La Roche	Commissioner of the government; works at the land tribunal in Saint-Marc; resident of Bwa-Mapou; nickname "Yaya."
Miracson	Chief CASEC of the zone.
Cassiodore	Known bus driver; influential person.
Kénol	Head of the local agricultural farm cooperative (*konbit peyizan*); community worker and activist.
Eugene	Owner of a local bar, club, and cinema; Rodny's, Mesac's, and Rosalvo's cousin.
Madanm Esther	Cook and owner of a small street restaurant.
Lily	Street vendor; Rodny's mother.
Fritznel	Friend of the family; born in the early 1980s; community activist.

Diego	Young man who used to harass and persecute Rodny.
Wilkens	Young man from the neighborhood; unstable and considered by many to be a *chimè*, a thug, a criminal; born in the early 1980s.

PROLOGUE

The stories recounted in this book take place in rural Haiti, mainly in the lower Artibonite Valley, in a place I name Bwa-Mapou, among the people that a certain urban elite call the *moun andeyò*, the outsiders. In 2016, four days after Hurricane Matthew destroyed the southern part of the island, and just over a month before the presidential elections that put Jovenel Moïse in power, a dear friend of mine, Basile Despland, took me to Haiti for the first time. He had lived there for a year and a half before. In collaboration with a group of young Haitians, he had helped set up a professional theatrical structure and a troupe of young actors. He taught classes, organized monthly participatory forums with villagers, and attended many *sèvis*, or Vodou services. We used to talk about all this a lot, having a shared love of anthropology, ritual, and theater. So, it was quite natural for me to follow him when he asked me if I'd like to accompany him to Haiti. I had just defended my dissertation in June. It was time to open new horizons.

I was lucky enough to be funded by the Swiss National Science Foundation (SNSF) to carry out in-depth ethnographic work between 2016 and 2021, which corresponds quite precisely to the Jovenel Moïse quinquennium (I'll come back to this in the Introduction). At the time, the overall objective was to understand social conflict at the crossroads of state and nonstate justice within everyday life in a so-called postcolonial context. My goals were to investigate how state law partly constitutes, and is constituted by, extrajudicial normative practices, and to account for different forms of legitimate and illicit violence and their entanglement. While this has remained central, things have changed too, as we shall see. These five years of research finally gave rise to this book.

At the heart of every book is a question of the choice of words. Of course, one doesn't choose every word. Certain words choose us, spring to mind and leave a lasting mark on the page; others are slips, unwanted. And they mean more than what we want them to mean, than what we intend. That is precisely why I'm responsible for them, for making their meaning intelligible. What better way to do this than to describe my relationship with them, to try to express why some of them matter? That's what I'd like to do in this Prologue, by making explicit the choice of words in my title.

■ ■ ■

As it happens, the title of my book came to me in the field when I was re-reading, as I struggled to find sleep in the sweltering humidity of summer evenings under the metal sheets of a roof that had been overheating all day, Henri Michaux's poetry collection *Life in the Folds* (2016). *Life in the Cracks* is a variation on the title he gave to his poems, written in the aftermath of WWII and his wife's death. His book is a text for a recovery that takes the form of a violent combat with itself, a fight within the twists, the bends, and the recesses. It is a devised refusal to abdicate in the face of a world in ruins. While it's obvious that his text is a tomb for his wife and a way of burying the hatchet of the war, it can also be read as the violent mourning of an ideal: His painful realization that there has never been, so to speak, a fully grown and formed world. It only comes in splinters, bits, and rubble, and is always to be grown and reformed. The energy that springs from this awareness is upthrust: It is indicative of something that rises up. While he does indeed stand up and fight, it must also be recognized that what makes him do so is not, and perhaps cannot, be determined; there's nothing really to point at. What there is, rather, is a swarming in the realm of the possible. He hears it and lets himself be traversed by its peculiar force. This is why one should not be misled by his willfulness and the strength of his turbulent voice. He's as much passive: He yields to the impulse of life itself when it yearns for movement, passage, and flow, even more so when it is blocked, threatened, congested, plastered, or petrified. With a gigantic kind of force, condensed in very small and repetitive acts, life nonetheless pushes on "by the way of rhythm" (*Par la voie des rythmes* is another of his book titles). The narrative and descriptive fragments in the chapters that follow bear the trace of this attention to the way in which life insists, sometimes violently, or despite the violence, independently of human will. Reading Michaux in Bwa-Mapou awakened my sense of how life follows its course, nonetheless, taking the blows, suffering the jolts and twitches of the ordinary, struggling in the turmoil, seeking to respond to the syncopations, one way or another.

What I call "life in the cracks" are these unexpected moments and places of life where something decisive happens and spurs a change: a variation of tone in the voice, an ill-received joke, a disdainful handshake, an improvised parody of one's own role, a caring hand on the shoulder, an absence of reply, the terrified look in a child's eyes. It is life in the interstices, as it were, life in the blanks, in the silences. These are moments, often tiny and unforeseen, when something significant is played out. Most of the time, they have nothing to do with the law, but it happens that sometimes they in fact do. And when they do, they are critical to the issues at stake. Yet, they are not moments of argumentation, decision-making, deliberation, or judgment, but they can bear a crucial relation with arguments or judgments. They are of particular weight, but not always perceived as such; they can be ignored or denied when our attention remains exclusively focused on what we believe a priori to be related to the law. Yet, if we are receptive to them, they can completely change the way we perceive a problem and thus respond.

My proposal in this book is to look at the law through life in the cracks. This means to change the prism through which law is studied. But before I say more about this, I'd like to say a few words about what motivates my questioning and critical rereading of certain traditions of thought. It has four main sources. First and foremost, the pressure comes from the people I've met and lived with in Haiti. By this I mean that I'm concerned above all with what concerns them on a daily basis, and not just when they're involved in litigation. The descriptions in my chapters will show the great diversity of these concerns, and, consequently, the difficulties encountered by the type of anthropology I am calling for. Second, the incentive came from professionals in the legal field (clerks, bailiffs, judges, lawyers, court janitors, commissioners, prosecutors, professors, and law students), with whom I had the opportunity to rub shoulders, with whom I conversed a lot, and whom I saw at work. Their more specific preoccupations, although linked to daily life, are also rooted in certain conceptions of law and justice that I cannot fail to address if I am to highlight the many ways in which the law lives in Haiti. Third, I was struck and provoked by the gigantic mass of documents of all kinds produced by legal scholars, policymakers, and political scientists, who regard the rule of law as a positive achievement, a desirable device of governance, when they are not outright overenthusiastic promoters of it. Fourth, I am of course also prompted to respond to what some of my colleagues in anthropology have written, particularly those interested, in one way or another, in law and politics.

■ ■ ■

Why did the law come to the forefront of my concerns in this book? I mentioned above that I had just defended my dissertation when I went for the first time to Haiti. In fact, I had just completed a decade-long research about how, in poor neighborhoods of Zanzibar City, spirits intervene in human affairs, sometimes as allies, sometimes as adversaries. If my initial interest was in the theatricality of therapeutic ritual devices, I soon came to realize that one can't understand what goes on in the ritual if one doesn't know what life is like outside rituals. Eventually, I became interested in how spirits are inherent to ordinary life, and that ordinary life is not in opposition to ritual—on the contrary, they are co-constitutive. Hence, I began to see that spirits were not only crucial actors in therapeutics, but also mediators in all kinds of contentions between neighbors, relatives, and friends, as I would later discover was also the case in Haiti. So, I finished my dissertation with the idea in mind that it would be interesting to take a closer look at the role played by spirits in conflicts, whether in triggering, in mediation, regulation, judgment, or punishment; and thus, in a way, their role in what might be called extrajudicial justice, which in Kiswahili is called "*sheria mkononi*," the "law in one's hands." This was my first incentive for a new research project on unofficial law. And as the SNSF was funding a project in Haiti and not Zanzibar, I ended up launching it in Bwa-Mapou.

My second motivation came from my discovery, right from the start, that the main targets of UN reform policies in Haiti since the fall of the Duvalier dictatorship have been the judiciary, the police, and to a lesser extent, the penitentiary system. This was accompanied by a relentless promotion of the rule of law. But why? Of course, it's no coincidence; but what exactly is the content of the argument? What is the ideology conveyed by those who defend the rule of law? And above all, what are the effects on the ground? I couldn't fail to be interested, especially given that, the further I got into it, the more I realized the impact it would have on everyday life. Indeed, the last links in the judicial and administrative chain—the peace courts and the municipalities, both of which are also the state's first point of contact for the rural population—are partly determined by the intervention of international actors. However, they are also partly determined by unofficial local ways of dealing with certain issues. This is the point at which we can see a mutual and conflicting absorption of state and nonstate law. And this porous yet rough contact zone is of particular interest to me as an anthropologist, since not only is it precisely here that the stakes are revealed, but it also is from here that we can question more conventional conceptions of law.

If we take a brief look at what underpins the discourse and practices of many professionals and those who view the rule of law in a positive, uncritical light, we see that it is based on a number of presuppositions that I'd like briefly to lay bare. There is in fact a certain theoretical tendency to regard law as something universal (even if culturally specific) that then applies to particular cases, something relatively stable (in its codified form), and an autonomous abstraction above everyday life (since it is supposed to be uninfluenced by worldly matters and applicable to all with authority). What's more, the idea of the rule of law goes hand in hand with the idea that the law is generally coherent, clear, and predictable (which is why some people optimistically imagine that the law can in fact resolve some of our problems). This implies, or presupposes, the idea that purportedly "lawless" societies are, on the contrary, unstable, incoherent, opaque, dangerous, and unpredictable. Whatever the tradition, say Hobbesian or Kantian, on which such a conception of law rests, its ideological foundation is that human beings need to be limited, I mean *juridically* limited. In the first tradition, the aim is to avoid a war of all against all while consolidating the power of a sovereign. In the second, it's about preventing reason from going astray and ensure freedom. In both cases, what must be avoided at all costs is lawlessness, because without legal limitations, human behavior would be totally arbitrary and lead to chaos, chaos to violence, and violence to tyranny. According to this perspective, laws are needed to arbitrate human behavior and contain the unreasonable excesses of reason.

Such a conception structures a distorted vision of the place of law in our lives. Indeed, it does not account for what the people I met in Haiti think and experience, nor for the issues raised by anthropology. Hence, as a response, I suggest instead to consider, not the law per se, but the most unexpected inflections within ordinary life. And this is not just a question of taking a close look, as others have been doing for a long time and with good reason, at how law is put into practice and used by the people, as opposed to works that focus on how law is fabricated by the legislators. In my view, it is also, and above all, about *not* taking the law, its applications, and its uses, *for granted*. On closer examination, not only is it unclear whether a law applies or not—and if it does, how—since the law and its applications are to some extent indeterminate; but it's not always a question of the uses of law. What's more, we realize that we do not know in advance where crucial issues will emerge that will relate, in one way or another, to the law. Indeed, what are we missing if we are too insistent and too narrowly focused on the law, whatever its manifestations? Being attentive to life in the cracks makes us available to other layers of complexities. It's an anthropology that has ordinary ethics and aesthetics instead of law as its focal point. The law is henceforth approached obliquely, so to speak.

Now, of course, there are the expected places to examine the law: litigations, courts, parliaments, codes, complaint letters, jurisprudence, conciliations, prisons, customs, and so on. And there are the now common fields of inquiry: human rights, international finance, domestic violence, human trafficking, indigeneity, asylum, or gender inequality. I am not disputing these, and I am interested in them, too. My approach is as valid for the studies of tribunals or activist movements or parliamentary deliberations, for instance, as for any other kind of human relationship. That said, in these cases, we take too much for granted where the law applies; it's a little too obvious that a legal anthropologist will work, say, on transitional justice, anti-terrorist laws, or alternative dispute resolutions. But even more than that, we take too much for granted that the question is one of the law's applicability—let's say, its uses, which include questions about procedures, processes, agency, settlements, dynamic reconfiguration of power relations, forms of subjectivation, etc. The challenge seems to me to be this: To stop considering the question of the law's applicability as central, in order to redirect our attention to all those moments and places that our obsession with the law's applicability causes us to miss.

There's a poetic sensitivity to anthropology here, I'd say, that shouldn't be overlooked—a sensitivity to the tiny, overlooked events that nevertheless make up the texture of human life.

■ ■ ■

Delving deeper into questions of law has inevitably led me to think about violence, and at different levels. On the level of the official and international narrative promoting the rule of law, Haiti is portrayed, in the lexicon of the United Nations, as a "failed" state. This is so, according to the narrative, because of Haiti's endemic violence. Consequently, Haiti is considered unable to become an orderly democracy precisely because of the violence inscribed in its culture. The cliché often naturalizes this supposedly culturally inscribed violence, making it appear as an irrefutable argument. But let's be clear: These are powerful and particularly perverse rhetorical devices designed to mask the production of violence by the very organizations that hold these discourses. I will show in what way they serve to legitimize military and civil intervention by delegitimizing the local population's claims. In fact, they justify the occupation of Haiti, thereby favoring the interests of corporations, mostly North American, to the detriment of the local communities' own interests. That's why this book sets out to unpack the contradiction at the heart of the rule of law: While ideologically the rule of law is understood as the means to limit violence and guarantee the stability necessary for democratic governance, in practice it is itself also the producer of the violence it aims to combat.

On the level of the everyday life, violence is multifaceted. The multiplicity of its forms will become apparent as the chapters, hence the context, unfold. It would make no sense to start to list these forms or characterize them now. What I want to emphasize is that from the point of view of life in the cracks, violence, whatever its form, never appears as an isolated, isolable event. On the contrary, it's there, interwoven, pervasive, diffuse, inscribed in the ordinary course of existence, sometimes barely palpable, sometimes spectacular, often muffled and present in the shadows, pulsing in the background like an eventuality ready to emerge. That's because it's inherent to an ordinary life that's been weakened from the outset—by which I mean, ever since settlers decided to bring in slaves after massacring the natives—by a national and international context that has at best maintained, if not aggravated, a state of great vulnerability to violence. Yet, ordinary life is both the place where violence is expressed and where care and recovery take place. Looking at violence from the point of view of the cracks means paying attention to the refraction of violence in everyday life, rather than being a spectator at its spectacle. And this reverberation can be felt in a collective prayer to thank the Lord for being still alive; in watching children stone a snake between two games; in observing a woman helping a drunk trapped in a coffin under construction; in dancing with toddlers to music accompanied by teenage gunfire; by noticing the disappearance of a judge just when the community needs him most; by holding the hand of a child who freezes in front of a door where he has seen a man lynched to death; or by hearing the silence of a mother who grits her teeth and swallows her condition to preserve her children. These moments, and many others, reveal forms of violence, the genealogy of which I'm going to trace in some cases. They also reveal what it is and what it takes to resist, to be solid enough to keep going in a world so often contrary to one's aspirations.

■ ■ ■

I hesitated for a long time to include in the title the word "resistance," so laden with the weight of a certain vision of history. The word seemed important for many reasons that will become clear throughout the book, but I was wary of using it thoughtlessly. Indeed, it raised a number of questions that I no longer want to avoid.

Three moments made me see clearly why "resistance" should be one of the threads that weave together the descriptions of these lives lived in the cracks that I offer in the book. The first was when Mirlanda, a friend in Haiti, told me, "Europeans say we're resilient, but we Haitians say we're resistant!" What's condensed in this sentence is enormous. I'd like to make just two points: On the one hand, the discourse on Haitian resilience is an exogenous discourse that most Haitians I know reject, and which serves above all to bolster a certain liberal vision of the subject (which itself serves the victimizing humanitarian policies so problematic in the region). On the other hand, the fact that most of the Haitians I've known themselves speak of their daily acts as acts of resistance—the very fact of continuing to live constitutes such an act—should challenge us about our ideological use of the term. Helping someone up, offering a bread roll to a pupil, giving up claiming what is owed to a person who is unable to repay a debt, bringing a bucket of water to a sick neighbor, or breastfeeding an abandoned child are not militant acts. But for the people I know, they are acts of resistance—acts of care as acts of resistance in the face of decadence. It's a micropolitics of the ordinary that may go unnoticed.

The second moment was when I realized that my friend Alix had in fact composed a poem entitled *"Rezistans"* in his first collection in Creole. I'd had my eye on it many times, as I was present at almost every stage of its composition; but I didn't realize what Alix had written until after I'd returned to Switzerland (proof that we sometimes miss something precisely because it's there, in front of our eyes, like Poe's purloined letter). I had read without reading; I hadn't listened carefully enough. Now my ear was ready and within range of Alix's voice.

Here's the poem I translated with him and with the help of writer Marie-Célie Agnant, first from Creole into French, then from French into English:

Isi ba lavi sèvi m devenn	Here on Earth life for me is but misfortune
Kòm si m te pitit manman pyan	As if I were yaws' child
Paske m te appran n lèt A	Because I've learned the letter A
Mizè rabi pote non bandi	The deepest misery is called bandit
Fè reklam simetyè	A one-way ticket to the cemetery
Anpil fwa m pran souri	Often I take a smile
Pou pansman	as a band-aid
Chak kè m ap senyen	Every heart I am bleeding
Lè solèy pa sèvi m sèvyèt	When the sun doesn't dry me out
Lang mwen souvan tounen mòp	My tongue often turns into a mop
Ki netwaye basen	that cleans the tears
Sou figi m	from my face
Pou swaf pa rayi m	So that thirst does not hate me
Wòch satiyèt zòtey mwen	The pebbles tickle my toes
Lè soulye m mande pip	when my holey shoes ask for a smoke
M pote flanbo nan panse m	I carry the torch in my mind
Pou ekri sou pachimen	To write on the parchment

M apran n akable	I learn that burdened
Pas sinonim endispoze	does not mean indisposed
Tonbe pa ti sè malkadi	The fall is not sister of epilepsy
Si se pou sa	But if it were
Tout fri mi tchimen	Every ripe fruit would drool
Pou jan mwen reziste ak chalè	My resistance to the heat is so high
Mwen ka yon bon kafetyè	I can be a good coffee pot
Yon kafetyè san mouda	A bottomless coffee pot

I take this poem to be a portrait of resistance; resistance against the heat of skeptical anxiety raised by Alix's understanding that it is not merely the world out there that has died, or is about to die, but the world in him—he carries the death of the world inside himself. When we exchanged voice messages again in December 2022 about the translation of the poem, he said, drearily: "*Rezistans* is a text that sums up my whole life, the dark moments of it. But I take care to endure."

Perhaps, if, as his model, the poet Georges Castera wrote, "The poem becomes an instrument / of percussion of daily life / an instrument of repercussion / of the days without feast nor destiny / the piece of evidence / of trials to come," (2006, 29; my translation) then Alix's poem beats the tempo of his time. It sounds to me like a measure of life in this world—*his* world—provided that we consider it as much a measure of the possibilities offered by language, *his* language. If the vocation of poetry is to bring words and the world back to life, then Alix is recovering the world with his words, breathing life into them.

The third moment was when I reread Michaux's *Life in the Folds*. With him, if humans do indeed resist, it's because reality resists too. And it so happens that reality sometimes appears as a block of oppressive, ill-intentioned obstacles. So, his war is a war against walls, vaults, floors, and ceilings. It's a never-ending battle against structures, limits, and foundations. It's a war on metaphysics, as it were, that has the look of a repeated attack on the frame—the cell. It is through poetry that Michaux resists the carceral condition of his thought, enclosed by obscure limits. His poems brought out an aspect of the concept of resistance that had hitherto been unclear to me: Resistance is simultaneously an inner resistance of thought to everything that bounds it, restricts it, compresses it, compartmentalizes it. It's a kind of cry: that of revolt, insurrection, insubordination, not so much against domination as against confinement. This resonates, as I hear it, with the cry of a certain spirit in Haiti.

Michaux's genius is in having renounced to obstruct the violent transformation life is to bring—the transfiguration of anger, outrage, and chagrin into something else. Call it pregnancy. This, too, is my sense of the sort of rebirth enacted when people ritually embody Ogou or Kalfou, the spirits of war and combat. Their dance steps ally with the crackling of the embers. "Drop your fear in the fire / Drop your tears in the fire / Watch them burn, burn," sings Dominique Fils-Aimé in "There is Probably Fire." The dancers' resistance to the heat of the flame morphs into something else. It ceases to be resistance. They end up embracing the fire, and some then become an ascending line; they become flame. This allegory says something about the heated times that Haitians are going through. Rage is exalted—transfigured. A burst of energy that has the force of a claim on life: "*nap goumen*," "we're still fighting!"; "*nap kenbe*," "we're still standing!"

Something was born within the breaches perhaps because some of the people I met in Haiti let themselves be greatly upset—upset with an intensifying expansiveness. Just look at what happens in the streets of Port-au-Prince when the people rise up, or within a household when a mother silently carries the burden of a whole family. Thinking of Haiti, there are countless reasons to be profoundly hurt and chagrined. But I also feel immeasurable gratitude for having had the chance to come into close contact with some of the most invigorating and inspiring people I've ever encountered. This book is dedicated to them.

"Stealing a march on the dawn,
I have opened the door onto the night."

—YANICK LAHENS

"the day calls
what to do with the dawn?"

—GEORGES CASTERA

"The day has barely dawned and
is already working on its night."

—JEAN-LOUIS GIOVANNONI

"Sleep lingers all our lifetime about our eyes,
as night hovers all day in the boughs of the fir-tree."

—RALPH WALDO EMERSON

INTRODUCTION

"The galley country sadly rows on the black pond
of small daily dramas."

—ANTHONY PHELPS[1]

THE FLESH OF DISCORD

Angly shows up on the front porch. It is the day after I arrived in Bwa-
Mapou. I was about to embark on my third stay, which was to last from
October 2018 to March 2019. Angly came to visit me, radio on his shoulder
and reggae on full blast. He's sweating and seems anxious. Without further
ado, he tells me that earlier in the year he spent five days in prison. An animosity with his neighbors had turned sour and escalated into open conflict.
They've had their share of disputes in recent years. While it's clear they don't
like each other, they put up with one another—until recently. Angly's version is that his neighbors despise him. He says he hasn't done anything to
them, and they're vilifying him and spreading stupid rumors. He claims
they dislike him not only because he's a Rasta, sells *kleren* (homemade rum),
and smokes ganja, but also because he has land that they're jealous of. "Did
I choose this life?" he asks me rhetorically.

One morning, he found three of his chickens dead in front of his hut.
Suspecting his neighbors, in a fit of anger he threw them beyond the pen
into the neighbors' garden, swearing. One of the neighbors replied by insulting him back. Angly realized at that moment that it really must have
been them that killed the hens, otherwise they would not have replied in
such a way. The neighbors then started throwing stones at him (he later

showed me the holes he claimed this had caused in the tin roof of his hut). He retaliated by throwing stones at them. Soon, other neighbors and passersby crowded around and tried to calm them down, but were not successful. So, people called the local CASEC, as they often do when a contention needs some arbitration. These are the members of the Board of Directors of the Communal Section. There are generally three of them per section[2]: a chief, an assistant, and a treasurer. They are the last links in the administrative chain and the first point of contact between the population and the state. Two assistants soon arrived. With the help of a passerby, they tried to subdue Angly, but to no avail. He defended himself fiercely. According to the account given to me later by Stanley, a friend and witness to the scene, the CASEC came to settle the matter amicably, but Angly was violent and reluctant to comply, whereas according to Angly, when the chief CASEC Miracson arrived, he tried to handcuff him. If they had come to settle things amicably, he wouldn't have had to defend himself; he wasn't going to let himself be handcuffed. One reason he invokes is that the CASEC are not entitled to arrest citizens, that only police and the judge are. He emphasizes that if they had called the police, he would've complied, but since he considered this to be an illegal arrest, an abuse of sort, he was ready to resist. "I must defend my rights," he asserts. "I know the arrest procedures, that's not the way you do it." Another reason Angly invokes for his resistance is that to him, Miracson is a criminal (*malfèktè*). Miracson is supposedly involved in shady businesses and would have shot someone dead. "Why do you think already two people have been lynched here since he was elected?[3] These are his contacts he wants to get rid of," Angly tells me. And to my question, "Why did the people then vote for him?" he answered: "Well, in Haiti, people choose those who have power, and those who have power are those who have the *bayonèt*." I also surmise that he didn't want to be taken away by Miracson alone, for fear of what might happen to him.

In any case, in defending himself, Angly dislocated Miracson's shoulder. He had no intentions of harming him, he says, but he would not let himself be handled by the man either. The CASEC then called the police. Angly finally complied and was taken to the Bouquet-Duvoisin police station, where he was held for five days until he was released.

Things calmed down, but the truce was short-lived. Over the next few months, Angly began to suffer from an ailment known to be the result of a spell. One of his legs became so swollen that he was unable to move without difficulty. This symptom was that of what is known as a "mystical attack" (*atak mistik*) brought on by a "blow of powder" (*koud poud*) (Meudec 2007). Angly had no doubt that this was the work of his neighbors, but he could not prove it. Fortunately, his father Odlon, a well-known *oungan*[4] in the area, was able to treat him and he recovered. In the end, he didn't fight back. They left the dispute at that.

When I first arrived in Haiti in 2016 to conduct ethnographic research on the intertwinement between official and unofficial ways of handling conflicts, Angly was a young man who had just turned thirty. He was a jovial and smiling type of guy, hanging around with ganja smokers and strolling the streets in search of small money to make. Consequently, he is also seen by some as a rascal and thus marginalized by part of the local community. His relations (although distant) with some youth who are known to be delinquent, involved in all kinds of small trafficking, armed and capable of violence,[5] adds to the feeling that he's not to be frequented too closely.

At the time, his main source of income was to break stones into smaller pieces. He used to sit for hours on a pile of stones under the burning sun handling a heavy hammer with bare hands and breathing in the dust. He often complained about body aches: His back and shoulders were sore; he was very tired; and he had headaches (which was unsurprising given the dazzling sun, the dust, and the dehydration). He was looking for something else to do, but times were hard: There was not much to do for which he could earn a living. And being uneducated, he could not aspire to anything other than basic manual jobs.

Angly has a son, Brisli,[6] born in 2010. The mother abandoned both after giving birth; she went to a city, a four-hour drive away, and never came back. Angly took care of the child with the help of others. After a while, he started living with a slightly younger woman, Judy. She adopted Brisli without too much trouble, as far as I know. They settled together on a plot of land where he could build a hut and stay. In fact, Angly's father, Odlon, being a rather influential *oungan* in the area, gave Angly a portion of the land he owned. However, as Angly was only one of thirty children his father had with many different women, he was given an almost uncultivable plot of land: It's been a long time since there was a tree, or little more than scrub on the plot. The earth has been washed away by decades of downpour. The soil is thus arid, barren, and very stony. Nonetheless, Angly, Judy, and Brisli live there in a decaying mud hut of about six to eight square meters, covered by a holed tin roof. The inner walls are covered with magazine sheets and political posters so the dust won't invade their space and make them sick (the crumbling of the walls often results in chronic or even acute rhinitis; in children, this can have important consequences on their lungs). When the sun is out, the heat inside becomes unbearable; they have trouble resting and sleeping in this confined and overheated space. When it rains, the noise on the tin roof is so loud that the occupants can barely hear each other. The combination of heat and humidity between May and September often results in fever and nausea. In addition, the roof is not watertight, so water drips onto their bed and runs inside along the compacted earth.

In 2023, they still couldn't afford to dig a hole for a toilet or other sanitary infrastructure on their plot. One had to go behind the bushes. They also do not have a kitchen; they make a small fire outside when the weather is fine, or inside when it rains. They eat when they can, what they can. They are worryingly food insecure, and among the most vulnerable to the rapidly changing situation (a small inflation has disastrous consequences on their life). And they do not have running water—they need to walk to a communal tap, about three hundred meters from where they live. When, during the dry season, the source has dried up, they need to go farther and sometimes stand in long queues. They get the power they need to charge their cell phones or Angly's radio by using a small portable solar panel. Neighbors help them sometimes, when they have not argued for one reason or another. In these conditions, the tension is often high.

It turned out that in 2016 Angly was able to quit his job breaking stones and start a small business: On a wooden tray, he sells cigarettes by the stick, small tubs of Dominican cookies, and shots of homemade rum. Judy also went into business: In a tiny corner of the market, on the floor hidden behind tarps between two bigger stores, she sells soaps and cheap beauty products. At that time, they had kindly asked if I could help them start their business, which I did. However, their business did not provide sufficient income. They were desperately trying to sustain a living. They did not eat as they should and could not send Brisli to school (being unable to pay for the fees and the uniform). This is when Angly told me, "Look, Haiti is destroyed (*kraze*).

There's no future for us here. I need to leave and search for life (*chachè lavi*) elsewhere, see what I mean?"

GRAY AREAS

This is an example of the kinds of conflicts that animate rural communities and the backdrop against which such conflicts erupt. Like everywhere else (Haiti is no exception in this regard), people live with neighbors they usually haven't chosen. And as is often the case, they don't always get along. Sometimes animosities are latent, expressed only in small, hushed gestures. Tensions exist, but that's as far as it goes. At other times, the situation worsens, and tensions escalate. Irritation, bitterness, and anger lead to outbursts of rage and violence, as in the case of Angly and his neighbors as I have described. Like in any community, there are official and unofficial ways of regulating and mediating conflicts; but unlike elsewhere, Haitians are not only deeply afflicted by a general anxiety and nervousness due to the violent consequences of international policy toward them, but have also generated specific ways of dealing with conflicts, given the particular situation. These dealings are first and foremost the work of the community before they become that of the state. Yet, Angly's example shows that, to some extent, it's unclear what comes under official law and what comes under unofficial conflict-regulation processes. There are contradictions, indistinctions, and a great deal of indeterminacy, which is of particular interest to me in this book, in that on the one hand they generate forms of violence, but on the other hand, create original and inspiring ways of living together. But these issues touch on more than adjudication, judgment, evaluation, choice, decision, values, agency, and deliberation. My approach to what is at stake in this case (and those I will present later) is far removed from the more formal, legalistic approaches.

Indeed, a certain trend in approaches to law emphasizes compliance with rules, principles, and codified legal procedures, often privileging structure and coherence over contextual considerations, with law seen as a more or less autonomous system. There's generally not much room for gray areas, vagueness, or indeterminacy in such a conception, not to mention the fact that the specific circumstances of a dispute are not always taken seriously[7]: On the contrary, it is believed that things need to be clearly defined (normatively), and the logic limpid, because, so one thinks, this is what ensures the consistency and reliability of legal outcomes, as decisions are supposed to be taken on the basis of clear procedures and established laws. Such an approach correlatively tends to downplay the importance of subjectivity in the various stages of procedures, and consequently also the role of discretionary power played by state officials. But above all, it fails to take into account specific issues that can only be understood by paying attention to the context. By generally setting aside ordinary ethical and political considerations, such an approach ignores what is at the heart of this book: The fact that the law only exists because we, humans, exist, and our language is what it is. It denies what is perhaps most important: That law is what it is only in and through human life, and therefore that law cannot be reduced to the legalistic conception I have just described. I will come back to this in a moment.

In contrast to this approach, I'm interested in questions that arise from everyday life, because these are issues that concern the Haitians I've met: What is it like to deal with my neighbors who hate me; what does it take to live with dignity a life that is constantly being ruined; how do I bear the burden of inherited grudges; do I really want to respond to the slights I suffer daily, at the risk of escalating the situation, or do I silently swallow the venom? There are no easy answers to these questions. No appeal to values, ideals of justice, principles, morality, laws, and procedures can guarantee a sure path to a solution to these human problems, nor assuage the anxiety of having to cope with that uncertainty. And we are certainly not judges of every moment of our lives. We're not always delineating, sequencing, and isolating individual acts, which we then submit for evaluation and judgment. That's just not how things work. And if we recognize that everyday life is a fine texture of messy subtleties and many contradictory movements never reconciled (Das 2020; Diamond 1997), then a door may be opened to the possibility of imagining differently the place of law and justice in human affairs.

Indeed, Angly's case shows the extent to which the law is interwoven with everyday life. As a result, it also shows that we don't quite know how and where it applies. Of course, we know *some*thing, but we can't draw a line and say that this is the limit, that here it's the domain of this law, and here it's not. That's why we have to remain open to surprise; legal issues may appear in unexpected places. In Angly's case, neighbors, passersby, and acquaintances (and later the family) got involved. They tried to defuse the conflict and calm everyone down. But as it happens, it did not work. So, they called in the authorities. First came the CASEC, representatives of the state as well as of the community, and then the police. And yet, things haven't been settled.

The CASEC have the special status of being both official and unofficial authorities. They are both administrators and local notables chosen by the people. Officially, their work is determined by the law on the organization of the communal section, issued by the Ministry of Agriculture, Natural Resources and Rural Development. In particular, this law sets out the mandate of the CASEC. For instance, they must contribute to and oversee the development, operation, and maintenance of structures established by the state; ensure the well-being and social, intellectual, professional, economic, civic, and cultural training of the population; or receive, study and transmit to the Municipal Council the grievances of the community. Their duties also include regulating the use of markets, cemeteries, irrigation canals, drinking water supply systems, the electricity grid (if there is any), roads and byways, and natural sites. And, more immediately relevant to our concerns, CASEC must ensure that the law is correctly applied in cases of arrest or detention in the section, and that citizens' rights are protected (Art. 12, al.17). They must also report to the relevant authorities. CASEC thus work closely with the Justice of Peace (hereafter JP) court and the police.

Unofficially, CASEC sometimes perform police or judicial functions where they are not legally authorized to do so, as is the case here. For example, they arrogate to themselves the right to arrest someone, or to confiscate property without a judge's warrant. They may also carry firearms without a permit, although they generally arrange for themselves to have one. While one part of the population grants them these de facto rights without further reservations, another part contests them. This is a legal gray area, which allows great latitude of movement, but also crystallizes a great deal of tension.[8] Angly's case is particularly illustrative in this regard. On the one hand, Miracson, as the head of CASEC, feels authorized to arrest and handcuff Angly (although he contravenes the law); on the other hand, Angly contests this wrongful right in the name of legal procedure: Only the police, or the judge in the absence of the police, can arrest him. When I asked Miracson what he thought of Angly's legal argument, he said he understood it, that he was even right, but that's not how things work here; if only the police or judges could arrest people, there wouldn't be any arrests. The situation is such, he says, that they can't assume their role. Police and judges are so underequipped, underfunded, and understaffed that they are generally simply absent, whereas CASEC are present and active in every communal section. They are therefore the only ones who can make arrests and carry out investigations. It would therefore be unreasonable, in his view, to obey the law too strictly; on the contrary, what is considered reasonable by him consists precisely in circumventing the law, but for the good of the community.

Now, the lines are further blurred by a darker aspect of the case. Rumors circulate that Miracson is, or has been, involved in dubious affairs. He is even said to be involved in violent crime. Whether this is true or not, it tells a lot about his ambiguous position. As is the case with many police officers who are also involved in criminal activities (some are notorious gang leaders), some CASEC also wear several hats. Indeed, their involvement in both state and local affairs puts them in a de facto position where they have to play on several fronts at once, and deal with forces that bend power in contradictory directions. Even if they are well-intentioned and eager to respect and uphold the law, they cannot escape the power relations within the community. This prevents them from being above reproach in the eyes of the law. Someone like Miracson, implicated in the most mundane as well as the shadiest affairs of the commune, can't help but deal with the pressures and threats coming from both the law and justice and the more underground world of the community. This includes, as we shall see throughout the book, a number of violent practices.

In a country like Haiti, there are a whole host of reasons why someone like Miracson feels invested with a police function when he's legally not authorized to do so, or why someone like Angly challenges his arrest in the name of the law when he's otherwise living a life that's in many ways illegal. In fact, Miracson has to prove himself as a guardian of community order if he wants to remain in office, whereas one of the challenges of someone like Angly is to avoid incarceration at all costs if he doesn't want to risk languishing and disappearing in the infamous halls of Haitian prisons, or else avoid the risk of finding oneself alone and handcuffed with someone one fears, like Miracson. These aspects are not trivial; they are central to the way in which the law is mobilized, contested, imposed, avoided, transgressed, and denied. This is what I mean when I say that the law has a life; it has a life insofar as it cannot be dissociated from ours, from our life as human beings. And the best way to realize this is to look through the cracks.

THE LIFE OF LAW

So, what is the connection between life and law? Or else, what is the life *of* law? The pertinence of these questions became clearer to me as I progressively discovered that matters were more complex and intertwined than what first appeared as a radical divide between the state and the people, or, as Michel-Rolph Trouillot (1990) puts it, a disjuncture between state and nation. While, in fact, there's no doubt that since Haiti's independence in 1804 and the first attempts to build and consolidate a nation-state, the country has been characterized by a fracture between, on one side, the state's official institutions and modes of governance that have reappropriated the repressive techniques of the colonizers and, on the other, unofficial and autonomous forms of social organizations that evaded the state's predation. On the ground, things seemed much more tangled: State and nonstate actors mingle and blur the boundaries between what is official and what is not (Kivland 2020).

Looking through the cracks thus allows us to see what is happening and what is at stake in such a tangle. And what is at stake is life, the possibility of pursuing. In other words, it makes us see that there is no notion of law without a certain notion of death. As a result, the opposition between official and unofficial channels loses some of its relevance. Other characterizations are beginning to emerge that make us see things differently. Yet, the study of the life and death of law is not simply a study derived from the plaintiff, as Laura Nader (2005) would have it, even if she had good reason to claim as such. It is infinitely more than that, for it must concern itself with order as much as disorder, reason as much as passion, peace as much as violence.[9] And where can we get a sense of this if not in the whirlwind of ordinary life?

Bringing the law closer to everyday life is nothing new. It's been precisely the business of anthropology from the very beginning: It looks at the various ways law is embedded in social practices. Despite their many differences, Malinowski (1926), Evans-Pritchard (1940), Llewellyn and Hoebel (1941), Colson (1953), Gluckman (1955), Bohannan (1957), and Nader et al. (1969) all have examined, in one way or another, adjudication and deliberation, dispute resolution processes, and ways of maintaining some form of social order in relation to different modes of informal, ordinary norm-making.[10] That said, in many cases, there is still some confusion as to what is meant by "ordinary" or "everyday life." Paradoxically, it appears that some regions of the ordinary tend to be somewhat left unexamined, as when (often male) researchers fail to take into account the perspectives of women and children and thus miss the immeasurable importance of the domestic in human life; or when we fail to capture that the ordinary is all but banal, for it carries within itself its own negation, its own forms of cruelty and horror; that the ordinary is itself both what constitutes us and what we flee from, and thus proves the most difficult to achieve. And when the ordinary is indeed rigorously examined, we sometimes witness the resurgence of conventional and unsatisfactory conceptions, little able to enlighten us on the complexity of what's at stake.

Allow me to illustrate this briefly with two examples, one from the social studies law and the other from anthropology. First, in their book *Law in Everyday Life* (1993), Austin Sarat and Thomas Kearns aim at examining how law both shapes, and is shaped by, the everyday. They take issue with approaches that confine law to formal institutions and see it as either constituent or instrument, by refocusing their analysis on mundane, ordinary contexts. This gesture is certainly to be welcomed, if our concern is for what concerns human beings. Yet, to this end, they draw on Henri Lefevre's perspective (besides Alfred Schutz, Jürgen Habermas, and Maurice Blanchot), which, while interesting in many respects, tends to reduce everyday life to repetition, routine, and monotony, whereas, as we shall see in the following chapters, the ordinary is infinitely more complex and interesting than that. Sarat and Kearns, building on this, define their zone of interest precisely there, adding habits, conventions, constraints, and restraints. Even more confusing is their vision of the ordinary as the (trivial?) domain of undramatic experience, as the place of the obvious, of what we take for granted and which, by the same token, "always sits just beyond the grasp of those who live in it and with it" (ibid., 6). I'm not going to counterargue at this point, except to say that people *do* grasp the ordinary in many fascinating and instructive ways for academics, that there are indeed ordinary dramas worth paying attention to, and that, if we do, we'll see that the ordinary is anything but obvious and routine.

The second example is the perspective developed by Sandra Brunnegger in *Everyday Justice* (2019). While it is also to be welcomed insofar as it proposes to redirect our gaze from the courts of justice toward the ordinary, it illustrates other kinds of limitations in that it is based on an altogether banal vision of the ordinary. If the idea of everyday justice is invoked, it is only to say that it must be considered in its context, i.e., that cultural, historical, and social differences, as well as heterogeneous points of view must be taken into account. So far, so good. Isn't this the bread and butter of anthropology? In addition, she claims, we must reckon with the fact that our vocabularies of justice and the different meanings of the categories we use are also derived from everyday life, and it happens that "the everyday is dynamic, contingent, and multiple" (ibid., 8). Of course, there's nothing objectionable about this. It could be said of any object of ethnographic inquiry. My questions are: Why give the impression that this is a discovery? Isn't this the point of departure rather than the point of arrival? If so, how else could we problematize the ordinary? What would be the next steps? *Life in the Cracks* as a whole is something of a response to that. And it will take the form of a portrait of both the law and the ordinary, say a portrait of the ordinary life of the law. And we'll see, as the sketches unfold, that such a portrait can only be, at the same time, a portrait of the violence inherent to both the ordinary and the law.

Hence, if one of the main challenges in my initial project was to show concretely and empirically the various points of tension and lines of force that run through the practice of law and acts of justice from within the everyday experiences of people, it quickly appeared that one does not know in advance where exactly these points are, and where the lines run (certainly not merely in expected places). This is why detailed descriptions of highly heterogeneous moments are so important in this book. Indeed, to look through the prism of the ordinary is, in particular, to look through the prism of all the astonishingly rich ways of addressing disagreements among humans, as well as all those moments of acknowledgment that pass in tiny interactions, sometimes almost nothing. As it happens, things aren't always played out where you'd expect them to be, for example in a magistrates' court, or at a neighborhood meeting. Often, something decisive is played out in a fleeting moment during a transaction in a corridor, in an improvised scene in the street, or in a silent exchange of glances.

This is why it is important to complicate simplistic oppositions between formal and informal law, legal and illegal activities, which would amount to adopting a nonlegalistic perspective on legality, a perspective on the judiciary that does not take judicial language as its starting point, especially not when the rule of law is seen as a positive, if not the necessary, achievement of any so-called "civilized" society. That's why I take issue with three main characterizations of the law that serve as the ideological basis for promoting the rule of law: First, that the law must be universal and necessary; second, that the law necessarily serves to resolve conflicts; third, that the law is the guarantor of order and justice. In the first characterization, the familiar argument is that laws must apply to all rational beings, at all times and in all places. And to do this, they must be posited a priori. They cannot be based on (empirical) experience, because then they would depend on particular circumstances, cultures, or individual inclinations, and would therefore not be universal. Laws must also be valid in themselves, in a necessary way, and not contingent (dependent on specific situations and personal desires), because they must always be just for everyone. What's more, insofar as they are normative (proscribing and prescribing), they cannot at the same time be descriptive of empirical experience, i.e., they cannot be derived from observation of the world (because observation does not show what ought to be). In the second and the third characterizations, the moral argument is essentially that the law—the law in its fairness, that is—guides human behavior and structures society in such a way that it can only lead to more harmony and less chaos. It strengthens social cohesion, assures justice, and guarantees order. Clear, codified laws and procedures, it is thought, provide effective mechanisms for settling disputes without major clashes. In other words, the law enables the peaceful resolution of conflicts that would otherwise erupt in violence. This is so mainly for the following reasons: a) clear laws provide precise guidelines, thus reducing the ambiguities and misunderstandings at the root of disputes; b) legal institutions act as neutral arbiters, avoiding as much as possible bias and prejudice; and c) the authority of the judiciary is combined with that of the police, who ensure that the law is enforced and respected, making dispute resolution both binding and effective.

This book will show how flawed, prejudicial, and unrealistic such a conception of the law is, hence how problematic the promotion of the rule of law is. Taking as my starting point, not the law and its application, but people's lives and the practical, concrete, and, dare we say it, real issues that confront them, I will focus instead on the ambivalence of the law. For while it can be the means by which parties in conflict settle a dispute, it can also be the source of much violence. Moreover, I will show that it can, not only hinder the resolution of conflicts, but actually aggravate them. And if we look through the cracks, as it were, it seems that the idea of resolution itself loses its force, for on closer inspection, there is no resolution if we mean that something is definitively resolved. If there is resolution, it is only provisional; and often the question is not whether things are settled or not. This was the concluding point made by Arnold L. Epstein in his article on the case method in the field of law, which I will rather take as my starting point. When he quotes the Bemba saying, "*mulandu taupwa*, a case never ends," it is to say that "it is not so much that quarrels are never wholly resolved, but rather that cases have their sources in the ceaseless flow of social life and, in turn, contribute to that flow" (2017, 230). Hence the daily work consists essentially in maintaining a livable life—and life in Haiti as I saw it is above all endurance. This involves, among other things, dealing with frustrated hopes—hopes placed in the law—which turn out to be disappointments. I wish to account for the profound dissatisfaction with the law as it stands and the solutions themselves. That's why, in what follows, I'll be asking in each particular case not whether the law is being applied, and if so, how, and if not, why, but rather what its place is in our lives as humans.

At this point, I would like to broach briefly just two ideas that will guide us throughout this whole book. First, the idea we generally have of what the law is, how it works, and the role it plays in our lives is derived from the way we picture what language is, how it works, and the role it plays in our lives. This is not something to be taken lightly, because it's the very way we perceive and understand what we, human beings, do and what happens to us that's at stake. Hence, second, our conception of language informs our conception of law. If we conceive language as determined by rules, as some claim—rules organized into a complete structure that determines: a) whether the rule applies or not; b) when it does apply, whether it is followed or infringed; and c) when no existing rule applies, that it is always possible to adopt a new rule to cover the case—we will be inclined to conceive law in similar terms. Yet, this is a misconception of language and what it is to be governed by rules, because on close inspection that's just not how things work. We need to ask ourselves why we were inclined in the first place to formulate such a conception of rules, and then, what the implications are of the fact that language—and thus law—do not depend on such a structure. And yet, the absence of such a structure of rules in no way impedes their functioning. Following or obeying or breaking or transgressing or thwarting or mocking a rule or, for that matter, a law—just like speaking, keeping quiet, or lying—are in themselves actions or activities that do not depend on rules or laws, any more than our wishes, intentions, desires, or decisions do.

With this in mind, it becomes possible to account more accurately for the multiple ways in which claims to legality, justice, and sovereignty are formulated and contested within the ordinary, with the aim of better understanding the dynamics that seem to prevent a strong centralization of power in the hands of the state. As Rivke Jaffe (2015) has rightly noted, the anthropological literature on the Caribbean needs to better understand these dynamics that lead to fragmented sovereignties and particular interlocking forms of violence and normative systems. As such, this is what this book sets out do, highlighting Haiti's plural legal landscape and the interconnection, or mutual absorption, between state and nonstate law. It aims to understand specific configurations of law, power, and violence. In addition, it explores more specifically some aspects of the processes that have impeded the development of a democratic state since the adoption of the 1987 constitution, after twenty-nine years of dictatorship, as well as the aspirations, desires, and alternatives that have emerged within local communities on the margins of formal institutions. And yet, while this remains a common thread for half the chapters, the book is not limited to this; its scope extends far beyond.

Hence, this book's main theme turns out to be less specific, or more fundamental, than law and justice: it is about human life, thus human death. My concern echoes Greg Beckett who attempted in his remarkable book *There Is No More Haiti* (2019, 9) to "think about what it means to struggle, to strive, and to try to live in a world that feels like it has already ended." Yet, unlike him, I am not so much concerned with the "crisis," its permanence and its effects, as with how life staggers on, wrestles, writhes in the cracks opened by multilateral and shifting conflicts that have lasted for decades. It is a question not only of being attentive to the impulses sustained by a "radical hope" for another future (Clitandre 2021), but also to what prevents or hinders the blossoming of such hope, and to what simply goes on more or less as usual, without being underpinned by hope, will, or any intention.

As it were, this book is about how life pushes on in the cracks opened by devastation. If there is no doubt that the critical events, which have been so detrimental to Haiti since its birth, must be recognized, and rethought in the light of new approaches, this book endeavors above all to trace, in the interstices of the ordinary, the small and uneventful moments when something swells and shrinks, thrives and withers, disrupting the rhythms of common life but also nudging it back on track. In a context of permanent crisis, daily life most often does not proceed simply and regularly. Living requires work, and that's no easy task. Yet, the work required is not that of a hero, and the task does not have the grandeur of a lion's heart. Rather, as we will see, small and creative acts of care and repair, experimentation and improvisation, are those that somehow make it possible for Haitians to pursue their lives and glimpse a future, however uncertain and vulnerable they may be to their milieu. The myriad of lives I encountered tussled to push on, bearing the traces of endless battles spanning across generations and seeping through all the nooks and crannies of the ordinary. Hence, what is it to endure in a context of so multiple and quickly shifting sovereignties? What does it take to go on walking on a ground that has been ransacked, devoured, and left behind eroded and fissured? How, after loss, do communities recover the ordinary and reinvent the task of living? And what happens when there's no aftermath, no end to violence and loss? What kind of future do they then imagine to be possible?

In Haitian writer Yanick Lahens's words, people fight "wars without victories, without outcomes and without glories." (2016, 36) As I will myself show in the pages that follow, people have their daily share of little deaths provoked by silent, uninterrupted wars going on behind the din of violence that erupts in broad daylight. "These are small wars," writes Lahens. "Wars in which we dig our defeats a little deeper every day" (ibid., 36). So "mistrust runs through our veins like an oozing liquid. Along with misfortune, mistrust is the only heritage that we, the defeated, truly share" (ibid., 42). And there, in the middle, are those who hodgepodge temporary solutions, patch up relationships, invent all sorts of schemes to repair the holes and tears in the social fabric. There are all these men and women, experts in resourcefulness, cunning, and small acts of kindness who, with or without confidence, do what needs to be done.

To live in Haiti today is to live under such radical contingencies (inflation, epidemics, coups d'état, interventionism, natural disasters, etc.) that it's hard to make sense of them. Something, resolutely, seems to be going on behind the scenes, somewhere to the exclusion of the Haitians themselves. Life is so uncertain that it's not that surprising that the skepticism that emanates from it brings hidden intentions into existence, whether behind political decisions or the seemingly innocuous glance of a neighbor.[11] Through its study of a certain condition of the human living in a political mist where dark and shifting forces operate, this book asks at each step what the political conditions are within which knowledge is produced, including that which is produced in and by this book, for knowledge can become as vital an issue as access to food. By looking at the complex intertwining of the lives of the people I encountered, I hope to be able to convey a sense of possibilities embedded in our forms of life, forms of life that generate particular forms of violence and death. If it does happen that life fades away and is extinguished, most often life inexorably continues in the faults of a numbing, wounding, and often deadly reality. In one way or another, it resists annihilation. Hence, what is needed, is an account of this resistance.

A ROUGH HISTORY OF RESISTANCE

A glance back in time will prove useful and teach us something about the forms of resistance that took root in Haiti and what kind of future people fight for. However, we'll be careful not to take this history as an explanatory factor for the present. Instead, let's consider it as partly providing the background against which certain aspects stand out and become salient. The depth of Angly's refusal to be handcuffed, for example, cannot be grasped outside a history of the people's resistance to the grip of a centralized power represented by the state. His gesture is permeated throughout by this memory. That's why I'd like to take the time to offer a few elements of this background for a better understanding of what follows, without which many aspects would be overlooked. What particularly interests me here is that resistance, which has taken the form of *marronage*, is not merely a matter of refusal and escape, but also, and perhaps above all, as we shall see, a care for others, a possibility of continuing human life in a context of annihilation.

I am well aware that resistance has become the bearer of a post-Marxist ideological charge that strongly influences a certain narrative of what politics is and how it works[12]: in such a narrative, resistance is above all resistance to domination and hegemony. I don't wish to deny that this is one of the meanings of the concept. Yet, it also means something else, less dialectical and ideological. I fully agree with Chantalle Verna (2017) when she urges us to add layers of analysis and complexify our understanding of the narrative that overemphasizes Haitian popular resistance to US imperial domination. First, because it is critical that we do not blindly adhere to predetermined narratives about politics, but rather pluralize the perspectives from the ground up so as to offer more nuanced understandings of the issues at stake. No doubt "Haiti needs new narratives" (Ulysse 2015). Second, because as Lila Abu-Lughod (1990) and Talal Asad (2000) made clear, we want to forestall the risk of nurturing a sentimental and triumphalist view of resistance, incapable of accounting for the complexity of the issues and often spreading stereotyped, and therefore impoverished, versions of reality. Third, because "Haitians have been more than victims or resilient agents in history. They have been central players." (Verna 2017, 5). So, to my ears, the word resistance has a different tone than what I usually read or hear in more conventional academic circles.

During slavery, the Haitian Revolution, and beyond, in a willful attempt to escape the reach of the centralized power, many people fled to mountainous and remote rural areas where they re-created inextricable webs of communities organized around a decentralized system of self-sufficient, small-scale, and kin-based farming economy, named *lakou*. This in Creole is a transliteration from the French "*la cour*," meaning "courtyard," but the concept has a much deeper historical and social meaning. It constitutes, as Jean Casimir (2020) makes us see, the foundation and the soul of the "sovereign people" over which state authorities didn't and still don't have authority. The *lakou* is generally occupied by an extended family, more rarely by several allied families, organized around common kitchen hearths, the sharing of domestic chores and childcare, cooperative work in the fields, and, often, Vodou services in which the various members participate.

At the entrance of a *lakou*, banners would be visible atop long wooden poles, announcing not only the identity and the ancestral spirit of the place, but also revealing the existence of a place of care from afar. Moreover, it indicates a place where certain contentions can be dealt with. Indeed, a *lakou* is a place where all kinds of problems and afflictions are treated. Their competences vary greatly, and range from conflict management to obstetrics, to pediatric care and the handling of behavioral disorders. The place often also includes a family cemetery as well as plots of cultivated land, which makes it a key site for the economic life of a family, each then connected by a complex system of markets. Not only have they constituted themselves as small collectives of mutual aid who share the fruits of their labor, but they have re-created forms of belonging, intimacy, domesticity, and solidarity that form an extremely important foundation of Haitian society (Barthélemy 1990; Hurbon 1988). Although the conjunctures of history and the structural violence have destroyed in part this way of life, its deep roots still contribute today to nourishing alternative modes of sociality. In fact, the life developed in these networks of *lakou* worked and still works to thwart and evade government policies and much of the state structures (Casimir 2020). Notably by producing, withholding, and interrogating knowledge, communities developed a great capacity to respond to contingencies they had not chosen. Throughout this book, we'll see how much day-to-day resistance is linked to this great ability of the *lakou* networks to react in ways that escape the grip of the state. But more than that, they've been the substratum for the blossoming and flourishing of new life possibilities.

The emergence of the *lakou* historically precipitated the collapse of the plantation economy, a process that Casimir calls "counter-plantation." In fact, the "Haitian peasantry . . . constituted [itself] in opposition to the processes of integration and assimilation to the commodity-producing plantation. [Its] culture was and remains a response to slavery, a form of self-defense responding to the abuses inflicted by modern, colonial society" (Casimir 2020, 351). One of the specific features of the Haitian Revolution, if one looks from below, is the destruction and radical rejection of the export plantation economy, whereas elsewhere in the Caribbean, the abolition of slavery did not entail the complete destruction of the colonial agrarian structures (Fick 1990).[13] Right from the start of the insurrections, in addition to abolishing the Code Noir,[14] the insurgents destroyed the mass production systems and divided the large plots of land into small lots for immediate use for food crops to meet the needs of the former slaves, now free and cultivating. As historian Marcel Dorigny points out in his preface to the French translation of Carolyn Fick's book, "freedom was not just a legal status, it was to transform the former slave into an independent peasant" (2014, 19). None of the measures taken by the big figures such as Sonthonax, Louverture, or Dessalines to reorganize the plantation economy were able to halt this reversal: "to be free was to have access to land for one's own needs" (ibid., 20). This implied a rejection of wage labor, which, like nowhere else, was made possible.

Yet, while marooning was the most significant and persistent form of resistance during the plantation system, there were no large, isolated communities of maroons, as was the case in other colonies with, for instance, the *palenques* in Colombia or the *quilombos* in Brazil (Price 1996). With rare exceptions, there were no well-defined, identifiable groups either, but rather shifting networks of small, fluctuating communities in regular contact with the enslaved who remained in the plains on the plantations, emancipated slaves, and free colored people; and for this very reason, the maroons were well-informed, resupplied, and difficult to capture. "In this vein, much closer attention ought to be paid . . . to the day-to-day marronage of slaves as an integral part of their life experience, to those fugitives who never joined the armed bands, but who were maroons" (Fick 1990, 239). In such a locked-in tyrannical system, this daily marronage can be described as a condition of clandestinity.

One of the legacies of *mawonaj* is a certain creative capacity of the people to reorganize themselves in situations of adversity and predation. Fick (1990) makes us aware that it is also a struggle to wrest back the human dignity of which the people had been denied. What's at stake, then, for us scholars, is the way we look at what happened (and, therefore, what's happening now in the light of that past), because we haven't always been attentive to those ordinary men, women, and children who were the artisans of that historic moment and of the shifts in history that followed. In particular, we have not always been able to see them as autonomous actors, with their own interests and objectives, often in contradiction with, or in direct opposition to, the path mapped out by their political and military leaders. Our obsession with heroic, generally male, figures (Louverture, Dessalines, Christophe, etc.) may have blinded us to the individual lives that not only made up what is often considered at best a vaguely defined mass of the people, but also were the impetus and driving force behind the movements that were to transform society. This is true for history, but also for anthropology: How attentive are we really to the ordinary, singular lives, both tiny and immense, that form the social fabric of the Haitian population today?

The afterlife of the maroon communities in the postrevolutionary period is interesting for the purpose of this book. In fact, these communities morphed into widespread unauthorized settlements that created their own clandestine networks of local authorities, which, as is still the case today, were enacted in large part by Vodou and secret societies and strongly connected by a constellation of underground and public markets (Gonzales 2019; Mintz 1959; 1971; 2011). These networks, by strengthening the ties among people, allowing the development of strategic intelligence, coordinating actions, disseminating false information to create diversion, circulating weapons and gunpowder and providing supplies, have contributed not only to avoiding forced or wage labor and taxation by keeping the state at a distance, but also to generating a sophisticated socioeconomic organization based on barter, smuggling, and mutuality.

Yet, let's not be misled. The movements that led to Haitian independence and out of which the later networks were born were not homogeneous nor consensual. Above all, the newly free people, as much as these later independent networks, had to contend with the international presence and pressures, particularly at a time when a republican government was being formed in Paris and intended to extend its power to the colonies.[15] So, from the outset, the insurgents progressed both by violence and by law, according to an ambiguous and contradictory local interpretation of the legal legacy of the Ancien Régime, in particular the protective measures of the Code Noir (Ghachem 2012, ch. 6). They had in fact to figure a way to consolidate their gain, that is, their rights. The different stages of the revolution, the transition to independence, and the first decades of the new nation were indeed marked by an omnipresence of law in the political culture of the insurgents. The law has been a central issue in the negotiations and processes at work. If in the early phases, it was a question of obtaining equal political rights for all and defining emancipation, it was then a question of legally guaranteeing this equality and the abolition of slavery, drafting a declaration of independence as well as a constitution. All this, nonetheless, was much more complex than what one often thinks, bearing the traces of conflicting interests and being subject to contingencies. Even before the birth of Haiti, the law was at the heart of the reflections and actions that would durably shape the face of the country.

This is particularly true of the early governments. Contrariwise to the peasantry and the *lakou* networks, the elite who formed the new state were themselves new conquerors. They followed the colonial models with the objective of reviving plantation economy (Dubois in Casimir 2020). So when Jean-Pierre Boyer, one of the military leaders of the revolution, famous for having reunited the Northern Kingdom and the Southern Republic into the Republic of Haiti in 1820,[16] figured he did not have the means to dislodge and subject the tens of thousands of reluctant peasants, he used juridical tools tactically to regain control over the fleeing population and restore forced labor. He set up the structure that has made up Haiti's judiciary system until today. However, the peculiar conditions under which he structured Haiti's judicial power have to be considered closely. After 1815, the French, considerably weakened by the Congress of Vienna, had to face various facts: Not only had they suffered a bitter defeat at the hands of the Haitian insurgents, but the British had taken advantage of the situation to take control of the seas and threaten to extend their commercial hegemony to the new nation. On the Iberian side of the island, upheavals were also taking place following the alliance sealed between Simon Bolivar and Southern Haitian Republic President Alexandre Pétion. France was also turning its attention to new colonial projects in North and sub-Saharan Africa, as well as in Southeast Asia. All this forms the backdrop to Charles X's decision, in 1825, to send Baron de Makau, his special envoy, to pressure President Boyer into accepting a compromise. It was under military threat—fourteen ships armed with 528 cannons were stationed in the harbor of the capital, ready to attack—that Makau imposed France's conditions. The amount and terms of the indemnity Haiti was to pay France in exchange for its independence, were 150 million gold francs of the time, equivalent to approximately 300 percent of GDP, or ten years of tax revenue, payable over five years on behalf of the former French colonists. It is clear that "the amount of the indemnity, its terms of payment, as well as the mechanisms advocated for access to funds, reflected on the part of France a desire to punish" (Jean in Dorigny et al. 2021, 14). In response, Boyer's government had no choice but to "resort to the Paris financial market to raise funds by issuing bonds" (ibid., 15). Haiti therefore suffers from a double debt: On the one hand, from the ordinance requiring the former settlers to be compensated for their losses; on the other hand, from the loan debt owed to the French bondholders. Added to this was a 50 percent rebate on customs duties for all ships flying the French flag. The strategy was clear: to ransom, isolate, and bleed the first state born of the emancipation of former slaves.

Pressed by all this, Boyer had no time to draw up his own codes of law. He therefore copied the French laws as quickly as possible, in order to impose an order aimed essentially at surveillance and streamlining production. Although he slightly adapted some provisions to local customs, the codes remained largely unchanged. He thus implemented the Napoleonic Civil Code (CC) in 1825. He also promulgated the Rural Code (RC) in 1826, designed to set out a very restrictive range of laws applicable specially to the countryside. For instance, it initially outlawed group labor and agricultural cooperatives (*konbit peyizan*) who practice rotational labor and are based on mutual aid relationships[17] (Freeman 2017; J. M. Smith 2001). The RC also forbade laborers to set up their farms and sell their production. In addition, it provided for the "*corvée*" (*kòve*), which allowed officials to force people to work, and set very restrictive working hours. The law was also designed to crack down on those whom it defined as "*vagabonds*," vagrants, people without a profession, and beggars, and calls for repression. A person therefore needed an official authorization to travel to a town or a city.[18] A system of rural constables was created in conjunction with the justice of the peace system, to enforce the new regulations, and monitor, control, and tax the peasants (Dubois 2012; also Chapter 3). Finally, Boyer adopted the Penal Code (PC) in 1835, which banned family-based and socially sanctioned ritual practices that played a central role in the life of rural communities.[19] At the same time, it condemned all festive and nocturnal gatherings, particularly Vodou services held at night. It likewise outlawed the production and use of "spells" (*sortilèges*), redefining legally certain objects used in rituals as witchcraft (Ramsey 2011). In the end, by criminalizing popular practices, the code ends up criminalizing the people (*pèp la*) themselves.[20]

Despite this, the local communities had developed such an effective clandestinity that they mostly escaped the grip of the judiciary, and even prevented the establishment of strong, centralized, and sustainable state institutions. "Over generations, Haitians had practiced and refined their resistance to various forms of coerced labor . . . [and] rural residents perfected techniques of evading government officials, living as much as possible beyond the gaze of the state" (Dubois 2012, 106). The mutual hostility has led to a deeply rooted suspicion on both sides. If, on the one hand, the ruling elite has and continues to develop a deep contempt for the peasants and urban working class, which they call "*moun andeyò*," "outsiders," or "*pèp la*," "the people," on the other hand, the peasants and working class have developed a profound mistrust of any state institution.[21] Even today, in urban centers as well, as outlined by Beckett (2021, 214; also 2014), "the much decried informality and statelessness of [cities like] Port-au-Prince is . . . partly the result of residents actively seeking ways to avoid the state, to not be governed by it even as they live in its very midst. . . . The perceived lawlessness and ungovernability of Port-au-Prince is not just the result of government failure or social exclusion; it is also how many residents have sought to reject the exploitative terms of their incorporation into the state." This long-lasting tension has created a breeding ground for all kinds of violence, from sabotage and guerilla warfare to embezzlement, kidnappings, and sponsored massacres.

According to Gérard Barthélemy's account (1990), what happened was the creation of a society, or modes of sociality, not so much against the state as next to it, coeval, collateral. The maroon resistance took the form of a creation of alternative social organizations. "In order to try to shed light on the workings of a reality that is inscribed in the most ordinary gestures and details of daily life, we must therefore look for what links the phenomena of agriculture, health, education, religion, and language within a global behavior that only seems confusing to us, or sometimes non-existent, because it remains misunderstood" (ibid., 17, my translation). This "behavior" for Barthélemy is characterized by three traits of a radical political imagination: self-regulation, equality, and the rejection of any form of subjugation. Yet, importantly, he tells us, its incentive was not underpinned by a preestablished egalitarian doctrine, an ideology, or structuring principles, nor guided by authoritative and prioritized organizations such as village or elder councils, institutionalized arbitration instances, casts or clans, communal regroupings, or small governments. And if we think of the notables, the secret societies, and the groups of *vodouizan*, they were themselves small and changing entities, scattered and independent of any superstructure, although networked and linked together. What we see is rather a type of organization made up of small and mutually permeable units that cohabit in terms of neighborhoods and that intersect and self-regulate at specific junctions such as crossroads, markets, water sources, and Vodou shrines. Not only was there no overarching structure, no general rule, that would organize the social world, but these modes of self-regulation had the effect, intended or not, of preventing any great accumulation of wealth and keeping the concentration of power in check.

But the peasant society has undergone many transformations. Today, it has to reckon with laws and modes of regulation inherited from state institutions for some of the matters concerning them. Administrators, courts, and to some extent the police are rather common actors in the valleys (much less in the mountains). As we shall see in more detail in the following chapters, they are more or less integrated in the village life and serve as a link between a relatively autonomous peasantry and the state or transnational structures to which their fate is inevitably linked. Yet, this is not without friction, as we've seen in the opening scene with Angly and Miracson. We'll see that at these precise points of contact, latent disagreements become manifest. These are the places and moments of disputes, grievances, and negotiations, but also of a mutual appreciation that serves as a gauge for assessing the potential danger and violence that could erupt. In such an uncertain world, which has seen a succession of particularly violent predatory power structures, rural populations have an interest in knowing the intentionalities of the state and its intermediaries, at the risk of not feeling which way the wind is blowing. That's why one of the challenges of this book is to unravel the stakes of such a gauge from within the ordinary.

OF VALLEYS, MOUNTAINS, AND CITIES

So, what does the ordinary look like in Bwa-Mapou? Let me first say a few words about the place. It borders the southern shore of the Artibonite River. The 321 km-long river flowing from the Dominican Republic into the Gulf of Gonâve, which is the longest on the island and the second longest in the Caribbean, has sadly become famous after the 2010 cholera outbreak; it was even nicknamed the "deadly river" (Frerichs 2020). Artibonite is also the name of one of the ten departments that compose the country, and is well known for its export-oriented mango production (Jayaram 2018), its rice paddies in the swampy alluvium along the river and the delta (Levy 2001), and also for its powerful mystical forces. In fact, this region is felt by many to be one of the sources of the power that gave the revolutionaries in the late eighteenth century the strength to fight and win against the colonizers. The Black Mountain massif separating the valley from the city of Gonaïves, the capital of the department, was a place of refuge for maroons (*nèg mawon*) and insurgents. The city is also called the City of Independence because it is where the independence of Haiti, on January 1, 1804, was proclaimed by Jean-Jacques Dessalines. The Artibonite's insurrectional reputation began a long time ago.

This reputation was reinforced at the beginning of the twentieth century and during the US military occupation (1915–1934). During a massive and violent expropriation campaign by American developers, the re-implementation of forced labor, and the conversion of the peasantry to salaried employment, aimed at reappropriating the land for foreign business purposes, peasants and farmers in the valley fought back. As "the U.S. administration rewrote Haiti's constitution, removing a prohibition on the foreign ownership of land and paving the way for the penetration of foreign capital and imported goods" (Beckett 2019, 28), the peasants were about to become consumers of imported goods instead of producers of their own food. Insurrections were organized. Their anger was channeled by local leaders who redirected the uprising against the central authorities in Port-au-Prince. Locally, small armies with sophisticated ambush tactics were created and consolidated their presence in rural areas. These groups later became squads of the "*caco*" rebellion, an organization of guerilla units fighting foreign power. The insurrections that had started in the Artibonite soon swept the country. The marines being shipped to Haiti had been warned: Haitians "might be inclined to resist" (Dubois 2012, 225).

Apart from that, the region is also famous for the violent disputes over resources and right to land. Therefore, it is the only department in the country to host two land tribunals, specifically designated to arbitrate litigations over land tenure, which is usually handled outside the grasp of the state institutions and regularly ends in bloodshed. Additionally, people of this region, just like Angly, are more generally known to be defiant and unsubmissive, as well as to include powerful Vodou practitioners—a conception that bothers some who try to shed the stigma, but which profits others who enjoy its effects and sometimes use it playfully. Hence, a certain spirit of resistance that infuses everyday life in the valley is indeed palpable. As we shall see, "resistance" means much more than "recalcitrance," "combativeness," and "rebellion"; it is also to endure, to withstand, to bear, and to cope with.[22]

In 2016, when I arrived with Basile who had been living in Haiti several years, we stayed with his former host, a middle-aged woman, Rénia, who was living alone with her son Adny (Despland 2021). She had no stable job, working sometimes at a local radio station and in an orphanage. She depended heavily on her daughter living in Martinique (and then in Corsica) and other kin from the diaspora. When I went back, each year between 2017 and 2020, it came to be that I stayed instead with the Artémis family. More details on this family will appear in the following chapters, but allow me to say a few words about them here, since they will accompany us throughout the whole book.

The small house of the Artémis family is located in Bwa-Mapou, a little upstream, on the first foothills of the Matheux mountain range, about a twelve-minute walk away from the main road that crosses the valley—the only paved road, even though only partially, in the region. Angeline and Frédéric, born respectively in 1982 and 1979, have two children together, Anaïca and Marley, born respectively in 2005 and 2009. Frédéric also has a son, Evens, from a former partner who lives in the poor areas of lower Port-au-Prince, and two other children who live in Miami, a boy and a girl, born from a previous marriage, whom I've never met. Often, one or two other relatives or acquaintances stay in the household for a while, a common habit in Haiti where the composition of households is often changing and recomposing. Angeline and Frédéric took great care and watched over me, not only rendering my research possible, but making my stay as pleasant and exciting as possible. They taught me how to go about daily life, and also schooled me on how to behave in different circumstances, how to be street smart and deal with so-and-so, especially in the trickier moments of the stay, when, for instance, the quickly shifting topographies of power made my route impassable; when the hands, holding the firearms, were ready to draw, be it for fun, intimidation, or battle; or when specific social obligations had to be diligently observed, and other times when they could be blithely ignored or subverted. Eventually, we became very close. Frédéric became the godfather of my son Naïm, born on October 14, 2022.

When I came to know Frédéric, he was earning a living as a bread merchant. He sold bread in Bwa-Mapou that he bought from a wholesaler in Port-au-Prince. He used to go back and forth between the cities two to three times weekly. The usual trip consisted of taking the first bus in the morning between 2:30 and 3:30 a.m. in order to arrive at dawn at the northwestern bus station in Port-au-Prince, at the border of the slums of Cité Soleil and Drouillard, before traffic jams made the entrance of the National Road No. 1 to the capital impossible. He would then take a *tap-tap* uptown to Pétion-ville to the wholesaler and carry the sacks containing buns or small baguettes all the way back to Cité Soleil. He stored the bags in a warehouse and would make two or three other trips to the wholesalers again. The bus station and the transport union being controlled by the local *baz*,[23] Frédéric had to bargain a deal: In exchange for a few bags of bread and a little cash, he enjoyed their protection. He had also introduced me to the local *chèf* and some of his "soldiers" so that they would know me. I would be "safe" each time I passed through there alone, at least before the conflicts erupted. Sometimes, Fred would stay overnight at his mother and sister's house, in a poor neighborhood downtown. But other times, he would take a bus back to the valley the same day with the bags stacked and fixed on the roof. He would arrive in the afternoon or evening and would go out again immediately, carrying the bags loaded with bread in his hands, for a first round of distribution. In fact, he would walk for miles on the stony paths of the hills to deliver the bread. He often found that his customers did not have the cash, so he kept careful records, which allowed him to return to all those who owed him money. This added tiresome walks. But what else was there to do? He privileged trust and mutual aid and was ready to sweat for that. When he finally got home, sometimes around 9 or 9:30 p.m., it would be no less than eighteen hours that he had been on the road and active.

For her part, Angeline is the administrator and bookkeeper at her uncle Robert's private school.[24] She occasionally teaches the lower grades. She also does administrative work at a public school in another area. Hence she could at least count on some form of salary, which is quite rare in Haiti, albeit small and always paid a few months late, if paid at all. But with the COVID-19 pandemic and the general degradation of the living conditions in recent years, the situation in schools has worsened to the point that they have had to close sometimes for several months consecutively. Many parents are not able to afford to pay school fees anymore, or are just unable to travel to the schools. Besides her job, Angeline generates a small income by making a spicy pasta for cooking and homemade peanut butter that she sells to acquaintances. She is also in charge of the household. Although Frédéric helps as much as he can, she does most of the housework: preparing breakfast; getting the children ready for school; buying what is needed at the market; cooking; cleaning; washing clothes; seeing to the children's needs; and meticulously managing the household's finances. She can also count on some help from her family: Anaïca has participated more and more as she's grown up[25]; sisters, aunts, nieces, and nephews, as well as some friends who are also neighbors, also provide support. But this means that Angeline is also always lending a hand to others. Finally, I'd like to mention that she is an active member of a local women's organization involved in community development and support for women. They have been able to access resources from international organizations, which has allowed them to provide some assistance to the needy families of the area.

As one can imagine, Frédéric's exhausting travels were not sustainable in the long run, not to mention the fact that he was taking a lot of risks by being on the road so much: He was at risk of accident, theft, kidnapping, or taking a stray bullet (*bal mawon*). In his late thirties when I met him, he was still in good shape, but soon began to show signs of deeper fatigue. In fact, the context really got worse after of the PetroCaribe scandal and the chaos it generated.[26] At times, the country was completely paralyzed for several days, sometimes weeks. Politically motivated assassinations and kidnappings were on the rise again, while state institutions were crumbling and armed groups were multiplying. Living with the Artémis family, I witnessed firsthand the disastrous impact of such a pace of life and uncertainty on Frédéric's health. After long discussions with family and friends, Angeline and Frédéric concluded that, in order to avoid the trips, it would be good to open a bakery in the village. They had given this a lot of thought. They wanted to create more than just a bakery. They had a vision: They wanted to create a place for the community, a "social bakery" that would not only provide food, but also a "taste for the future," as they put it. They wanted to make the well-being of the community their daily bread. In an idle community, they said, young people are more than others vulnerable to lethargy and forms of violence. They are at risk to themselves and to others. Only an educated and active community, they said, could prevent decline, violence, and destitution. It was clear to them that peace in the community could not be imposed by rules and law; and there's nothing one can expect from state institutions. A peaceful community would become possible only if people opened up toward each other, cultivate caring relationships, and reinvent modes of living. The aim with this bakery was to cultivate from below a communal intelligence. To do this, Frédéric said he'd first have to instill a taste for learning, encourage young people to take an interest in themselves and the world they live in, whet their appetite for things, and inspire the desire to initiate projects. If he could manage to open up a little bit of a future horizon for them, the whole community would benefit. And one direct benefit is that people forge links, get to know each other, and create conditions conducive to a slightly more serene life together. Yet, this is no easy task.

Eventually, the project went ahead. Since the bakery was close to the main crossroad, it very quickly became a spot where a handful of regulars would meet and hang out (including me). Frédéric had set up a few chairs on the porch. Just next door, Madanm Esther had a food stall and prepared *fritay* (Creole fried food). Across the street, Lily had her mini-grocery store, with cold drinks, including beer, and small bottles of rum. Next to her, a guy had set up a phone recharging stand. So, there was everything you needed to have a good time with friends at the end of the day.

This conviviality, this way of creating a pleasant and safe social space, was part of Frédéric's vision of what this place should be. And not just for friends and customers, but for the youth too. Indeed, during breaks or after school, some kids would spend a little time there. It was an opportunity for Frédéric to talk to them in his spare time. They talked openly, often joking, but also tackled serious issues. This allowed him to get a feel for what was on their minds, and to guide and advise them if necessary. Sometimes, he would give them small jobs, like going to deliver a bag of buns, or buying kerosene at the market. They exchanged services. It worked well. This mutuality has to be considered against the fact that some children go to school with empty stomachs; many don't eat their fill. So, Frédéric's policy was to sell quality bread, *pâtés*, and sandwiches at low prices, whatever the conjecture (even if that meant he would earn less or lose money); sometimes he offered what he had. Providing cheap, accessible, and quality food in a country where half of the population is chronically food insecure and a quarter of the children chronically malnourished,[27] was for him an act of resistance against *misè*, misery.

But with this new structure, came new challenges. First, he had to find the right flour, because the quality of flour on the market varies enormously. And sometimes he couldn't find any at all. Second, he needed to have help to knead the dough and put the dough through the mill, all by hand. Since it's extremely tiring and difficult work, it's not easy to find hands able and willing to help with this kind of work, and what's more, at inconvenient hours (before dawn, or at night). Third, he needed to be able to make bread that satisfies customers. Other breads are already available, and people are used to them. It's not easy to arrive on the market with a new bread and make sure it's to the customer's taste and that it's cheap. Finally, to these ordinary challenges were added the occasional problems caused by blockages, the main one being access to raw materials: not only flour, but also sugar, butter, and propane. Sometimes nothing was available at all. And if, thanks to his connections, he could find some, the products were very expensive (prices sometimes doubled or even tripled).

After some time, he was able to buy a propane-powered artisanal bread oven, with a capacity of four trays on which he could bake about fifty rolls each (two hundred per batch), before investing in a second oven. Since he used to make the dough by hand, he employed two teenagers to help him, but by March 2023, he was able to buy a motor and set up the dough-kneading machine. The mechanization of the system allowed for greater efficiency and less effort, but it also created greater risk. On Easter Monday, April 10, 2023, Frédéric got his left hand caught in the machine. His fingers were crushed. He stayed more than a month in a rural hospital surrounded by a war between armed groups, with Angeline by his side supporting him and providing him with what he needed (but therefore not at home taking care of the household). The doctors tried to heal his wounds and restore partial use of his fingers, but it became clear that the flesh around the bones was not going to recover, and the risks of necrosis and infection were too great. They finally had to amputate his index, middle, and ring fingers.

In these valleys, mountains, and cities, I very much navigated these networks, following the tracks of the contentions of different natures that arose around me, allowing myself to take side roads. This led me to inquire into different sections and neighborhoods, in the surrounding villages, as well as in the city of Gonaïves and in the poorer neighborhoods of downtown Port-au-Prince. I obviously had in mind what I had learned from situational analysis and the extended case method applied to the field of law. Yet, since I tried to work without a preconceived idea of where and what exactly I should be looking at, I mostly improvised, following the traces of what had happened and the lead of what was about to unfold. This method organically organizes itself in concentric circles, expanding unforeseeably in a sort of fibrillary network, thus keeping me open to the unexpected, the accidental. Hence, I inquired, not only among a great heterogeneity of interlocutors and collaborators who very much transformed my questions as I was moving forward, but I also came across a wide variety of documents, ranging from UN reports and drafts of legislative reforms to personal letters of accusation, WikiLeaks cables, and children's drawings.

So, for example, it was by playing with children that I learned certain gestures that adults make (when the children reenact them) and that I had failed to notice. Or it was through neighborhood meetings that I gained a certain sense of the complexity of assessing certain allegations. I was also led to participate in numerous Vodou services where, for instance, testimonies were heard in connection with ongoing cases. This method led me to follow, say, students in their classes at the law school; devotees on pilgrimages to historic sites of resistance to the state; or my family during carnival, where mock trials were improvised in the streets. I had settled myself the methodological goal of taking an interest in everything that interested those with whom I shared my time. All this to say that I tried to work deliberately without prejudging the parts and the whole, how they are connected, and the specific nature of the variations at play. I simply allowed myself to be instructed, at each stage, by the people I met along the way. It required patience, attention, and a certain willingness to let oneself be surprised. But at one point, however, I simply couldn't go on.

I left Haiti for the last time on March 4, 2020, on the last flight to Paris and just two weeks before the first total shutdown due to the COVID-19 pandemic. Since then, three times I have wanted to go back, and three times I was prevented: In December 2020, the persistence of the pandemic made it impossible; in May 2021, the flight from Paris that I was supposed to take had not yet been restored; and in November 2021, as I was in the Haitian corner of Mattapan, South Boston, with friends from the diaspora celebrating Thanksgiving, just a week before my departure, we took a common decision to cancel my flight. We concluded that, since the kidnappings had spiraled totally out of control since Moïse's death[28] and that the roads leading from the airport to Bwa-Mapou were blocked in several places, it was too risky for everyone. How did we get to this point?

FOREIGN OCCUPATION, INSTITUTIONAL REFORM, AND STATE COLLAPSE

At the time I began my research, the global context was heavily marked by judicial reform influenced by foreign intervention. Indeed, when I started this project in 2016, UN armed peacekeepers were planning to withdraw after officially thirteen years of military presence, whereas the United Nations' bureaucratic management would eventually take the lead and continue its so-called "nation-building" project. It has been a long time since Haiti was declared a "failed state" by the international community; thus, it was also declared incapable of self-governance and of reforming its own institutions. It therefore was (and is) said to need foreign assistance. Officially, The United Nations Mission for Justice Support in Haiti (MINUJUSTH) ended its mandate on October 15, 2019, handing over to the United Nations Integrated Office in Haiti (BINUH). The pervasive presence of the United Nations since roughly the fall of Jean-Claude Duvalier has had at least six important consequences in the judicial field. First, the United Nations' priority was the creation of a civil registry, which was seen as a first step toward population control, a precondition for establishing citizen rights. Second, after the dismantling of the army in 1994, it led to the creation of the Haitian National Police (HNP), trained and monitored even until today partly by foreign agencies. Third, in line with the promotion of human rights, the United Nations prompted the government to create in 1995 the National Penal Administration (APENA), responsible for overseeing all matters relating to the prison system.[29] Fourth, it gave birth in 2007 to the Superior Council of the Judiciary Power (CSPJ), an organ in charge of selecting and appointing magistrates, and issuing recommendations. Fifth, the same year the School of Magistrates was created, which was designed to standardize and unify the training of the jurists. Sixth, the United Nations supervised Haiti's first in-depth reform of its criminal code, disclosed in 2020, which was to be followed by a new Code of Criminal Procedure. All this took place under the supervision of the United Nations and bilateral agencies, which so profoundly shaped contemporary state institutions.[30]

Yet, as I sought to conduct research on the judicial cultures of the country, the Haitian state was in such advanced decay that I had to refocus my attention. In fact, I found myself in a position to witness the breakdown of the state apparatus. As a final blow, the COVID-19 pandemic, followed by the assassination of President Jovenel Moïse on July 7, 2021, have caused the main institutions to collapse: The Parliament was made null and void in January 2020. There were no longer any elected officials to sit in Parliament. Ariel Henry, backed by the Core Group,[31] awarded himself the position of prime minister the day after the death of Moïse and constituted a highly contested de facto government without elections and with no legal basis, whereas economist Fritz Jean was elected president after the Montana Accord,[32] even though controversially, but has never been able to assume that role. All this has taken place while more than two hundred armed groups were operating within the country, with, at the time, an estimate of 600,000 clandestine military weapons in circulation. By November 2024, they were controlling over 85 percent of the capital city and, according to the International Organization for Migration (IOM), an estimated 700,000 people are internally displaced, half of which are children. Moreover, the health system is bankrupt and largely out of use; public education is almost nonexistent; public infrastructure such as roads, water pipes, power supply, or waste management are in ruins or never existed; the police are either inoperative, understaffed and insufficiently equipped, or corrupt and at the service of the political wishes of all sides[33]; and the justice system is similarly clogged, ineffective, mismanaged, and subservient to shifting political powers.[34]

As can be imagined, my interlocutors, even those employed by the state, have a widespread feeling that public institutions are not trustworthy, if not downright noxious. A similar feeling is conveyed in many accounts. Greg Beckett's friend in Port-au-Prince, Luc, for instance, says, "The courts do nothing. The courts, the police, the government—they're all corrupt" (2019, 32). These are words one can often hear. Could it be, then, that the promise of peace and democracy—let's say, the promise of freedom, of modernity—has been so blinding and disappointing and hurtful that it has carried within itself its own forms of barbarism, backwardness, and monstrosity?

For most of the population, Jovenel Moïse embodied the most deplorable version of Haiti (Dougé-Prosper and Schuller 2021; Schuller 2021). As journalist Arnaud Robert (2021) wrote, Moïse's death by fire can be seen as the culmination of the worst debacle in the country since the fall of the Duvalier dictatorship in 1986. But what about all the anonymous deaths that it obscures? What about the lives that continue in the mess—literally and figuratively—left by the countless governments that have succeeded one another over the years? I had not imagined, when I started conceiving this book, to what extent its content would echo current events.

In the messages I received following death of Moïse, I read: "*Nap kenbe, malgre peyi a nou pa konn sa k ap fèt, n ap tann, pwoblèm ekonomik kap kraze nou,*" "we are holding on in spite of the fact that we don't know what is going to happen in the country, we are waiting, (it's) the economic problems (that) are crushing us." Or, "*Nap tann, nou pa ka fè anyen kounyea. Nap swiv,*" "we are waiting, there is nothing we can do for the moment. We'll see." Some people don't even really care; they have other, more pressing concerns that occupy them in the immediate future. After all, wasn't Jovenel Moïse the president that most sectors of public and community life wanted to see gone, tried for corruption, embezzlement, and crimes against humanity? Nevertheless, this death is that of a president: It is symptomatic of a situation whose effects are numerous and whose impact on daily life is considerable.

Haitians are accustomed to saying that everything in Haiti is political; at least that's what I kept hearing. As one would expect, there is the politics of politicians and big men. Without a doubt, it shapes part of the future of this country. However, there is another form of politics at work, which has little to do with ballots, international diplomacy, referendums, or guns. It is one that takes shape in the streets, schools, homes, fields, and backyards. Such politics of the ordinary, of the domestic, are embodied in a way of life, a way of being, a voice, a memory, a gesture, an object, and is depicted in the chapters gathered in this book.

THIS BOOK'S COMPOSITION

It is against such a backdrop that I conducted research and wrote this book. What initially guided the project was the idea that, by studying disputes and case processing while paying close attention to the ordinary dynamics of imposition, appropriation, and resistance to state law in a postcolonial context, I would get a clearer sense of the tensions inherent to legal pluralism, changing norms of justice, and informal regulatory practices. The general endeavor was to understand how a specific body of codified civil and criminal law has been institutionalized, amended, and adapted to local realities, how the contemporary social changes influenced such institutionalization, and how the locals' everyday reality has been modified by such legal norms. In turn, I was equally interested in how daily living and local practices influenced and changed state law. The three chapters (2, 3, and 4) at the center of the book are the result of that moment of research.

Chapter 2 revolves around the complex relation between legal and extrajudicial means of managing the consequences of a homicide. Through the detailed description of what followed the death of our neighbor, I was interested not only in the way in which litigants formulate changing and competing claims about their rights, obligations, and expectations, but also in the fact that they act in ways that are not based on any explicit claims or rules. However, I'm less interested in the devastating manifestations of overt violence than in the everyday struggles and latent conflicts that rustle underground, and that people have to deal with, which I call "the silent wars of the ordinary." Through meticulous attention to detail, I draw a different picture of what commonly counts as law, as well as the ways in which people relate to the judiciary. My ambition is to allow for another understanding of the making of ordinary legality by demonstrating how the silent wars of the ordinary are intrinsically constitutive of such making.

If the focus in Chapter 2 is on conflicts seen as the visible face of long-lasting wars simmering beneath the surface, in Chapter 3 I take the matter up again by looking, this time, more closely at the complex concept of peace at work in the everyday lives of the people I met, which I confront with more conventional views of peace. In fact, Haiti is seen by foreign funding agencies as well as by most of the media as a "failed" state that needs "help." What ensues, is usually a rhetoric of "peace-building" that takes the form of advocacy for "democracy," functioning as a justification for all kinds of interventions in domestic affairs. In this context, the rule of law is pictured as the necessary and unavoidable means by which Haiti would attain sufficient "peace" and "stabilization" to enable a democratic transition. One aim of this chapter is thus to make explicit a number of assumptions and the underpinnings of this normative view, as well as its effects on the ground. To do so, I propose a close look at the concept of peace within everyday life, especially in and around JP courts. By adopting this gaze from below, one will see that the promotion of the rule of law and peace can indeed, contrariwise, lead to destabilization, violence, and the reproduction of inequalities.

Chapter 4 challenges and complements some well-established ideas about law by emphasizing the theatrical character of conciliations and lawsuits, and the way it instructs us on the sort of relations instituted with state law. I will do so by tackling four aspects of the problem. First, I will consider the court, and other related spaces, as spaces where some of our concepts are projected, tested, and discussed, concepts such as ownership, heritage, suspicion, trust, and tolerance. This will bring me to discuss, secondly, the idea that, if the court is a place, not only for rational and cool-headed reasoning but also for the passionate expressions of human concerns, then the court constitutes an arena where improvisation plays a greater, or perhaps different, role than we habitually think of. Hence, thirdly, if the court is a place for the performance of the orality of the law, rather than for the mere application of the written word, then we would have to reckon with the fact that liveliness is a matter essential to law. Finally, a darker picture will appear if, to get a sense of what happens inside the courts, we venture outside and look at what happens in the interstices of ordinary life, for the playfulness that can go with the practice of law coexists with the violence it can generate.

As the situation deteriorated to the point that the judiciary almost stopped functioning, I had to redesign my project. The situation changed so quickly: Courts were inoperative sometimes for months, even years; some were looted, evidence was stolen, and the infrastructure destroyed; employees became unable to practice, since they were often unable to travel, unpaid, and under threat of death. Many have been killed. Moreover, I often could not meet up with the people I was supposed to meet or travel around at will. Cases were either dismissed, reported, abandoned, or just interrupted, and the people involved would simply disappear. And when I saw the disillusionment on my friend Alix's face—he who was about to graduate from law school and had envisioned serving his country by becoming a lawyer fighting for the rights of the disadvantaged, who was now trying to keep his head above water by selling phone cards and pills for a few pennies—I could not but reorient myself after such a sight. As it turns out, this book became more an ethnography of a moment of institutional failure and collapse seen from within the margins of the state. From there on, something else began to rustle. It became important to convey the way people still stand up and go on, despite decades of unending strife and backlashes. In their own manner, they resist, aspire, dream, and struggle for a better future; but they also endure disappointments, discontent, frustration, and rage. And all this, in one way or another, has something to do with the place the law occupies in their lives. It has therefore become important to convey a different sense of what it means to be human; that is, what it means to lead a human life in those circumstances.

This has become the theme of the other three chapters (1, 5, and 6) that surround the three central chapters I have just presented. Chapter 1 takes the form of a chronicle composed from notes that I compiled in a diary on how violence appears in the interstices of everyday life. By paying heed to the details of ordinary interactions and the swells that affect communal life, I tried to capture something of the atmosphere of Haiti's recent history, in which it has become difficult to breathe, thus, to think. There are people who walk in silences too compact to be penetrated, who push on silently, withdrawn from the world; others who stir in a swirl too molten to be approached, whose raw nerves ignite endless sparks. Others oscillate between fighting and retreating. But all are affected by the violence that reverberates in unexpected regions of human experience. It is this refraction that I want to make tangible in this initial chapter, which also serves to set the scene.

This state of muteness, of subjection, of withdrawal from the world in which one moves as if in a trance, a world that resembles a waking dream or a nightmare, has a name: *zonbi*. Chapter 5 takes the emergence of the figure of the zombie in the reform of the Penal Code as a point of departure. It then looks at what it means to live a life in which zombies have a place, including in law. In fact, zombification became a main issue among the commission tasked with drafting the new code. By paying attention to the different contexts in which the Haitian zombie appears, including cultural works such as literature, carnival, and cinema, this chapter discusses how realism can be thought in relation to anthropology's interest in the nuances of everyday life. Attention to forms of corrosion internal to the ordinary allows us to understand how a concept like "zombie" offers a means of investigating human life.

This investigation ends with a sort of meditation on what it is to live up to one's finitude in a world that has collapsed. By juxtaposing heterogeneous scenes from quotidian life, Chapter 6 traces the combat for life in a world that has in some ways already died. Through its attention to minor characters, this chapter shows different aspects of the forms of death that permeate Haiti's everyday landscapes and the impulses that arise from them. It draws on different, elusive ethnographic moments when, for instance, a drunken man lays down to nap in a coffin, or when people nail charms on a tree trunk in the cemetery to avert or provoke death, but also on fragments of the story of Rodny, a young man who, from bewitchment to prison, brings us back to the question of our subjection to fate. This chapter notably takes up an ancient philosophical theme, that of learning how to die, which I reread from and through the ordinary. Thus, this chapter aims to show that considering what matters is not so much prompted by spectacular events as it is by minute details and the uneventful.

This whole book is an opening onto a horizon of possible thoughts; at least that's my aspiration. Indeed, one of the challenges is to imagine the extent to which people cope with disappointments and disillusionment by reinventing themselves and their relationships with each other. Life finds its way. One of the questions that thus arises in such a context is, as Frédéric and Angeline put it: How can one still nurture a "taste for the future?" This book sets out to show how some people have found ways to breathe new life into the present and make the future worth fighting for.

1

"WE'RE HOLDING ON!": A CHRONICLE

"We are torn between the greed of knowing
and the despair of having known"

—RENÉ CHAR

"Words cry tonight."

—KERMONDE LOVELY FIFI

"but how to tell
the words are crazy"

—GEORGES CASTERA

"Writing is as fragile as living."

—LYONEL TROUILLOT[1]

PREAMBLE

This chapter is written in a different form and style from the other chapters. Indeed, the following text is a chronicle composed from notes recorded in a diary I kept during one of my stays in Haiti, between October, 2018, and February, 2019. It thus follows a diurnal rhythm in which seemingly unrelated events and small facts begin, as the days go by, to acquire a certain significance in relation to one another. This tempo of writing, and the posture that went with it—to record what seemed important at the time, without prejudging or applying criteria other than those emerging from the experience itself—made it possible to elucidate certain aspects generally unseen of the violence in Haiti. At the same time as it can be read as an encounter with the world of Bwa-Mapou, the rural area where I lived and in which the research was conducted, it is also an account of the lives of its residents during dark times.

The narration begins on October 27, three days before the start of the Feast of the Dead, and ends on November 18, the date of the anniversary of the victory of Dessalines's army in the 1803 Battle of Vertières that led to Haiti's independence from the French colonists. Between these two dates, on November 13, 2018, the massacre of La Saline took place, presumably sponsored by the PHTK, Jovenel Moïse's political party in power, and led by the troops of Jimmy Cherizier, known as Barbecue. The detailed investigations of the National Human Rights Defense Network (RNDDH), the Fondasyon Je Klere (FJKL), the Center for Human Rights Analysis and Research, and the Harvard Law School International Human Rights Clinic are eloquent and corroborated by public and media opinion.[2] There is no quantifying the succession of large-scale atrocities that have taken place in the history of this land. The one in La Saline was perpetrated in the wake of the political massacres of the post-Duvalier years; but since the fall of the regime, this event stands out for its extreme cruelty and magnitude. What did it herald? I have no clear answer, but one thing is certain, the killings went on, intensifying, and moments of respite have become ever fewer since.

I was a few miles away from the event when it took place, but I didn't know it right away, and only became aware of it later, when I began to feel a certain contraction in the minds and bodies around me. The atmosphere was not quite the same anymore; nor was the air we breathed. "For some time now," wrote Yanick Lahens back in 1997 (2019, 165), eleven years after the fall of the dictatorship and during a period of great instability, "the silences have been heavier to bear, and the dreams were lost along the way." A wave of violence had already knocked out "thirty years of a revolution on the march, followed for nearly a decade by a fallen democracy. . . . The revolution of the father and the son had given birth to monstrosities."

In 2018, the nature of the pressure seemed to have changed again. It left no one in peace, as if old demons that were thought to be dormant had begun to stir. The late President Jovenel Moïse—assassinated in his bed on July 7, 2021—had raised fears of the worst by taking measures that seemed to lead more and more clearly to an authoritarian and autocratic regime. Among these measures, let us note a few: On January 13, 2020, he ratified the nullity of the Parliament (which no longer exists) and thereafter governed by unconstitutional presidential decrees; on February 7, 2021, when his presidential term was coming to an end and elections were due to be held, he simply stayed in office and refused to organize the elections; while resistance was coming together on several fronts, he used force and extreme violence, mainly with the help of hybrid armed groups (both police and criminals) who acted as henchmen, to intimidate and silence opposition outbreaks. In addition, there was the unprecedented creation of a coalition of the most powerful armed groups in Port-au-Prince, called the *G9 an Fanmi e Alye*, the G9 Family and Allies, as well as an armed group of violent dissident police officers, the Fantòm 509. Unsurprisingly, the violence has continued, claiming thousands of lives since, and causing over 700,000 internally displaced people.

Among the citizens who suffer from this situation are friends of mine who, in one way or another, are affected by this violence. By some effect of resonance, the shifts in the nature of the conflict between the power in place and the population have also changed the way I perceive it. Certainly, there comes a moment when a reality imposes itself brutally: It is the shock, the bombshell of reality, as it were; but something was already smoldering for a long time, with a sort of trembling light inhabiting the ordinary gestures. It is this rustling that I try to make heard in these lines.

The violence of the events that have followed one after another since 2018 is hardly imaginable and opposes any wish to grasp it. There is a difficulty here with some part of reality, with which understanding is at odds. Something resists the mind's will to get a hold on what eludes it and leaves us speechless, as if we don't really have a concept for that, or the concepts we do have—those of "human being," "love," "dignity," or "life," for example—have been abused and mutilated (see Benoist 2021a; Das 2022; Diamond 2003). It is as if the order of language itself had been shaken, perverted, and bruised. It seems to me at times that some of our concepts are as good as dead. Writing this text in French before translating it into English, then, has turned out to be a way of reviving the words that are dear to us, the concepts that matter, without which we would be, perhaps, condemned to be only zombies (see Chapter 5).

One of the effects of this violence is that it prevents us in part from seeing clearly, from thinking, and therefore from writing. It is as if there was a difficulty there which concerns not that which one ignores, but the excessiveness of what one knows—its madness. This chronicle is therefore an attempt to respond to this difficulty by accepting that we do not look such a massacre in the face, but rather see its reflection in the mirror of daily life. It is then necessary to listen to the silences that reveal as much the tremors of violence as the shivers of love.

The decision to place this chronicle as the first chapter is guided by the desire to give a sense of the pulse of everyday life before focusing more specifically on issues of law and justice, because it is from *within this* everyday life, as I said in the Prologue, that we will understand the issues at stake in the following chapters.

CHRONICLE

Saturday, October 27, 2018, Bwa-Mapou. The afternoon light is so white that I can hardly keep my eyes open. In the distance, clouds still cling to the bald hills that surround the valley. It is the end of the cyclone season. Over the next few weeks, the sky will gradually recover all the intensity of its royal blue, the clouds departing, leaving only the sun and the wind to scorch the spirits, and the dust to dull the dreams.

I arrived three days ago. To take the pulse of the situation, I linger at the crossroads of the Grande Rue, the only paved road that crosses the village, and that connects the Dominican Republic to Saint-Marc, to Gonaïves, and to the Arcadian coast. I buy two Comme Il Faut cigarettes from Angly, who sells those by the stick, and shots of a *tafia* twist—homemade rum in which herbs and barks are macerated—at a rickety old wooden workbench. He's settled in front of a building under construction, a building destined to become a police station. It will remain unfinished for several years. In 2021 it will be occupied by a patrol for about two months. After the murderous raids carried out by armed groups in the valley against other precincts, the police will flee before they too fall victim to the assaults. For the moment, the reinforced concrete skeleton houses hashish smokers and young people deported from the United States by what was coldly named ICE (US Immigration and Customs Enforcement) following the attacks of September 11, 2001. I smoke while listening to the news of the moment, but I have to go. I am expected at Ariel's *kay*.[3]

Along the road, I pass in front of Mesac's store, where he sells phone cards, USB keys, and services: photocopying, printing, layout, text processing, photography. I stop for a moment to chat. Stanley is there too. We talk about Mesac's next stay in Florida, where he works illegally in the tomato fields or in the orange groves.[4] We laugh too. But when I ask what's the latest news, their faces darken. They tell me a lynching took place earlier this year.

A group of three young men broke into a local resident's house and stole a motorcycle, using violence against the owner. Things went wrong. Two of the accomplices managed to escape, but the third was caught and beaten up by an angry crowd. When the alarm was sent, the CASEC and notables[5] of the area intervened to prevent the situation from degenerating. They locked the thief in their office while waiting for the police, while outside the tin gate, the crowd grew. When the police finally arrived, they had to fight their way into the compound. As they were about to leave in the direction of the police station with the young man, who was already quite badly injured, in the back of the pickup truck, the crowd destroyed the metal gate and entered the courtyard. Under the helpless eye of the CASEC and the police, part of the crowd pulled him out of the vehicle into the street and stoned him. The corpse was then dragged by a rope to a corner of the cemetery where it was burned.

I remain speechless.

Mesac specifies it is the accomplices of the young man who provoked the crowd, who incited them to kill their fellow man, essentially by fear that they would be denounced. They allegedly participated in the lynching themselves. They know only too well, he tells me, how a prisoner can yield under pressure and rat out his companions. Stanley, suddenly wound up, adds, "But the CASEC are also involved! They arrest some and not others, even though they know very well what is going on. They are corrupt, too! Besides, one of them, Miracson, has already killed before."

I go out alone in the street to smoke my second cigarette. A phrase from Jean-Euphèle Milcé's *Alphabet of Nights* (2004, 102) comes to mind: "The Artibonite, a valley full of holes, shadows and cemeteries."

A grandmother walks in front of me with her granddaughter, whom she is holding by the hand, while a motorcycle passes right by her, dragging concrete irons on the ground and spitting sparks. A *tap-tap*, a pickup truck that serves as public transport, driving in the opposite direction leans to the side, with its load of goods and passengers returning from the Pont Sondé market. Everything seems to have moved back at a certain distance as if retreated into a distant, odorless, abstruse hinterland.

"Mako!" The scrap metal dealer across the street snaps me out of my reverie. He shouts with his visor raised on his forehead, almost offended that I looked in his direction without seeing him.

Mesac then appears on the doorstep and tells me that at 4 p.m. a meeting between various local leaders is to be held in the new market. The brand-new building has been erected by a priest who is also chaplain to the local police force, the same force that I later learn is bound to be involved in the armed conflicts that will soon erupt in the valley. The aim of the meeting is to generate ideas for the development of Bwa-Mapou and to discuss the community's future. I make my cigarette butt fly and turn around: "All right, let's go!"

There must be about fifty people there. I know some of them well. There is Malcolm, a former student of the Faculty of Ethnology in Port-au-Prince; Rosalvo, Mesac's cousin, director of a vocational school; Mathias, a well-known *oungan* from the area who practiced in Brazil; Mirlanda, a *manbo* and candidate in the departmental elections; Rénia, a radio host and activist in the Baptist church, with whom I lived for a couple of months in 2016; and Kénol, the director of a development center for peasant agriculture. The meeting has already started. I and my two companions sit quietly in the back. The discussions are passionate and revolve around citizen participation, hypocrisy in politics, and organization. Some point to specific development problems in the area, such as the state of the roads, the provision of electricity, or access to education. Others look for blame. Mirlanda complains about the proliferation of mystical attacks, that people are hateful and only think of attacking each other through occult means. "This is the real reason for Haiti's underdevelopment," she says. Others would like to separate from the commune of Bouquet-Duvoisin (of which the area is a part) and become autonomous. Despite the differing opinions, everyone seems to at least agree that it is necessary to transcend personal interests in order to think of the good of the community; but no concrete decision is taken. After several hours of discussion, another meeting is scheduled in a few months, without an action plan. We leave the room, empty-handed.

It is dark when I arrive at Ariel's house. The *sèvis*[6] has already started. I am welcomed by Simbi dlò, the serpent *lwa*, doctor and guardian of the springs and water points. He welcomes me to Haiti.

Sunday, October 28. In the late morning, I go with Frédéric for a meeting in the office of Miracson, the head of the CASEC of the area. A shiver seeps through me when we pass the new metal door into the courtyard. The same courtyard where the young man, a few months earlier, was taken from the hands of the authorities to be killed. Right there. This silver door made of corrugated iron and impeccably new in the middle of an old, dented metal fence is a witness. It attests to the violence of which we are capable. It is the irreducible trace of it.

Monday, October 29. Since this morning, I feel muddy, almost nauseous. Without being really sick, I am down. I turn over in my bed for the umpteenth time when suddenly I hear the children coming back from school, so cheerful and alive. They come storming into my room, without paying any attention to my condition, begging me to accompany them to the river. They say they have no school this afternoon. I tell them that I am not well, but at their touch, my torpor quickly dissipates.

After enjoying a dish of rice with black pea sauce accompanied by herring, and having swallowed a fruit juice made from soursop fruit, we run with full stomachs to Cherline's yard to pick up the cousins and friends. In two shakes of a lamb's tail, the flock is ready to leave in the direction of the Zephyr, the small river which flows not far from there during the rainy season.

As soon as they arrive, some of them undress and jump naked with their arms in front of them into the fresh and transparent water that comes down from the hills. The afternoon is spent playing in the water of the pool dug by the children, throwing themselves into it, doing dangerous jumps, apnea competitions, and human pyramids. The little ones stay on the edges, while the older ones are proud to contest the current or jump into the deeper part. The teenagers are overjoyed. The boys have fun fighting each other. The girls, imitating the washerwomen, make rhythms by beating the water like a drum. Then they throw themselves on the boys, or the opposite, to make themselves fall into the water; but it is actually to touch each other. Discreetly, the bodies remain entwined for a few seconds. The boys press their naked torsos against the backs of the girls who have kept their shirts on, hugging them, before pushing each other away and laughing.

A few meters away, below, some women accompanied by young girls are washing clothes. They look at us, amused, and whisper among themselves. A little higher up, a naked father soaps himself several times while his little daughter is busy alone in a small basin that he has built especially for her. Then a peasant appears between the high grass with his mule, a machete hanging from his belt. He stops, amazed, and looks at us for a long time. I smile back at him. His face lights up. He leaves, laughing.

At dusk, I go with Fred to the bakery. He has to prepare the dough for the next day's breads, and sell his stock of the day. Stanley joins us.

—*Sa k ap fèt baz pam?* (How's it going, brother?)

—*Nap kenbe!* (We're holding on!)

Under his falsely cheerful air, he looks sad. Three folding chairs are set up under the awning that overlooks the busy evening street. Without a lamp, the street is illuminated from the side by the few cars and motorcycles that pass by, but especially by the noisy trucks that arrive in a hurry, with defective headlights and brakes, from the Dominican Republic. The dust they stir up blurs the already dim light. We hear them more than we see them.

I cross the street to buy three Prestige at Lily's. The beers are not very cold. I feign discontent, and blame her for not taking care of her customers.

—*Ann mete plis glas nan frizè la! Yon Prestige ki pa frèt sa pa bon machè!* (You need to put more ice in your freezer! A lukewarm Prestige is really disgusting!)

—*Dakò cheri, men banm di goud an plis!* (Okay honey, but it'll will cost you ten gourdes more!)

We laugh.

As I hand Stanley a beer, I can feel his energy is low. He probably hasn't eaten. He has little means and sometimes does not even eat a real meal a day. Without saying anything, I go to Madanm Esther's, just next door, to get some pieces of *fritay*—plantains and fried pork.

Stanley tells us that he is back from the hospital. He accompanied a friend's wife to visit the friend who had been shot in the leg a few hours earlier. The story begins with the arrest of a certain Cassiodore, an influential bus driver who travels between neighboring Dominican Republic to the east and Gonaïves to the north. He was arrested at the border, which should not have happened because of his privileges. Suspecting his rivals of having bribed the border guards to stop his business and destroy his reputation, while they went on their way without hindrance, Cassiodore immediately called his contacts to block the road to other buses coming from Pont Sondé, Saint-Marc, and Gonaïves. A barricade of stones and tires was to be erected near the house of Stanley's friend, the mechanic. Looking for anything they could find, Cassiodore's henchmen broke into the mechanic's yard to take the tires he was storing there. He firmly resisted and a fight broke out. After shooting him, the assailants left with what they were looking for.

While Stanley is finishing his story, my phone vibrates in my pocket. Mesac is calling me from Cité Louverture in Port-au-Prince. He is nervous and excited. "It's too tense, man! There's shooting everywhere!" I ask him what is going on, but he is vague. A conflict has broken out between the gangs in the area. "*Nap pale!*" ("let's talk again!"). He hangs up.

Fred then pulls out his phone and plays a two-minute recording he received on WhatsApp. It's continuous automatic gunfire. Apparently, it is happening right now in Portail Léogâne, a stone's throw from downtown, not far from Cité Louverture. A few blocks away is the Village de Dieu, the stronghold of a certain Arnel Joseph, leader of an armed dissident group, called "baz" by the locals, and "gang" by the media and politicians.[7] Fred's brothers and friends are informing him that the shootings have spread to the Marché Salomon and Route des Dalles, as well as to different areas of the neighborhoods of Carrefour-Feuille and Martissant.

Arnel is the leader of the Bicentenaire (officially called Harry Truman Boulevard), a highly strategic area in the lower part of the city. He was reportedly shot at while driving through the area. "So he's fighting back," I'm told. Fred and Stanley are cautious: It's hard to know what's going on, but it doesn't bode well. When armed groups in different parts of Port-au-Prince start a war, it has consequences for the whole country. The affected area is not only the epicenter of the national market of Croix-des-Bossales from where the vast majority of merchants from all over the country, including those of Bwa-Mapou, get their wares, but also the only transit axis between the north and south of the country. If a war breaks out in this area, the whole country is paralyzed.

I would learn much later that Arnel Joseph was arrested by the National Police (HNP) on July 22, 2019, and incarcerated in the Croix-des-Bouquets prison. On February 25, 2021, he would escape with more than four hundred prisoners after a mutiny. He would be killed the next day by police during a checkpoint in L'Estère, in the Artibonite, not far from where his gang will have established after being relocated from Village de Dieu by rival groups.

Around 1:00 a.m., I am awakened by a good dozen gunshots on the main street. Despite the fact that I am staying with Fred and his family, in the hills about a ten-minute walk from the road, I hear everything. The sound echoes far into the silent night at this hour. The next day, Fritznel will tell me that it was just a bunch of kids having fun; but he will add that it is also to intimidate the justice of the peace and the CASEC, since there are cases involving them. Others will tell Fred that the skirmish was caused by thieves who were chased by armed citizens. No one around me will try to unravel what really happened, as if it were pointless to pursue a truth that will in any case never reveal itself as one and unique.

Tuesday, October 30. I spend the afternoon in Cherline's yard with one of her aunts, Régine—who would die on February 1, 2020 from an *atak mistik*, a mystical attack[8]—and a young girl, a local *manbo*. While the leaves of *lalo*, a kind of spinach, are being sorted and prepared for the next day's succulent dish of pigs' feet and small freshwater crab, we talk about everything and nothing, we make jokes. Cherline is a talkative person and doesn't miss a chance to tell stories. She knows that I am interested in Vodou and occult affairs. So, she asks me, "Have you ever seen a *lougawou*?" I answer that I have not, but I have heard of them. She retorts that it is possible to see them.

"But it is not so easy!" interrupts Robert, who passes in the court.

She continues. There are plenty of them in the area, especially young girls who try to get away with it. They go to the *bòkò* to buy *wanga*[9] and potions to attract the men they want. "This makes them more attractive," she says, as the *manbo* imitates a young girl strutting her stuff. Indebted to the *bòkò* for their services, the girls find themselves in the position of having to pay off debts that they cannot assume. The *bòkò* then demands that they bring back the blood of newborns or young children. When a person reaches this point, they have become a *lougawou*. I ask if there are not also men who become *lougawou*. She says yes, but it is rarer. She calls these men "brunettes."

Cherline has three daughters, born in 2004, 2014, and 2017. All of them had been victims of *lougawou* attacks when they were young, to varying degrees. Two became very sick and one almost died. Hospitalizations and local medical treatments, including care by members of her religious community, the Redeemed Church of the Lord, were not enough. Finally, remedies concocted by an *oungan* allowed her daughters to survive.

Cherline continues. She tells me the story of her grandfather, born in 1922. We are currently in his yard, which Cherline inherited. He was a section chief during the Duvalier dictatorship. On several occasions, he was attacked by a *lougawou*. Using his knowledge of *mistik*, he captured the creature in the form of a turkey and locked it in a room. With his skills, he was able to change it back to its human form. She was an old woman, a neighbor. He then attached her to a tree in the yard and beat her with a stick; "hard and long," Cherline adds. She gestures with her hand and frowns. Her expression is violent. She looks at me and nods: "Yes, when you beat a *lougawou*, it doesn't feel anything! That's how you know it's a *lougawou*!" The grandfather eventually brought the woman to the police station, where she was imprisoned. Many people then went to the police to complain, accusing her of causing other misdeeds. She became the perfect scapegoat. On the one hand, the case was inadmissible under the law, which does not recognize the kind of crime the woman is accused of. On the other hand, there was a risk that she would be lynched on her way out and that would have made waves. The police, Cherline tells me, preferred to execute her themselves. It seemed to suit everyone.

Wednesday, October 31. In Cherline's yard, the children gather. As long as there is water, Wednesday afternoons are reserved for playing in the river. As I wait, I feel behind my back the tree that this woman was tied to. I shudder.

The kids run down the slope toward the Zephyr at full speed. They shout and throw words in the air in a lilting Creole that gets lost in the almond trees that line the path. The older ones run without worrying about the rocks. These offspring of the Haitian countryside have grown up with stones under their feet and stars in their eyes.

They run with their chests puffed out for the simple pleasure of racing. No winner. No losers. Their joy is contagious. I start to run too, taking the little ones by the hand. An afternoon at the river is worth celebrating! At the corner of the neighbor's house, the most agile jump over the irrigation canal that crosses the road. The others jump from stones to ledges. I walk in the mud, like an idiot. One of my sandals gets stuck. The children laugh.

The water of the rice field behind the candelabra fence overflows and floods the last part of the path before the river. The stones are slippery. I yell to runners ahead to be careful, that they will get hurt, but I can't see them anymore. I slow down and walk cautiously with the younger children in this rocky and soaked recess.

The smaller ones jump into the river with carelessness and move painfully up the weak current of this stretch of clear water, sandals in hand, in direction of the group of elders. I follow them, with this strange feeling all of a sudden that something is happening. The bodies are clustered higher upstream, on the shore. I see abrupt, tense gestures, and hear cries still, but not the same ones. The joy has not disappeared, but it has darkened.

The ferocity of the older children has fallen on a snake, already torn apart by the stones thrown at it. The little ones look on, stunned, at the spasms that still agitate this body of wounded leather. The older ones laugh proudly as they throw the last stones to make sure that the snake is truly killed.

I stammer out a silly remark, something like, "But why did you do that!" I can only receive in return an answer as stupid as my question: "because it is a snake." That is all. I don't have the courage to pursue nor the desire to play the sanctimonious adult. And I especially don't want to destroy what should be, and will be for them, a happy afternoon at the river. The older children are already splashing around in the pool again. The little ones are hesitant. Some of them are still stunned by the corpse. A disturbance has set in. I think of the man who died under the stones. And of so many others who died in this way, whose memories have been erased by the stories of the deaths that follow them.

When we get to the pool, the boys want to play with me. They would like me to jump into the water and invent acrobatics for them to do. The girls ask me to take part in a contest of who can stay the longest under water. But my heart is not in it anymore. I sit aside on a rock and I watch them have fun. What difference is there between children and adults? And between a snake and a human being?

Coming up from the river in the late afternoon, I find Robert, Sony, and Fritznel in Cherline's yard, drinking. They invite me to join them. Sony hands me a cold Prestige from a big cooler, and with the other hand, a glass of *kleren*, an artisanal rum. They are already quite drunk. You can tell this by the wide gestures they make with their arms, their bloodshot eyes, and the volume of their discussion.

They talk about politics, development, justice, the role of the diaspora. I catch on the fly the issues at stake in the discussion, which revolves around the demonstrations that have been taking place throughout the country since July. Sony waxes lyrical about how the situation has only gotten worse since he returned from the United States a few years ago. He lived in New York and Miami in the late 1980s and the following two decades. While crisscrossing America as a heavy truck driver for a not-so-transparent

Sicilian construction company, he learned a lot about doing good business behind the administration's back. In the ghetto of East New York, he says he learned how to kill with one blow, with his bare hands, by tearing out the glottis of his opponent. After being married to a Palermo woman and divorced, he married Régine. He has two children from his first marriage who live in Miami. Port-au-Prince is less than two hours away by plane, so he often flies back and forth. He has a green card and a pension from the American union, which allows him to live comfortably in Haiti. He doesn't like the way the country is going and denounces the laissez-faire attitude, laziness, and opportunism of the Haitians, in front of whom he places the Italians: hard-working, ingenious, and smart. He ends his speech by uncapping four beers with his teeth.

When the discussion turns to local affairs, they start talking about secret societies, especially the *sanpwèl*, the "hairless." These societies fascinate as well as frighten the population. Associated with occult rites that contribute to the mystery surrounding them, the *sanpwèl* feed the imagination and stories that frighten. It is said that they are cannibals, and that they possess extremely powerful mystical abilities. They come out mainly at night, after midnight, and "*yo fè bagay*," they "do things," especially in the crossroads.

Among the places that are essential in the geography of Haitian mysticism, there are the crossroads. "Each crossroads places itself at the listening of the defunct passions," writes Milcé (2004, 25). These are places of residence and "work" of many *lwa*, including Legba, also called Master Crossroads, the old cripple who "opens the barriers." He is responsible for the paths and roads, guardian of the gates and fences, bearer of the banners of the societies associated with the Vodou sanctuaries. He is the one who indicates the way. He is also the interpreter of the other *lwa*. The *sanpwèl* also work at these crossroads with the *lwa* called Kalfou, Kriminel, or Bossou-twa-Kòn. I have sometimes heard strange sounds on the surrounding paths during the night, suggesting the passage of the *sanpwèl*. In the early morning, one can sometimes see in a crossroads the remains of what was played out there during the night: burnt wax, remains of bones, sometimes charred, small pieces of colored cloth, traces of flour or ash. It is said that if you walk late at night and you come across one of these groups, you can't go back. You need either a password that only the members know, or something to offer in exchange for a pass. Otherwise, you risk much.

Cherline warned me that you can be kidnapped and have your blood sucked. Others have told me that they can give you a *kout lè*, a mystical "blow of air," by releasing the secret contents of a bottle; you can die from it. The impossibility of establishing a boundary between reality and fantasy feeds the fear and fascination for these groups. The *oungan* and the *bòkò* that I know well have reassured me that if ever I should meet the *sanpwèl* at night, I would have no problems, that they would ensure my safety.

Two weeks later, Cherline will come to see me in my room to tell me about a dream—a "nightmare," she will say. It was night. Somewhere in Bwa-Mapou, both of us were hidden on the edge of the road, she on one side, I on the other. We saw each other, but we didn't talk, when suddenly a *sanpwèl* group passed by. A single woman was in the street at that moment. As they passed, one of the *sanpwèl* opened her belly with a dagger and continued on their way. The disemboweled woman left screaming and holding her guts in her hands. In the dream, Cherline and I looked at each other, stunned. She will tell me that the "*sanpwèl konn fè sa*," that "that's the kind of thing they do": They kill and eat humans and animals that are in their path. Sometimes they call us by our first name three times in a row, so we must not answer, otherwise we make ourselves vulnerable to their fate. She herself has been called several times.

Sony pours me another drink. I am starting to feel a little muddy, but I concentrate so as not to miss anything. Angeline's uncle, Robert, a former mayor of the commune who now runs a large private school in the area, says that *sanpwèl* used to play a key role in local affairs. "Now things have changed." When he was a kid, Robert says, they had powers they don't have today, including the ability to protect certain areas and attack others, much like an organized vigilante group. At the head of the societies is an emperor who has guards, judges, lawyers, and inspectors under him. The hierarchy within these societies mimics that found in the state. They may be called in to arbitrate disputes or more covertly employed to attack. Sony adds that when he was a young resident of the neighboring commune, there was visible collusion between the *sanpwèl* and political power. During the *sanpwèl* festival on January 6—which is officially the Feast of Kings, but unofficially the Feast of Emperors, during which societies go out into the streets, pass through the *oumfò* of the region, and ritually perform their power—he recalls seeing senators, ministers, and government commissioners. It is not uncommon today for senators or local politicians, as well as the police, to "visit" during Vodou services, especially to "shake hands." I've seen it for myself on several occasions. These groups have considerable influence in the region. They constitute an alternative power to the state without which the officials cannot exercise theirs. Robert and Sony conclude that the power of *mistik* is indeed at the basis of the victory of the Haitian Revolution—otherwise how could slaves have routed the troops of the invincible Napoleon? But it has weakened considerably. Today, it is more firearms than *mistik* that make the rules of the game. But guns have their own magic.[10]

Intoxicated, I go home. It is already dark, but fortunately the house is right next door. Two gunshots burst, very close. I find Angeline in the kitchen, who tells me that it is probably Robert's .22 Beretta. As a former magistrate, he has a permit to carry weapons. And sometimes, when men are drunk, they like to shoot in the air for fun.

Thursday, November 1, Port-au-Prince. With my eyes closed, I relieve myself on a hill of still-smoldering garbage, enjoying the first rays of the sun that warm my face. I was cold in the bus, speeding along the still deserted provincial roads with open windows. It is almost 6:30 a.m. when Fred, Stanley, and I arrive at the bus station in Cité Soleil. We left Bwa-Mapou around 3 a.m. The day that awaits us will be long.

When, in the bottom of a suffocating bistro of the Rue de la Réunion, we finally sit down to have breakfast, it is past 9 a.m. We are hungry, so we order everything that is ready: ground corn purée, chicken liver soup, bananas, plantains, avocados, potatoes, and passion fruit juice. Fred takes a beer. Then a second one. Stanley and I catch up with him. We eat without talking. The TV in a cage above our heads is broadcasting a Café Philo program on the theme: "Parapsychology and zombification." We listen with one ear, but tiredness and appetite divert our attention.

All Saints' Day is an important date in Haiti, where both Catholic saints and the *lwa* of Vodou are celebrated. It is also the *fèt gede*, the feast of the *gede* spirits, the conveyors of the dead souls, the agents of Bawon Lakwa and Grann Brigit, the couple in charge of the cemeteries, guardians of the dead.

We go to the grand cemetery of Port-au-Prince in the early afternoon, under a blazing sun. On the road, we walk on traces of soot still visible, witnesses of the tires burned in recent days. There are still some irretrievable wires and especially many stones, ready to be reused. These are the marks of the recent anti-government protests and conflicts between rival factions.

On July 6, Prime Minister Lafontant had announced an increase in gasoline prices of nearly 150 percent. Within an hour, Port-au-Prince was barricaded. The thick smoke of burning tires dulled the horizon. Riots broke out everywhere. A week later, under pressure from the street, the government resigned. Then, the price of gasoline dropped, but the question on everyone's lips was: "Where is the PetroCaribe money?" "*kòt kòb PetwoKaribe a.*" This question foreshadowed the scandal that would come to light in January 2019, when the first report of the Superior Court of Accounts and Administrative Disputes (CSCCA) on the management of projects financed by the PetroCaribe fund would be published.[11] It would reveal that the highest officials in the state were setting up a large-scale embezzlement scheme. This report and the two that would follow would prove a misappropriation over a period of ten years, involving several presidents, first ladies, prime ministers, various other ministers, judges, senators, and directors of organizations and companies. The embezzlement, estimated at $3.8 billion, would become the largest corruption scandal ever uncovered in Haiti.

Perhaps a truce has been negotiated for All Saints' Day, who knows? In any case, there are no demonstrations today, and no gunfire has been heard for the moment. Yet, this area is the epicenter of the current conflicts.

Above the entrance gate to the cemetery is written: "Remember that you are dust."

Malcolm, who worked in the administration of the cemetery while studying ethnology at the State University of Haiti, joins us. He gives us the tour. We buy bags of water, some *balèn bouji* (candles used in Vodou services), and we enter the cemetery which, at this hot hour, is still fairly empty, but will not delay in filling up.

There is a certain path to follow, a bit like what I saw the year before during the pilgrimages to Saut d'Eau or to Limonade. On the way, we pass by small groups perched on the tombs or in the shade of a tall stone stele a little further. Here, people gather around a *gede* with a nasal voice, black glasses turned upside down on his nose, and a purple T-shirt. With a face whitened with talcum powder and a bottle of *kleren* full of chili in his hand, he jokes and tells stories that make people laugh. He takes his audience to task and improvises sung verses. There is talk of *gwo zozo* and *langyèt*, of "big cocks" and "clits." Elsewhere, there is a *manbo* sitting on the ground, visibly ridden by a *lwa*,[12] who administers treatments to people in a small circle who appear one by one before her.

In a corner of the cemetery is the altar of Bawon Kriminel where the *vo-douizan* come to make offerings and prayers. The artist who built it, Guy Pierre, took care to write his name, his cell phone number, and his status as a *bòkò*, in large white letters on a black background, right in the middle of the wall above the cross. Several of the *gede* present are performing in front of a large audience who waits to see what will happen. The *gede* jeer and insult personalities, as well as other *lwa*. They do not stop swearing. They make speeches that I don't always understand, but which people are quick to record on their cell phones. Suddenly, a local TV crew arrives. They ask to speak to the artist. A filmed interview is improvised in front of the altar, while the rest of the event takes its course. A man next to me is indignant and exclaims that this is intolerable, that he should not use this event to promote himself. He protests against what he considers to be an outrage to the spirituality of the moment.

As we leave, we are thrown to the side by a band of enraged *gede* who run singing obscene words and who are followed by a group of entertained spectators. Among them, a patrol of female scouts, teenagers, and especially many boys who want to dance with the girls. A little further on, we pass several groups of *ounsi*[13] in long ceremonial dresses who follow their *manbo*. Their attitude differs: They are absorbed in a ritual to which they attach great importance. They also publicly display a more delicate manner, obviously less shameless, to celebrate the dead. But it is the *gede* who are the real kings of the feast.

It is difficult to make one's way through. A now-compact crowd obstructs the narrow corridors between the tombs. In front of the altar of Bawon Lakwa—one of the figures of the triad of the Barons (Lakwa, Sanmdi, and Simtyè), the kings of the gravediggers and guardians of the dead—people line up to enter the space of prayer and libation. Further down the path, people gather in front of the tomb of Grann Brigit, Baron Sanmdi's wife, on which a cake with icing sugar has been placed. Behind them, on the large white façade, the couple is painted; they have skulls as heads. They are holding hands, she, dressed in a blue dress and wearing a bandana, and him, dressed in a black jacket with epaulets. Both are smoking pipes. They look happy. Above is written, "Happy Birthday to all the dead."

Friday, November 2. I step outside with swollen eyes and a heavy hangover. I am the last one up. We slept in downtown Port-au-Prince in a room of a dozen square meters where Fred's mother and his sister Lovely are staying. Two of his brothers, who slept on the floor with us, have already left. Stanley and Fred are looking at their phones. Lovely brings me a steaming cup of coffee. I sit on a brick in front where the first rays of sunlight warm the city. Two little girls are playing in front of the neighbor's house with a blonde-haired Barbie doll that's missing both her arms. People appear in the narrow alleys—these corridors they call *moridò*, the "death-alleys"—and disappear just as quickly. A kitten tied to a tree with a torn piece of cloth tries to climb up the trunk but keeps falling backward on its buttocks. Lovely prepares a bucket of water for me to wash between the carcasses of cars strewn in front of the house.

Fred has some things to take care of. We will return to Bwa-Mapou in the afternoon. So, Stanley and I go for a walk. We end up sitting in the Sainte-Anne plaza, down the street. He tells me that the news is not good. Supposedly six men were killed near here in the early morning, including the leader of the gang of the Croix-des-Bossales, as well as his right-hand man. Stanley knows nothing more, but says that there will be reprisals.

I will learn later that during the night of the 1st to the 2nd, around 8:30 p.m., while celebrating All Saints' Day, the inhabitants and the gang of the La Saline Project were attacked by a coalition of two armed groups, Baz Nan Chabon and Kafou Labatwa. The bar where we were drinking was less than three kilometers from the scene of the attack. At least five people were killed and nine injured. This first raid foreshadowed another. I would not know until later that the events Stanley is telling me about would lead to the so-called "La Saline" massacre on November 13.

It's getting hot. We buy bags of water from a merchant sitting on the ground, and we sit on the low wall in front of the basketball court where some bare-chested young men are playing. We watch silently, when suddenly automatic weapons detonate, a few blocks away. It's time to leave.

On the bus, on the way back to Bwa-Mapou, I think about the end of yesterday. Passing by the stadium, after our visit to the cemetery, we bought some fried fish to accompany the beers we were going to drink in front of the bar on the corner of Rue Joseph Janvier and Rue de la Réunion. A wooden bench and a stool were set up on the sidewalk as a table. The only real table available was occupied by a group of fiery domino players. We stayed there drinking for hours, watching the street. We got carried away in debates and laughed a lot. At the same time, the killings were taking place. We spoke loudly to make ourselves heard over the music blasting from the speakers at full volume. The guys from G-Shytt rapped their song "Balèn Bouji"—as if in echo of our trip to the cemetery[14]—before going on with Niska and her "*lougawou*":

> *Gade malfektè kap chache maje mwen . . . Yo pa ka manjem . . . Pa pè lougawou! Tout se lou . . . Tout se lougawou!*

> [Look at the evildoers, they want to eat me . . . but they can't . . . I'm not afraid of werewolves! They're all us . . . all werewolves!]

The hits from last year and this year followed one after another. Roody Roodboy sang:

> *Nèg Site Solèy gen manch nan men yo! Bèlè Delmas 2 gen manch nan men yo! Pele Simon gen manch nan men yo! Grann Ravin Ti Bwa gen manch nan men yo! Yo pete! Yo pete! Yo pete!*

> [The guys of Cité Soleil have weapons in their hands! Bel-Air and Delmas 2 have weapons in their hands! Pélé Simon have weapons in their hands! Grande Ravine and Petit Bois have weapons in their hands! They detonate! They detonate!]

Fantòm had also joined the choir by unloading his words before the musical register changed for a long session of *compas*:

> *Tatatatatata! Si w gen 9mm yo, mete yo anlè! Si w gen 3/80 yo, mete yo anlè! Si w gen glock ou byen manch long yo, mete yo anlè! Si w gen SM14 ou byen Gary AK mete yo anlè! Dechaje! Dechaje! Dechaje!*

> [Tatatatatata! If you got 9mms, put them up! If you have 3/80s, put them up! If you have Glocks or rifles, put them up! If you have SM14s or Gary AKs, put them in the air! Empty your magazine! Empty! Empty!]

As soon as I arrive in Bwa-Mapou, I go to wash myself with the fresh water coming down from the hill. It'll get me back on my feet. I am exhausted, but I draw on my last resources, because I can't miss the *sanpwèl* tonight.

It is already 8:30 p.m. when we arrive at Bois d'Eau's, the *bòkò* leading the ceremony. He calls himself "Bawon" or "Emperor," like the leaders of secret societies. In the village, he is known as a *bòkò* affiliated with these groups. Today, he organizes their outing to close the Feast of the Dead. His *mèt bitasyon*, the "master of his compound," is the *lwa* Bawon Sanmdi, guardian of the cemeteries and chief of the *gede*. When we arrive, the festivities have already begun in the *peristil*.[15] The *lwa* Kalfou are dancing frantically in the fire with firebrands in their hands. The crowd shouts. Incandescent and ephemeral spirals are drawn in the night. Sparks fly out from the eccentric movements and are immediately extinguished. Something burns inside.

Saturday, November 3, Bwa-Mapou. The news from Port-au-Prince is bad. Much of the lower part of the city is barricaded. No vehicles are circulating, except for a few reckless motorcyclists and rare pedestrians. Some say that there are demonstrations against President Jovenel Moïse; others that it is the gangs clashing. Others still say that it is all at the same time.

In the afternoon, we go to the cemetery for the last stage of the Feast of the Dead.

Sunday, November 4. Fred and I had planned to spend the evening in Mathias's *peristil* where the annual feast of Ogou Batala, the *lwa* of fire, master of the forges, of lightning and of war, is taking place. It is his *mèt bitasyon*, his "house master," and his *mèt tèt*, his "headmaster." But we give that up. We prefer the serenity of our own house. We stay at home to play UNO with Angeline and the children. I go to bed with a peaceful heart and the feeling that this family is also in a way my own.

Monday, November 5. This morning Fred is waiting for his shipment of bread from Port-au-Prince. This is the first time he has asked his son Evens to take responsibility for buying the bread from the wholesaler in Pétion-ville and sending it to Bwa-Mapou. Evens, in his early twenties, lives with his mother in the slums of Port-au-Prince. He is a good young man, but his father is worried about his whims. Fred tries to keep him busy so that his son doesn't stay in the neighborhood and hang out with the guys from the *baz*. He is afraid that one day things will go wrong. So, he taught him where and how to buy bread in bulk, carry it to the bus station, and load the vehicle firmly enough so that the bags don't get lost on the way, but gently enough so as not to crush the buns. However, that day the barricades on the roads prevent the buses from moving. The bread will eventually arrive in the afternoon. We need to change our plans.

Around 11:30 a.m., we go to the school to pick up Angeline and go to the credit union for a loan. Fred would like to start a bakery and stop commuting between Port-au-Prince and Bwa-Mapou. The family is exhausted from the fatigue, the stress, and the dangers. Making bread in the village would be a good thing.

After dropping off the papers at the cashier's office, the three of us sit for a while under the awning of Fred's store. Lily brings us three beers. A procession of *vodouizan* passes in the street. They pray, sing, and dance behind an ox which they walk around the village. With the sun at its zenith, sweaty faces sparkle. Among the women with beautiful colorful dresses is Barbara, the daughter of Bois d'Eau and Stanley's godmother. She stops for a moment to greet us. Today is a big day: It is the "tour."[16]

In the evening, we meet again in front of Fred's store, as we so often do. Stanley, Wilbert, and Malcolm are there, each with a Prestige in hand. Malcolm has returned from Port-au-Prince. He shows us a video on his phone: In the middle of the street, a woman straddled by a *gede*, naked under her dress, which she has pulled up, is dousing her sex with rum from a bottle filled with extremely hot habanero peppers. At one point, she takes some peppers out of the bottle to rub her crotch with them, without visibly suffering. A small audience watches, amused, and is challenged by the *gede* who does not seem bothered in the least. Malcolm explains that the *gede* come from a world where it is cold, the world of the dead, that's why they need warmth. They like it. And sex too, of course: They love life! Why else would they bother to come among the living?

Tuesday, November 6. While Fred is inside the store doing his accounts, Alix and I are talking under the awning. As part of his law studies, he had to do some practical work in court. He tells me that *mistik* is widespread in the courts of justice. He recently witnessed a case where a young, inexperienced lawyer was mystically "probed" by his opponent, which caused him to lose his abilities completely and to remain mute. The other won. "Some people think it's psychological," he says, but Alix insists that this is precisely what mystical power is: Someone has the power to block someone else and to diminish the other for their own benefit.

In the evening, the sacrifice of the ox of the "tour" takes place at Bois d'Eau's *lakou*. The feast is beautiful.

Wednesday, November 7. At dusk, we meet as usual in front of the store to drink a few beers while looking at the street. Alix tells me about the Haitian judicial system while Fred finishes selling the rolls inside. He tells me about the administrative difficulties of a decadent and dysfunctional bureaucracy. Talking with him, I am reminded of a discussion I had with Stanley some time ago. It started with a trivial question about his birthday. He told me about the fact that many Haitians do not have papers and do not know their birthday because they do not have a birth certificate. This is often the case for girls whose fathers refuse to recognize them. Sometimes it's because they can't afford it; other times, because they would be forced to acknowledge adultery. Often, it is both. Furthermore, obtaining a birth certificate requires a voluntary process. It is costly and can be complicated for those who live far from the cities and transportation. First, you must go to the hospital, which is supposed to issue a paper with which you then go to a civil status office. Without this, there is no record and therefore no identity papers. For many, it is a real ordeal which, if all goes well, can last a few days, if not weeks or months, or indefinitely. All this, of course, is extremely costly in terms of time and energy, but also unaffordable financially for the poor families. And if the father refuses, no record can be issued.

All this comes to mind at the same time as I think of all those dead, those thousands of lives that shine and fade away without ever having been recognized by the country of their birth.

I think back to a poem by Lyonel Trouillot (2015) that I read once while sitting at one of the small round tables in front of a bar on the sidewalk of an alley in Paris. Basile and I had just come out of Tschann's bookshop. We were drinking our second pint of beer. It was October 10, 2016. Hurricane Matthew had just destroyed, on October 4, the departments of the south, Nippes and Grande Anse, and the postponed elections were going to give the victory to Jovenel Moïse. The weather was good enough to linger in the street for an hour or two. The next day at dawn, we left Orly for Port-au-Prince. It was my first trip to Haiti:

All I can offer you
On the other side of the sea
Is a silence that wrecks.

I had not taken the measure of these words. The intuition that there was something there that was addressed to me accompanied me for a long time; but I was not able to receive what this poem had to offer. I was *lòt bò dlo a*, on the other side of the sea, on the far side, where these words could not be heard. Today, I am on the side of silence, and I hear the wreckage.

Thursday, November 8. Angeline's birthday. Festive meal at noon. Otherwise, everyone goes about their business.

In the afternoon, we go to Bouquet-Duvoisin with Fred to meet two judges. They do not come because of barricades and check points manned by armed groups on the road. So, we return to Bwa-Mapou. We have another appointment with Enock Saintil, the incumbent judge who was suspended for looking into a suspicious case involving the nephew of an influential senator. With a few phone calls, the senator had the judge disbarred for five years. He is not at the meeting. We go to find him at his home. He is ill. We reschedule for Saturday.

Friday, November 9. Adny came to see me this morning. Since I planned to go down to the bakery, I take his hand, already strong for a child of eleven or twelve years old, and we start walking. When we reach the CASEC courtyard, his hand grips mine so tightly that it hurts. Adny freezes for a short moment, as if petrified. He looks at the new metal sheet, then pulls me in the opposite direction. We're not going to pass that door of death.

I will later learn that Adny was there the day of the lynching. His childlike eyes saw everything.

Saturday, November 10. I follow Fred on the narrow, rocky paths that crisscross the hills. We make the rounds to distribute his bread. We are surprised by one of the tropical showers, as sudden as they are ephemeral. Around us, there are only fields and trees, which do not protect enough. We run. Nearby, there is an *oumfò*. We take refuge in the *peristil*. An old man sits there, impassive. He is the *oungan*. The rain makes a deafening, shattering noise on the roof. Another man appears and brings us two chairs. We try to exchange a few words, but the rain is too noisy. We remain in silence to look at the waterspouts by the frame of the door. A woman comes and tidies up her stall. The *oungan* asks her for a packet of menthols. He gives us each one. Fred refuses politely. I smoke them both with the old man, until the rain stops. We get up to go on our way. Fred offers them a bag of bread to thank them for their hospitality.

This afternoon, it is planned that we should speak with Judge Saintil, but he calls and says that he had to go to Saint-Marc in a hurry. Another missed encounter.

Sunday, November 11. At the end of the afternoon, I sit down in the shade of Robert's school, which is also his home, and share a few beers with him. We talk about education, jealousy, and resentment between people. He explains to me that he has been the victim of several mystical attacks. After one of them, for which he was not prepared, his right leg swelled up for three months. His knees are still damaged. Several times, he has found gris-gris in front of the school's gate or in the courtyard. They even tried to burn down the school—his house. He shrugs his shoulders: "what can I do?"

Monday, November 12. Before dawn, Fred, Stanley, and I leave for Port-au-Prince. Fred has some bakery business to attend to. I have an appointment tomorrow at the Ministry of Cults. Stanley is coming with me. A few days ago, in Bwa-Mapou, I met by chance a retired member of the ministry who was visiting an acquaintance. He asked me questions about my research, and we talked about justice and Vodou. He seemed interested. He gave me his phone number, as well as the private number of the head of the legal department of the ministry. He assured me that he would be able to help me.

Tuesday, November 13, Port-au-Prince. In the maze of alleys of Delmas, I look for the Ministry of Cults with Stanley, which had to be relocated after the earthquake of January 12, 2010. We are received by the director of legal affairs. His reception is rather friendly, although he is suspicious. The fact that I have been recommended to him by a friend, a former executive of the administration, helps, I think, to reduce suspicions, but he still takes a lot of precautions. He begins by telling me that he is a Protestant, but that he will speak on behalf of science: "I will be neutral," he says. When I ask him if I can record, he hesitates and then approves, but warns me that he will not speak, as I asked, about informal justice, and that he will only answer questions that concern the mandate of the ministry.

At the end of a not-very-fruitful interview, he introduces me to his colleague in charge of the Bureau de Liaison et de Structuration du Vodou. I find myself alone in his office. He is much more relaxed. We have a friendly conversation about the role played by this office, created in 2003 following Aristide's decree for the national recognition of Vodou as a religion in its own right. At the end of the conversation, he tells me that if I want to do a *lave tèt*, the first step of an initiation, I have to call him, and he will organize it for me. He gives me his cell phone number.

In the evening, after I wash, a kind of eczema starts to cover my thighs, my calves, and my arms. I have some on my hands too. Red and hot patches which become bigger and bigger cover progressively all my limbs. I have an allergic reaction; but to what?

Without any answer and without any other alternative, I go to bed with a feverish heart and a worried mind.

That night, the La Saline massacre took place. An alliance of seven armed gangs, composed in part of police officers and ex-police officers, entered the neighborhood in public vans and armored vehicles of the Departmental Operations and Intervention Brigade (BOID). They massacred men, women, and children in their homes and on the streets with machetes and firearms and burned down more than 150 houses. According to local NGO reports, at least seventy-one people were murdered (including eight minors), two missing, five shot, and eleven women raped. I would learn this only a few days later.

Wednesday, November 14. I slept badly because of the eczema that has spread to my whole body. I now have it on my face, back, chest, feet, and penis. Fred and his brother tell me that it is probably the water I washed with. In this area of Delmas, the water is brought in by tanker trucks that transport the water from outside the city. The problem is that sometimes the trucks stay for weeks, even months, in the sun before transporting it. All kinds of living organisms can then develop in the water and allergic reactions are not rare. Except that on a *blan*, a white, it really shows.

The crossing of Port-au-Prince under the sun and the return trip by bus to Bwa-Mapou are excruciating. The gigantic patches that cover me itch all the more when I move and my clothes rub. The perspiration and the dust do not help. This is without mentioning the swollen feet, trapped in my shoes that scrape the surface of my skin with each step.

I am hoping to get some rest when I arrive, but the two neighbors across the street spend the afternoon insulting each other and fighting in front of the house. They are screaming in a state of hysteria that borders on trance. A small audience eventually gathers on either side, including many children who, in the process, learn the insults, invectives, rudeness, and the art of poking the other where it hurts. Suddenly, one of the neighbors takes up a stone and advances. The children leave running and the adult onlookers become agitated. Some intervene to avoid blood. Then the other neighbor goes into her house and comes out with a knife. Now, it is the husbands who intervene. It is not long before they also begin to fight.

Thursday, November 15. It must be 9 o'clock in the morning. The sun's rays are filtering through the foliage that surrounds the house. My coffee is still steaming on the table. I am enjoying a slice of bread with *manba*, the delicious peanut paste that Angeline made last night. I write down in my notebook the memos I scribbled yesterday on small pieces of paper. Suddenly, the quietness of the morning is broken by shouts and knocks. The neighbors are again in the street, violently insulting each other. They are shouting, clapping their hands, and turning on themselves. The young audience soon gathers around them. The men make sure that they don't get into fights. It lasts a little over an hour, after which they turn their backs and go home. It gives me a headache.

Friday, November 16. Nothing to say today. I don't want to think or remember or write. Let me be left alone.

Saturday, November 17. I usually get up before dawn, but this morning I had to drag myself out. The children are already in class and Angeline in the office. I find Fred, slumped on a plastic chair, watching a rerun of yesterday's Le Point program. The guest is Jean Renel Senatus, better known as "Zokiki." He is a lawyer and senator, president of the Justice and Security Commission of the Republic. The theme: gang violence, politics, and corruption. I hesitate to sit next to Fred. I think I should watch, take notes, take an active interest. It's my subject of study, after all. But I can't. Not this early, not like this. These first moments of the day are so precious. I can't waste them listening to politicians bamboozle the listeners by selling their nice speeches on TV sets. It already makes me nauseous.

Angeline left me some black coffee in a pitcher. I grab a banana and a roll and go out on the porch. Sitting on the parapet, I soak the bread while listening to the world of Bwa-Mapou in the background. A thin wisp of smoke rises from the house below in which a woman shouts, perhaps at her child or her husband, who knows; or is she angry at herself? In the distance, the dull, nervous pounding of the mill engine accompanies the distant hustle and bustle of the market. Hidden in the thicket, two dogs talk as if they know something that we humans do not. Behind me, the streams of empty words are still coming out of the speakers. Zokiki is in the middle of a trick. I wish he would shut up. Sometimes I miss the time when all this—TVs, batteries, political broadcasts—didn't exist, a time when we took the time to listen to the breath rising inside us at dawn, and in the evening, to let the night stir inside.

I lean to the side. Water overflowing from the drain dug by the neighbors is running between the banana trees in our garden into the pile of rubble that should be used, one day, to build an extension to the house. I move to get in line with the first rays of the sun that shimmer through the leaves of the coconut trees. When a light breeze stirs them, and a ballet of light rays and shadow begins, they make a noise like crumpled paper, and give the strange impression that a score is being written. Someone listens at the borders of the intelligible.

Two hundred and ten years ago, the founding father of Haiti, Emperor Jean-Jacques Dessalines, was assassinated. For two years, he and his men resisted the assaults of the thirty-five thousand soldiers of the Saint-Domingue Expedition. Napoleon aimed at reconquest and wanted to restore slavery. The revolutionaries first defeated the troops of General Leclerc, then those of Rochambeau. Determined to wage war, the latter brought in hundreds of Cuban dogs specially trained to hunt down *cimarrones, nèg mawon*. But the dogs attacked the French as much as the rebels.

The French lost the war definitively at the site of Vertières on November 18, 1803.

2

THE SILENT WARS OF THE ORDINARY

"the dead man's kin never cease
'to have war in their hearts.'"

—EDWARD E. EVANS-PRITCHARD

Chapter 1 focused on quotidian moments surrounding mass slaughter and extreme violence. While the event itself is somehow absent, it remains discreetly present in all sorts of ways through the multiple echoes it has had in people's lives. In a way, its possibility was already brewing long before, as if the budding of certain events first needed a particular terrain to develop. That's why I've focused on what ordinary life looks like in the present circumstances, rather than concentrating on the massacre itself. In this chapter, I'd like to continue to follow what rustles beneath the surface, the almost imperceptible undercurrents that are felt through the tiny cracks of everyday life, in order to get a more nuanced and complex picture of the making of ordinary legality. More specifically, I will describe in detail the aftermath of the murder of our neighbor by two local teenagers. By looking closely at the consequences in relation to a certain horizon of possibilities, I hope to show some of the ways and reasons why certain disputes are handled outside the grip of the state, even if the state is present throughout, but mostly present in its absence. We will see, however, that neither state procedures nor nonstate ways of resolving the dispute have satisfied the parties involved. The "solutions" worked out during the conflict were not solutions at all; or they were, insofar as they momentarily made it possible to avoid a further tragedy, i.e., a generalized brawl between two rival districts that would undoubtedly have ended in bloodshed. In some respects, the conflict has not been resolved, but neither has it led to further open violence. Yet, while it was already fueled by previous latent conflicts, it also undermined future relations and the togetherness that could have made for a more serene and peaceful cohabitation. A threat persists. But before going any further into characterizing the problem, here's the beginning of a story whose plot I'll try to reconstruct, piece by piece.

THE DEATH OF A NEIGHBOR

The sun has not yet risen. Everybody in the house is still asleep. The chilly air of this Monday, January 7, 2019, made the dew turn into heavy drops that drip from the leaves of the shrubs invading the front porch. They will soon evaporate in the azure sky of winter.

I tie my shoelaces and walk down the canal that circumvents the fields full of young pea seedlings; no water runs through it. It does not always, but I miss it. I savor these mornings when the water streams quietly and feeds my ears with its music.

I pass the ghostly marketplace and go down the narrow pathway behind the brothel to penetrate the *lakou*, a family compound of Vodou practitioners, where each morning I train. Cutting across the courtyard where ceremonies take place, I walk by the tomb of Bawon Sanmdi, whom I salute, he the great master of cemeteries and patron of the *gede*, the spirits of the realm of the dead.[1]

By the time I reach the gym, the daylight has settled in. The place is outdoors and shady, loosely bounded by a few wooden planks and steel sheets, through which curious children peep as goats hop back and forth. The devices are either rusty old machines brought back from the United States by former emigrants or homemade weights. The gym is located between an earthen hut that stands as a home for spirits and a small wasteland where, amid the smoke of a fuming heap of garbage, carpenters build coffins.

A few regulars are training already. The atmosphere is much livelier than usual. The young men, the carpenters, and the neighbors are passionately talking about what happened the previous night.

January 6 commemorates the day of the Epiphany, when the Three Kings followed the shining star and praised the arrival of the new Messiah. In the Artibonite Valley, it is also known as *fèt sanpwèl*, the feast of the dreaded secret society.[2] It is the day when the kings of these societies (they actually call themselves "emperors") come out in the open (yet only at night) and show their spectacular power.

The men are interested in how many *sanpwèl* groups were present at the feast, what the ambiance was like, if the *Kalfou* spirits that mounted them had danced well in the fire, or how important it was to announce yourself before leaving if you cared about getting back home alive. Since I was not present, I listen carefully while I do push-ups. They also share their astonishment that, in the current situation, everything went well. "What do you mean?" I ask. "Usually it ends up in fights; people throw bottles and stones and fire with weapons to frighten the *sanpwèl*." They argue that there are rivalries between various groups, in that case between the secret societies who partly control the zone at night and act as community police, but also run illicit businesses (and sometimes act as mercenaries, employed to harm and kill), and other groups (notably of young people, some of them former inmates in the United States and deported, and pointed by many as thugs).[3]

The discussion then deviates and revolves around the recent explosion of gang violence in Port-au-Prince. The young men training are very committed to elucidate, for instance, how Arnel, the most wanted leader of Village de Dieu, a *geto* of the capital, could get away with all the wars that have erupted in these parts of the city. They are also concerned with the exact circumstances of the recent assassination of the five policemen in Martissant (another *geto* in the capital), one of whom was a relative of my host family and who was killed by an axe blow to his neck at 10 a.m. while he was bringing his daughter to school. It seems to matter how much these policemen were themselves involved in gang activity and if they died like others die when a deal goes wrong.

The sun is halfway up in the sky when I reach home again. Angeline is about to go to work at her uncle Robert's school where she is an administrator. She is late, but on her way out tells me that the solitary neighbor from above, a man in his eighties who used to come by from time to time to chat or buy things at the small shop nearby, was killed on Saturday afternoon by two adolescents, seventeen and eighteen years old. The police eventually caught the youngsters on their way to the Dominican Republic. They are now in custody.

Angeline left without making any further comments. Freshly washed, I sit down on the front porch with a dark coffee and a piece of bread. I need to catch up with my notes, but I just sit there thinking of that man.

However, my quiet moment is soon disrupted. Around midday, Anaïca comes back from school and tells me there is a crisis meeting just down the stony alley in front of Cherline's *lakou*. "The whole family is there; you should go too," she said.

The climate is tense. Men are complaining about the dead man's family, the neighbors who live about three hundred meters further up the hill. Women loudly partake and make demonstrative commentaries, while children are mostly silent. Sometimes a joke makes people laugh, but soon, they all plunge into arguments again.

Some of the men are drunk. Bottles of *kleren*, homemade rum, are passing from hand to hand. Some pairs of eyes are reddish and vitreous, gestures and speech are slightly unsteady, and I can smell the alcohol on their breath as they yell. Johnson, a neighbor in his thirties, stands next to me for a while. He is calm but under the influence of alcohol and has a visible 9 mm handgun on his belt that he takes in his hands from time to time only to put it back. Children discreetly and unfailingly follow all of the slightest movements of the gun. Wilkens, twenty-eight years old, is there as well. "*Sa se chimè pa nou*" ("This is our chimera"), Angeline once told me, referring to those young people from the slums of Port-au-Prince who were hired during the time of Aristide as "hidden hands," and used as contract killers to protect the interests of political parties. The pockets of his oversized jacket are filled with bricks and stones. I understand that the people prevented him from wearing a firearm. He is too agitated, nervously going back and forth, very clearly willing to fight. He had been involved in criminal activity in the past (something people know) and is considered as the most uncontrollable of all those in the area. Yet, he is a neighbor who is willing to help in daily tasks, a nice guy when he is not causing trouble, and ready to defend what he perceives to be the interests of the neighborhood, even though he may do exactly what contradicts these interests.

Angeline is there as well. She came back from work earlier. She is evidently upset, as is her sister, Cherline, along with other relatives living in the area. Her uncle Robert who owns the school in which she works is there as well, slumped in one of the few chairs brought out by Cherline. He is a well-known personality in the village, for he was the mayor of the commune about twenty years ago. Now he heads one of the most important private schools in the area and organizes many cultural activities, such as soccer tournaments and parties for youth. Virtually everybody knows him, and he is respected by many because of his investment in the community, yet also resented precisely because of that. Robert is what in rural Haiti one calls a "notable," one who is listened to, has authority, and is capable of gathering forces. People call these leading community figures when something goes wrong. The police, judges, or lawyers also convene them in order to shed light on issues in an ongoing investigation. So I stick around and try to recompose the fragments of the story. It roughly goes as follows.

On Saturday afternoon, an argument between the old solitary man and the two suspects turned sour. The juveniles were hired by a landowner to water the fields—a job, I was told, they would do for a 100 HTG each per occasion, which is less than $1.30. The old man eventually showed up and decided to irrigate his fields as well. However, he opened the sluices further and redirected the water the others were using. It could have been the case, I was told, that the old man may have used (or abused) his age privilege to prioritize his fields. Either way, the fact is that his action triggered hostilities.

This season is very dry. It did not rain for two months, and it might still not rain at all for several months. Household economies depend on the peas, more or less the only profitable crop at that time of the year. These plants do not like rain but have to be watered, and the irrigation system is quite well organized in the valley. Nonetheless, conflicts often erupt during this time. The period running roughly from January to April is the worst of the year, for this is when most of the fights and killings among peasants occur.[4] The anxiety of having to properly irrigate the fields and the tensions arising from the unequal distribution of water inevitably generate disputations, some of which are settled in special land courts; but others—most of them—are handled outside the grasp of state justice, many of which end up in direct confrontations, occult attacks, and vendettas.

It is unclear what exactly happened, but it seems like, at some point, the argument started going wrong when, in the midst of insults, the old man took a stick to chase the young men and might have hit them. He then ran away and withdrew into his home. However, it is said that the youth forced the locked door open and killed the old man inside his garden. He was found dead, half lying in the canal. The circumstances of his death remain obscure. Some say he was hit by a stick in the neck and would have died on the spot. Others claimed that he had been choked first, and still others said that he had been drowned in the channel that passes through his compound. (In

February 2020, Angeline and others told me that the old man, no doubt under stress, might have actually died from natural death—a stroke or something of the kind—and wounded his head after he fell. People are unsure whether he was actually really assaulted in his home or not. But there has been no further inquiry, and people went on with their lives. The youths are still in jail, unlawfully held captive, waiting to be tried.)

Soon after, some relatives of the old man, including two of his grandsons, law students at the university, smashed the part of the canal on the old man's land (where he was found dead) and filled it with earth and debris. It now became clear to me why there was no water running this morning.

In the alley, everybody is waiting for the police, who are supposed to come with a warrant at 2 p.m. Nobody expects them to be on time, but the stakes are high: The channel has to be unblocked as soon as possible. The peasants depending on this canal (about seven hundred but possibly up to 1,000) have not been able to water their fields at least since Saturday. Some of the seedlings are starting to turn yellow. They might not survive another twenty-four hours. The fertilizers the peasants use burn the plants if the earth is not wet. To make matters worse, people all depend on short-term credits they have received from local union banks, refundable after six months, to pay the workers who help them plow the fields, to buy the seeds and the fertilizers, and to plant. The domestic economy completely depends on their ability to harvest the sufficient amount of peas to pay back the loans and to meet the basic needs for the household. Time is running out. It is now a matter of hours. In January, night falls around 5:30 p.m.

As we wait, more peasants gather, restless. Faces are stiff. Most are returning from the fields carrying spades, rakes, axes, machetes, screwdrivers, or pocketknives. Anxiety rises, especially among women and children. This does not bode well. Weapons start to become too numerous.

All of a sudden, Wilkens leaves, enraged. He comes back after a while swearing and rolling two old truck tires. He wants to make a burning barricade one hundred meters away in the alley at the crossroad with the path that leads up to the old man's house where another group of people is gathered around the deceased's family. This junction marks the border between two neighborhoods: upward, where the mourning family lives, and downward, where we live. Both camps are separated by about 200 or 300 meters, but the inhabitants cannot directly see each other since there is a right-angled corner in between. A few observers have been dwelling there for some hours, where they can examine the situation on both sides. The authoritative males eventually dissuade Wilkens from lighting up the tires, imposing physical force upon him. The tires remain on the side.

At some point, there is agitation among the small group of observers. A few seconds later, a group of about six or seven men turn the corner and walk straight toward us. The mothers jump up and cry at their children, commanding them to lock themselves immediately inside the houses. A delegation led by the son-in-law of the deceased man wants to sit down with Robert and negotiate. They are welcomed by some and slurred by others. However, three of them sit down with Robert and a whole crowd surrounding them, while others just stick around, arms crossed. Wilkens, evidently wanting to battle, insistently provokes some of them. He has to be kept at bay by other men but eventually a fight starts—hopefully nothing too bad.

Some punches and mean insults are exchanged, which is enough for the neighbors to want to cut short and leave. Everybody becomes more nervous. People shout and gesticulate. The son-in-law and Robert still try to talk in this noisy ambience. The delegation asks for an amicable settlement. They make jokes, appeal to the complicity of their neighbors from below, and ask for comprehension. Their suggestion is that Robert should choose a group of men to go up there and dig out the channel, and everybody thus avoids having to deal with the police and the justice system. However, Robert and the people who support him refuse. This affair cannot be settled that easily now. They have gone too far, and the risks of a deadly confrontation if they go up there are too high. The group leaves, angry and anxious.

The issue is not a small one. The murder happened in the late afternoon on Saturday. On Sunday morning, Robert, Judge Saintil, and a few others went to talk with the family of the deceased and try to convince them to unblock the channel they had broken the previous evening. The judge read the Civil and Rural Code before them. In fact, according to the Chapter IV, art. 36, RC., and Chapter 1, law no. 14, art. 522 and 523, CC, the general servitudes and obligations are applicable to irrigation issues; because streams, springs, rivers, and lakes are part of the public domain of the state, the owners of a property through which water runs are not allowed to cut the flow of water to the properties downward, and if both parties cannot agree on the allocation of water, they are compelled to go to court. But the grandchildren refused to comply, and apparently, they were very presumptuous and cocky. Robert disliked the arrogance and the aggressivity of the two young students, behaving as if they had the power to defy a whole neighborhood. However, what bothers Robert and the others above all is that they have not only broken a further part of the channel in addition to the part they broke on Saturday, but they also bought bags of cement to mortar the canal definitively.

This canal was born out of a collective initiative. Both neighborhoods met in 2017 and planned the construction of a cemented system of channels in place of the gullies where the water would run, carry material, and erode the soil; the stream could not be controlled. It cost a considerable amount of money to buy the sand and the stones, as well as to hire trucks to carry them. During several months of collective work, after they were finished with their own matters, the peasants volunteered to contribute to the project without pay for the benefit of all. Hence, many people involved in this collective effort feel personally attacked; Robert has good reasons for being upset since, as one of the wealthy people of the area, he has invested a huge amount of money in the project.[5]

What is at stake now is beyond what initially appeared to be an impulsive act of rage, which everyone told me they were ready to understand and accept (since they all would probably have acted similarly out of anger). The issue becomes of another kind: It seems like the grandsons have the firm intention of not letting the water run through the canal anymore. Moreover, they accuse the people from below to have plotted to assassinate their grandfather. The nature of the conflict has changed.

Soon after the meeting on Sunday, Judge Saintil disappeared. It turned out that, a few hours later, he fled, afraid for his own safety. He told Robert that he could not handle the case, which he said was beyond the competence of the JP court (*tribunal de paix*), and wanted to bring it before the lower court in the capital of the district, Saint-Marc. The people here, however, think he does not want to be involved since he comes from the upward neighborhood and is afraid to take sides. The people that surround me now call him a wimp, a coward, and a sissy. They say that, if this is what justice is, then they had better make it themselves.

On Monday morning, people found the doors and windows of the local courthouse nailed with wooden planks. I am told Wilkens expressed his wrath against the justice system and decided by himself that the court should be shut down until this case is resolved.

That same morning, Robert went back up to see the neighbors, this time with the court clerk. Nevertheless, the grandchildren stubbornly maintained their position. The talks were at a dead end. For the people downward, the police now have to come, but they seem slow at arriving.

So, here we are, waiting in the alley, arguing if this is a civil or a penal case, if the acts of the grandchildren can still be repaired through a conciliation procedure, or if they deserve a fine or a prison sentence. There are people who want to do things according to the law, whereas others just want to go up there and fight them if necessary. Angeline cries out repeatedly: "We want legal water, not illegal!" Others respond, "Who cares? We want water. That's all!"

It soon becomes clear that the police will not come. There is no point of waiting any longer. Around 4 p.m., Robert and a small group of leaders decide to go to another judge and ask for a warrant that would allow them to enter the private property without violating the law and uncork the canal. I jump in the pickup truck with them. On our way down the main road, we come across Yanick La Roche, the commissioner of the government who works at the land tribunal, a well-known resident of Bwa-Mapou. Everyone calls him Yaya. The police called him and sent him instead, he says, to settle the problem. Fair enough. We all go back up to where the sitting is taking place and prepare to go up to the neighbors. Robert asks Johnson to take out the magazine of his gun. He hands it to Cherline, who conceals it in her house. The children's eyes follow every move.

The encounter is tense. The grandsons and other men are waiting, angry. Yaya asks for their version of the story, which more or less coincides with what the people around me were recounting, and then he goes around the compound to assess the damage. He concludes by saying unconvincingly that, in order to avoid any further issues, everybody should come together and, instead of uncorking the canal, build another that circumvents the property. Robert and the others firmly protest: This is no option since it would take at least a month, assuming that everybody works together on the project, which is not likely to happen. In the midst of a moment of confusion, Yaya leaves, and we follow. Back in the alley, the commissioner insists, without addressing the immediate issue, that they have to plan an alternative solution and drives away. People are very upset with him. After about a half an hour of anxious deliberation, they envision no other solution: They have to go up there again and uncork the canal by force if needed.

As dusk is slowly gathering over the valley, we all leave on foot. The silent convoy led by Robert, Johnson, and other men reach the late man's house, where a group of kin and neighbors stand. The power balance is in our favor: We outnumber them, and the men are extremely determined to dig out the channel. Nobody could stop them at this point. Hence, the neighbors mutely watch them enter the compound and free the water. Nobody utters a word. By the time they finish, it is dark. We all leave as silently as we arrived.

TROUBLED WATERS

What are the effects of this murder? The fact is that it acted like a catalyst, triggering multiple responses that revealed what was dormant and pending in the relationships between the people and parties involved. Now, what may we learn about the relation between the specific issues at stake and ordinary legality by paying heed to how this chain of events is rooted in both the actual everyday and in the field of possibilities emergent from it? At one level, the question of justice for the dead man becomes a question of justice for the broken infrastructure. But more than that, it becomes a question of justice for water, and water is life. So, it's a fight for life. And at this level, for peasants, the state has little or nothing to do with it. At another level, the state exists in its modes of appearance and disappearance, materialized by bodies. Yet, it also exists as an aspiration as much as an adversary. But things are more complex than the idea of a "society against the state." First, because the state can also go against the state itself, and because it is obviously not homogeneous. To understand this, we need to have some sense of the complex rhythms that make up this event.

The varying intensifications of the rhythms composing the sequences of the event are the moments when the daily wars people fight silently show both their destructive and creative potential. I call the "silent wars of the ordinary" the battles of peasants having to generate an income by cropping their lands, the struggles of mothers having to keep crumbling households together, or the combat of younger generations having to bear the weight of a dark past and trying to make a life despite the gloomy prospects. They also include all antecedent events that have fueled mutual hostility between people and that may have been passed on from one generation to another. Bitter resentment and desire for vengeance may nourish long-term and latent animosity, even though compensation is often accepted, and feuds are rather quickly settled. Hence, these "wars in the hearts" that Edward Evans-Pritchard mentions in the epigraph I cited from the *The Nuer* (1940) not only sneak into the most mundane matters, pervading relationships between neighbors in ways that may at times lead to full-blown and deadly conflict, but also give rise, as we shall see, to spaces where concepts such as "rightness of behavior," "intentional wrong," and "state responsibility" take shape. Therefore, on one side, they trigger harmful and even deadly actions, but on the other, they also enable productive encounters and solidify certain ties between people. The question of the manner in which the ordinary is inhabitable is linked to the question of the way one dwells within these everyday rhythms, and these may be rather noxious. Henceforth, if there is a point at which they become uninhabitable, the problem then becomes the following: What work is there to be done to reinhabit these rhythms, that is, to make the ordinary livable again?

I would like to ask these questions in relation to the particular occasion to which the murder gave birth, in which the fabric of both state and unofficial law could be unraveled and stitched together again. The vagueness of these shifting boundaries not only enables litigants to make changing and competing claims over their rights, their obligations, and their expectations but also makes the people act in ways that do not rest on any explicit claim or rule.[6]

These questions have taken a particular weight since the violence that erupted a couple of weeks before my arrival for my third stay, at the end of October 2018, considerably changed the environment in which I was to inquire. The civil unrest and the open political and armed war drastically impacted the daily lives of everyone. Displacements became problematic, the risks of being assaulted or blocked were high, the price of staples increased, and a particular kind of anxiety was pervading relationships and affecting the people's health. The crisis undermined the country's basic functioning. The conundrum was such that many institutions stopped working; the justice system was not spared. After a court clerk of the prosecutor's office and two lawyers were brutalized by police on October 4, 2018, the lawyers of the Port-au-Prince bar all went on strike for more than two months, which not only deteriorated the already fragile relations between justice and police, but it also impaired the entire system based on the collaboration between the two. Consequently, this conflict incapacitated the state institutions in their ability to deal with the situation of a country on the brink of civil war.

It is in these circumstances that I was involved in several conflicts affecting my friends or host family, including the case I have just started to describe. These cycles of almost unending political strife and the lingering insecurity are the ebbs and flows with which the people I lived with face in their daily lives. It is against such a backdrop that the story I tell below unfolds.

A FEW COMMENTARIES

In order to better understand the stakes, let me outline a few critical points. First, the case indicates that the question of the boundaries between state and informal law is directly related to the question of how the web of relationships works. The judge, Enock Saintil, for instance, originates from the upper neighborhood. He grew up there and knows the bereaved family. Yet, he also knows the people downward and is a friend of Robert and others. It is thus not surprising that he refused to address the case, even though it was his duty, and fled to Saint-Marc, fearing for his safety. When he took the pulse of the whole situation, he realized that it could easily get out of hand, and his own life could eventually be threatened. His way out was to redirect the case toward the lower court, arguing that it was beyond his purview. But to my knowledge, no suit was ever filed.[7] For his part, Yaya, the state commissioner, is kin related to the grieving family (and they have the same last name, La Roche). This certainly played a role in the fact that he compromised the quest for a legal settlement since he took sides without negotiations and imposed an unacceptable solution to the benefit of the people upward. Robert is also related to several residents directly affected by the shortage of water and is a well-known personality. As a former mayor and current director of a school, he is particularly prone to portray a positive public image of himself and promote peaceful means to solve conflicts. All these facts suggest that one has to take into account the complex interplay of social and political forces in order understand the legal issues at stake: Some ask for justice and repair, others want to fight, and still others want to preserve their kinship ties or their privilege in the neighborhood.

Second, one has to acknowledge the general dissatisfaction with the solutions proposed. Take, for example, Wilkens's seditious act of shutting down the courthouse. This was not an isolated act by a single angry man. On the one hand, he undoubtedly had help; at the very least, he was able to do this only with the consent of part of the population. On the other hand, his gesture reiterates an old seditious gesture described by Michel Foucault.

In a debate with the Maoists on popular justice Foucault had in 1972, he says: "In the great seditions of the fourteenth century onwards, the agents of justice are regularly attacked, as are the agents of taxation and, in general, the agents of power: the prisons are opened, the judges are chased out and the courts are closed" (2001, 1212). For Foucault, the tribunal "has the historical function of grasping [popular justice], of mastering and curbing it, by reinscribing it within institutions characteristic of the state apparatus" (ibid., 1208). This function is known to Wilkens and others; that's why closing courts, intimidating judges and, in other cases, forcibly opening prisons, are known and practiced acts.

Take now the proposition to circumvent the property. It was not acceptable for the people downward, but to free the canal was not tolerable for the people upward. Yet, at least one party had to compromise. In the end, the force of numbers and determination of the people downward compelled the people upward to accept a solution with which they were unhappy. However, this solution did not satisfy the people downward either since the crops had been already damaged by several days of drought. People also lost time and energy arguing and looking for a solution and became exhausted. Moreover, the grandsons, in particular, revealed a different face than what the people in the area were accustomed to. How will they cope now with what happened? How did this shift of attitude change the whole set of relationships between the neighborhoods? Their attitude and defiance may not be so quickly forgotten. Some people became resentful. It might be that for some of them, another silent war has started, even though by February 2020, things seemed to have cooled down. The relations between the neighbors had at that time returned to normal, more or less; they greeted each other politely, and sometimes sat down and chatted; but for how long?

Third, it is important to note that there are many reasons why the people are reluctant to appeal to the formal legal system. Most do not have the money to pay the legal services (attorney fees, displacements of the members of the court, situational analysis, transcripts, hearings, clerk taxes, etc.). The procedures often take too long. Paperwork is in French and the majority only speaks Creole. A significant number of people are not able to produce civil identity documentation, and, most importantly, they do not actually perceive the court to be an adequate, reliable, fair, and efficient place to solve cases. Most people I spoke with—including sometimes officials themselves—do not see the judiciary as impartial, but rather as a partisan system generally indifferent to the plight of the poor and the peasants; they are thus often unwilling to use it. There are also important geographical constraints that limit access to courts. Some areas of the commune where I lived are only accessible by foot or on the back of horses or donkeys and are about eight to nine hours away by foot from the first tracks, but this is not relevant in my case. However, it is equally important to note that, at times, it may be the judiciary itself that refuses to handle a dispute, as was the case here. What's more, Louis Marcelin and Toni Cela (2020, 2), for instance, mention a certain number of "key drivers of instability and challenges to the legitimacy of institutions that enforce the rule of law," such as "an archaic legal framework"; "the politicization of the police and judicial system"; "poor governance with inadequate oversight"; "corruption"; "lack of access to justice in rural areas"; and "land rights issues." These are undeniably factors that hinder the enforcement of the rule of law, but there are many more. For example, since police cannot guarantee the physical integrity of the magistrates, they are constantly threatened; and there are indeed many cases of assassination of court members. No later than August 28, 2020, Me Monferrier Dorval, the president of the bar of Port-au-Prince, was assassinated in front of his home by anonymous shooters. In March 3, 2020, two unidentified bikers shot dead bailiff Jean Fenel Monfleury close to Pétionville's court of peace. On January 7, 2020, deputy judge Antoine Luccius was similarly shot dead in Tabarre. This happened exactly a week after bailiff Bob Dolcine was killed by several shooters in front of the gate of Port-au-Prince's courthouse on Bicentenaire. On January 8, 2020, the National Association of Magistrates (ANAMAH) and the Professional Association of Magistrates (APM) called for institutional guarantees for safety and a harmonious functioning of the judiciary, but who will guarantee safety when policemen themselves attack jurists? On January 20, 2020, Samuel Madistin's lawyer's office was attacked and six vehicles in the parking lot burned by hooded and armed men who were part of a violent crowd of angry policemen demonstrating in the streets; and on March 9, 2020 Durin Duret Jr., judge at the court of appeal of Port-au-Prince, member of the Superior Council of the Judicial Power (CSPJ) was assaulted in his car by armed uniformed policemen demonstrating—they shot toward his car, violently hit it, punctured the tires, and took his keys. These are only a few examples among the many that show how pressured the actors of the justice system are.

Conflicting parties often intimidate the magistrates. Thus, "judges and state officials may neglect legal rulings due to fear of retaliation and the absence of state security forces to protect them" (Report 2012). Hence, one has to understand Judge Saintil's lack of motivation to intervene as part of a broader picture: They are often not paid, or paid after months of arrears; they lack safety and the means to enforce the law; and they do not have the documentation (birth certificates, land titles, usufruct, etc.) to properly adjudicate cases. This lack of professionalism and transparency, the bureaucratic mismanagement, as well as the production of false documents, bribery, and the impunity of certain people cause litigants to refrain from dealing officially with certain issues. According to a report entitled "Options for Land Tenure Dispute Management in Rural Haiti" (2012), less than 5 percent of the land is registered by the National Cadastral Office (ONACA) or the General Directorate of Taxation (DGI). This has a direct influence on the way people perceive their rights over land and their legitimacy to reclaim the prerogative in the use of irrigation. Most land titles are not formalized and have been transmitted through oral contracts, usually with the presence of a local notable playing the role of a witness.

Moreover, even though plaintiffs may go to court to settle disputes, and even though the case may be adjudicated, it does not mean that the conflict is over. Indeed, depending on the outcomes, the losing party may still continue to look for reparation, or retaliation, by using, as is often the case in the commune where I lived, occult means; there are many cases of people who commission a *bòkò*, an expert paid to manipulate vengeful powers, to cast spells against the opposite party after the verdict (also Cavender 1988). Actually, conflicts are managed primarily through family meetings with the presence of one or more notables, and according to my observations, most often disputes are settled before they escalate into violence.

INFORMAL WAYS OF SETTLING DISPUTES

Before returning to the experience of generalized insecurity in the next section, I would like to emphasize the relation between the circumstances in which certain forms of violence occur and the jurisprudence to which the people involved refer to. It is critical, for our purposes, to recognize Haiti's changing, heterogeneous, and pluralistic legal landscape, and therefore to acknowledge the tenor of the many internal tensions between state and nonstate laws, rules, and conventions, and various informal social regulations.

In this case, the state's institutions—in particular the courts and police—are important, not so much because of what they do but rather due to their absence or their inability to enforce the law. Without a doubt, their failure has decisive consequences for people's trust in a centralized power, as well as for the claims they make regarding justice. Nevertheless, the state laws and the institutions supposed to guarantee their enforcement are not the only legal resources they have. There are deeply rooted social regulations or, say, habitual ways of handling conflicts that are not formalized a priori, but these rules do nonetheless lay out a spectrum of what is conceivably and reasonably acceptable or tolerable and what is not, and which asks for justification. This is the case, for instance, when at some point, the people downward consider that the grandsons have crossed a limit, motivating the people to ask for legal help. This perspective gives the event another texture, another kind of seriousness. The moment the grandsons are endowed with another sort of intentionality—they are now considered ill-intentioned, while they were initially seen as just having expressed excessive rage—is also the moment the course of events and the nature of the problem change. From then on, grief and anger, for example, will not be accepted anymore as mitigating circumstances, as they were the first day; this breach of the rules of conduct led the grandsons to be held accountable for their acts in another way than they were the day of the murder. As a consequence, some people downward have started asking for legal sanctions, and some want to handle this by themselves by engaging in a fight, whereas others want to reestablish good relationships (even though this might involve some form of punishment). This is the point when the destruction of the canal shifts from being conceived of as a civil case to becoming a penal issue. As long as the offence is defined by the damage (an injury to the particular interest of one of the parties), it is not clear whether it is a civil or criminal case. The fact that water is used improperly, irrigation rights are disputed, private vengeance is exacted, and that then the matter is brought before a judge, shows that the question cannot be decided so easily. What I mean when I say that there has been a major shift in the way the parties involved have conceived the case is that the moral texture of the case, so to speak, has changed. Henceforth, punishment rather than reparation became the horizon toward which they were moving.

The literature on the subject has accustomed us to frame the problem in terms of a balance between codified law and informal regulations, which, in other words, is the problem of commensurability between state and non-state, or customary, law (F. Benda-Beckmann 2002; Chanock 1985; Corrin 2019; Merry 1988; S. Roberts 1998). This is, for instance, the question at the heart of Jaquelin Montalvo-Despeignes's (1976) ethnography of informal law in rural Haiti. The author examined juridical acculturation by showing how the application of the Civil Code had to be constantly negotiated with respect to the application of informal rules and modes of handling public and private matters. By considering the relation between the law and different social and economic structures, Montalvo-Despeignes argues that we are more likely to understand the articulation between different sources of law and their internal organization.[8] Through his Maussian- and Marxist-influenced perspective, to some extent, he is right. Yet, considering codified laws and informal regulations in an overly dichotomous way might obscure the ways in which, in the flow of ordinary lives, they are mutually constitutive and often vaguely defined. The problem here is not merely of a balance or commensurability between the two—since there are no unitary "twos" (Benton 2002)—but of responsiveness: How do people respond to the problem at hand?

There are, of course, established and well-known conventions internal to the rural community that dictate, for example, who negotiates with whom, what the protocols of negotiations are, what role notables play in such an affair, and so forth. Notables, in particular, have an important role to play, not only as arbiters, but also as "those who know." They have the authority to establish, or decree, what is "notorious," hence the "notoriety" of a fact, a case, or a matter. In this, they are surely in part heirs to an essential notion of medieval European law, in which the "notorious," by designating what is manifest, seen and known by all, dispenses with the administration of proof. The notables, therefore, by establishing the notorious fact, establish obviousness before all—a flagrance. Flagrante delicto can thus be actualized by them, even when no reliable witness is able to testify what happened at the time of the offense.[9]

Yet, less clearly identifiable conventions that are nonetheless part of practically regulated behavior also guide, for example, the way someone like Wilkens should be considered and handled, as well as how one should behave with machetes or with firearms in those circumstances. Furthermore, chains of reciprocal services are also very important modes of regulation, and do not necessarily go through the kind of clientelism used by the notables. For example, the fact that the two neighborhoods recently met, planned, invested in, and collectively built the canal raises the question of what kind of offense it is for the grandsons to break up what the people below helped build. How should one appreciate the fact that they decided that, from the day they blocked the canal on, the water would not run through their late grandfather's compound anymore, thereby imposing the construction of another canal that should bypass the property? Is this admissible? If yes, under which circumstances? If not, then why is it not appropriate, and with what consequences? What sort of offense is this? Even though the immediate issue at stake for the people downward was to make the water flow again, the whole affair took unexpected turns. Something seemed to be at stake during the heated discussions in the street, where one of the issues was precisely to determine if the case fell under civil law—and should therefore be handled by the conciliatory tribunal— or if it was penal and thus had to be brought to the lower court.

Yet, what interests me here more than the deliberative discourses is that there was something going on in a minor key, in the shadow of the disputes, so to speak; there were modes of address whose affective tenor and aesthetic quality revealed what was implicitly at stake. When the son-in-law sat down with Robert and argued about the reasons the people downward should accept an amicable solution, there were gestures, bodily postures, attitudes, as well as manners of behaving and speaking that influenced the way people viewed what was going on that had nothing to do with the content of the argument. For example, there was a moment when they started to play, parodying their own roles in front of the curious audience, exaggerating their own respective stances, unduly reinforcing their opposition, to the point that it became a funny spectacle to watch. It seemed to matter to keep the audience on the lookout. Moreover, by mimicking their own positions, almost mocking themselves, even though the seriousness had never left the scene, they established complicity and reminded the audience of their friendship. After all, they are neighbors, are they not? They never really had any serious issue before, and this fact matters. Their theatrical performance thus had a particular meaning: "Maybe we all have gone too far. Maybe we got carried away. Let us not forget who we are: neighbors. We do not want to fight, do we?" It was simultaneously meant to entertain the crowd, amuse the children, display theatrical talents, and show competitiveness. Serious-ness does not prevent playfulness.[10] Alfred Métraux (1955) had noticed in the context of Vodou how much the rituals had "dramatic elements" incor-porated in their very functioning, and could indeed be seen as ritual com-edy. If we do not consider Vodou as disconnected with other kinds of social rituals such as the one I describe, we can imagine how much such a meet-ing can turn into a sort of theatrical performance. Yet, it was still a battle, and Robert clearly won. No doubt, he was the one who made people laugh and ridiculed his sparring partner. Having shown no skills at all for that kind of game, the son-in-law, now bulking and upset, became angry again. Since Wilkens had been mean and provocative with other members of the delegation, they now had good reasons to leave and abandon their efforts. What happened in these interstices had certain kinds of effects that, by elic-iting a whole chain of unforeseen events, were critical to settling the dispute. All these elements, when we look at law exclusively through the prism of codified texts, judgments, and rational deliberation, go unnoticed.

DAILY LIFE IN INSECURE TIMES

These fine nuances have to be reinserted in the context in which they occur (Das 2013; Han 2012). The stress and suspicion caused by a hazardous situ-ation no doubt influenced the daily life of the people I met, and thus the way law is lived ordinarily. Indeed, local conflicts are unavoidably related to many others, and cannot be understood if we do not also look at the more general picture of the weak and dysfunctional state apparatus (Hauge et al. 2015).

Roughly during the period I describe, between October 2018 and Febru-ary 2019, there was widespread civil unrest against the governments Jove-nel Moïse had put in power. An outbreak of armed conflicts between various groups operating on behalf of the state or opposition parties, as well as in their own interests, led to a lingering climate of insecurity (*ensekirite*).[11] Er-ica James (2010) described such a climate in the aftermath of the coup years (1991–1994), which she saw as the direct consequence of a "terror economy": A systemic transformation of the suffering of people into a source of profit through acts of intimidation, destruction, theft, torture, and murder. Even though the political context of her inquiry is quite different than mine, her work is instructive to understand how "criminal actors [including officials] have begun to capitalize on the chaos in order to expand their traffic in persons, drugs, and illicit goods" (ibid., xxi), thereby resulting in "ongoing political and economic insecurity" (ibid., 3). By examining "the paradox that many of the efforts to rehabilitate the nation and its citizens, and to promote democracy and economic stability, inadvertently reinforces the practices of predation, corruption, and repression that they were intended to repair" (ibid., 7), she pointed out that the internal dynamics of the quest for sovereignty cannot be dissociated from a "terror apparatus" that has a history at least as long as that of Western capitalism's inaugural act of predation: slavery. Hopes for changes have been systematically discarded.

During my stay, civilians were targeted by other civilians, but the police were accused of corruption and collusion with gang activity as well; which meant they were accused of being involved in the kidnappings, the shootings, and the killings. As for the justice system, it was clogged, either because its actors were themselves partisans or because they simply could not do their work without the police ensuring their safety. They were caught in a system from which there was no escape, having the choice between relinquishing their responsibilities (because they are the target of repeated threats and acts of intimidation) or yielding to the bribery and compromise. The question of whether the judicial system will be able to do anything is critical in thinking about state sovereignty and the autonomy of justice in a postcolonial democracy.[12] In short, the state institutions had become almost inoperative, which gave free rein to whoever could exert their power by force. It created a climate of anxiety beyond Port-au-Prince, which affected rural areas. Many armed groups started proliferating and operating in the valley, accompanied by an increase in banditry directed against buses carrying civilians in rural areas (muggings and rape), which in turn, toughened the attitudes of the villagers toward marauders and encouraged them to be extremely fierce with thieves if they caught them. Moments of respite alternated with moments of turbulence.

In one instance, the whole village where I lived was isolated for up to nine days consecutively. Burning barricades had been placed at both ends of the unique paved road that crosses the village, and vigilantes were guarding the spots. Some were anti-corruption demonstrators, but others were paid to create mayhem to destabilize the government. Some turned out to be themselves taking advantage of the situation and stole from the most reckless who would want to pass (often to siphon from the gas tanks of cars or motorbikes, taking the opportunity to steal cash and phones). Barely would anyone leave or enter the village. The household economies being dependent on the capital's markets, the situation very quickly triggered a general climate of nervousness.

The events leading up to the current situation in the lower Artibonite Valley further illustrate the proliferation of violence, rural insecurity, and the inability of the state to intervene. The lower Artibonite Valley has always been a major strategic issue, and thus subject to violent competition (Levy 2001). However, in the last three years, irrigation in particular has become the object of rivalry between armed groups, especially in the delta that has become the scene of violent clashes. Pont-Sondé, for instance, features an important market (on which Bwa-Mapou depends), various depots and credit unions, and is the main center of commercial activities in the delta. In 2018, the hostilities began in earnest when the powerful armed group of Arnel Joseph, which controlled part of the neighborhoods of Village de Dieu and Bicentenaire, at the southern entrance of Port-au-Prince, was dislodged and chased out of the capital, and some of its members moved to Joseph's native commune in the delta, Marchand Dessalines.[13] The geography of power was suddenly changed. Immediately after, vigilante brigades as well as other groups emerged or were reinforced, and competed for control of the main roads, the Pont-Sondé market, and, of course, the irrigation canals.

The Artibonite River, which drains nearly 9,000 square kilometers as far as Pont-Sondé, is the largest watershed in Haiti and the neighboring Dominican Republic. The Artibonite basin concentrates 90 percent of the country's hydroelectric production, has the largest surface area of irrigated land (about 32,000 hectares), and is one of the most populated in Haiti (Levy 2001). The Artibonite produces two-thirds of Haiti's total rice production. By June 2019, more than 2,000 farmers had already been forced to abandon their land and would soon be followed by others. The situation worsened after Arnel Joseph was killed on February 26, 2021, and new competing groups emerged. Robert Moïse, the CASEC assistant of the first communal section of Marchand Dessalines, expressed during an interview for Ayibopost (2021) the urgency of the situation affecting the people who make their lives in the basin: "To better suffocate their rivals, the gang [of Savien] decided to block certain irrigation canals. Thus, they intend to fight the enemy gang of Jean Denis, by blocking the Dessalines Canal. Thousands of families are thus deprived of the water necessary to grow rice." Besides rice, onions, melons, tomatoes, sweet potatoes, corn, finger millet, cassava, cabbage, yams, pomelos, beans, and peppers do not grow anymore in dried out areas. About 5,000 irrigable hectares are affected by the drought imposed by the gangs. The Organization for the Development of the Artibonite Valley is unable to clean the canals, and no official authorities intervene.

In response, the local population rose up, but the armed groups fought back. On August 3, 2020, a crowd, angry at the assassination of a boy by the hitmen of the Savien gang and despairing of the deprivations imposed, set fire to the vehicle of the former senator of Artibonite, Jean Willy Jean-Baptiste, before they blocked the National Road No. 1. Exacerbated by the passivity of the police, the citizens also attempted to set fire to the premises of the National Institute for Agrarian Reform (INARA), which houses law enforcement officers assigned to the Organization for the Development of the Artibonite Valley (ODVA). In other areas close to Bwa-Mapou, vigilantes tactically blocked the communication channels in order to control the comings and goings, to capture suspects, and confiscate ammunition. But the gangs did not remain passive. On October 21, 2022, heavily armed members attempted to storm the Petite-Rivière de l'Artibonite police station. On October 31 the same year, the town was ransacked once again: five food stores looted, fifteen houses burned, dozens of commercial businesses emptied, the generator to supply the drinking water network stolen, and hundreds of people abused and wounded, some killed. A little more than a week later, fifteen people were killed in a raid on the town after some rice vendors suspected of being accomplices had been lynched. And no later than January 25, 2023, six policemen were killed in the neighboring commune during a raid by the Savien gang allegedly supported by other policemen.[14] These uprisings or battles have just made it worse: Always more canals are blocked or diverted, more land dried out, and more peasants and families displaced.

All this happens as reports, dating back to September 2022, by the Food and Agriculture Organization of the United Nations (FAO) and the United Nations World Food Programme (WFP) speak of "catastrophic levels of hunger recorded for the first time in Haiti" where "nearly half of the population" without access to food, fuel, markets, jobs, and public services "is currently facing acute hunger."[15] Official reports state that 4.7 out of 11.7 million people in Haiti are currently acutely food insecure (which means 3+ on the scale of Integrated Food Security Phase Classification, IPC), including

1.8 million facing emergency levels of food insecurity (IPC, 4), and several tens of thousands have been classified as being at the highest level (IPC, 5).

Therefore, when the people of the valley spoke about the climate of *ensekirite* (insecurity) in 2018 and 2019, they were not only describing a situation, but they were also expressing their foreboding; they were foreshadowing the events to come.

It is characteristic of a climate that it suffuses every aspect of life. Similar to most people, Angeline and her husband Frédéric were of course not indifferent to what was happening in Port-au-Prince, on the roads, and in the neighboring communes, not only because they have relatives and friends in these areas most affected by urban violence. But also, because, since Frédéric is a bread merchant, his income completely depends on his being able to go back and forth to the capital (at least twice a week, but often three to four times); and this meant that he had to take the National Road No. 1 and pass several areas controlled by violent armed groups and vigilantes, and risk being stopped and mugged, if not more. Besides personal safety, food insecurity was very much part of the problem.

Shortly before Christmas, on December 20, 2018, Angeline organized an *aksyon de gras* (a personalized "Thanksgiving") at her home to acknowledge the good dispositions of the Lord toward her family. She invited about twenty people, most of whom were members of the religious group to which her sister Cherline belongs, L'Église Rachetée de l'Éternel. The *aksyon* (the action) lasted for a couple of hours during which prayers, songs, dances, and speeches were performed in a circle in the parlor. At some point, during a blessing that might have lasted a half an hour, in which everyone would pray aloud and individually, generating an intense cacophony, I heard several people mention "bandits," "insecurity," "weapons," and "violence." I also heard sentences similar to the following one: "With all these thieves now, thank you, Lord, for giving us peace." Later, Angeline expressed all the distress that the situation described in this paper had raised. She stood up with the sort of presence that would silence everybody and started her speech with our undivided attention. Sobbing, she expressed her profound gratitude to the Lord for having ensured that her family had remained healthy, that nothing had happened to Frédéric, who was traveling so often to Port-au-Prince, and that he had not been killed and was still there—a father for his children and a husband for her. Her words drew tears from us.

The question of how a sense of justice can still be cultivated in such a context takes a particular shape for Angeline, Frédéric, and the family. Their daily struggles have led them to be as lawful as possible when they have sufficient reasons to believe that the law can help them maintain a livable coexistence with their neighbors. In the case at hand, there are indeed arguments in favor of a conciliatory procedure in the peace court; for instance, it would help prevent a potential deadly brawl, publicly reaffirm their legal right to access water, and manifest the rightness of their behavior by showing that they comply with the law and refuse to use illegal and violent means (in that sense, they aspire to a democratic nation-state). Yet, they also have good reasons not to file a lawsuit, as they told me, since the actors of the judicial system are not only corrupt and taking sides but also quite inefficient in solving these kinds of cases. From their perspective, it is useless to try. They have no time to wait for the court to do its work (if it does it at all). The combined pressure of time and the overall life conditions have to be dealt with immediately. Such pressure intensifies until it becomes a matter of hours, or minutes, in which they cannot but respond by appealing to alternate modes of doing justice.

LACK OF JUSTICE, DENIAL OF DEMOCRACY, AND THE SEARCH FOR PEACE

The epigraph at the beginning of this chapter is a quote from *The Nuer*. Reflecting on their political systems, Evans-Pritchard wrote, "the Nuer have no government, and their state might be described as an ordered anarchy" (1940, 5). He then argued, "Likewise they lack law, if we understand by this term judgment delivered by an independent and impartial authority which has, also, power to enforce its decisions" (ibid., 6). I am relatively unsure if all Haitians I met would say that they have a government; some would probably argue that they have none, or they might say that what is called a "government" in Haiti is no government at all or maybe a zombie-like government. Possibly, some among them would agree with the idea that their country works more or less like "ordered anarchy." However, they would certainly deny that they lack law and would not consider "judgments delivered by an independent and impartial authority" as such a relevant defining criterion of what counts as law.

What counts as law is inherently related to what counts as justice. But, as Marcelin and Cela (2020, 3) write, "to what extent does the population's understanding of 'justice' converge or diverge with those of formal institutions? How does this inform the ways in which marginalized populations interface with, circumvent or resist formal institutions?" I have tried to make explicit the ways in which, and the reasons why, people feel compelled to take judicial or extrajudicial actions, some of which may be violent. I have also shed light on the dissatisfaction of the conflicting parties involved, while they still try to maintain an equilibrium of some sorts that prevents direct confrontation. To finish, I would like to emphasize one last important point: The general disappointment and disillusionment with the state goes hand in hand with a feeling that what they have been denied is actually a fair and democratic justice.

There is undeniably a sizeable gap "between national-level and local-level processes, actors, and dynamics" (Donais 2015, 44), such as between a ruling elite and a majority of poor citizens, which in many ways not only jeopardizes previous attempts by the state and international organisms to promote and enforce the rule of law, but also hinders the current justice system, and tends to ruin the people's expectations of a brighter future. As Timothy Donais remarks, on paper "Haiti is well positioned in terms of local-level democracy" (ibid., 47), if by that we mean that its territory is organized into communal sections, municipalities, and departments, each being an administrative entity "constitutionally mandated to ensure coordination and control of public services" (ibid., 48). However, on the ground, the least one can say is that democracy has never worked the way it is supposed to. The people I met thus all have more or less good reasons for avoiding the judiciary.

Some scholars broached the question of the peace-building processes before and after the earthquake of January 12, 2010, by emphasizing how important it is to include local level dynamics and agencies in the analysis (Carey 2005; Donais 2015; Hauge et al. 2015). Their dissatisfaction with state-centric approaches and liberal theories arises from what Donais (2015, 40) identifies as "conventional understandings of both agency and change," which do not enable a clear-sighted view of what is currently happening in Haiti. Indeed, one of the problems with the tenants of Western liberal approaches, besides their top-down perspective and relative indifference toward the everyday lives of people of which they know very little, as well as their insistence on the necessity of intervention and assistance from external actors importing peace-building models, violently, if necessary, is their assumption that popular neighborhoods or rural areas are ungoverned, if not chaotic. By thinking so, they completely miss the fact that "these areas have actually developed their own system of security and governance, although sometimes involving criminal activities" (Hauge et al. 2015, 264)—but they are criminal first and foremost in the eyes of the state. In the ebb and flow of ordinary life, there are no easy, ready-made answers to the conflicts that undermine communities.

With this chapter, I hope to have shown how an in-depth ethnographic approach of ordinary life can open up a different perspective on the study of law and justice in context. Even though I imagine well how important it is for someone like Marcelin (2015, 253) to think of anthropology as a discipline that "seeks to play a meaningful role in contributing to a better world, one in which justice and fairness, human dignity, and democracy play a central role," I am less sure than he is about the role anthropology is indeed to play in this world. But I do believe that close engagement in local affairs and care for the daily lives of the most vulnerable, rather than overarching and dispassionate perspectives, can complement the analysis of institutions that other disciplines endeavor to conduct, and thus contribute to fostering a more complex, perhaps better, understanding of the current issues at stake in Haiti.

3

THE MANY FACES OF PEACE

"I'm afraid of peace."

—ALIX

In Chapter 2, I was interested in the effects of a murder committed after a dispute over the irrigation of pea fields. I paid heed to the thresholds of violence and the thin line that marks the difference between concepts such as "dispute settlement" or "conflict resolution" and the everyday efforts to maintain a sustainable life, which cannot be spoken of in terms of "settlement" or "resolution." Rather, the making of a livable life often means having to go on despite unavoidable violence and without being able to "resolve" anything. This is epitomized in expressions such as *nap brase* (we're struggling), or *nap goumen* (we're fighting). The focus was on seeing some conflicts as the visible face of long-lasting silent wars simmering beneath the surface. In fact, people have a history with each other, as well as with the state—a history fraught with violence of all sorts. This is an important fact because it partly determines how people deal with their differences. It cannot therefore be ignored or simply dismissed in the study of law and justice.

In this chapter, I would like to take up again this question of what it takes to sustain a life, this time taking a closer look at the day-to-day work required to achieve some form of peace. As much as it may be said to have been achieved once, peace is never achieved once and for all: It is a constant challenge and a never-ending work in progress.[1] Starting with a case of goat theft brought before a local court, I'm going to untangle, one by one, some of the threads that link local practices and the interventions of international actors. Indeed, local ways of operating, their ways of working together to build a more or less peaceful community, are partly shaped by the way in which the legal landscape has been organized by outsiders. It cannot be denied that everyday life and possibilities have been profoundly transformed by decades of institutional structuring overseen and controlled by all sorts of foreign actors, not least the United Nations. More dramatically, however, sometimes what it takes to achieve peace requires forms of violence. What's more, peacemaking can become an argument that justifies violence (Kelly 2006). Locally, this is the case when, as I showed in Chapter 2, people like Wilkens fight violently in the name of peace to settle scores and restore the balance of power between neighborhoods. Yet, on a national and international level, this is also the case in the peace-building projects. In this chapter, I endeavor to show that the rule of law, conceived in theory as prerequisite for a lasting peace, and promoted by all official institutions—especially the United Nations—not only often does *not* bring peace, but also contributes to fueling violence and conflict. Although on one side the practices that accompany peace-building projects and the language through which it is carried out strongly contrast with the ordinary, unofficial, practices and language the local communities use, on the other, they meet, notably through the JP courts; they partly absorb each other. What are the effects of the international and national legal language on the daily dealings with conflicts? How do they shape the local practices and language, and how are they also contested, reinterpreted, appropriated, or subverted?

As Tobias Kelly wrote about the Oslo Process, "the language of peace . . . should not blind us to the continuing violence" (2006, 4). An important part of this chapter is to characterize the international legal language that the Haitian state and many local organizations have largely adopted (or been forced to adopt). An equally important part will be devoted to demonstrating the inability of this language to account for what happens in everyday life, where inequalities not only persist despite all the efforts, but even seem to have deepened. I will focus on some of the specific mechanisms by which international interventions have helped to produce, rather than alleviate, the tensions and violence that stand in the way of a functioning nation-state and institutions (Lombard 2016). Part of my argument is that peace-building in Haiti is not so much disrupted or hindered by so-called endemic violence as it plays an essential role in creating the conditions of possibility for such violence.

A tenacious prejudice about Haiti is that the violence perpetrated on the island is endemic and deep-rooted: In other words, violence is seen as culturally specific (M. Trouillot 2003). Such a view not only tends to naturalize Haiti as a violent place, but also eclipses the role played by unending political ostracization, massive foreign meddling in domestic policies, and unquestioned paternalistic discourses that invalidate Haiti's capacity to govern itself, all of which serve to keep Haiti subordinated. Ironically, this perception prompts foreign funders to sponsor programs and reforms, supposed to contribute to ending the violence, which ostensibly hinders the development of what is called a "war-torn" or "post-conflict" (or "failed") state into a democracy; yet, as I will show, the violence is sometimes stimulated, if not created, by these same funders' policies. The face of peace is sometimes war.

STOCKBREEDING, THEFT, AND EVIDENCE

Let's start with a case brought before a reconstructed court of justice funded by the United Nations. On December 14, 2018, a gathering is taking place in the shadow of a leafy almond tree in the courtyard of the Justice of the Peace (JP) court in a communal section in the lower Artibonite Valley. The infrastructure is nowadays out of use. In 2012, the department that was tasked with the justice reform of the United Nations Stabilization Mission in Haiti (MINUSTAH) had "renovated" the existing buildings and built a few others in order to enhance the court's capacity: a hearing room that would accommodate up to twenty people, a reception room, and an office for the appointed judge, the deputy judge, and two court clerks. The UN peacekeepers described their mission in these terms: "to counsel and provide technical support . . . to enhance the capacities of magistrates, judges of the peace, court clerks, and bailiffs, and to accompany the modernization of the Haitian legislation."[2]

Only six years have passed and the floors of the building have already collapsed. Some members of the public who were standing on it when it happened were wounded. Moreover, the equipment furnished by the United Nations, especially the four air conditioners and a 32 kW generator, are broken, out of use, or stolen. The buildings were haphazardly planned and made, with scandalous negligence, out of cheap, precast material. The damage is such that hearings can occur only outside, under the blistering sun, and must be rescheduled if it is raining.

In the face of the failure of the joint work of the state and the United Nations, the court employees and a group of citizens had come together in a collective effort and, without any help from the state, had invested their own time and money to repaint the walls surrounding the yard and make it look "good." They also bought a new generator.

When Frédéric and I enter the courtyard, about thirty or forty people are standing in a compact circle around two wooden benches, on which the conflicting parties are seated. Behind each one, two armed policemen wearing bulletproof vests, obviously bored, are slumped in metal chairs with earphones inserted in their ears, looking at their phones. The judge and the court clerk are seated in front of the contending parties. At his side, two attorneys are handling their notes and wiping the sweat off their faces. The plaintiff, a woman in her late twenties or early thirties, complains that one of her goats (*kabrit*) is missing. She explains that she had inquired with the CASEC of the zone. The CASEC, I remind the reader, is the communal supervisory board (Conseil d'Administration de la Section Communale), the very end of the chain of officials. People usually call the board members themselves "CASEC," and often confer with the chief of the board if they have any issue or grievance before they go to the police or to court. During their inquiry, the CASEC had found witnesses who had told them that this man, the accused (sitting on her left-hand side), had sold it and that the people who had bought it had already butchered and eaten the animal. Thus, she accuses that man, who is of more or less the same age, of having stolen one of her goats. Her attorney goes on to explain that, in order to sell the goat, the legal procedure requires that the man would have needed a pass for the animal, as well as his own ID or birth certificate, which he had said he had lost.

The title of acquisition of an animal is called *lese-pase pou bèt* (pass for animals) and is issued by the Ministry of the Interior and Territorial Communities and the Ministry of Agriculture, Natural Resources and Rural Development. Every commercial, as well as noncommercial (gifts, inheritance) transaction involving animals is supposed to be formalized by this mandatory document, which specifies the characteristics of the animal: the sort of animal in question (cow, sheep, horse, goat, donkey, mule, or pig), its official register number, its sex, color, and tagging, and its origin and destination. The document is numbered, and it declares where the transaction took place: in which communal section of which commune and in which department.

The owner (*mèt bèt la*) has to write down his name, national identification number, address, and signature, as well as a testimony (*temwen*). It is also mentioned which CASEC is in charge of the communal section (with his phone number). The document is dated.

This document must be seen as part of a more general trend, which consists in inscribing judicial power (and therefore the state) in writing, and imposing it through bureaucracy, against the orality of informal property laws. In the informal mode, any contract of sale generally requires only a *temwen*, a witness, the person who testifies to the sale and can guarantee the "deeds" of ownership. The *temwen* is generally a notable, or someone empowered by this type of authority, or at least a person whose "*pawòl donè*" (word of honor) is trustworthy. The *pawòl donè* is a very important aspect of social relations in the rural area, where it is said that "*moun de byen achte chwal san papye*," "people of honor buy horses without papers." Yet, art. 1126, sec. "On testimonial evidence" CC stipulates that no witness will be admitted without a notarized deed or private signature for any dispute exceeding 16 HTG. Of course, we have to bear in mind that the written word and all forms of bureaucracy are the specific hallmark of the state, by which I mean the hallmark of the state's repressive apparatus. Implicitly, this also means that in such a context, the appeal to *papye* (paper) arouses a kind of suspicion: Bureaucracy worries more than it reassures. Hence, for many peasants, it is to be dodged, subverted, or fought.[3] Yet, the past decades have been detrimental to these habits. Sales made by former owners are often no longer recognized by their heirs, and become a source of endless conflict. As many people have told me, a part of trust and honor has disappeared, giving way to other types of logic. Invoking contracts, notarial deeds, signed letters, and papers of all kinds has become a custom for many of the younger generations, as is the case here. This is an example of how the people adopt the state's legal and bureaucratic language and practices.

Of course, then, papers can also be falsified, lost, or destroyed. In this case, it seems the man had usurped or invented another identification number, either because he did not want to be identified or actually had no ID, as he had claimed (the judge checks the ID the man had used to sell the goat and finds it does not exist in the records). The police arrested the man after the woman filed a complaint.

The accused provides a line of defense that the woman has no evidence whatsoever and no proof of what she purports; her accusation is thus said to be totally unfounded. His lawyer asks bluntly, "Where is the body of the offense? Where is the corpse of the animal? You said that your goat had been stolen, sold, and slaughtered [insinuating that she might be lying and using the court to take advantage of his client]. Are you at least able to show us the skin so that we can certify that it is indeed your goat? No, you're not."

She replies that she obviously does not have it, because she is not the one who slaughtered it, and time has passed, and the skin is now lost. The man's lawyer proceeds, "but then what makes you say that it's your goat?" Her lawyer replies that she knows that it's hers because of her inquiry with the CASEC and the corroboration of witnesses.

The contention evidently revolves around the problem of adducing evidence—the pass, the skin, and testimonies—which are the missing pieces. The man goes on to claim that the goat was his, that he had bought it when it was small and raised it, but that unfortunately the title had been lost. He adds that he also lost his ID and his own birth certificate (one of which at least is required to lawfully complete the transaction).

At the time of the investigation, the woman who had bought the goat from the accused had showed the police agent that she did possess a pass, but it turned out that the registration number of the animal inscribed on it did not exist in the official register; nor did it match the number the man gave to the court.

Given the contradictory claims and the confusion—which triggers some jokes from the attorneys and the judge, and laughter from the audience— the judge decides to keep the man in custody while an investigation is conducted. He had previously (orally) requested some hearings with the witnesses and the buyer, but they had all refused to show up in court. So, he now instructs the clerk to produce an invitation letter, which is the step before issuing an official court summons.[4] If they still refuse, the judge says, he will issue a subpoena and give the order to the police to coerce them to come to the court. However, that is surely no easy job, because they first have to find them, and then, make it happen.

After everyone has left, Frédéric and I sit down in the shade with the judge. We had asked him if he would be kind enough to spare us a moment, and he was happy to oblige. He tells us that he is highly suspicious of the man, because it seems very unlikely that he has suddenly lost all three documents at once (the pass, his ID, and his birth certificate). He also mentions the attitude of the man, which is not quite trustworthy, whereas the woman seems to speak with outright earnestness. Nevertheless, he adds, he is a judge and does not want to rely on his own impressions. Still, he tells us, it is quite clear to him: According to the way both parties pleaded, it looks to him like a common case of theft and the usual strategies of exculpation. The case will be easily settled in court, he says; yet, he adds that the settlement might well not be that easily accepted by the parties, and that further issues could add up. That is not his problem anymore, though, unless they come back to the court.

We are here at the core of ordinary matters. Goat theft and killing, like the sabotage of the irrigation canals, are major issues in this region. As it happens, the provisions in art. 119 to 130 RC determine procedures for repair in case of devastation by animals, but not in the case of slaughter; yet, animal slaughter is a common practice among peasants.[5] Indeed, people still practice free breeding on a large scale, even though it is formally forbidden by art. 84 RC.[6] Goats freely go about with three long sticks hanging around their necks in the shape of a triangle to prevent them from going through bushes and gates into the gardens. Yet, they still manage to find ways and do enter the fields. When they damage the plantations, the owner of the plot often either kills the animal, which might trigger a contention with the owner of the goat, or reports the incident to local officials. If the animal was slaughtered, an agreement is usually found informally by negotiating the share of meat each party is to receive. The aggrieved party might also capture the animal and call the CASEC, who will keep the animal in a gated yard that serves precisely this purpose until the case is settled. However, it often happens that goats are also stolen. People might seek reparation for the wrong, but they might also be prompted to seek vengeance, or both. Theft easily triggers fury and rancor, which might not be easily diffused.

An example of the sort of violence triggered by the invasion of cultivated fields by free-breeding livestock, was shared with me by Miracson, chief of CASEC from the communal section of Bwa-Mapou where I lived. In May 2018, he received in his office a man who had descended from high up in the mountains (about a six- to eight-hour walk on stony and slippery paths). The man claimed he had something important to say, but on condition of anonymity: He feared retaliation. Indeed, five days earlier, he had witnessed a murder.

Around 10 a.m., as he was walking in his hamlet, he noticed some unusual movement in a backyard. He peeped through the bushes and saw two men he knew apprehend another man he knew as well in his own garden: They cut off his head.

According to Miracson's rendering of the witness's version, the story roughly goes as follows: A cow owned by one of the suspected murderers ate and ransacked a large portion of the plot owned by the neighbor. Perhaps the cow loosened its knot by moving and set itself free, or the owner did not moor it at all; in any event, it was walking around untied. May is the end of the dry season and the beginning of the rainy season. The animals have had little to eat during the winter and hunt for fresh grass or seedlings. The peas and other vegetables have arrived at maturity or are still growing. For the cow, they are food, but they are also among the most precious of goods for those who cultivate them. If cultivators lose their harvest, it may be that, not only is the main income and staple food for the upcoming six months or so lost, but they are strongly indebted to the local union bank where they usually take out short-term loans, payable after six months, to buy the seeds and the fertilizers, and pay the workers. Such a situation could indeed be catastrophic for a family that has no other source of income. Under enormous pressure, the owner of the plot retaliated by putting fertilizer in the grass and alfalfa of the cow, and thus killed it. When the owner of the cow discovered the carcass, he and an accomplice, enraged, penetrated the other man's garden and killed him with a blow of a machete to the neck.

Soon after the witness statement, Miracson went to Judge Saintil's house to get a signed warrant. The next day, with two other CASEC, he walked up the mountain to summon the accused to come down into the valley and be questioned by the judge. The geography plays a critical role here. One can only access the remote hamlet on foot or on the back of a donkey or a mule. It takes a tiresome two-day walk back and forth. A visiting official would also need to sleep somewhere and eat and drink, none of which was likely to be provided to them by the local people. It is risky too: Up there, if things go awry, there is no escape. A judge or a police officer could easily be put in danger. So generally, the peasants only have to intimidate the officials if the matter is sensitive and they do not want the state to intervene; this is enough to discourage them from undertaking the trip. Contrariwise, the CASEC, being mediators between the state and the people, are generally welcome.

In these kinds of cases, however, the CASEC can play the role of police. They can be given a special status by the judge that allows them to use restraint measures and to arrest someone, which they normally cannot do. Eventually, the three CASEC were able to inquire in the zone, interviewing relatives, asking neighbors for information, listening to hearsay and rumors, and spending some time among them to get a sense of what happened. Miracson then tells me that he started to become suspicious of one of the accused when he saw that, not only did he avoid going to the burial of his neighbor, but also acted strangely in their regard. He tells me the man was bizarre in the presence of the mourning family (with whom he is related by marriage); he was elusive, not offering the usual questions like "how are you?" or "how can I help?" or the sorts of affections that characterize normal behavior in these moments. Miracson took this to be a sign of his culpability. The two suspects were eventually taken to the precinct.

There was not enough proof with which the judge could appreciate the case. On the basis of some small pieces of evidence gathered during the inquiry and the growing sense that the case was more serious than first thought—probably involving family histories, long-nourished resentment, and buried conflicts—and thus could get out of hand, the JP court finally decided that it was beyond its purview and sent the two accused to the lower tribunal, which is also the criminal court, in Saint-Marc. What initially could have been a civil case, regulated by the Rural Code (law no. VI "On Stockbreeding," section "Devastation of fields and capture," articles 119–13), became penal. The JP judge hoped this court would have the means to inquire more deeply (with police assistance); but he also sought to unload a complex and probably intractable case. In the end, Miracson told me bluntly, the police did obtain avowal from the accused by "giving them a little electricity" (*bay yo yon ti kouran*). He explains to me that they were actually tortured by police, as if he were explaining the simplest and most banal procedure. "It just helped them to solve the case quicker," he said. What would have taken weeks or months of inquiry was finally "solved," so to say, in a few hours. Both men have been put behind bars in Saint-Marc. Miracson sees this as a victory: He has played his role successfully.

It's interesting to note at this point that the Creole concept of "*kouran*" has multiple aspects. While in the case discussed here it is used to mean torture and the violent extortion of confessions, in other circumstances it is also used to mean the neutralization of violence. Indeed, *kouran* can also be a lever for healing and resolution, as shown by what happened in the evening of precisely that same day. Around eight o'clock, I am at Wilbert's, a neighbor and *vodouizan* apprentice in his late twenties, for a little chat in the dark when a young pregnant woman arrives unexpectedly and complains that she's in pain and that her child isn't developing. Wilbert tells her to go bathe at the back of the house. Meanwhile, Wilbert, his younger sister, and her daughter, a neighbor in his thirties, and I gather in a circle in the backyard in front of the dried, cracking remains of a tree that has a white and dirty teddy bear nailed to it. Wilbert lights candles and spreads a powder. When the pregnant woman returns, naked under a loincloth she's tied around her chest, the little conclave begins to sing, pray, and invoke the *lwa*. Meanwhile, Wilbert prepares a mixture consisting of a fried, skinned, and stinky sardine; homemade rum; coconut water; talcum powder; and pieces he scrapes from a small block of chalk and a block of indigo. After a little while, he's mounted by a *lwa* that greets everyone. He introduces himself to me as Bossou Twa Kòn[7] and says: "So, you're my horse's [Wilbert's] friend?" I answer positively to his rhetorical question; he seems happy. We share some rum. He then asks the woman her name and place of origin, as well as the names of her father and mother. Bossou then places a yellow handkerchief on the floor, around which he lights candles and in the center of which he places a bowl with the potion. The woman undresses and stands upright on the cloth, her feet on either side of the bowl. The neighbor then washes her with the stinking mixture. (Wilbert's niece holds back a barely sketched grimace.) He smears it all over her round belly, breasts, back, shoulders, buttocks, thighs, and feet, using determined, skillful gestures, as if he were washing a child and had no time for it. Bossou then tells her to get dressed without washing off the mixture or removing the pieces of fish sticking to her body. Under her dress, he ties the yellow cloth around her waist and pours rum over her head. He then asks her who persecutes her in the neighborhood. She gives a name and says that this person is hurting her. Bossou then prays, digging a groove on a few white candles with his fingernail in a spiral motion. He gives her one and asks her to keep digging the furrow with her own fingernail, saying clearly who her stalker is and what she's doing to her. The woman does this silently, as if to herself. Once she has finished, Bossou calls another *lwa*, Danbala Wedo, the serpent spirit of fertility and growth.[8] He says he'll send Danbala to sneak up and bite the accused to stop her. Bossou takes the trouble to point out that it's not a question of hurting her (of course not, since Danbala is good), but that it's a matter of warning her and preventing her from committing other harmful acts in the future. He adds that Danbala will also camouflage himself and stand nearby, "like an electricity pole." With his power (*kouran*), he will burn away her evil intentions and attacks. His electricity will neutralize the threat. Bossou greets us and leaves.

I won't comment further on this moment, except to say that it illustrates the complex texture of human relationships. The question of whether this or that form of violence is justified or not, or whether there might not be other possible avenues—imagine for a moment that the suspect in the case described above had been taken to Danbala rather than to the police station—is a question that can only be asked and understood within the thickness of a particular context. So how do the different communities and groups of people perceive and conceive what living together means and entails? What notion of peace is there at work among them? And is there a relation between these very local cases, the way they are handled, and the global pressures trying to impose the rule of law in Haiti?

FRAGILE EQUILIBRIUMS

Haiti is known to have endured the presence of one of the biggest and most enduring UN peacekeeping forces in world history. In particular, between 2004 and 2017, the MINUSTAH occupied the republic, in the name of peace, with no less than 10,000 soldiers. The first sentence of the UN Peace Operations Year Review of 2004 reads, "the year 2004 witnessed an unprecedented surge in UN peacekeeping operations, widening prospects for ending conflicts and raising hopes for peace in war-torn countries." Seemingly galvanized by the 2001 Nobel Peace Prize attributed to the United Nations and Kofi Annan "for their work for a better organized and more peaceful world,"[9] the review praises the United Nations' success at bringing "peace and democracy to Namibia, Cambodia, El Salvador, Mozambique, and East Timor." Haiti was to follow.

As I went on reading more documents produced by UN agencies and other organizations, as well as academic articles on the subject, it soon became evident that a certain rhetoric on "peace-building" actually not only reinforced the belief that Haiti's main problem was its own culture of violence, but also promoted the rule of law as the necessary and unavoidable means by which Haiti would attain sufficient peace (or "stabilization," which is another word in the UN lexicon) to enable a democratic transition. Since Haiti was pictured as incapable of doing so itself, it needed the "help" of foreign forces.

Hence, one aim of this chapter is to expose the underpinnings of such discourse, as well as its effects on the ground. We need, on the one hand, to untangle the discourses that justify specific forms of violence in the name of peace and, on the other hand, to take a critical look at the culturalist discourses that portray violence and lawlessness in Haiti as both cultural and endemic characteristics. The extreme political instability and violence that plague Haiti today are not accidental. On the contrary, although the internal politics are strongly marked by a culture of predation and mismanagement, the disorder, as I will show, has been largely stimulated, if not generated, by international coercive forces.[10]

First, I will provide some details of the Haitian justice system and the way Haitian people relate to it. Second, this view from below will enable me to shed light on the structure of the argumentation, as well as on the assumptions underpinning international discourses, to show how far such a view is from what actually happens. The discrepancy between the ideology promoted from above and the daily reality that the people live in should inspire us to reflect on how such a mismatch also enables forms of violence. I would like to finish by depicting how people carry on even in the ruins left behind by foreign "aid" (Johnston 2024; Katz 2013; Schuller 2012). They do not give up. Many still strive for something they call *lapè* (*la paix* in French), searching for moments of calm and quietude between the spans of overwhelming tension. The search for the fragile equilibrium that makes life livable continues interminably.

Yet, this search for peace takes sometimes a form that is imposed by outsiders. Here, one must reckon with the fact that the ordinary vocabulary of *lapè* is heavily affected and transformed by the lexicon of human rights, law, and peace-building. It's no coincidence that Haiti was named the "Republic of NGOs" by the media, under the yoke of a "humanitarian empire." There are so many NGOs in Haiti—whether local, national, or transnational—that a very large proportion of the population has dealt with them at least once in their lives. I don't think there's a person in my immediate circle in Haiti who hasn't been, or isn't, in sporadic contact with them. As a result, the language conveyed by these NGOs is partly adopted locally, if only because it has to be mastered to gain access to the resources of these NGOs. Take, for instance, Lakou Lapè, an NGO doing community work in the poor neighborhoods of Saint Martin, Bel-Air, Nan Cocteau, and Martissant. It was created in 2005 by Concern Worldwide and Glencree Center for Peace (both from Ireland). Among its partners, the United Nations, the Haitian state, Inter-American Foundation, the American Jewish World Service, the European Union (EU), and the National Endowment for Democracy. On its website, Lakou Lapè defines its "mission" as "building a more peaceful Haiti by transforming violence and conflict starting from the individual, to communities, and to Haitian society as a whole." Its "vision" is "a peaceful and prosperous Haiti through the forging and deepening of human relationships across deep cleavages to collectively build a society that is more inclusive, equitable and just." They emphasize that "peacebuilding begins at the individual level in order to transform one's community." (Note the emphasis on individual responsibility, to the detriment of the structural conditions that have created the current situation in Haiti.) They organize "trainings," "meetings," and "workshops"; they have a "staff" and a "board," "facilitators" and "community mobilizers," as well as "executive directors" and "chairs." They specialize in "dialogue facilitation," "mediation," and "negotiation." Their language is one of "empowerment" and "responsibility," "outreach" and "facilitation." Yet, interestingly, they mingle this liberal lexicon with vernacular concepts such as "*lakou*"[11] and "*rasanblaj*" (assembly, regrouping, enlisting, compilation, reunion, assemblage, mobilization, ceremony, protest). "Lakou Lapè remembers and honors histories of the traditional *lakou* and respectfully brings together (*rasanble*) Haiti's children as family in the *lakou* in order to dream and collectively construct a peaceful and just Haiti. . . . It was a space that maintained peace, promoted a unique sense of mutual social responsibility and cared for the well-being of every member." Thus, vernacular language is also entering the mainstream of NGO discourse. That said, with the balance of power clearly to the disadvantage of the Haitians, it is the language of international diplomacy that comes to the fore, not the Creole.

In what follows, I will concentrate for a while on the JP courts because they are particularly important today as somewhat intermediary spaces between the people and the state. They operate in a gray zone; they are neither always fully in line with the promotion of the rule of law conveyed by the ministry and the council in charge of the judiciary, which partly espouse the United Nations' incentive, nor do they fully adopt an alternative, more informal way of handling local issues. Theses courts are a privileged theater in which the tensions related to the various inflections given to the concept of peace become visible.

THE JUSTICE OF THE PEACE IN HAITI

The primary scope of the JP courts is to maintain relative peace within the community by offering a space for conciliation and mediation in local civil affairs. Its official function is to adjudicate civil cases, settle disputes, and mediate arrangements supposed to prevent the escalation of tensions into private vengeance. Their mandate is to ensure civil peace and prevent civil conflicts from turning into criminal cases. As one might suspect, matters are far more complex. What "peace" actually means is unclear; thus, it cannot be as evident as some might think that the courts necessarily contribute to maintaining it within the community, nor that people go to the courts to find some kind of peace (Rubbers and Gallez 2012). To compound matters, in Haiti *lapè* is also a word that bears the weight of a long and dark history of violence.

The French system of the JP courts (*tribunaux de paix*), also called "proximity justice" (*justice de proximité*), was adopted in Haiti, as I wrote in the subchapter "A Rough History of Resistance" of the Introduction, by President Jean-Pierre Boyer, who ruled between 1820 and 1843. The administration of the newborn country required the adoption of codified laws and a judicial system capable of not only managing internal affairs, regulating agriculture, and enforcing nationwide order, but also of streamlining production. The JP system, in coordination with the constables, the rural police, and the military, enabled him to quickly organize property rights and rationalize agriculture in order to generate wealth. I remind the reader that, in fact, his country was under great pressure after he had ratified the decree of April 17, 1825, issued by King Charles X, which stated that the inhabitants of the French part of the Saint-Domingue Island had to pay off 150 million of the old francs in order to indemnify the colonial settlers against compensation for what they had lost (Dorigny et al. 2021). Thus, Boyer, having neither time nor the means to invent and elaborate his own codes, implemented the Civil Code in 1825, the Rural Code in 1826, and the Penal Code in 1835, all largely drawn from the Napoleonic codes and other precedents. He slightly adapted them, although without any major changes.

The JP courts as we know them today were created in France in 1790 and, notably, conceived to uniformly enforce the new Civil Code on the whole territory, apply standardized procedures, and manage small litigation that would not threaten public order: that is, to keep in check potential disruptive conflicts (Follain 2003). Their mandate was to handle all sorts of ordinary contentions by attempting to mediate, negotiate, and arrange situations rather than imposing sanctions or using coercive force.[12] This new jurisdiction was characterized by simplicity, rapidly executed procedures, and an effort to treat all parties equally. Yet, its roots lie deeper in history and its functions appear less obviously reparative. As Michel Foucault showed (2019, 149–82), institutions of peace were consolidated in medieval society, when, in conjunction with the penal institution, their functions were: (1) to put an end to the institution of vengeance and ban private warfare; (2) to appropriate wealth in an indirect and regulated manner through better-organized, better-run, lucrative tax levies in the form of fines, forfeitures, redemptions, remissions, pledges, and court costs (replacing violent plundering); (3) to ensure the conditions favorable to trade by protecting individuals who could afford the state's services; (4) to control and limit the circulation of weapons, and concentrate them in the hands of the legitimate authority. Before that, in a moment of transition between Germanic law and the modern judiciary, "The act of justice is not organized by reference to peace and truth [as it would later be the case]. To effectuate an act of justice is rather to pursue a war according to the rules" (ibid., 116). An act of justice is an attack: It has the form of a battle. "All this clearly shows that the course of the judicial act continues to preserve a warlike character ... in front of a judge who above all had to authenticate the course of the 'combat.' ... In its dramatic staging, the judgment is still a struggle, an episode of the war, a rivalry" (ibid., 130).

In the Middle Ages, the idea that justice was about "*pax*" and truth was then imposed, notably through the confiscation of the right of some to arms. And in the face of defiant groups, all this can only be achieved by the intervention of armed forces. Concomitantly, an army of mercenaries emerged, serving the judicial authorities, the ancestors of what later would become the police. This is what allows Foucault (2019, 170–71; also Polat 2010) to write: "it is through war that the peace institutions can be established. . . . Recourse to the army of mercenaries made it possible to establish peace through war."

In Haiti, if it is true that the JP courts' original functions remain intact, they are also, as we shall see, mostly unable to exert their functions. The role they play primarily, to my view, is one of intermediary. In fact, they are presently at the forefront of the judicial system and play an important role in communal life, along with other institutions or habitual ways of handling contentions. People more voluntarily defer to kin, friends, and neighbors, but also to the local notables, depending on the issues. Notables are usually older and respected men within the community, more rarely women: a retired official, a schoolteacher, an *oungan* (Vodou priest), a *manbo* (Vodou priestess), or a *doktè fèy* or *pè savann* (old herbalists and wise men considered to be guardians of traditions and ritual formulas); a priest, a pastor, or any clergyman; a CASEC; or the court clerk, the bailiff, or the *jij de pè* (judge of peace). Litigants rarely file a complaint at the police station because the police are not only feared by many and known to be inefficient but are generally absent. In most communal sections with which I am familiar, there is no police station to which one can report, except in my example, where it turns out that the court is a block away from the precinct. What prompts people at times to appeal to the court rather than to settle disputes with the help of other community leaders or the police is a complex matter. Before I get to this, let me briefly provide a few details about the overall organization of the judiciary, and the operational principles at the end of the chain.

The JP courts are managed by two institutions. First, there is the Ministry of Justice and Public Security (MJSP), whose mandate—fixed by a decree issued in 1984 under Jean-Claude Duvalier's fading dictatorship—is mainly to submit bills, organize the judiciary system, and control the courts. Second, there is the Superior Council of the Judiciary Power (CSPJ), created in 2007 under the occupation of the MINUSTAH and the second mandate of René Préval, whose task is chiefly to appoint magistrates; manage the material and financial funds; receive the magistrates' grievances; and provide information and recommendations about the state of the magistracy.

According to a document produced in 2015 by the CSPJ, the national territory is organized into eighteen jurisdictions, each administered by a lower court. There are four main judiciary offices: the JP courts (numbering 179), the lower courts (18), the courts of appeal (5), and the court of cassation (1). Additional courts exist with specific functions: a juvenile's court, a chamber for commercial matters, two special land tribunals, a labor tribunal, the superior court of accounts and administrative disputes, and a military court.

The territorial authorities of the Haitian state are organized in concentric circles. The smallest administrative unit is the communal section, above which are the commune, the district, and, finally, the department. For instance, Bouquet-Duvoisin, the commune in which I mainly conducted my research, has six large communal sections and two JP courts (Bwa-Mapou is a what people call a "neighborhood," informally regrouping two sections). At the very end of the chain of officials are the CASEC and the communal supervisory boards, which are usually composed of three men: a chief, an assistant, and a secretary-cum-treasurer. Communal sections are, in fact, the backbone of social, administrative, political, and economic life in Haiti, even though they are nowadays largely marginalized and left behind.[13] Communal sections paradoxically place the CASEC at the forefront. They are usually people from the zones, elected by residents, and have a deep knowledge of the problems plaguing the community. They work closely with the JP courts and police (if any) and provide essential help with investigations and arrests.

Now, what does it look like on the ground?

A BLURRY CONCEPT

One morning, roughly a week after the session in court described above, I was waiting out in the courtroom of another section of the same commune. It was quiet. The sun was already pounding down hard on the tin roof. A court clerk was reading some documents in the office. The judge had not yet arrived. A lone woman, waving a piece of paper in front of her face, was patiently waiting for her case to be heard. She eventually left when it became obvious that the other party was not going to show up. The head of the three court clerks working in that JP court was also lingering, obviously bored, so we started to chat. He told me that he had been working in that tribunal since 2005. The court was full during his first years of work. "Now," he said, "people don't come any more. There is too much insecurity, and trust has been lost." He went on to explain that people feared bringing their disputes before the court not only because the courts and the police could not guarantee their safety, but also because appealing to the judiciary might worsen the issue. "Settling" a dispute in court might not be settling anything. Once the court sessions were over, he said, the resentment between parties usually deepened. People often attacked each other afterward, in one way or another, even though the case was supposed to be resolved. The court could not prevent people from getting even, and it did not have the means to be coercive. The clerk told me the accused, even when found guilty, often resisted and refused to comply. The judge, the clerks, or sometimes the police, could do nothing to force them to cooperate. Some litigants just walked away under the eyes of the officials, ready to use force or violence to escape the clutches of the judiciary. According to him, people had no respect for the laws because they did not fear the institutions and tended, more and more, "to dispense their own justice" (*bay tèt yo jistis*).

A couple of weeks later, Frédéric organized a one-day seminar on the theme, Democracy and Social Justice. In fact, he had been active in the community for many years, mentoring adolescents and organizing occasional activities for children, public forums, and workshops of many kinds. His commitment to the community had taken a new turn since, a few years before, he had opened his "house of bread," which he calls a "social bakery."[14] Not only did he welcome many young people, who came to buy sacks of bread or pass the time and with whom he had time to chat individually, but with the money he earned and the reputation he acquired, he also organized events he perceived to be mutually educational and, thus, a contribution to a peaceful community. His conviction was that education, knowledge, and awareness would help appease some of the tensions that plagued the community. Hence, he seized the opportunity of my presence to invite teachers, nurses, lawyers, artists, notables, and community leaders, many of whom I had come to know more or less already, for a one-day seminar held in a classroom of the school owned by Robert, wife Angeline's uncle. He asked me to conduct the seminar, which I did.

One of the points of discussion revolved around what the court clerk had told me: Conflicts were essentially dealt with outside the courtroom. This point was unsurprising since it was obviously the case in most parts of the world. Another was the way in which the litigation was addressed, often by notables, such as heads of schools, elderly community leaders, retired officials, or religious leaders, in places like someone's courtyard (*lakou*), in churches, in schools, in Vodou compounds (*oumfò*), or near specific sources of water, some of which are the homes of certain spirits (*lwa*) who help people to reach settlements.[15] The participants also mentioned that certain moments of social life were important, such as the *jèn*—a particular Vodou ritual—during which participants create a space called *temwayaj* (testimony) dedicated to the expression of grievances. This is something I had witnessed myself. Participants also expressed their reservations and a certain anxiety about unofficial means of doing justice, because many of these means were viewed as dangerous, getting easily out of control, potentially and ultimately leading to injustice, death, and further war. This is the case, for instance, when mobs are created and the logic of deadly vengeance is at work or when people recklessly or malevolently manipulate *fòs mistik* (mystical forces). However, it appeared that such dangers and effects had nonetheless to be reckoned with if the community wanted to handle disputes itself. In the end, all participants emphasized that justice, social order, and cohesion were the product of education, culture, and collective intelligence rather than of law. The court simply did not appear to be such a privileged site at which to find peace.

Yet, the picture is darker than first it appears. Local communities know all too well that the discourse of "peace" is also an instrument of power and a justification of violence that works more often than not against their interests. This knowledge obviously generates much resistance among the population. Indeed, the codification of the law, by enabling the settlement of the standards for homogenization and the rationalization of conduct, served from the very beginning to consolidate the centralized power (Cabanis and Louis Martin 1996; Foucault 2021, 2009; Collot 2007; Petit 2003). Historically, "law proceeds from the state, namely from the legislative sovereignty of a prince or a nation" (Supiot 2009, 27).[16] Not only is the codification of law intrinsic to the centralization of the administration of power, but it is also partly designed to serve the interests of a ruling elite against those of the poor and the peasants (Payton 2018).

There are deep historical and internal tensions between centralized authorities—whose attitude is defiant, authoritative, and predatory—and the islanders. However, the turf wars have been fueled largely by the outside. Hence, in such a context, rural residents have often responded by thwarting the state and its allies' attempts at control by creating alternative livelihoods.[17] Plausibly, the JP courts could be used today to keep an eye on local affairs and potential dissidence in areas out of the control of the state. After all, the initial scope of their implementation by Boyer was to keep records of what happened in the countryside (Schneider 2018, 123). People today are generally quite aware of such a possibility, even though many are unafraid of JP courts, since the whole state apparatus lacks the means to enforce control and since the police cannot guarantee the safety of magistrates. This state of affairs strongly conflicts with the JP court's role as a peaceful arbitrator and its position as an actor that is supposed to be close to the population. The so-called justice of proximity is actually often far from home, and peace is often close to war. The courts are not only far from the homes of many people geographically, especially those who live *nan mòn* (in the mountains), they are also distant in terms of their language (French) and rationale, which is often alien to the everyday language (Creole) and modes of thinking of the people. My example at the beginning of this chapter shows, notably, how potentially alien to the people involved are concepts such as the probative value of a document or the burden of evidence, or a specific conception of causation (notably determined by the appropriateness of criteria). Yet, Haitians are nonetheless subjected to such language and rationales. The strong impression of alienness that emerges in certain key moments when the magisterial (and esoteric) legal language is disclosed in courts adds to the already deeply felt impression of remoteness that is generated by the state itself. Yet, in the JP courts, the use of formal language (usually in French) alternates with colloquialisms, jokes, undertones, sayings, and so on (in Creole), showing that the JP courts, for all the seriousness and technicality of the language of law they convey, are perhaps nonetheless not so far from the playfulness of ordinary language (as I will show in detail in Chapter 4).

How close to or far are the judges and attorneys themselves from the language of the institutions they represent? I personally witnessed (but it is also systematically underlined in various assessments of the judiciary in Haiti) that jurists sometimes do not possess the codes of law to which they refer, and, if they do, they often do not have the official standard but copies of codes or, even more often, compendiums of codes in which not every law is to be found. This is no surprise since the official codes are sold only in the few big cities and at prohibitive prices. The majority can barely afford the compendiums; thus, even in law schools, the courses are based on the copies and compendiums, since the students will hardly ever have the standard code in their hands. To this must be added the fact that some magistrates have not been to law school. Even if today the superior authorities try to appoint judges who have been lawyers, there is a lack of professional lawyers, according to some observers. However, this state of affairs is not necessarily problematic from the point of view of the people. As long as the magistrates at the level of the JP court can translate the law into their own words (regardless of whether the translation is accurate), it is somewhat acceptable. Furthermore, if the judges consider the specific problems people have (in contrast to high magistrates originating from the bourgeoisie, who often lack sympathy or feel disdain for the poor and the peasants), then it is even better. Most people hardly expect more from the courts. This is why the courts are seen as a buffer zone between the state and the people, also working with the community to forge a common language regarding, for example, respect, theft, dissimulation, reparation, lying, cunning, and so on, that is neither fully the language of the law nor fully everyday language.

Most of the judges and clerks of the JP courts I met tried their best; their effort is not in question. They did strive for peace within the communities in which they often lived. However, they were also subject to enormous pressures. They were themselves citizens and sometimes residents of the villages and neighborhoods in which they worked (or close by), and they were thus part of the everyday life and relationships within those communities. They too were entrenched and bound to cope with many forces they could not contradict.

The specific potential for violence embedded in some of the cases could scare off a judge, as mentioned earlier. This is, notably, because the police do not have the means to fulfill their mandate. Many disputes occur far from the precinct, and it happens often that the police never show up. They fear for their own safety. Sometimes they take sides and decide not to intervene for partisan reasons. Often, they just have no gas in their pickup truck, so unless someone sends them money via a cellphone transfer system, they will not move, or else, as they themselves told me, they might just be unwilling to sweat in vain.

The pressures on the *jij de pè* come from all sides. They are intimidated by the parties or the people in their surroundings. The bullying can be verbal, but also physical to some extent. For instance, the judge might be unable to reach the place he is supposed to inspect because a few men are standing firmly in the way with hoes, shovels, machetes, and hammers. Some judges I spoke to told me that sometimes men even push them physically, such as malevolently knocking their foreheads with their rigid index fingers, to make them step back. A common kind of threat used in the Artibonite is deemed "mystical" (*mistik*), which can take many forms. It is actually very telling that on the official webpage of the CSPJ, in the section devoted to presenting the professions linked to the JP courts, the *hoqueton* is said to be the one who is not only the janitor of the court, but also the "one who makes sure that nobody puts *pwa grate* and other sorts of spells [*sortilège*] in the office of the judge."[18]

Magistrates are also intimidated by the lawyers, who are known to also use occult means to pressure them and to influence a decision or a judgment. *Yo sonde w* (they probe you), which means they are influencing the power relation "on another level." Then *yo fè bagay* (they do things), implying that they use occult forces. If the judges are not careful enough, or not protected, they can easily succumb to the pressure. These are not small matters in Haiti.

In addition, a major menace for their integrity comes from the streets and the political circles of influence that leverage their position with either bribes or direct physical threats (at the hands of henchmen). In one communal section, the CSPJ suspended the appointed judge from the bar for five years after he ignored pressure from an influential senator, Youri Latortue, and went on adjudicating a case involving that senator's nephew. The CSPJ was quick to suspend the judge, and most of the other judges and court clerks were muzzled.

I name the senator because his case is very telling. Several classified Wikileaks cables from March 27 to November 20, 2006, target Youri Latortue. He is highly suspected by former US Ambassador J. A. Sanderson, US Ambassador J. Foley, and a Haitian judge of being implicated in murders, kidnappings, and an attempted coup, as well as drug, weapon, and other contraband trafficking; being in cahoots with illegal armed groups (notably the Cannibal Army) and for having stimulated criminal associations; owning illicit businesses (nightclubs and movie theaters), not to mention theft (of telephone poles and utility boxes), unfair competition, influence peddling, intimidation, and embezzlement (notably during the large-scale flooding of September 2006, when he allegedly intercepted and stashed food supplies and then redistributed them on his behalf for political interests). Latortue was president of the Senate when I met him a couple times in 2017 and 2018. I have myself collected testimonial evidence that he used to grant favors to women who slept with him, such as giving them cash or helping them to find jobs. On November 4, 2022, the US Department of the Treasury's Office of Foreign Assets Control (OFAC), along with the government of Canada, identified Haitian nationals Joseph Lambert [the sitting president of the Haitian Senate] and Youri Latortue for

having engaged in, or attempted to engage in, activities or transactions that have materially contributed to, or pose a significant risk of materially contributing to, the international proliferation of illicit drugs or their means of production. Lambert's history with drug trafficking covers two decades. During this time, Lambert used his position to lead and facilitate the trafficking of cocaine from Colombia to Haiti and to facilitate impunity in Haiti for other narcotics traffickers. Lambert has also directed others to engage in violence on his behalf. His drug trafficking, corrupt tactics, and continued disregard for the rule of law have contributed to the continued destabilization of Haiti. Like Lambert, Latortue has also had lengthy involvement in drug trafficking activities. Latortue has engaged in the trafficking of cocaine from Colombia to Haiti and has directed others to engage in violence on his behalf. OFAC coordinated closely with the Drug Enforcement Administration on this designation.[19]

In other cases, it is not uncommon that judges, clerks, bailiffs, or lawyers are assaulted, wounded, or sometimes killed: Me Monferrier Dorval, the president of the bar of Port-au-Prince, was assassinated in front of his home by anonymous shooters; Me Fritz Gérald Cerisier, the substitute for the government commissioner at the Port-au-Prince lower court, was shot dead in his car; bailiffs Jean Fenel Monfleury and Bob Dolcine, as well as Deputy Judge Antoine Luccius, were all killed by several shooters nearby courthouses or their home. The list could go on and on.

The oppressive and deceptive character of the state is something most people are aware of and contend with on a variety of levels. Their disillusionment incites some to simply avoid all contact with the judiciary as much as possible, others tactically use these institutions for their own purposes, and still others fight them violently. Nevertheless, many express a strong yearning for a functional justice system, equal rights, and democracy. The dream of and hope for peace and a fair justice system working on behalf of the interests of the poor and vulnerable, rather than safeguarding the power of the elite, are very much alive. They aspire to something other than a justice system in tatters.

THE INTERNATIONAL RHETORIC OF PEACE

The particular role the JP courts are to play in society is notably defined by a certain conception of "peace"—and thus of what constitutes an offense, a settlement, a punishment, and so on—which may be more or less ideologically inflected, depending on who conceives it. Official discourses usually take the form of a "philosophy" of the justice of proximity: The JP system is said to contribute to the peace within the community because it is said to be close to the people (attentive to their particular problems), simple (there is little paperwork), rapid (the aim is quick resolution), rather inexpensive, and equitable. Yet, the long-lasting foreign presence in Haiti has had considerable effects on the Haitians' conception of peace. The money and energy invested in Haiti, especially by the United Nations, profoundly modified the country.

Less than four years after the fall of the Duvalier dictatorship, the United Nations began to occupy Haiti's institutional and geographical terrain. Between the 1990s and 2020s, one mission followed another. First there was the United Nations Observer Group for the Verification of Elections in Haiti (ONUVEH), then the International Civilian Support Mission in Haiti (MICIVIH). At the same time, the UN Security Council deployed the United Nations Mission in Haiti (MINUAH), followed by the United Nations Support Mission in Haiti (MANUH). The latter gave way to the United Nations Transition Mission in Haiti (MITNUH), which in turn gave way to the United Nations Civilian Police Mission in Haiti (MIPONUH) before the International Civilian Support Mission in Haiti (MICAH) took over. Following the 2004 coup d'état against Jean-Bertrand Aristide, the Security Council judged the Haitian state to be bankrupt and sent in MINUSTAH, a force of several thousand blue helmets. This presence coincided with the introduction by the United Nations of a new strategy that took the form of counterinsurgency military offensives conducted jointly by the police and the army. While missions are generally determined by "Chapter VI: Peaceful Settlement of Disputes" of the UN Charter, MINUSTAH is now primarily governed by "Chapter VII: Actions in Case of Threats to the Peace, Breaches of the Peace and Acts of Aggression," which states that the Security Council "may take such action by air, sea, or land forces as may be necessary to maintain or restore international peace and security (despite Haiti being no threat to the international community). Such action may include demonstrations, blockade, and other operations by air, sea, or land forces of Members of the United Nations." From now on, war serves peace.

As such, MINUSTAH marks a departure from previous missions: (1) it is the first peacekeeping mission specifically designated as a stabilization force; (2) it is the first whose activities are not related to an ongoing armed conflict; and (3) it is the first to have been asked to use the new methods, not against armed parties in a conflict, but against groups of civilians labeled by the governing bodies as "gangs" or "criminals" (L. Reed 2007).[20] This new discursive formation "gangsterizes"—and therefore criminalizes—young men from the slums. As a result, it justifies a heavy-handed intervention: Armed men and armored vehicles are deployed in strategic areas and raids of rare intensity are conducted in neighborhoods that were otherwise important pools of pro-Aristide voters. In one of the first raids, on July 6, 2005, approximately 1,400 heavily armed men entered the shantytowns of Cité Soleil at dawn to dislodge or kill alleged "gang" leaders. In the twelve hours of what has been dubbed "Operation Iron Fist," the peacekeeping force fired no less than 22,700 rounds of ammunition and seventy-eight grenades into one of the world's most densely populated neighborhoods, killing at least twenty civilians and injuring dozens more (Mobekk 2017; Pingeot 2018). This is just one of the many raids conducted by MINUSTAH between 2004 and 2007 that led, in the name of peace, to the occupation of Haiti by a so-called "interim" multinational force.

The UN presence was to last. At each deadline, the Security Council extended MINUSTAH's mandate. After the earthquake of January 12, 2010, the council decided to increase the military contingent to 8,940 soldiers and police to 3,711 police officers.[21] The mandate was extended twice more before it was finally lifted on October 15, 2017. The tanks and helicopters then left the island, and no more peacekeeper patrols were seen in the streets. As one mandate gave way to the next, the council simultaneously created a new entity, the United Nations Mission for Justice Support in Haiti (MINUJUSTH). This was to ensure the strategic plan for the development of the national police and to "assist the Haitian government in strengthening the institutions of the rule of law."[22] In 2019, the council once again changed the UN presence in Haiti, and replaced the MINUJUSTH with the BINUH, the United Nations Integrated Office in Haiti. Its mandate was planned for an initial period of twelve months, starting in October 2019. However, the COVID-19 pandemic, the extreme political instability, the assassination of former President Jovenel Moïse on July 7, 2021, the wars gangs waged against each other and the civilians, and the dramatic food crisis, convinced the Security Council to extend the mandate of the BINUH several times again, lastly until July 15, 2025. It will be thirty-five years since coalitions of international forces occupied Haiti.

The official mandates of the successive missions in Haiti, despite their variations, have all been about building a state sovereignty strong enough to ensure a protected and stable socioeconomic environment. This is what is called, in UN jargon, "state-building." This way of seeing the United Nations as a guarantor of the rule of law stems directly from the concept of "failed state" that experts apply to countries when they are deemed to have lost sovereignty over their territory, their legitimacy in public decision-making, and when they are considered unfit to guarantee minimum public services and to engage in international dialogue. With such criteria, the experts ignore the role played in this "failure" by international actors. Moreover, they reduce and simplify a complex issue that requires a contextual and nuanced analysis. Indeed, by taking the Organisation for Economic Co-operation and Development's (OECD) development criteria as a standard, the vision that stems from such a discourse fails to consider local sociological, political, and urban specificities. This blatant ignorance of the terrain thus encourages the violent application of peace plans. Moreover, by justifying UN tutelage, such discourse legitimizes external intervention and occupation.

After the end of the Cold War, but above all in the past two decades, this lexicon of constitutional liberalism entered the language of mainstream political discourse and international affairs, abandoning, "in the same gesture, another key aspirational vocabulary of the postwar settlement: social welfare and an accompanying register of solidarity, economic equality, social justice, and so on" (Humphreys 2010, xii). The United States Institute for Peace (USIP), which is active in Haiti, could not be clearer; subsection 7.2 of its "Guiding Principles for Stabilization and Reconstruction: Rule of Law," is titled, "Why Is the Rule of Law a Necessary End State?"

The notions of "rule of law" and "peacekeeping" are omnipresent, even repeated excessively in the official publications of international, private, or bilateral agencies such as the United Nations, the International Peace Institute, the United States Peace Institute or the Crisis Group, as well as in a number of academic articles and reports.[23] They are often accompanied by a conquering vocabulary and missionary rhetoric. Based on the assumption that Haiti's problem is its endemic culture of violence, the rule of law is generally seen as the only way to "pacify" or "stabilize" the country. Only in this way would Haiti complete its democratic transition, which began in 1986 after twenty-nine years of dictatorship. But since the Haitian government is considered by the international community to be incapable of carrying out this transition itself, it must accept "help" from those who are imposing it.

There is an optimistic tendency among advocates of the rule of law to view the judiciary as the first line of defense against mayhem. For instance, James Wilets and Camilo Espinosa (2011), by relying on a conception of the rule of law defined essentially by the World Bank and the United Nations,[24] perceive the law as being simultaneously predictable, transparent (thus legible), and coercive, which thus enables governance and promotes order. As these authors write, "the United States and the United Nations have begun establishing conditions to promote and create the rule of law in Haiti" (ibid., 211). Their article ends on an enthusiastic note: "The United States has played a significant role as well in promoting the rule of law in Haiti, and the U.S. has provided the means so that international organizations can conduct seminars advocating the rule of law, and reinforcing fundamental principles of governance" (ibid., 206.) America's imperialism has not yet uttered its last word (Pierre 2023).[25] Moreover, their article makes clear that the promotion of the rule of law accompanies the promotion of capitalism and liberal values so that, faithful to the World Bank's injunctions, investments are encouraged. In short, the implementation of the rule of law in Haiti appears as the Trojan horse that smuggles in the laws that stimulate international free trade and secure (foreign) corporate interests. As Ugo Mattei and Laura Nader plainly write, law has incrementally been used "as a mechanism for constructing and legitimizing plunder" (2008, 1). And the rule of law rhetoric is "used as a cover, a camouflage, or as propaganda when engaging in lawless or criminal operations" (ibid., 4). This trend is not new, however: US meddling persistently favors US businesses.[26]

What I am rather interested in here is why this kind of ideological perspective on the rule of law is also seen as "essential to building peace in post-conflict states" (Wilets and Espinosa 2011, 186), as if without the rule of law, "the written words of the Constitution [would be] trumped by political practice" (ibid., 191). The authors surmise that Haitians are incapable of self-government. This idea that the (ex-)colonized populations are not yet mature enough for self-government, and thus need the "help" that is given to them through structural adjustments plans, humanitarianism, the training of administrators, and so on, is not as outdated as some might think; it underlies many of the reports and articles, sometimes written by former US military or administration officials, that authoritatively describe what they perceive to be the internationalization of "gang" activity.[27] Their interpretations serve to legitimize a discourse that portrays these groups as major destabilizing agents and an insurgent threat to world order. They have become the new terrorists to fight.

This paternalistic promotion of rule of law is itself the product of precisely the political maneuvering it is supposed to keep in check. Interestingly, but unsurprisingly, Wilets and Espinosa's perspective relies on Manichean dichotomies that oppose, on the one hand, the government and the judiciary (as well as the police) and, on the other hand, "criminal gangs" (2011, 196) and "criminal enterprises" (ibid., 200); or, if you will, the good and the bad guys. Of course, the rule of law is meant to keep the good guys in. The discursive and interpretative framework for the problem is thus settled.

The authors' simplistic view justifies and legitimizes the promotion of a certain conception of peace that derives directly from their imagining the rule of law to be the superior and necessary device that secures order against anarchy, a view consistent with the Hobbesian idea that what makes the law supreme is its unsurpassable capacity to prevent dog-eat-dog warfare. In slightly different terms, this is the line followed by the authors of two briefings sponsored by the United States Institute of Peace—which also hosts the International Network to Promote the Rule of Law Community of Practice (Albrecht et al. 2009; V. O'Connor 2015). The purported characteristics of backwardness are roughly described as being "endemic poverty," "corruption," "malfunctioning and weakness of the justice system," "high level of crime," "drug trafficking," and "uncertainty about what the law is." In short, the picture is this: Haiti, being in a state of anarchy and chaos, is a "failed state"; hence, Haiti needs foreign aid to bring some law and order to this mess.

The logic is clear: Law guarantees order, order ensures security, and security ensures stability, which leads to peace, and peace facilitates the transition to a democratic nation, a prerequisite for beneficial international trade[28] (Carey 2005; 2012; Fatton 1999; Krever 2011; 2017; Mattei and Nader 2008). The criminalization of certain sectors of the population also serves as a lever for legitimizing the militarization of humanitarianism and peacekeeping missions (Fassin and Pandolfi 2010; Greenburg 2013; Neiburg 2017;

Müller and Steinke 2018). The offensive action of peacekeepers against "gangs" was officially included in the MINUSTAH mandate in 2006. But while its original mandate was to prevent civil war, a series of allegations and investigations reveal crimes committed by MINUSTAH soldiers and police: corruption, rape, sexual exploitation and abuse of under-aged minors, illegal arrests and detentions, summary executions, torture, property violations, illegal firearms sales, arson, drug trafficking, and false testimony. In addition, as a result of negligence by a Nepalese battalion that defecated in a tributary of the Artibonite River in October, 2010, nearly 7 percent of the population was infected with cholera, which killed more than 10,000 people.[29] The United Nations has not yet compensated the Haitians for the damage caused. While they condemn and claim to be fighting crime, UN soldiers and Haitian police have broken countless laws and many of their actions are criminally reprehensible. This raises the question of the extent to which the foreign intervention itself is not in part perpetuating and even triggering the violence and chaos it claims to be fighting.

"The expressed intent" of building the rule of law in Haiti, according to the one briefing, is "crucially" to "ensure that the justice system serves all the people of Haiti (rather than the rich and powerful)" (Albrecht et al. 2009, 5). Such an endeavor is consistent with the seventeen global objectives defined by the United Nations for sustainable development in the world, but also with the necessary conditions to achieve the rule of law defined by the USIP.[30] Most of these objectives are those of the BINUH in Haiti, among which is the promotion of "Peace, Justice, and Efficient Institutions" (objective 16) to guarantee the access of all to the judiciary.

Such a tendency to view the judiciary as the privileged and democratic site where litigations among citizens are resolved rests on a few conventional assumptions about disputes that, to end this section, I would like to challenge. The main idea from which this tendency derives is that peace is the product of a "resolution" or "settlement." Thus, first, it is assumed that a dispute has a definable beginning and ending. Second, that it can thus be precisely characterized. Third, that once clearly characterized, decisions can be taken, and judgments made. Fourth, that through decisions and judgments, the dispute can be properly resolved. Fifth, that once resolved, it is over. Sixth, that the courts are exactly the place where this happens. And finally, that the courts necessarily contribute to the establishment of peace and order in the community. Such a view is coextensive of the broader dogmatic, transcendental, and functionalist picture of the law as that which is vital, and thus necessary, to the regulation of human society: Without it, society would be gripped by generalized civil war (Supiot 2009, 24). But have we forgotten that this picture was imagined by Hobbes as a working hypothesis, a fiction meant to elaborate a theory—a myth?

However, disputes cannot be that easily defined; they are often signs of deeper conflicts. In fact, a feud might have started long ago and might continue long afterward. Sometimes, internecine divisions have existed for so long that one does not even know anymore why the people are fighting, and sometimes the unending cycle of grudges has begun only recently. At other times, issues are not so serious and are resolved rather quickly. In my initial example, we do not know when the contention really began or when and where it will end. Did it start with the theft? Or with the complaint? Or did the parties have former issues? Is one of them really seeking reparation or preparing to retaliate? Or is it a warning? And how sure can we be that, after a judgment and a punishment, the fight will not go on or even worsen? How much do we know? Delimiting the boundaries of a case is a matter of authority and arbitrariness. In everyday life, there are no such clear-cut boundaries.

The normative perspective on the rule of law is of little help to understand the issues at stake in concrete cases or the complexity of the intertwining of power relations. To be sure, there are many cases in which the attitudes and actions taken by courts do exactly the opposite; that is, they contribute to blurring the characterization of a conflict. Moreover, not only do they sometimes *not* contribute to resolving disputes, but they actually feed the feud and participate in the production of inequality, disorder, and violence. In the case I describe in Chapter 2, the court performs by its absence; the judge's refusal to take up the challenge posed by the conflict—his "wimpiness," according to the people outraged by his defection—contributed to the escalation of the tension. The doors and windows of the courthouse were nailed shut with wooden planks by one of the conflicting parties, firearms circulated freely among litigants, and the police did not dare to arrive, even though they were insistently called upon (which imparted an additional layer of impunity to those ready to be violent). Although bloodshed was avoided in this case, the judge's inaction could have led to a disaster. It happens that the so-called peace court triggers hostility, deepens differences and inequalities, and conflicts with local ways of reestablishing some sort of calm and ordered coexistence.

JUSTICE AND POLICE AT THE CENTER OF CONCERNS

As mentioned, the police and the justice system are seen by most peace promoters as key institutions in the realization of the liberal project. Following the dismantling of the Duvalier police and the demobilization of the Forces Armées d'Haïti (FAd'H), and in conjunction with the effort to disarm and then disband parallel militias, the Haitian National Police (HNP) was created in 1995 under the supervision of MINUSTAH. It was trained, monitored, supervised, and developed with the assistance of various foreign agencies (Lemay-Hébert 2014; Podur 2012; Sprague 2012), as is still the case today. Still under the control of MINUSTAH, in 2007 the CSPJ was created. As for the School of Magistrates, provided for in the 1987 constitution, it only acquired its true legal status in December 2007 under the leadership of MINUSTAH. This shaping of Haitian institutions by the United Nations can be seen even in the law itself, since the reform of the Penal Code, disclosed on June 24, 2020, which was soon to be followed by a new Code of Criminal Procedure, initiated under MINUSTAH's mandate, was actually implemented under the supervision of MINUJUSTH, which assisted the CSPJ in drafting the texts.

Some of these changes have been, from a certain point of view, a remarkable step forward (Carey 2001). For instance, the Magistrate School is an important achievement and has contributed to women's rights and their progression within the profession (Tøraasen 2022). The outdated Penal Code no doubt needed to be adapted to the reality of today, although there are serious doubts about the new version's adequacy. Moreover, a modern state is certainly unlikely to function without an adequate police force. That these were important matters to take care of in a modern state is hard to contest.

Yet, the reality on the ground looks quite different depending on what, and from where, one looks. On Sunday, January 23, 2020, Frédéric traveled to Port-au-Prince from Bwa-Mapou, as he usually goes there for his bread business. Because of a fever, I stayed home in Bwa-Mapou. Throughout the day, Frédéric gave me and his wife Angeline news: The situation was tense on this first day of carnival. First, in the Rue de la Réunion, a group of hooded and heavily armed men spread panic. Then, in the city center, a demonstration of policemen who claim the right to form a union degenerated. A giant shootout broke out in several areas between armed, hooded, plainclothes police officers; the military; and young men from the surrounding neighborhoods. Shortly afterward, the prime minister decreed a curfew. The next day, the streets were empty. Wisps of black smoke rose into the air everywhere. There was almost no public transport, and the inhabitants hid in their homes. Frédéric found a motorcycle cab to get to the bus station, but on the way he and his driver were stopped by barricades of burning tires and armed men. They were activists demonstrating against the government of Jovenel Moïse. The motorcycle negotiated its way through. Frédéric managed to take his bus but it was stopped at the exit of Cité Soleil. After intense and long negotiations, the driver paid his right of way. Frédéric finally arrived, safe and sound, but exhausted from a harrowing journey.

In April, as I was back in Lausanne, my hometown, Frédéric tells me on the phone that a mutual friend's bus was stopped by an armed group on the way from the village to Port-au-Prince. After the passengers were robbed, the men attacked our driver friend. He was shot and killed, and three passengers were injured. In March, a childhood friend of Frédéric's, a small businessman in Port-au-Prince, was also killed in a kidnapping attempt. Frédéric's voice is muffled as he tells me this. The burden is heavy.

A few months later, we hear Mario Andrésol, ex-captain of the FAd'H and ex-chief commander of the HNP, advocating for an uncompromising military response to the "gangs" (Alphonse 2021), while a dissident faction of the HNP, by forming the Fantom 509 group—the militant group for a police union—has itself constituted into an armed group mimicking the style of the "gangs." Fantom 509 has demonstrated violently (and armed) in the streets several times. So, I wondered: What does it say, that Andrésol advocates logistical assistance and counterinsurgency tactics imported from the United States, France, Canada, Honduras, El Salvador, and Colombia, after revealing in the press that some of the police, as well as the then-president himself, Michel Martelly, were involved in cocaine trafficking from Colombia? (Abi-Habib 2021a; 2021b; A. Robert 2018).

Officially, MINUSTAH's agenda regarding the establishment of the HNP is essentially technical, tactical, and logistical, the goal being above all to train men with new intervention equipment. When the HNP was created, the MINUSTAH insisted on incorporating former FAd'H soldiers and ex-paramilitaries. In 1987, shortly after the fall of the dictatorship, the same reclassification mechanism had already resulted in the incorporation of former *tonton makout* into the new government. In the 2000s, former combatants from groups active in the 1990s were not only rearmed and remobilized, but were offered a new career in policing. This obviously had the consequence of weakening a police force that was supposed to ensure the security of a democratic state, undermining the legitimacy of the HNP in the eyes of a large part of the population, and spreading corruption.[31] Without a doubt, the pitched battle on April 23, 2020 resulted from this deleterious recompositing of the police force.

Another symptom is the Jimmy Cherizier, aka Barbecue, phenomenon. He was a former police officer trained by UN-mandated agencies, fired and yet still in the professional circuits, who was known to be the head of an armed group in the areas of Delmas 2–6. He created the first federation of armed groups in Port-au-Prince, the *G9 an Fanmi e Alye*, the G9 Family and Allies, ostensibly to enforce security and peace and to restore a decent life to the ghetto. Even if he publicly denied it, he was said by many to be close to the ruling party, the Parti Haïtien Tèt Kale (PHTK). Former President Jovenel Moïse, like others before him, supported illegal armed groups to leverage his position through the political influence these heads of armed groups were capable of exerting (or negotiating) in their neighborhoods. Since February 6, 2019, Cherizier is the subject of an international warrant for murder and criminal association. According to several reports from human rights associations, he is also allegedly involved in several massacres of civilians, including the "La Saline" massacre on November 13, 2018 (see Chapter 1). Over time, his coalition has become even stronger. Since October 2021, the G9 controls a large part of the capital's resources and communication routes, including the Varreux terminal, the main point for the delivery of oil and import goods, without being worried by the authorities.[32]

Like the police, the judicial system today is still not working any better. On the contrary: Road blockades, lack of coordination between the police and the judiciary, intimidation, influence peddling, delayed salaries, bureaucratic mismanagement, limited access to fuel and hyperinflation, among other things, are all hindering its proper functioning. Many courts are falling into disuse or are simply abandoned because armed groups prohibit access. During investigations, it happens regularly that court offices are broken into and evidence and court records stolen or destroyed. Even more seriously, as I wrote earlier, in recent years many judges, lawyers, and court clerks have been sequestered, injured, or executed.

One should then ask: What are the effects of the reforms and transformations imposed in the name of peace? It seems clear upon closer inspection that the United Nations has contributed to reinforcing the dynamics that it set out to change. Moreover, the foreign presence has largely contributed to the formation of powerful and extremely violent groups that have become key players in Haitian political, economic, and social life. The policies of "consolidation of the rule of law" have also made Haiti even more dependent on foreign trade and encouraged inflation, which today leads to food insecurity for more than half the population. It is therefore difficult not to see behind this rhetoric of peace a practice of war (Curtis 2014). The UN rhetoric of democracy and world peace seems to be a distraction from the many ways in which international forces ignore or fight civil society, especially the most disadvantaged, and contribute to increasing violence and inequality.

ALTERNATIVE PEACEMAKING

Conceptual boundaries are not as clear-cut as some believe (Brandel and Motta 2021). At some point, it becomes difficult to distinguish formal from informal—or official from unofficial—laws and procedures. Even if we can, they do meet at some point and absorb each other in the ordinary (Das 2020, ch. 8). As shown in the examples, the court partly integrates everyday language and habits and unofficial ways of handling conflicts, and the people learn and incorporate into their lives some official procedures and ways of conceptualizing law and conflict resolution. Furthermore, the same acts that are viewed by some as criminal are viewed by others as legitimate, and those viewed by some as legitimate are viewed by others as criminal. The law can also be used to suspend rights and even institute the suspension of rights (Agamben 2005; Das 2022; Mattei and Nader 2008). Similarly, peace might at times have the physiognomy of violence and oppression (Armstrong 2014; Branch 2014). Chelsey Kivland (2020) shows, with much delicacy, how much young men in the *geto* desire justice, peace, and emancipation. She equally shows how these aspirations can work against their goodwill. In the name of peace, violence is often said to be necessary. How else does one imagine *defans lejitim* (self-defense) and the achievement of *jistis*? As Roland, a leader and political figure of the Bel-Air *geto* says, "politics has never been about peace. How can you be about peace when the majority of people live in hunger? This is an agent of misery, not peace! . . . we are here to defend our right to democracy. In Haiti, that means not just what's on paper but also who controls the bayonet. And for us the bayonet is the force of the street" (ibid., 112–13). Indeed, many poor people's claim to democracy goes with a sharp awareness that force and violence might be necessary to contest an unequal social order partly fueled by international meddling. I fully agree with Kivland when she questions "the presumed separation of violence and democracy" and aims to understand "the manifold and conflicting ways in which violence—as sign and practice—has been part and parcel of imagining, making, and maintaining contemporary democracies" (ibid., 114).

This is why we should not be too quick to consider the JP court as the locus at which peace is to be found. We should be mindful that, if people dare to venture into a courthouse, they do not leave their ordinary lives outside the door. And once the session closes, peasants hurry back to the fields to irrigate before dusk; the youth hang around the crossroads, make jokes to pass the time, and wait for job opportunities; mothers start the fire to get the next meal ready before the children come home from school; men look forward to finding a drinking companion to sip rum and play dominos with in the shade of a flame tree. Others nervously think of a plan to retaliate. Despite all the goodwill of the judges, lawyers, and court clerks, the answer to the question of what will in the end diffuse a conflict and bring some kind of peace, no matter how provisory or durable, is out of their reach. This does not mean, of course, that they do not play a role. Rather, I should say that if there is something like peace at some point, it is not so much the result of the enforcement of the rule of law, than the slow and unending work *of* the community, *within* the community. The enforcement of the rule of law, contrary to what is emphasized in the conventional discourses, ends up harming the less advantaged people more than it helps them. Above all, it conveys a picture of the role and place of law in our human lives that is misplaced; we do not comply because we are threatened and do not obey because we are coerced. In my example, the threat of punishment would not have prevented the man, if found guilty, from stealing the goat, nor would it necessarily prevent him from committing further infractions. The witnesses who are reluctant to show up in court might not be more willing to show up *because* they are suddenly coerced—some will, others not. Perhaps it is even the threat that encourages illegal behavior, and some will be all the more tempted to transgress or escape when they are threatened or coerced. That the correct application of codes of conduct and standards of procedures will lead to peace and order is just a story we tell ourselves. Things are different on the ground.

It is no surprise, then, that informal or customary justice, as was the case during European colonization in Africa, has been perceived as problematic by those who promote the rule of law; and that it has been seen at some point as what hinders democracy and the progress of a certain civilizational project (Humphreys 2010; Greenburg 2013; 2017). Yet, it is true also that the United Nations has come to acknowledge what it calls the "informal justice systems" (IJS) as an empirical reality, and increasingly integrated them into its reflections. It does indeed recognize now that they "form a key part of individual's and communities' experience of justice" (UN 2015, 7). The advantages of IJS as perceived by the United Nations are above all their flexible structures and processes, cost-effectiveness, local pertinence, and outreach to grassroots communities. It is willing to take these IJS more seriously, yet always in "an effort to ensure international norms and standards" (ibid., 7). While it readily admits that "both types of justice systems [formal and informal] can violate human rights, reinforce discrimination, and neglect principles of procedural fairness" (ibid., 7), the fact remains that, in the end, international legal standards should have the last word. More than that, a complex programming was conceived that seeks to inspect, assess, monitor, and oversee the IJS in order, so it says, to make them more transparent and accountable (see the 2015 study report). Even though the United Nations now tends to include more and more local perspectives and draws tools from them—as is the case with the Community Violence Reduction (CVR) program—in the end, the strategy consists of controlling local practices and imposing a legal order that is, it has to be said, little in tune with the interests and needs of local communities.[33]

It is interesting to note that historically, the CVR was first mandated in 2006 in peace operations conducted in Haiti. It was specifically meant to "reorient its disarmament, demobilization and reintegration (DDR) efforts towards a comprehensive community violence reduction programme adapted to local conditions . . . [it] focused on reducing gang-related violence in selected neighbourhoods of Port-au-Prince through the following four principles: mitigating risk factors that contribute to insecurity; promoting capacity development of state institutions and supporting rule of law; empowering civil society and facilitating dialogue with government authorities; and mobilizing and empowering women to engage in project activities" (CVR n.d., 5–6).[34] While these are, of course, respectable principles, the strategy was also of another kind. In linking the CVR program to the achievement of the United Nations' Sustainable Development Goal no. 16 on "Peace, Justice and Strong Institutions," it placed the CVR program in the Disarmament, Demobilization and Reintegration Section of the Office of Rule of Law and Security Institutions. We should be reminded here that at the very birth of the modern state's repressive apparatus in the sixteenth century, there was disarmament of the masses. The issue is critical in Foucault's (2015) analysis: After a series of important seditions, the popular masses had been selectively disarmed by the royal power, who then rearmed the privileged supposed to keep the potential revolts in check. The consequence was a concentration of armed control in the hands of a few who would, later, be policing the territory, to the detriment of the population, who has been dispossessed. That the CVR program is part of the United Nations' offices that concern disarmament and security cannot be considered casual, especially not when we know that part of the weapons in circulation in the underground market have been introduced by the successive UN missions. Hence, if the United Nations seems to give some credit to local ways of handling conflicts, it does so insofar as it contributes to achieving the objectives it has set itself.

In everyday life, extrajudicial means of handling conflicts and informal ways of safeguarding relationships between humans who have all sorts of reasons to express their indignation, wrath, grudges, and claims are nonetheless what makes it possible for them to go on; in some cases, these ways contribute to ease people's suffering and might lead to some kind of provisional pacification; in others, they harm and worsen the situation. The people I met mostly did aspire to live together in relative serenity, but they also knew that moments of calm alternated with moments of turmoil, upheaval, and havoc. What's more, not everyone is willing to compromise to find peaceful solutions. Some fight hard, or part ways for good.

Frédéric, the litigants, and the judge all improvise in the face of unending hardships. Sometimes they succeed, sometimes they fail. Nevertheless, they keep on going. If they were applying predetermined criteria to solve their problems and progress in their ordinary affairs, as advocates of the rule of law argue, they would just not be able to live, simply because these a priori criteria could not have accommodated all possible projections in further contexts. They would stumble at every step over the hardness of reality. People know very well that no a priori criteria exist that can assist them and, thus, also how little they can rely on the judicial rationale to solve anything at all. Ordinary people give us quite a different picture of peace when it is seen more as an aspiration to move forward and keep heads up. In everyday life, indeed, *nap brase* (we're struggling); *nap goumen* (we're fighting); *nap kenbe* (we're holding on); and *nap swiv* (we'll see what happens).

4

THEATRICALIZING THE LAW

"To demand that the law be fulfilled, every jot and tittle,
will destroy the law as it stands . . ."

—STANLEY CAVELL

We've just seen how complex the issue of peace becomes once we vary the scales of analysis and reckon with different layers of reality. What constitutes context is a major question. In fact, according to a certain tradition of thinking, context is overarching, all-round, panoptic, as it were. Everything that happens is somehow contained and determined by the context, which is always beyond immediate experience. In this sense, it is transcendent. And since context has been elevated to the status of an explanatory factor by a certain social science, it is also the necessary focal point; I mean that it is necessary to reach context in order to make sense of—or understand or explain—experience. One consequence, or premise, of such a conception is that our ordinary experiences always seem to lack something, as long as we haven't reached the context. Or, more precisely, it seems that the knowledge we draw from experience is incomplete as long as it is not knowledge of context. Another correlated consequence, or premise, is that reality is perceived as divided: There's the way reality appears to us in our ordinary experience, and reality as it really is. But these two modes of reality are not symmetrical. Appearances are not only deceptive, and therefore suspect, they are also insufficient. They do not satisfy our desire to know. That's why we imagine that we should go beyond them, since an appearance is always an appearance *of* something. So, some kind of impulse drives us to know that thing beyond appearances, which we imagine to be the real thing

(Brandel and Motta 2021). This attraction to the beyond is a function of having conceived reality as hidden behind a veil or a screen which we should lift and look beyond, because that's where the essence, the true knowledge, lies, or so we think.

Now, the point I want to make with the help of Jocelyn Benoist (2021), is that what's important, what's at issue, is our capacity to develop a *perspective* on reality. I've just described one. "Now, this capacity is something that is only exercised within reality . . . for we cannot mean anything without meaning it from *somewhere*. . . . This is a point about context. Once again: context is not so much an external constraint on meaning—as if reality, so to speak, struck meaning from the outside—as it is the manifestation of meaning being *effectively rooted* in reality, as well as something that contributes to the constitution of meaning itself" (ibid., xii–xiii). Hence, the perspective I've just described is profoundly unsatisfactory. The problem with it, is its blindness to the very fact that everything it means—that there's a world of appearances opposed to reality; that one can and should reach beyond the world of appearances; that context is overarching, etc.—is at once emergent from reality and constitutive of it, of its space of possibilities. So, whatever the perspective, it cannot be external, or it wouldn't mean anything. What this leads us to understand is that what's at stake is what *we*, humans, say, mean, and do. And what we say, mean, and do, is *in* reality, *in* the world.

Consequently, our questions become relevant only in a particular context. Yet, I do not know what the context is beforehand, I mean before my experience of reality. This is why the context only appears, or reveals itself, as we go along. It manifests itself, as it were, when we experience the world in certain ways. In this sense, context is all but overarching and panoptic. On the contrary, it is always incomplete, partial, fragmented. In Chapter 3, for instance, I did not immediately realize how much the local issues around peace bore a relation to the reconfiguration of the institutional structures by foreign agencies. I had to experience certain things first to begin to see certain aspects and make certain connections between them. I first had to experience *that* trial for *that* robbery in *that* peace court; have *that* conversation with *that* clerk at *that* moment; participate in *that* seminar with *these* participants; lead *that* kind of life with *that* family (Artémis) and *these* particular neighbors, and so on. Only then did I begin to understand the specific context. Yet, it's not up to me to understand things one way or another (as if understanding were a matter of choice). The fact is that I'm in situations under specific circumstances, and I begin to understand what they are only to the extent that I "get in the game," so to speak. I have no exteriority to the context. Hence, the problem is not of reaching context beyond experience or going behind the veil of appearances, but of adjusting our questions to make them relevant to that particular context—because they might not be tuned in and be out of place, or simply irrelevant. But what criteria do I have? Where do they come from? As it happens, that context requires me to give reasons for thinking things in a certain way; it demands that I justify my knowledge.

I have tried as far as possible to justify the relevance of my sense of the connections between modes of peace in the Bwa-Mapou community and international peace policies. There can be no doubt that the international community was very much involved in building Haiti's state institutions, especially in monitoring the judiciary and the police, and thus influenced what I was witnessing on the other end. This is why, besides the detailed ethnography, I felt it was important to lay bare the mechanisms by which peace can be legitimately, yet violently, imposed. As it turns out, these peacekeeping and state-building efforts, contrarywise to their objectives, have ended up playing a role in the collapse of state institutions and the spectacular rise of violence. This is why, perhaps, the chapter may thus have given the impression of a predominance of political issues and of the omnipresence of state and international institutions. While it is true that I have set myself the task of examining in depth international and state policies, I have also attempted to counterbalance this impression by showing a less politicized politics, let's say a politics of the ordinary. And here we see that state institutions are not omnipresent, on the contrary. But they're not absent either.

In this chapter, I'd like to reflect more specifically on the question of the aesthetics of law and, in so doing, on the links between aesthetics and politics. I will examine how the stage of legal power is in fact a stage of political power, related in all kinds of ways to other scenes of the politics of the ordinary. In an illuminating note on Foucault's course on penal theories and institutions, Claude-Olivier Doron underlies that "the conditions of representation, 'the systems of restriction' and the very rules to which the play of elements are subjected in order to be represented, entail that some forces, among the most important, are absent from the scene, an absence which betrays the underlying relations of force as much as the way in which the represented elements effectively function" (Foucault 2019, 53, n. 16). In Haiti, in fact, the civil power performs in some ways by its absence. The game is partly determined by the rules fixed by a remote judiciary power, and conforms to its alien language, gestures, and formalities. Part of the formal judicial language and mode of reasoning is absorbed in the ways with which everyday issues are handled. Yet, the scene of the juridical power also enacts the language, practices, gestures, and procedures called "customary," "popular," or "informal." By looking this time at the theatrical character of conciliations and lawsuits, in relation to the other forms of theatricalities in everyday life, I not only hope to challenge some common assumptions about the practice of law, but also to depict from another corner the life of law.

OPENING ACT

On February 18, 2020, an older man requests a hearing in a local Justice of the Peace (JP) court, a small derelict building on the wayside of the only paved road that runs through the Artibonite Valley. He opposes his sister. Fewer than twenty people are attending the session, sitting on loosely aligned benches. From what I can tell, most are relatives or friends accompanying one party or the other. Many have come dressed casually; others, still in working clothes and carrying tools, seem to have taken a break from their fields to attend. It's mid-morning; the peasants have been working for five or six hours already. The judge, dressed in a dark suit, sits in front of the audience behind his massive desk, clear of anything except a folder and a handbook of law. Next to him sits the clerk behind a much smaller desk. Two attorneys are also wearing dark suits and ties; they face each other in front of the judge and the clerk. A space is left vacant in the middle. I have been invited by the judge to take a place on the bench next to the man's attorney. We sit on the slightly elevated floor dedicated to officials, delimited by a low wooden brim.

After a very short opening, and without delay, the judge asks the man to recount his version of the issue first—since he is the one who "invited" (*envite*) the other party in conciliation (by filing a petition). Timidly he starts to speak; the judge cuts him short and asks that he stand when he does so. Nervously holding his cap in his hands, he accuses his sister, seated next to him, of preventing him from ploughing and benefiting from the land on which she lives but over which he claims rights. He says that it was their mother's plot, and that before dying she authorized him to work on it. Now that she's gone, he complains that his sister does not want him there anymore. Then, the accused woman is asked to speak out with her version of the contention. She contests her brother's claim on the grounds that this portion of land is hers and has always been, since their mother had given it to her and she lives on it. Therefore, her brother has no right to take advantage of "her" plot.

The attorneys are then asked to plead. A spectacle starts. I am watching, amazed. The tension and the excitement immediately increase. The woman's younger lawyer shows off in a sort of sermon in Creole interspersed with French formulas of eloquence, overplaying his own role with emphatic and dramatic tones. His opponent is less given to such excesses but is soon swept up in the game as the other goes on provoking. They both start to quickly gesticulate, bawling, sweating excessively, interrupting each other indecently, demeaning the other with grotesque interjections, using lame arguments, and giving in to sheer sophistry. Now and then, a misplaced quote from Montesquieu or Marx punctuates their pleas. In their trance, they are so extravagant that they openly insult each other, and even abruptly cut off the judge when he urges for calm, as if they no longer had any awareness of their whereabouts—in a court, supposed to have its rules of decency and standards of conduct. But perhaps, I think, they know exactly where they are: This may be precisely the place where such behavior is to some extent permitted, even expected. In any case, it markedly contrasts with courts I know back home in Switzerland, where attendants' and jurists' behavior tend to be dispassionate, and kept in check: They privilege the purported rationale of the written word over the feared eccentricities of oral persuasion. Lost as I am in this contrast, the man's lawyer jolts me from my thoughts, outraged, when he almost hits me during his performance; his hands wave in such fury, as if they'd been given the mission to orchestrate his voice, which is on the verge of breaking. People in the audience watch, mesmerized, as this play full of incomprehensible words and crooked arguments unfolds before them. Some of them wince and frown, others smile, still others laugh discreetly as if they were watching a show.

Nothing really comes of their pleas. The woman's attorney threatens with idle talk and exaggerated indignation to sue her brother in the lower court for home invasion, property law infringement, and defamation. The brother's lawyer, aghast, responds by asking desperately if common sense and a little good will wouldn't actually do better for both parties. After all, this is a court of conciliation, isn't it?

The judge, undaunted, stops them without raising his voice. "This quarrel will lead nowhere. The issue lies somewhere else," he says peacefully.

THE FEAR OF THEATRICALITY

This scene is played out in Bwa-Mapou's JP court. It is commonly assumed, as I said in Chapter 2, that the JP court's primary scope is to offer a space for conciliation and mediation in local civil affairs. Its function is to adjudicate on civil cases, settle disputes, and find arrangements that are supposed to prevent the escalation of tensions. Its mandate is to ensure civil peace and avoid the turning of civil litigation into criminal cases. More broadly, the judicial rationale, according to Western, modern, liberal standards, conventionally conceives the court as the primary locus of the search for and the production of truth (Suresh 2023), which is supposed to be the basis for a reasonable judgment. The court is thus supposed to guarantee fair justice (Besnier 2017; Foucault 2001). Such a view is coextensive of our conceiving the court as a place where decisions are made, judgments produced, and disputes settled on the basis of preestablished criteria.[1] The whole procedure is thus imagined as guaranteeing fair treatment of parties by maintaining the cool-headed and impartial appreciation of facts. It is the rationality of procedure itself that justifies the ends—that is, the judgment; and in turn, the judgment implies and produces the legitimacy of procedure (Das 2022; Nield 2019; Olivelle et al. 2024). The idea that the JP court should be the least coercive possible is a function of its proceedings being accepted on the grounds of the perceived fairness of the court. And yet, there are surely matters in human affairs, thus in courts, other than truth-seeking or judgments or decision-making. What exactly is at play in the scene above?

I'm interested in these small moments when something arises, spurs certain events, and questions a certain view taken for granted thus far. At first sight, it emerges from my introductory example that what is being played (the performance) and what apparently is at stake (the dispute), do not seem to meet. This gap, I contend, is not so much a paradox or an anomaly than the symptom of the inadequacy of our way of perceiving what happens. In response, I would like to emphasize the theatrical character of conciliations, or lawsuits, and the way it instructs us on the sort of relations instituted with state law. The history of the practice of law in the Western tradition shows how familiar we are with the idea that the court is an agonistic scene where a contest takes place—which is not unlike a sporting competition, with hints of humor in addition (Huizinga 1980; Peters 2022). Hence, we are used to imagining what happens in this space as an enactment of a desire to win. It is thus not so surprising that today, students in Haiti and elsewhere learn sophistry in law school (and often also acting techniques). But if the Sophists knew already well how to generate wealth out of such a desire, sophistry certainly cannot be reduced to calculation. Our modern suspicion and even fear of seduction, persuasion, influence, and the effects of rhetoric have deep historical roots. Plato had already drawn up the first indictments against the influence of rhetoric in judicial reasoning, privileging instead the search for truth and virtue through deliberation. Yet, imagining sophistry to be mere rhetoric, as Plato may have wanted his readers to believe, is too simplistic (Cassin 2014; Pepe 2020), for the anxiety it raises among the defenders of the metaphysical quest for an ontological truth only shows how powerful sophistry is at questioning—and undermining—our fundamental assumptions about justice.

The late medieval tradition also bequeathed to us the conceptual proximity between the figure of the judge and that of the soldier because the judge (and to a great extent the soldier) rules by divine right and the court becomes a place of the metaphysical manifestation of God's judgment. The judgment is legitimized by its celestial anchoring. Both figures are in the business of just judging, which then, in criminal trials, was the business of just killing (Whitman 2008). Yet, one who perceives law and play in dual terms, opposing order and reason to chaos and folly, the way we have been accustomed in modernity to oppose the rule-bound exercise of judgment to the arbitrary, improvised play of instinct, might be blind to other ways of imagining the relation between order and free play, or the law and turbulent improvisation. At stake is the normative vision of the discipline and order that law is supposed to represent. Even though scholars of heterogeneous backgrounds have underscored many kinds of connections between theater and justice,[2] there are ways in which law and theater are related that have been overlooked. I will shed light in what follows on some of these ways.

In professional circles, this closeness between law and theater is often countered or denied. Although legal actors are aware of the theatricality of the practice of law, and often even master it, they tend to moderate its presence and effects. In fact, the performance of such temperance is itself part of that theatricality: Of course, law's own performance is theatricalized, but it should not be too much, because otherwise, justice loses its power, and if it is not enough, it is not justice. "Such debates about legal theatricality . . . lie at the heart of legal theory, defining what counts as law and what does not" (Peters 2022, 9). Indeed, justice must be seen—literally "theatricalized"—in order to be what it is, i.e., the righteous application of law, but must not be seductive, as it would lose its legitimacy.

This (almost erotic) ambivalence that lies at the heart of the practice of law is tied to a deep suspicion of eloquence that becomes the marker of manipulation and the masking of dubious intentions. This suspicion and refusal are even foundational of the legal profession itself. In the mid-thirteenth century, ecclesiastical and civil authorities began to prescript norms and regulations for the conducts of advocates and proctors. The field of law was starting its professionalization, thus leading to the institutionalization of professional oaths and specific obligations and behavioral standards.[3] Failure to comply would be punishable by law. These ethical aspirations remain largely unchanged to this day. "Modern oaths of admission to the bar strikingly resemble their medieval counterparts, as do the assumptions about proper lawyerly conduct implicit in codes of professional responsibility" (Brundage 2008). For instance, the current code of professional conduct of the British Columbia Law Society[4] states that a "lawyer's conduct should at all times be characterized by candour [that is, truthfulness and sincerity] and fairness" and that s/he should maintain "a courteous and respectful attitude." Additionally, a lawyer "should not attempt to deceive a court . . . nor attempt to curry favour with juries by fawning, flattery, or personal solicitude."[5] These provisions are supposed to prevent iniquitous influence that is the point at which justice turns corrupt (Biagioli 2019). This kind of influence is imagined to be precisely the risk engendered by theatricality.[6] In France too, for example, the Criminal Law Procedure provides legal provisions that are supposed to prevent lawyers from indulging in passions and moderate emotional excess, by encouraging a temperate and self-controlled behavior (Besnier 2017). The very fact that, for instance, in the US *Standards of the Legal Profession* (Ball 1975, 82), it is stated that "a courtroom is not a stage; and witnesses and lawyers, and judges and juries and parties, are not players," and that "a trial is not a drama," of course makes us see it precisely as that.

This particular fear of theatricalization (of corruption) is a concern that emerged with the rise of Christianity, contrariwise to the practice of law in ancient Rome, which fully assumed its ritualized, performative, and oral character (Bettini 2022). That reason and just judgment may be corrupted by passion and influence is a particular issue raised by the advent of modernity. Some of its roots lie in the debates surrounding the formation of the theological canon law of the late Middle Ages, where the problem of just judgment, that is, just killing, in criminal trials (determining when blood could be lawfully shed) was a problem that concerned above all the protection of the soul of the judge from the Divine Judgment. Avoiding passion on one side, and following correct procedures on the other, was meant to guarantee judgment beyond all reasonable doubt, and thus keep the soul safe from burning in Hell (Whitman 2008). These matters were serious, as are today the issues related to professional ethics. This notably shows how the court is *not* a stage in a theater on which actors play roles in front of an audience who, after the play, go back tranquilly to their ordinary lives. There are important differences that must be acknowledged. One among them, and not the least, is the degree of violence of, and entailed by, the performance itself: In a court of law, the accused who has been fined or sentenced to prison must, after the end of the trial, pay the amount due or be escorted by the police back to his cell, whereas on a stage, when Athena joins the jury in the trial she has set up herself, and gives her voice to Orestes, leading to his acquittal, the actor playing Orestes is no freer than before, nor is he in anyway guilty of the murder of Aegisthus and Clytemnestra once the play is over. And the actor playing Athena's judgment is not at risk of being judged by the Divine, nor by his conscience. Indeed "theatrical performance is not anchored in violence in the same way in which legal performance is" (Rogers 2008, 441).

In what follows, I articulate four points that challenge or complement some well-established ideas about law. My first point is that the court is one place among others where our ordinary concepts are forged and put to work and tested. In this specific case, this applies to concepts of territory and property, but also with concepts such as heritage, suspicion, trust, and tolerance. The blurriness of the boundaries of concepts then sets the stage for improvised, inventive productions of new spaces of application of these concepts. This should lead us to my second point: If the court is a place, not only for rational and cool-headed reasoning, but also for the passionate expressions of human concerns, then how are we to perceive what is going on in tribunals? What are the matters expressed, and in what ways? The third point is a direct extension of this: If the court is a place for the performance of the orality of the law, rather than for the mere application of the written word, then we would have to reckon with the fact that liveliness is a matter essential to law. Finally, to get a sense of what happens inside the courts, one will have to venture outside, and look at what happens in the interstices of ordinary life. A darker picture will appear in contrast, for the playfulness that goes with the practice of law coexists with the violence it can generate.

THE WORK OF CONCEPTS

After examination of the record, it turns out that the land in question in the process mentioned above is what the law calls a "state-owned property," which none of the civil parties had fathomed. According to the documents available, the land was indeed "owned" by both parties' mother for twenty-four years, until the state reclaimed it as its property after the fall of the Baby Doc's regime, in 1986. It appears now in court that the mother had not known—or perhaps had refused to recognize—that what she had considered as her land was actually not hers (anymore). Thus she positioned herself, illegitimately, as the one legitimate to cede it to her daughter, who has also been living on it for decades, and who has built her *lakou*, her family compound, there.

When the judge asks the parties if they understand what "private property of the state" means and entails from the point of view of law, it seems to me that none of the parties get it right, including the attorneys, who have quite differing understandings of the concept. Maybe they misinterpreted the legal provision or made a strategic use of the law's vagueness[7] (Endicott 2022; 2014; 2001; Asgeirsson 2015). Whatever the case, the judge takes the time to calmly explain the stakes, as a patient teacher would, by carefully reading the text of law, translating into Creole what it means, and commenting on it as he proceeds. He reads from an updated version of a compendium of codes, the transcription of articles 5 and 6 of the Decree of July 14,

1989, included in Chapter III on "Usufruct of Rural Properties" of the law no. IV of the Rural Code of 2009/1962, which allows the Ministry of Economy and Finances to proceed to a systematic survey of all arable and available lands of the private domain of the state, and to establish the cadastre in order to distribute them to the needy families.

After the state had reclaimed the land, the judge explains, the mother, as the head of the family, had no other rights over it than to live and work on it, and benefit from her work. The law is very precise, he emphasizes: The plot cannot be divided, sold, given, or transmitted to her children. He goes on to explain with great tact that the daughter's claim over the land, and thus her refusal to share it with her brother, is surely comprehensible but has no justification in regard to the law. It is also understandable, he says, that, given the tumultuous situation in Haiti and the lack of proper bureaucratic management, there is no formal contract between the mother or the daughter and the state to be assessed in court. The judge therefore takes for granted that an oral contract was passed, and that it was tacitly renewed every nine years. He then introduces a subtle but crucial detail: The nature of the contract grants de facto usufruct. Since the daughter was already living on this plot at the time of the death of the mother, she, as well as all other siblings in equal terms, benefit de facto from the same usufruct; this would not have been the case if no one had lived on the plot. In such a case, the members of the family would have been able to exploit the land until the end of the ongoing contract, after which the state would have been in the position to restart the procedure of attribution and consider any other demand. This means that the daughter cannot reclaim this plot as "her" property *because* she lives on it; she is now in the position of the mother, compelled to share it with her brothers and sisters. The judge then explains the legal concept of de facto using the following analogy: If an unmarried man and woman live together for years, as they would if they were indeed married, and everybody knows them and refers to them as a couple *as if* they were married, then they are considered married de facto by the court. So, in the present case, he tells the audience, this means that even though the mother died and the law says that the land cannot be transmitted, the daughter and her siblings can benefit from the same renewable usufruct contract as the mother did *as if* they all were now their mother.

After his minute characterization of the case, the judge encourages both parties to be reasonable citizens: They should get together, talk, and reconcile. "You are brother and sister after all, aren't you?" he says. "You can handle this amongst yourselves. Try at least!" He still mentions that if they cannot settle their contention, they can initiate a dispute settlement procedure in one of the two special land tribunals in Saint-Marc or Gonaïves, but insists that he does not advise them to do so. In his opinion, it would be a great loss of time and money, and would not resolve anything, but rather would probably worsen the situation; he's seen many cases go awry. To him, the only viable solution here is an amicable reconciliation.

As soon as the session is adjourned, the people in the court, as well as the attorneys and the clerk, stand up and shout and argue. The tension quickly rises. The judge is the only one who remains calm and looks on from behind his wooden desk at the mayhem with a resigned face. The small and angry crowd moves out of the courtroom into the yard. A couple of minutes later, a fight starts between the court clerk and a young man, a member of the defendant's family. Eventually people separate them. They keep insulting each other in the street for a few minutes, before the man leaves with the defendant and the rest of the family. The judge looks at me, hopeless, and says: "This is how it is, you know. I cannot do anything more. There are issues beyond my grasp," evoking the fact that many peasant families have long histories of rancor that plague them; much more is at stake, it seems. Before I leave, I ask him why the court clerk was fighting. He tells me that the court clerk is the son-in-law of the plaintiff and, since the outcome has turned out to be in his favor, is thus accused by the defendant of taking sides.

The details of the specific legal issues in this case are of great interest and would deserve a more serious treatment than I can offer here. Instead, I would like to emphasize the details of the aesthetics of the court justice because, as Julie Peters (2022, 5) puts it, "law's aesthetic power is essential to its force." So, what kind of stage is a court? What do the dispositions of space, objects, and people tell us about what is taking place: officials (me included) taking their place on a slightly elevated floor delimited by a low wooden brim facing the audience sitting on loosely aligned benches, or the compendium of codes displayed on a massive wooden desk with nothing else on it except a thin folder with documents? What is the use of body language and style? How are we to understand the fact that the law is read out loud, in such a way, at that very moment? What kind of enactment of authority do we have here? And how does the audience behave? What are the different atmospheres and ambiances that distinguish different moments? All these aspects of the situation, and many more, are indicative of something going on. If, on the one hand, there is a careful scenography of the impartiality of the law by the professionals, on the other hand, at some point expressions of emotions and passion are given free reign, so to speak. Hence, if we acknowledge the tension between the vindication of a cool-headed approach to social conflicts and the fact that the lawyers, and later the audience and the clerks, allow themselves outbursts, then we are compelled to nuance our conception of the law, its procedures, and its rationale. Most importantly, perhaps, we then cannot blindly take the justness of justice for granted anymore. Our criteria are at issue. A certain picture of fairness and reasonable judgment—thus injustice and unsound judgment—will have to be redrawn.

Milner Ball (1975) writes that the "judicial theater is itself a continuous way of saying, in things and acts within appointed spaces, what the law is" (ibid., 109). Indeed, but it is also a continuous way of "making" what the law is to become in certain circumstances. Figuring out what the law is, what it does, what it implies, what it presupposes, how I am to relate to it, *in a particular context* and caught *within particular issues*, is a matter of our learning, and thus of our capacity to be educated on, important matters pertaining to our life in a given society. And in some occasions, going to court might actually be a fitting way to learn something about these matters.

The fact that on some occasions people actually do go to the JP courts in a country whose institutions are known to be authoritative, dysfunctional, and corrupt, if working at all, and thus barely trusted, should perplex us. In fact, "a puzzle remains . . . how do we explain the faith people put in the law to put limits on violence, when decades of experience in the postcolony has shown that much violence actually resides within the law?" (Das 2022, 14). The distrust of, and even the hostility toward, the judiciary and the laws inherited from former settlers has deepened in the past years, which has all the more stimulated alternative means of handling contentions[8] (Montalvo-Despeignes 1976; Paisant 2003). However, for some issues, like the ones I describe in the case here, people are still prompted to appeal to the JP court, even though the court does not necessarily appear to be the right place to settle the case.[9] How come, then?

One partial answer is to say that the court is one place where our ordinary concepts are at work and put to the test. In this case, concepts such as property, inhabitation, and territory, are dealt with, and these are heavily loaded concepts in Haiti.[10] There is a relation between the content of the complaint and the performance of law itself. The performance delimits conceptual territories (of the state) as much as the space of application of the law (Sarat et al. 2006). But of course, these territories are not fixed once and for all. They move, and the boundaries move too. We would have to remind ourselves that there is a "before" the conciliation, where not only did something stand in need to be addressed specifically in a JP court, but also where something that happened long ago—which may not have had much to do with this man and his sister but with deeper movements in history— nonetheless triggered the contention emerging today. We would also have to imagine that there will be an uncertain "after" the mediation, where further grievances might appear, or silent grudges might start to poison relationships, or perhaps an agreement might be found. The court is thus a place where a *language* for certain kinds of issues is learned, formed, transformed, searched for, transgressed, tested, and dealt with (Endicott 2021); in this case notably a language of property rights, infringement, and succession; but also, a language of love, trust, rivalry, betrayal, contempt, intolerance, and ruse. Learning such a language means learning the comportment and the attitude that goes with it, that is, a way to behave. The learning of a language implies a constant readjusting and transformation (extension and restriction) of the reach of other concepts we already have. This search for the adequacy of their application in, or projections into, further contexts is never-ending but not unlimited (Brandel and Motta 2021). How will this new concept of "private property of the state" enter the lives of that man and that women and change what they perceive as their respective rights over that plot of land, or cast doubt over their sentiments toward one another, or alter the way they view their mother's intentions, or complicate their understanding of the state's legitimacy? The search for intelligibility involves not only the learning of a specific language, but also a test of the fitness of the concepts we already have in our lives. And this happens in practice, performatively, that is, theatrically.

As shown here, people notably go to court to find the appropriate language to address issues that touch on notions partly defined by state institutions, but that have not yet been fully absorbed into the ordinary language of the people affected, and perhaps will never be. I do not deny that there may be strategic reasons for "inviting" someone to appear in a JP tribunal, which also testifies to the capability of citizens to make smart use of state institutions. But to think merely in terms of strategy, which implies that one would have already defined the case and the goals and known the ins and outs of the questions at stake, is to avoid accounting for the uncertainty of our projections. Strategy and pragmatism do not fully encompass the reasons why people show up in courts. There are many aspects to such a problem like the one at stake in my example, of which people do not have a sense; even the lawyers seemed surpassed. If there may be strategy, it does not exclude that the plaintiffs also show up to gain knowledge (about their ignorance perhaps), and improve their skills for comprehension of the web of issues they are caught in. The court, with its apparatus, is a place where human beings encounter each other on specific grounds, and where they redefine their interests, learn from each other, and stake their future.

PASSIONATE THEATRICALITIES

The kinds of issues that end up in conciliation affect people and sometimes demand to be voiced out loud. The court thus also appears to be a place where passions can be lived, where human concerns can find expression (C. Smith 2013). In this case, the litigants do not themselves express their grievances in court (but they express them outside the court rather harshly)—they are merely asked to make a sober and concise statement. Instead, it is their legal representatives who express on behalf of their clients their indignation, frustration, anger, or sentiment of injustice. Litigants are spoken for—say, interpreted—by their representatives. The fact that a "representation" is required "before the law" is an essential aspect of the law; but then the "law" and "representation" are not two distinguishable instances anymore: The performance *is* the law, and law is the performance. Moreover, the fact that the lawyers' pleas are so virulent tells us something about the sort of space in which we find ourselves in courts. What do the lawyers' modes of pleading and the judge's poise tell us about what is going on? What are we to understand from the sort of dramatic excess that characterizes the battle between the parties? Quite an easy answer would be to say that the lawyers in the earlier scene acted out their competitiveness or rivalry, and demonstrated their ambition, their willingness to win. It is easy because it is trivial. As Pierre Bourdieu showed decades ago, "the juridical field is the site of a competition for monopoly of the right to determine law," which establishes "a social division between lay people and professionals" as well as "the separation between judgments based upon the law and naïve intuitions of fairness" (1987, 817). And of course, such a competition is acted out, performed: Theatrics just creep in as soon as human beings start to act, be it in courts, churches, schools, or other institutions that produce and organize the norms, the sources, and the interpretations granting their own authority. Yet, this solution leaves unanswered the question about the expression of law in particular circumstances.

The young lawyer was disturbingly and disproportionally provoking, even threatening the other party. It seemed that he got carried away to the point that he had lost sight of the fact that this was a court for conciliation, not a battle zone where one would purposefully feed the feud; but it could have been an intended maneuver. In any case, he was clearly unwilling to accommodate the interests of the parties, and uncompromising when the older lawyer and the judge suggested that the issue should be settled amicably. At some point, he outraged his opponent when he adopted a sarcastic tone followed by a smirk. His attitude was all the more scandalous in that it did not seem to matter to him that a relationship between siblings was at stake, something that the older lawyer emphasized. Moreover, he demonstrated that he was unwilling to meet his professional obligation to act with respect, civility, integrity, diligence, and courtesy (International Bar Association 2011), and that he did not care about his accountability as a legal representative (being subject to fines for contempt of court), or about his responsibility to do as much as he could to avoid the escalation of tensions (since this is the mandate of the JP court). He was embodying the conception of law as a battle, where some win, and others lose.

On his side, the older lawyer was expressing frankness, and presented himself as an incarnation of reasonableness and morality. Yet, he too got carried away by the provocations of the younger lawyer, who was seemingly content to have engaged the older man in this stormy jousting (was it a trap?). Both allowed their modes of expression to escalate very quickly to the point that their ecstatic dispute took on a melodramatic touch (Brooks 1976; Cavell 1996). The smiles and concealed laughter of the audience (including myself) showed that something changed the physiognomy of the issue. That these serious issues are handled with such an extravagance, made the whole event become funny to some extent, but also grotesque and ridiculous.[11] Not all were ready to laugh, though. Why did the theatrics of the lawyers not exasperate the judge, who was not even offended by the lawyers' attitudes? He could have, I suppose, sanctioned them (he did not seem to lack the authority to do so). How are we to understand the fact that he let them put on such a show?

I was scandalized, as it were; this says something about my own prejudices and the way they shape my perception of what is overly theatrical in these circumstances; what is a sign of egotism and hubris, and thus an abuse of the court process; what is tolerable or not in a court. Ball (1975, 97–100) underscores how disruptions in the ordered sequences of a trial in the United States can become so absurd that they end up confusing completely the parties. Unending interferences make the lawyers lose their cues and their focus to the point that even their roles dilute into something else, and reason may be lost. If it can become a technique and be used strategically, my sentiment was rather that something was getting out of hand and making them lose touch with the issue at stake, something that not only released uncontrolled passions and overran reasoned deliberation but also increased the excitement around issues between a brother and a sister that rather needed to cool down. The lawyers' show seemed to matter more than protecting their clients' rights and settling the dispute.

Other people in the room may have been scandalized too, but there are surely important differences with how such an event might appear to them. One would have to see the relation, for instance, between the fact that this performance in court had a particular tint that was parodic, being reminded that, theatrically, parody is used, by negation, to make the truth appear, which is a great sophist technique by the way. And the fact that judges and lawyers are also carnival characters also matters. During carnival revelries, indeed, improvised parodies of trials in the streets attract crowds (Gordon 2010). Costumed judges, lawyers, court clerks, and bailiffs will sit in the middle of a street grotesquely debating the administration of a contested proof or the verisimilitude of a testimony in an imagined case that, of course, is not unrelated to the quotidian issues the people face. One would thus have to recognize a continuum between different modes of play to get a sense of how dramatic and parodic behavior sneak into real courts. More generally, everyday life is infused by a sense of seduction that takes many forms. The *bann a pyè*, the street brass bands, for example, must seduce the crowds by generating a feeling of togetherness, by unleashing a collective energy; they will be judged on their capacity to arouse such a feeling

(Kivland 2020). Outside carnival, heated debates may be improvised in the streets that become spectacles attracting and cheering up bystanders. There is a certain pleasure taken by the debaters in their competition over the power to seduce the crowd. These micro-events do not so much disrupt the flow of ordinary life as they uplift the tired minds of people struggling to make a living. Hence, there could be a relation between all this and what happened in my example, that would open up the possibility of seeing it also as a show, a sort of parody, an amusement of sorts—yet without reducing it to that—through which the law itself, and state institutions, are ridiculed from the inside (Lipset 2004). If indeed the parody breaks the theatrical illusion insofar as it shows the artifice, contrary to what is often admitted, it does not really break the theatricality, but displaces it, as if, in a way, the show was playing behind the scenes. Going one step further, we could even imagine that the sort of excess played out, perhaps ironically, hints at something more profound: Could it be that what is somehow ridiculed is the magisterial and transcendent character of law, its overarching and remote presence? Could it be a sort of ironic defiance of the all too serious (perhaps insane) perception of the metaphysical force of law? Could it be seen as a parodic enactment of the authority drawn from the transcendence of the law? If so, this representation can also be seen as an ironic enactment of modernity itself, let's say of modernity's overconfidence (or blindness) in its own reason. I leave open the question of whether we can speak of postcolonial critique.

THE LIVELINESS OF LAW

These questions bring us to the idea that the court is a place for the performance of the orality of the law, which is my third point. Liveliness, as it becomes obvious, is a matter essential to the law. Italian anthropologist Maurizio Bettini (2022) brilliantly shows how, in ancient Rome, the *enunciation* of the law was essential. For our purpose, this observation is pertinent for many of our legal concepts originate from the Roman conception of the *vocal* character of law, like our concept of "summons," which in French is *"acte de citation"* (act of citation), itself derived from the Roman concept of *in ius vocare*; or the concept of advocacy developed from the concept of *advocatio*, to assist in a court; or else to avow (*advocare*), to call upon you, to convene. They all have something to do with the orality of the voice (*vox*). An important feature of it is the centrality of the verbal: Acts such as a command, a decision, a designation, a claim, a judgment, or a sentence can be effective only through the thorough observance of the pronunciation. "It is above all the spoken word (*parola*) that makes the law" (ibid., 59). Indeed, it constitutes the essential conditions for the very existence of these acts, as well as their effectiveness.[12] "In sum, for the Romans, the spoken word—its very sound—was not a superfluous or accessory component of the *ius* (law), but was directly part of its substance" (ibid., 60–61). It is the very range of the voice's sound, the "phonic harmonies" (ibid., 4), that determines the act (i.e., to give a sentence its quality of sentence, and not, say, turn a sentence into a joke). It is therefore not only a question of style (although style is certainly a very important matter), but a question of the very existence of the law (and its functioning). For that to happen, it was necessary to be physically present and exchange dialogically the spoken words (*verba*). For an act of justice to be efficient, the presence of parties was indeed mandatory, for no written act could supersede the oral exchange. Whatever act, it had to be voiced out loud.

Now, the frisky energy with which the lawyers pleaded in that small courtroom that day, the pleasure and relative satisfaction they seemed to draw from it, and the enjoyment (nonetheless ambiguous) of the audience (including the clerks, the judge, and myself), tell us something of the kind of event that is taking place. One will have to reckon with the fact that "creativity and improvisation with legal technicalities lie at the heart of the trial process" (Suresh 2023, 15). This means paying attention to human expression, let's say the more or less delicate or coarse ways in which the human voice can be heard. If "to improvise or to experiment is to make an attempt at creating a community" (Benoist 2019, 277), then their show was not only deplorable in that it had little regard for the possible effects on the relationship between sister and brother, but also enjoyable to some extent because it gave the audience a sense of what it is to be alive together—alive within the uncertainty and the bounds of what can be perceived otherwise as an austere and lifeless formal law. What is it that, in a dispute of this sort, at some point awakens a smile and arouses laughter? I have noticed in the circumstances otherwise more serious described in Chapter 2 that, even under the imminent threat of death, something in the flow of microevents spurs the transformation of faces; fleeting smiles surface, and even laughter erupts more or less bashfully, on faces otherwise sullen and stiff and cranky. The aspects change. Something shines in moments of darkness.

In this case, I would risk going so far as to claim that the floor was open for the lawyers to vest their authority over the play (shown by the complacency of the judge and the clerk, or at least their unwillingness to sanction them), a play in which their authority notably derives from the fire they can spark (the problem they illuminate, or the moment of cheerfulness they create); call it an elusive moment of human accord, a reassertion of commonness.

I have witnessed similar moments in other court sessions, often also during informal exchanges in between more formal performances. For instance, that same month of February 2020, I was waiting with a small audience in a JP court in the city of Gonaïves for the judge to arrive. The lawyers of both parties as well as a clerk were there already, standing in the middle of the room between the people watching and the judge's empty desk. Unlike us, they wore dark suits and ties and shining leather shoes and smelled of perfume. Hands in their pockets or carrying a code of law, their heads high, they were prancing, empowered with self-confidence. They started discussing loudly about issues in broken Creole, interjecting complicated French expressions as well as typical Latin idioms used in classical rhetoric. The more they carried on, the more animated they became. They started making jokes, now in a perfectly understandable Creole. These were clearly meant to make the audience laugh. The judge being slow to arrive, their show went on, becoming more and more theatrical: Their bodies became more expressive, more expansive in their movements. They started to occupy the whole space, going now from one place to the other, laughing intrusively or arguing with grand gestures. The intensity grew and amused most of us, even though some seemed annoyed by it, or by the late judge perhaps. In this interstice in a busy day, a fleeting moment of warmth and fun had relaxed most of the stiff faces. After about a half an hour, the clerk got a call: the judge wouldn't come. They all promptly left the room.

I believe that kind of performance bears some relation to what a priest, an MC, or a brass band notably does. By demonstrating publicly their mastery of eloquence and rhetoric, they show proof of their expertise and oratory prowess and enact their charisma. Thus, they not only secure the support of the audience, but also bring people together; and what better than a smile or laughter to embody our togetherness? Call it seduction if you will. But rhetoric has its violent effects when it silences the voices of others (especially women and men of lesser social status) and concomitantly performs masculinity by enacting the power and virtues associated with masculine dominance (Harrington et al. 2019). The lawyers may also ignite an already tense situation and then violence could flare up. Obviously, in the case of the sister and the brother, not only did the lawyers not succeed in creating the conditions for an accord—they may have been carried away by their own fervor—but they also could not extinguish the blaze. The conciliation ended in a confused scuffle and a ratification of the parties' grudges.

Beyond the stakes internal to the case, there is a more general issue with the place the court of justice occupies in a society. From the perspective of a conventional view of the modern state, it plays quite a definite role: In principle, it is the organ that interprets the law to make sure it is applied as equally as possible to all, ensures that the laws are enforced, settles disputes in accordance with national and international standards, and provides advisory opinions on legal questions. Now, as it happens, courts can be, and are, used for many other purposes. For instance, they can protect the interests of an elite (for example, corporate law); enforce state policies even when they are in flagrant contradiction with the law (for example, asylum law); create diversion to cover responsibilities (for example, ICTR, the International Criminal Tribunal for Rwanda); or stage a public show to reassert common values (for example, the "Paris terror trial"). In so-called postcolonial states, other uses of courts shed light on what courts are. Alan McPherson (2012) shows, for example, how and in what spirit local courts in Haiti were used to fool the US officials during the occupation of 1915–1934. Litigants and Haitian magistrates made smart use of courts during times when a foreign force was trying to implement a more efficient and coercive judiciary system, one more punitive. They mimicked what was expected from them, staging trials of defendants, except that in the end they favored those criminalized by the United States by lightening the sentences and mitigating the punishments, if not squarely freeing them from charges. They turned the outcomes to their advantage.[13] The courts thus became places where the law simultaneously was applied scrupulously (yet ironically) and where the US authorities were fooled and outplayed. Courts were thus diverted from their initial purpose to become places of resistance and transgression, as were the churches by Vodou practitioners.

My example too does not fit the determinations of the taken for granted conception of what courts are and the role they play in society. What's more, if we do not look closely at "how the courts are bound up in the daily lives of the people," as Arnold L. Epstein (2017, 229) has already made it clear, we will fail to recognize the place of law within the community. We also need to focus our attention on aspects rather than the dispute processes. Part of the issue is how we picture, not only the relation between the justice system and other state organs like police and Parliament, but also between what happens inside the courts and what happens outside, reckoning with the fact that the borders between them are porous.

THE PLAY OF LAW OUTSIDE THE COURTS

In February 2020, I attended with Alix, then a fourth-year undergrad student, some classes on criminal procedures and on human rights at the Law School of Gonaïves. These classes took place in the evening. The large space, with approximately three hundred seats, was overpacked. Dozens were standing on the sides and at the back or sitting on the floor. We arrived shortly before the beginning and went to the back, where a group of friends was waiting for us. The sweltering heat was unbearable. The sweat was dripping on all faces. The course started in a tense and confused ambiance. The group tried to concentrate for a little while, but soon gave up. They started to make fun of the university and their conditions. At some point, noticing how sweaty I was, one of the students handed over a bottle of Toro (a locally made Red Bull). I was quick to take a huge sip, happy to quench my thirst, but immediately realized that I had just taken a mouthful of warm *kleren*, artisanal rum. I almost spat it out and had to cough.

They laughed, happy to have trapped the *blan pentad*, the "white guinea fowl." I laughed at my naïveté with them. After this little farce, a couple of circles started to form in the back. Clandestine bottles of alcohol were circulating, and while the professor was lecturing, other debates started to raise the students' passions. In one group, questions were raised concerning agency and responsibility when a person is mounted by a *lwa*, a spirit. One student asked Alix: "When a *lwa* dances in your head [possesses you], is your mind gone? Is it absent, or is it somewhere still there? Is your mind there but somehow asleep, or on standby, while the spirit rides your body and speaks in your place? Or is your mind still on the watch, active alongside the *lwa*?" Issues revolving around the limits of responsibility of the subject were at stake. A complex discussion ensued about the gray zones of law when it comes to matters pertaining to the influence and effects of the presence of spirits among humans. Everyone in the small conclave had something to say, and most had divergent opinions on the matter, which they felt they had to express in oppositional modes. A related question was, to what extent is one really mounted by a *lwa*? Because obviously one can fake it. The stakes of the question, for them, were to figure out how much one was liable and responsible for one's acts under certain circumstances. Specifying these circumstances was a core issue. Another then came up with the example of zombies, asking to what extent the criminal procedures are valid in the case of someone who is the victim of a *kout zonbi* (a specific spell that captures one's agency). Such a person would not be entitled to file a complaint, since it would be inadmissible in court for at least two reasons, they surmised: Because a person who is bereft of her agency cannot sign a complaint in her own name, and because the nature of the alleged crime is not recognized by the law (see Chapter 5). Another replies, "So either we deal with these things outside the tribunals, or we change the codes."

The professor went on, while they improvised in the back oratory jousts and tested their rhetoric skills, their knowledge and ability to argue for or against, regardless of whether they believed what they were defending. I had participated in other circumstances in many of these informal disputes, but also in more formal debates in colleges, universities, and TV shows. It appeared quite clearly that the dominant picture of thinking was one of argumentation and debate (Mézié 2019). This is notably how students learn to be lawyers. In many ways, being a jurist is precisely about play, oratory performance, and seduction skills. Students also know how much the (materiality of the) text matters (Latour 2010), and thus how important it is that they learn to use, refer to, quote, and manipulate it in the right way at the right moment—it is much about the effects, whatever the accuracy or pertinence of the quote. Fair play and sincerity will be important at some point, but one learns very early on that it is surely not enough to be fair and sincere in a court. Students equally know that a great deal about what one has to learn lies not in codes, doctrines, and procedures taught in class. Their readiness to play, their promptness to follow the excitement, their capacity to respond on the spot, their agonistic prowess, are all competences acquired in the flow of a form of life that values such things as play, experiment, improvisation, inventiveness, pleasure, and entertainment. And since "one who improvises *tries* something, and every trial calls for an assessment" (Benoist 2019, 273), improvisation becomes an exercise of judgment.

Hence, what plays out in my example is to be thought in keeping with what happens outside, in other moments of life. Not only does this then put into question common notions of justice and law, but it forces us to rethink the specific theatricalities that color the situations in relation to each other. How much would we understand of this moment in court that I described if we had not connected it to how students learn and practice law at the threshold of the classroom or in their daily life, or still to how people generally are inclined to play, argue, and parody social roles? The fact that such a possibility exists, that these lawyers might embody ironically or parodically their own role and by the same token the justice system itself, is important to consider. It is not just a side effect or an epiphenomenon, but it is critical to how we think about justice and the law. Aesthetics interlace with ethics and politics.

A DARKER PICTURE

Putting into perspective the taken for granted concepts of law and justice from the standpoint of Haiti makes us rethink them in their performative dimension. As I have made explicit, the law is theatricalized, and this theatricalization is essential to what law is and the place it has in our human lives. It notably allows a "systematic derangement of our power of judgment" (Benoist 2019, 276) and thus unsettles our reliance on fixed criteria. Yet, the performance has different tones, or inflections, depending on the situation. To conclude, I would like to offer a few musings about how the peculiar aesthetics of justice in Haiti generates, conveys, and displays various kinds of violence.

The courts, despite their significance and necessity, are also places where people put immense pressure on each other, leverage their influence, seek to gain power, extend their cronyism, extort money from the vulnerable, insure wealth, and exercise control. What happens in a court, no matter how theatrical or comical or dramatic we may call it, has consequences beyond the court. This is where the analogy with the theater stops: People convicted in courts will pay fines or go to prison, actors not so. People in courts might get hurt, seek revenge, or even be killed, actors not so. The theatricality that characterizes the performance of law is connected to the ordinary lives of people in very different ways.

Something regarding Haiti's history seems to indicate that it is critical, if not vital, for some (vulnerable) people to know more about how the state functions and to have a sense of its hidden agenda. To some extent the state must be legible, and its modes of functioning known, for them to make their lives livable. This is historically comprehensible in a country whose state is constantly jockeyed by the major northern powers and is itself maneuvering against its own citizens. Therefore, we might want to consider that people go to court to *learn* something about a state that allows itself to ignore its population and still go on governing, with violent and coercive means if necessary. The judiciary is undoubtedly an ambiguous system, to say the least. In Haiti, it is strongly marked by a systemic violation of laws, corruption, and an ineluctable partisanship. The generalized violation (by police and the courts) of the arrest procedures and the laws regulating the conditions and time of custody shows this. The large-scale and years-long detention of suspects, who have never appeared before a judge or gone on trial, unduly and unlawfully incarcerated on mere accusations, is common and dramatic.[14] Clientelism also plays a critical role in the attitude of the courts. Judges and commissioners sometimes (are compelled to) enact the decisions taken by senators or other high officials. Judges, clerks, bailiffs, or lawyers are themselves pressured, and sometimes assaulted, wounded, or killed. This is where theater stops on the threshold of another kind of reality. The actors of the judiciary are subject to enormous pressures from all sides: from competing fractions of the government, from international interference, or from the streets. They are submitted to political maneuvers all the time and are often forced to relay different kinds of political clout. The oppressive and deceptive character of state justice is something most people I know are aware of and contend with on different levels. Nonetheless, in an ever-changing world, they need to keep on figuring out where they stand in relation to the state's agenda.

Hence, on the one hand, many people show the sense they have of the farce of all this oratory spectacle. "*Se kanaval*," "it's a carnival," I heard law students say about the judiciary. Indeed, Haitian politics are carnivalized, as much as carnival is politicized; this is not news (Kivland 2020). The whole system may appear as a send-up, a vast and insane comedy, or perhaps madness. On the other hand, people generally still aspire to justice and peace, and many yearn for another kind of system that would not just sound like a bad joke. This is notably why people still go to courts, as did the woman and her brother. Some might want to settle the issue informally, even with the recourse to violence. Others still hope that an arbitration organized by a state institution could do its job. There is a double-sided perception that law and justice are at the same time crucial and necessary to the functioning of a decent democracy (at least it is part of the concept of, thus of the aspiration for, democracy), and yet the people's disillusionment and disappointment are such that they cannot take law and justice too seriously.

5

INNER FORMS OF CORROSION

I am teeming with corpses
Teeming with dead rattles
I am a tide of wounds

—RENÉ DEPESTRE

Zombie, I'm not afraid of you
I know you're a human being

—EDWIDGE DANTICAT

At the end of the day, it was all just a question
of the mysteries of death—our common fate

—RENÉ DEPESTRE

WHEN ZOMBIES ENTER THE LEGAL ARENA

As we have seen in the previous three chapters, over the past two decades
Haiti has undergone many important institutional changes, many of which
have been monitored and supervised by foreign states and organizations
(Johnston 2024). The judiciary, in addition to the police and prison system,
has been the main target of these efforts. Yet, the outcomes are dismaying:
By the United Nations Development Programme's (UNDP) own admission,
"The Haitian justice system is largely dysfunctional and unable to fulfil its
mandate as a critical third branch of government" (February 2023 fact sheet).
The UNDP underscores that Haiti is now ranked 136th out of 140 countries
on the WJP Rule of Law Index, and that over 90 percent of Haitians have

recourse to informal means of justice, outside of any state intervention. While the judicial system is currently out of order, patently attesting to the failure of decades of investments, the UNDP still plans to invest $20 million more for the judiciary in Haiti between 2023 and 2028.

Important institutional changes include the reform of the Penal Code and the code of criminal procedure. The UNDP was early to launch the project entitled "Appui au processus de réforme de la justice en Haïti à travers la réforme du Code pénal" ("Support for Justice Reform in Haiti Through Reform of the Penal Code"). This was back in 2002, under Aristide's first mandate and with MICAH's collaboration. This project was explicitly aimed at promoting "the reform of Haitian criminal law . . . and related legislation." In fact, these bodies of codes dated back to 1835 and were never reformed, even though there had been a few amendments. The idea of a reform, however, was not new. In 1959, François Duvalier set up a commission to assess the possibility of overhauling the codes. This was a year after he had declared a state of siege and required Parliament to govern by presidential decree. It was also a year after he banned opposition parties and created the brigade of National Security Volunteers (VSN), better known as "*tonton makout*." In 1977, his son, Jean-Claude Duvalier, created again a commission designed to reform the codes. In the same year Haiti ratified the American Convention on Human Rights. It was also during these years (1973–1980) that the regime was in the process of installing the Corps des Léopards (Duvalier's paramilitary force) as a general police force, and that arbitrary detention, torture, and extrajudicial executions increased considerably. It seems that in such a context, the very idea of criminal law reform is linked to the establishment of an autocratic and repressive regime.

After the fall of the Duvalier dictatorship, although the 1987 constitution enshrined individual and civic rights and guaranteed the independence of the three powers of the state, the Penal Code and criminal procedure remained virtually intact, "outdated, archaic and liberticidal," according to the UNDP. In the eyes of the international community, for Haiti to become a democratic country, reform was a priority: The codes had to be brought into line with the new constitution and adapted to the reality of a new rule of law. In the 2010s, two entities tasked with reforming the criminal justice system, one set up under President René Préval, the other under President Michel Martelly, have merged and pooled their respective work. A new entity was created tasked with drafting the new Penal Code and code of criminal procedure.

The reform was finally drafted and adopted under Jovenel Moïse's mandate, albeit in obscure conditions. The Penal Code was disclosed on June 24, 2020; the code of criminal procedure is still awaiting disclosure, and they are not due to come into force until 2024, if ever. The publication was widely publicized and debated. Some of the changes were met with an outcry. For example, several parties and organizations have drafted an anxious statement denouncing what they called an illegal, undemocratic reform (without prior debate), which they believe calls into question the essence of the moral and cultural values of Haitian society. In particular, they deplore what they (mis)interpret as the legalization of abortion, as well as the reduction of the age of sexual consent to fifteen. The aim, they claim polemically and vociferously, is to encourage the corruption of minors, and to decriminalize pedophilia. The Episcopal Conference of Haiti (CEH) strongly decried the new text, soon followed by The Protestant Federation of Haiti (FPH), which launched a petition to revoke the code, claiming that it decriminalizes incest, recognizes and admits zoophilia, as well as child prostitution, underage drinking, and homosexuality.[1]

Following much criticism and heated debate, the members of the Presidential Commission for the Reform of the Judiciary publicly defended their reform project. They highlighted that the guiding principles and methodology adopted conform to all the international conventions ratified by Haiti. As stipulated in the constitution, the provisions contained therein became part of national legislation as soon as they were ratified. They also claimed that the committee's reflections also focused on the compatibility of Haitian culture with the content and requirements of the human rights philosophy formulated in the international conventions ratified by the National Assembly. Throughout the drafting of the code, the committee says, it has examined all the documentation on Haitian habits and customs, the influence of religions—"including Vodou"—on the Haitian way of thinking and social practices.[2] In addition, the committee focused on the nonexistence of a Haitian doctrine in the field of law in general, and criminal law in particular, and at the same time on the considerable influence of French doctrine on the practice of law in Haiti. Commission members claim they have had an eminently participatory and inclusive approach that has enabled them to gather suggestions and observations from participants in the various workshops, on a variety of themes particularly in areas such as zombification, voluntary interruption of pregnancy, rape, sexual harassment, discrimination, the scale of penalties, the criminal liability of corporate bodies, crimes and misdemeanors against persons and property, and environmental offences.

This reform is the starting point for this chapter. As we shall see, it is significant in several respects. However, it is especially of interest to me because it has made headlines by placing the issue of zombification at the center of the debate. That a postcolonial state such as Haiti has an interest in discussing in the legal arena a concept as vague and complex as zombification, is in itself a fascinating subject. But my aim in this chapter is not to discuss at length the details of reform, which would lead me to discuss technicalities and legal issues that are of little relevance here. In what follows, I will rather track how and why the figure of the zombie entered the field of law, and how the issues around such a figure in law are related to other kinds of issues concerning agency, political violence, gender, death, and resistance in ordinary life. It seems to me worth looking closer at what the concept of the zombie says about the conditions of (non-)existence in Haiti. Based on the questions raised by these debates, I'll extend my thoughts to examine the scope of this concept as it unfolds in everyday life. Some people in Haiti end up being demeaned and silenced, some no longer fully awake to themselves and their condition as human beings, others so aware that they end up isolated, withdrawn from the world. What does, then, the figure of the zombie reveal about these forms of inner corrosion? What is the context for the emergence of such a figure?

THE MONSTROSITY OF DEATH IN EVERYDAY LIFE

In 2017, the Haitian Senate launched new consultations in view of the reform in some African countries. During September 15–22 that year, a delegation of three Haitian senators made an unusual diplomatic visit to Benin. The explicit purpose of the journey was to learn from the Beninese government about juridical tools for legislating on Vodou and witchcraft crimes. The delegation attended a two-day workshop on criminal law, as well as meetings with local ritual experts and the president of Benin's supreme court. At the end of a session at the Haitian Embassy in Cotonou, where attendees were shown Wes Craven's horror movie *The Serpent and the Rainbow* (1988)—inspired by the ethnobotanist Wade Davis's famous sensationalist book on zombies (1997)—one of the three Haitian senators, Jean-Renel Senatus, also a jurist and the president of Haiti's Commission of Justice, Security, and National Defense, declared that, among all the issues Haitians must wrestle with, zombification in all its forms is one of the most pressing. He added that traditional forms of justice that do exist are insufficient and often used to harm. This is why, he said, Haiti needs to redefine clearly what a zombie is, reform the outdated penal law that was derived from the Napoleonic Civil Code, and give the government new tools to address these issues.[3] Eventually, the Senate commission did not have the opportunity to submit the results for Senate approval.

At the same time, in Bwa-Mapou, as I followed the local people's activities, I was struck by how much creatures such as zombies (*zonbi*) or werewolves (*lougawou*) were embedded in people's everyday lives.[4] They were mentioned in a wide range of contexts to refer to apparently many different things. It became progressively obvious: they were there, almost everywhere. I read about them in the newspapers, saw them on TV, or heard about them in a casual conversation in the neighbor's shack. Someone would say, "These people from the government do nothing—these bureaucrats! They're like dead and they're paid! They are zombies!" In a neighboring village, at a packed Catholic church during the patronal feast of Mount Carmel I heard behind me two elegantly dressed old women quarreling over pew seats and starting to insult each other with phrases like "You're a werewolf!" or "You're a dead body! You carcass! You zombie!" Or, as I drank rum with young men as their mates sewed under a tarp, I listened to the endless diatribes on zombies, followed by heated debates about the different possibilities of using them as a working force or employing them as slayers, about whether those who would use them are good people or not, or whether one who was not their target and not a Vodou expert can actually see them at all, which called into question the knowledge one can claim to have of them. Often as the sun set, when the children were heading back from the river where they went to play, I found myself sorting the vegetables I had collected earlier in the garden alongside women from the family with whom I was living, and I listened to the issues they had, as mothers, with the *lougawou*, a vampiric creature who is said to drink the blood of children and sometimes sucks them to death. Almost half of the children roaming around in the compound were victims of *lougawou* attacks during their early childhood: Many fell ill, and some came close to death without medical explanation. The children themselves would test their own fear and courage, imagining *lougawou* lurking in dark and stony alleys of the hills as they headed home after a local football match. And since zombies are manipulated in rituals, I encountered many references to these figures in the Vodou cures or ceremonies I attended and in my conversations with Vodou practitioners. I also met them in Haitian novels, which refer to them now and then, if not featuring them bluntly at the center of the narrative, as in the works of René Depestre (2017), Edwidge Danticat (2015b), or Makenzy Orcel (2021).

These are just a few examples of the pervasiveness and seriousness of the presence of these monstruous creatures in Haiti. They are generally elusive and equivocal, generating all the more concern as they thwart all attempts to clearly define their behavior. Thus, one can consider them as figures of doubt. They give, so to say, a physiognomy to skepticism (Motta 2023). They can also be understood to be the forms our anxiety takes. Something's there that in turn creates disquiet, challenges our reason, puts us to the test—they make uncertain what seemed assured, shaking our certainties, inciting us to revise our judgments, to perceive otherwise, to pursue other kinds of knowledge, and to reinterpret what happens to us. Sometimes they may ignite curiosity, and yet, at other times they dampen or quell it. Zombies displace the limits of our comprehension of the world but remain mysterious. That says something about their importance. Hence, they require us to be humble in their regard.

No wonder, then, that the figure of the zombie worries legislators and politicians alike. Nor is it surprising that they haunt the legal arena, as they call into question the normative scope of the law. Zombies appear in all sorts of circumstances: Sometimes where they're expected, like in the movies, sometimes where they're less expected, like on the street or in our dreams. They live in speeches, imagination, and literature; they also live in homes, cemeteries, factories, courts, prisons, and asylums. As much as their presence is ubiquitous, the people also have motley perceptions of zombies. One can make fun of them, use them as insults, imagine them as workers or henchmen, or mourn them as the lost, caught between the living and the dead and in the grasp of deadly powers. It is said that zombification happens when forms of death corrode vital ties, leaving nothing more than wrecked beings dwelling in between the realms.[5]

Haitians commonly distinguish between two types of *zonbi*. The flesh and blood *zonbi* are people whose death has been duly recorded and who have been buried, usually after having been poisoned, but they were later found living in a state of lethargy and idiocy; this is the type that worries the legislators. The second type is *zonbi mistik*, referring to the wandering souls of dead people who did not die properly or were snatched by corpse washers and sold in bottles on the black market of occult objects (Degoul 2006; Depestre 2017; Hurston 2009; Lucas 2004; Métraux 1972); this type is too far removed from any legal grasp. But, as we will see, there are many more kinds of zombies.

Before we go any further, it will be fruitful to first consider how we, as anthropologists, receive and respond to what people do and say about their life and experiences. All the previous examples raise a particular, and in many ways fundamental, question for anthropology and the humanities in general: What would it mean, and why is it important, to give a realistic account of the lives of others, avoiding the excitement that often leads to clichés and fantasies as well as the reductionism that flattens the very thickness of reality and obliterates the issues people do contend with? The whole history of our discipline shows us how the "other" can be and indeed has been cannibalized (say, eaten by the eye of a distant observer) and carnivalized (e.g., folklorized, turned into a spectacle, exoticized) by anthropologists. Let's not repeat history.

A REALISTIC SPIRIT FOR ANTHROPOLOGY

All anthropologists are concerned with reality, and we all claim to say something relevant about it. Yet, even after we learned to inhabit the worlds of other people, nothing seems more challenging and difficult than to convey and make relevant a certain sense of reality that matters (Motta 2019b). And "realism" here would mean something like a kind of attention to particulars. It might be that certain stories ask the question of their account with a particular acuity, and here I am thinking of the sort of demand placed upon Saidiya Hartman (2008, 9) by the archive of Atlantic slavery, asking her to look for an "aesthetic mode suitable or adequate to rendering the lives" of those who have been forever silenced (see also M. R. Trouillot 1995). Her approach, then, is to attend to the quotidian practices as they shape the contours of day-to-day life. She looks at how "an expansive register of minor gestures, ways of sustaining life, caring for each other, undoing slavery by small acts of stealth and destruction, communal dreaming, sacred transport, acts of redress, and faith in a power greater than master and nation made it possible to survive the unbearable while acceding to it" (Hartman 2022, xxxii). Importantly, she tries to "illuminate the terror of the mundane and the quotidian rather than exploit the shocking spectacle" (ibid., 2). One of the issues is, as she underscores, to propose alternative accounts to the grand narratives that continue to hold sway over our imagination. Another issue is, I suppose, how we redefine our attitude toward certain dimensions of the real.

The kind of question I want to address here is not ontological (do the zombies exist or not); metaphysical (what is their essence); semantic (what is it that they refer to); or merely epistemological (what can I know about them); but rather *grammatical*—what would we say when. A grammatical investigation, for Ludwig Wittgenstein (1986, §90), is an investigation directed toward the possibilities offered by our life in language, not a syntax analysis or a description of a set of defined rules. In Stanley Cavell's interpretation, Wittgenstein's method is to look closely, not only at what is said, but "what we should say in a given case, and when we should say a given thing." The request, then, is "not that we predict an occurrence, but that we imagine one" (Cavell 1999, 146). And imagining it depends on our ability, as ordinary speakers, to project words into new yet unimagined contexts, i.e., to try, to experiment, to improvise, all the things we've been doing so ordinarily since we've learned our first words. Hence, a grammatical investigation is no more but no less than an appeal "to what we should say when, to how words are normally used" (ibid., 167). It is not just the grammar of our language as such, but the grammar of a whole form of life of which language is an integral part, as well as a generator. We're not just looking at words or meanings (however we conceive them), but at the reality that both gives them life and is determined by them. This includes practices, habits, breaks in habit, gestures, steps, rhythms, glances, silences, but also the details of the worlds through which we walk, the perception of a luminous intensity, the colors of the sky at dawn, the musicality of a stream, the shape of an ambiguous friendship, the physiognomy of a reproach, or the seriousness of a threat. So, investigating grammatically the concept of the zombie in Haiti will require a close look at life circumstances in which it appears.

To figure out the importance of the zombie in the Haitian context, one will have to reckon with the background of a whole form of life—legal, religious, practical, mythical, literary, imagined, aesthetic, ideological, poetic, and moral. In fact, "what experience shows you about reality is a matter that you will have to determine in complex ways that cannot be read off experience itself" (Diamond 1991b, 1006). Hence, what there is to be seen in that reality depends on a certain experience of the form of life and the language that brings zombies into existence. So how are zombies brought into existence? And what are their modes of existence?

Reality is not something stable that awaits definition. It is rather perceived, thought, imagined, shaped, composed, assembled, reconfigured as humans go about their daily lives and face new challenges, ordeals, and problems they have to make sense of. Thus, the objects of our thoughts change as we change and as context changes, and morph into something else that acquires a place in our lives and means something to us. The reality of the *zonbi* is thus to a great extent indeterminate, even though we will see that it can be quite narrowly restricted by the normativity of our language (Benoist 2013), for instance by the legal discourse. Regardless, the multiplicity and specificity of its aspects, just like the aspects of figures such as the vampire, the unicorn, or the dragon, makes it a particularly interesting object to think with.

The questions addressed to the *zonbi* in the Haitian context are much richer and more interesting than simply asking "does it exist or not?" For instance, a set of questions one can come across in different settings of daily life concerns how one detects its presence and deciphers its intentions: How do I recognize it? How does it sound? What difference does it make if I encounter it in a dream at night, rather than when I'm awake? Are there different kinds of zombies? How can I make sure it is indeed one? If I can't, then how do I live with that uncertainty? Another set of questions follows: What will it do to me and my loved ones? What are its intentions? How can it be "doing" and "wanting" to do anything at all if it is the kind of being deprived of agency?[6] How can it nonetheless free itself from its subjugation? How can I prevent its harmful effects? Can I domesticate it? If so, how can I? And can I use zombies for my own purposes? What kind of purposes? What responsibility, then, do I have in using it? In sum, the question for the anthropologist becomes: What is it to describe forms of life, hence forms of death? And how are we to do such a thing with tact?

The rightness of our ethnographic descriptions is a key issue. In my case, I take the question of rightness (or adequacy or tactfulness) to be of a particular relevance, not only because many scholars grapple hard with it—this tells us something about the difficulty of the problem—but also because the tumultuous history of Haiti's relation with Western countries asks that we write with care; and it might be that writing with care means something like "being realistic." Even when anthropologists aim at providing some kind of reasonable account of zombies, exerting themselves to find the right pitch, it turns out that their goodwill is not sufficient. I take a risk I am not unaware of here by associating (again) Haiti with zombies. The history of the relationships between Haiti and the West, especially the United States (Dash 1997), can be seen as one of denigration of Haitians; and such disdain has partly been conveyed through the figure of the zombie, a representation of rough colloquialisms, and insulting stereotypes, notably produced by the media and the American film industry[7] (Dayan 2004; McAlister 2012; Ramsey 2011). To me, however, this is a sufficient reason to reopen the record.

Now, there is another reason I see rightness to be an important feature of the problem of realism. If we accept that when we say, "there is nothing we cannot say," that does not mean "we can say everything," and when we say, "there is nothing we cannot know," that does not mean "we can know everything" (Cavell 1999, 239), then the ethics of realism becomes this: We must mean what we say (Cavell 2015). And if we are misled, "we must not suppose that this means [we] have been led to say the wrong thing—as though there was a right thing all prepared for [us] which [we] missed" (Cavell 1999, 239). Rather, we must take this as an exhortation to revise our sense of what matters. Let me recount a different zombie story here.

SOMETHING ABOUT NEIGHBORS

During summer 2017, Alix, Stanley, Frédéric, and I traveled all the way from Bwa-Mapou to the Jacmel Valley, overlooking the south coast of the island. We went to the village where Frédéric grew up before moving to the capital city when he was a teenager. We visited *matant mwen*, his aunt, who raised him. The four of us stayed for a couple of days with her (who lives alone), as well as Gasner, her grandson, and his wife, who, as it happened, were visiting too.

After we traveled all the way back home from Jacmel to Bwa-Mapou, Frédéric, Angeline, and I sat quietly under the night sky and sipped dark coffee. Frédéric asked, "Did you notice anything bizarre this morning when you went to pee in my aunt's backyard?" He had heard me go out into the pitch black of the early stormy morning. Puzzled, I asked why I should have noticed anything. I only needed to chase away a goat that sought refuge in the shack when the rain poured down, that was all. "Well," he said with a placid, grave, and slightly enigmatic tone, "my aunt told me that there are *zonbi* in the backyard."

He then asked for my opinion about what to do. As I inquired further, he told me his aunt was recently in conflict with the neighbors over land and water issues. There were many small events in the past weeks, which had escalated into full-blown hostility by the time of our visit. Two of them stood out. One was the theft of the aunt's yam. Her small plot of land, about fifteen minutes from her house by foot, was ransacked a week before our arrival.[8] The other event was the neighbors' refusal to dig a gully on the border of each parcel of land to drain the rainwater. Although all the houses were built on a steep hillside, the aunt's house was particularly vulnerable to water since it sat on a downward slope where the land was not correctly leveled to allow for rainwater drainage. Therefore, the water that penetrated the earth uphill would seep right into her house. With each party holding doggedly to their position, the situation was deadlocked.

The aunt accused the neighbors of having stolen the yam from her and colluding to make her life unbearable in order to push her to leave. There had always been arguments, Frédéric said, but the relationships were overall cordial, even friendly most of the time. It was only recently that the disputes intensified and deteriorated the ties, resulting in a bitter and resentful interaction in which the old woman mercilessly insulted the neighbors. After that, they no longer spoke to each other. Moreover, since the altercation, she claimed to see *zonbi* roaming around her house, which she said were sent by the neighbors to threaten and scare her off. Her grandson, Gasner, and his wife, both believing her, reinforced her suspicion and sought means to neutralize the threats through Vodou remedies. Gasner's wife is a *vodouizan*, an active Vodou practitioner; one of her spirits (*lwa*) confirmed that there were indeed zombies in the aunt's home. Frédéric was more doubtful. He did not deny the possibility that they were there, but neither did he take it at face value. He was cautious and ambivalent, at the same time showing openness and reluctance. He remained calm and tried to get his mind around the matter. He said that he tried to stay up all night to hear them (he didn't say "to see") but fell asleep.

I answered that if a *lwa* noticed the presence of *zonbi*, I would organize a ceremony to interrogate the *lwa* to find out more. Frédéric agreed. He thought that they should seek a *remèd*, a remedy, but insisted that the matter, being a minor dispute, should be settled amicably, although the grandson and his wife considered it a serious conflict that could not be resolved by talk. The grandson had also told Frédéric that besides zombies, *sanpwèl*—members of a well-known and dreaded secret society (*sosyete sekrè*)—came almost every night to dance and beat drums nearby, a story corroborated by the aunt, who confirmed having heard the uncanny rhythms and songs of the *sanpwèl*. In the rural context, it does indeed happen that delegations of these societies make forays into one's backyard or perform rituals incomprehensible to most in the streets, especially in crossroads. This is partly why people fear them and usually do not dawdle in public late at night. These groups generally appear only after midnight and disappear before dawn, roaming around like gangs of specters and speaking an undecipherable ritual language. They may as well be allies of some *bòkò*—a Vodou expert in the domain of *lwa achte*, tradable spirits—to threaten or fight against enemies, or to arbitrate an unsolvable conflict. In fact, the *sosyete sekrè*, such as the *sanpwèl*, have long existed and assumed alternative (judicial) order. Today, especially in rural areas, they assume at times the role of police (vigilante), arbiters in disputes (adjudication), and tax authority, without appealing to the courts or any state administration. They constitute in many respects a "parallel 'nighttime' legal order" (Ramsey 2011, 17). But they are always ambiguous, for they are also at times hustlers, dealers, smugglers, and contract killers. There are in many ways shapeshifting paramilitary organizations. Their occultism makes them particularly prone to criminal activity. They are also like marauders, going around at night surveilling certain zones, and one would eventually hear them beat strange rhythms, chant unknown songs, and speak an odd language as they address the *lwa* Legba and Kalfou, the guardians of barriers and pathways and masters of crossroads, as well as all the other spirits dwelling there at night. These societies are notably experts in manipulating a *lwa* called "Kriminel," specialized in punitive actions.

One can pay these *bòkò* for such things and therefore indirectly employ detachments of these secret societies for occult jobs. Frédéric was well aware that all this might be happening to his aunt, but he was not fully convinced. He explained that, if it was true that she was capable of cruelly insulting the neighbors and that her yam was indeed stolen, she also easily felt persecuted and besieged. Angeline shared in Frédéric's doubt; at the end of our conversation, she expressed her skepticism and her frustration, saying that she "can't believe" it and that what counts, in the end, is our faith in God.

Let me now step back and say a few words about Gasner whose nickname is Bwa Gede. Bwa means "wood" in Creole, and *gede* are the spirits of the realm of death (Métraux 1972, 112–16). Hence, his nickname can be taken to mean "one whose life is contingent on the *gede*," but also "the erect penis of the *gede*." Indeed, the local way of calling an erect phallus is *bwa*, a wooden stick, and a *zonbi* who is brought out of his lethargy into a normalized human state is said to have become *bwa nouvo* (new wood).[9] The *gede* are those lecherous and uncouth spirits dwelling mostly in the cemeteries under the patronage of Bawon Sanmdi (Baron Saturday), Bawon Lakwa (Baron the Cross), Bawon Simityè (Baron Cemetery), and Grann Brigit, gatekeepers of graveyards. Characterized by their insatiable sexual appetite and debauched behavior, they mock people, use lewd vocabulary to make the audience laugh, and love wild sex.[10] Yet, despite, or maybe in virtue of, their eccentric and unrestricted behavior, they are said to tell the truth straightforwardly, especially those concealed truths that embarrass people. The *gede* come out in droves and mount[11] people during the Toussaint, All Saints' Day, which is locally called "*fèt gede*," "the *gede* revelry."

From the mid-1990s until the first years of the new century, Frédéric had spent several years of his young adult life in Martissant, a shantytown of Port-au-Prince. He was trying to generate a small income by working with a younger brother in the barbershop managed by his cousin Danley, the father of Bwa Gede. On November 1, 2002, Danley went to the cemetery for All Saints' Day; he brought some black coffee to the dead, but while there he stumbled and fell. Frédéric told me that this was bad omen (but none of them felt so at the time, he said). A few days later, when Danley entered the shop, he noticed a bizarre smell; he said he could smell a *zonbi*. Frédéric and his brother laughed at him; neither of them took him seriously (Frédéric's aunt discouraged him from learning about or participating in Vodou and did not want him to be raised in the proximity of these matters). The next day, Danley noticed the same odor. The day after, Danley told his cousins, when he opened the shop in the morning, he found a young and silent girl behind the door, odd-looking and wearing rags. Without saying a word, she escaped. In the late afternoon, after closing the shop, Danley stopped by a street vendor. He bought something from the vendor but dropped it on the floor. He bent down to pick it up, and when he got up again, someone came from behind and shot him in the head.

Frédéric paused for a few moments before speaking again. "It had to be a punitive expedition," he said, "or so we thought." It seemed to have the signature of a local gang. There were many envious people around, and a lot of weapons. The shop was running pretty well, so there must have been issues Frédéric and his brother were not aware of. But the events turned out to be of another nature. That mysterious girl, who was she? Why did she appear that very day? And what about the slayer, whose identity was never established? That seems bizarre, since an execution-style assassination in such a crowded slum in the late afternoon would not have been without witnesses. But neither the vendor nor the bystanders had been able to identify the assassin. Frédéric told me they started to think of another kind of attack: a *zonbi* expedition. "Expeditions" are said to be mystical attacks (*atak mistik*); some of them are called *ekspedisyon lanmò*, a "sending of dead," which could involve a sending-off of *zonbi* killers. The *zonbi* can be used by some *bòkò* as henchmen to kill someone.

Danley left two orphans behind, a girl, Melodi, and a younger boy, Gasner (Bwa Gede). Having been very close to Danley, Frédéric took care of his children as if they were his. Approximately a year after his death, Frédéric dreamed of his cousin: Danley told him to prevent his son (Gasner) from riding the bicycle and that he had better sell it. So, he did as he was told; he warned the boy not to ride anymore and that they would sell the bike the next day. The boy did not heed his words and continued to ride in the courtyard until he crashed the bike against the wall and bent the front rim. It remained in Frédéric's mind as a sign of an ongoing threat.

In 2005, Frédéric was supposed to go with Danley's children to the Mardi Gras carnival in Jacmel, in the south of the island. But on the night before they were supposed to travel, he had another dream. Danley appeared again to discourage them from going and cautioned that there would be trouble. But the youngsters, aged thirteen and sixteen, insisted. They had yet never been to Jacmel's carnival, which is known internationally for its exquisitely creative celebration (Danticat 2002; Depestre 2017). There was no way they were going to miss it once more. Frédéric gave way to the pressure and told them that if he managed to pass his exams at school early enough, they would go; otherwise, they would give it up. But even before Frédéric entered the classroom, around 11:30 in the morning, he received a message on his cell phone: "See you in Jacmel, we're taking the bus." With two friends, the teens had decided to go on their own. Around 2:30 p.m., Frédéric received another message: The bus crashed in the mountains. Three of the four juveniles were heavily injured. Bwa Gede escaped unscathed. He helped extract his sister Melodi from the wreck. She survived, but one of her ears was severed in the accident.

During the years that followed, Melodi had several miscarriages. Each time, her father would come in her dreams to tell her she would not have children yet. Eventually, a ritual was organized to appease the roaming spirit of her father, after which she had her first child, who was born in 2013.

During the rest of my stay with Frédéric (about three more weeks that year), the aunt's situation did not evolve much: She was still complaining about the *zonbi*, the *sanpwèl*, and the neighbors. Bwa Gede and his wife had not yet found the means to counteract; and Frédéric was busy with selling bread. A few days before my departure, Frédéric and I went to Martissant where Melodi lives with her son and where her father had been killed. It turned out that Bwa Gede was there as well. The four of us stayed, chitchatting for a while during a downpour. We drank a local brew and spontaneously embarked on a discussion I did not initiate about zombies: Can those who are not their target actually see them? Are there different kinds of *zonbi*, some "physical" and others "mystical"? How do they actually act if they have no agency of their own? And so on. Frédéric and I both contributed some money for the aunt. Shortly before leaving, I expressed my bewilderment: Why would the neighbors want to harm an old lady in such a way? They say it is jealousy; they believe the neighbors think she has more than they do and want to make her pay for that.

SOME ASPECTS THAT MATTER

Given the vast number of possible angles from which to discuss this story, I will focus on only a few points. First, note that in my example, zombies do not necessarily have a human shape or resemble anything close to what we imagine to be the "walking dead." While in some circumstances, zombies can be perceived as humanoid (like the girl Danley saw in his shop), people do not always have a clear sense of what they look like. Their physical form is less of a question for some: Frédéric's aunt, or Frédéric himself, for instance, was more concerned with the sound of the zombies. This is also clear in Depestre's poem "Cap'tain Zombi," taken from his *Epiphanies of the Voodoo Gods* (1977), in which a zombie picks up and reveals reality through sound. He hears the dead bodies of his people as "a black artillery howling / in the cemetery of my soul" and urges the white world to listen "to the volleys of our dead." He asks to be heard: "Listen to my zombie voice / in honor of our dead. . . . Listen white world / To my zombie-roaring / Listen to my sea-silence." So, let's not assume we know how zombies would appear, or presuppose that the question of their silhouette is always pertinent. It may be that my example is one in which a different kind of zombie is involved.

Second, human relations take shape in particular ways. Understanding this situation is a matter of lending an ear to the subtle nuances, particular tones of voice, that come to matter to people and that, thereby, come to matter to us: They express "the dawning of an aspect," in Wittgenstein's terms (1986, 194–206; also Laugier 2010). Because there is always a question of the point(lessness) of perception—some sounds are considered trivial or insignificant, whereas others are highly critical—the problem is not resolved by training to perceive more but by being more discerning. What we are taught here is that we must lend the right ear. How, then, do these sounds, voices, and silences relate to the expression of what matters in human life? Here, I am also thinking about how words can become poison for the ear. If, on the one side, we must account for the possibility that the aunt's home might have been poisoned by her neighbors, on the other side, did she not drop poisonous words in their ears when she insulted them? And I cannot forgo establishing an analogy with the way Claudius murdered his brother, King Hamlet, by dropping poison in his ear; and how then the ghost of the king further drops poisonous words in the ears of his son by burdening him with knowledge he cannot endure and that debars him from existence (Cavell 2012). No doubt the story I just recounted hints at ordinary tragedies.

Third, it should strike us how ordinary the issues at stake are: draining rainwater; respecting properties; being robbed; having to deal with unwanted neighbors; jealousy; family responsibilities. The kind of problem the aunt has with zombies (having to face the menace of unfamiliar and hostile forces that sneaked into her peaceful garden) cannot be separated from the kinds of problems she is having in her life as a whole. My point relates to forms of becoming and their varying intensities within the ordinary, but of course it depends on which conception of the ordinary we rely upon. One can view the ordinary as the site of habit and routine, a sort of dull space in which the mere repetition of days can be perceived as reassuring or threatening, but that is, in either case, quotidian in an eventless flow of time. Yet, ordinary life might also be understood as that which is the most difficult to achieve and dwell in. From this perspective, the numbing and toxic effects of repetition are not considered anomalous as such, but are part of the very condition in which we live our lives. There would be no escape: Each flight being in itself part of reality, yet symptomatic of the difficulty of living in it. In either case, the ordinary would bear the traces of previous transformations, therefore enabling change to varying degrees. Thus, forms of becoming would be inherent in the everyday (and not dependent on, say, fantasy or artistic sublimation), regardless of the fact that they are at times perceived as "silent transformations," to borrow a phrase from François Jullien (2011), or as a brutal conversion. The ordinary is the site of movements growing and declining, rousing and sedating, thriving and shriveling, or "waxing" and "waning," as Bhrigupati Singh (2015) puts it. And this is something we hear more than we see.

Fourth, an important aspect of the hearing or listening to within ordinary life is that it brings to the fore the creative and destructive forces at play, each containing in its own movement the opposite force. If a creative thrust is also one of undoing, a destructive impulse equally renews. In that sense, zombies are signs of both an annihilating and a generative power. Would they then be heralding a potential destructive force, but also inviting to avoid it? Through resonance, we would hear not only what happens, but also an announcement of what is coming and becomes. This is not merely seen. A focus on the rhythms and magnitudes of the forms of life people inhabit would enable us to sense their specific quality in terms of a tendency toward suffocation or breath, hurly-burly or harmony, dissonance or accord. We would get a sense of something teeming, or swarming "on the surface of great depth," as the poet André du Bouchet aptly writes (2011, 53). Something is sensed that is heard rather than seen, which indicates the sort of dynamic of "what comes"—is it a swarm of killer bees or just a bunch of flies? Is it a crowd ready to kill or a harmless gathering of nervous neighbors? The question of recognizing "what comes" and "what becomes" is at the same time a question of the forms of our agreements and disagreements. Through the ear we can perceive the potential corrosive forces revealed by

these sounds (e.g., forces eroding the relationships among neighbors or causing an aunt to become sick), but also the empowering effects of being disposed to lending an ear in such a way (kin ties are strengthened, family
members may take care of the neighbors' concerns on behalf of the aunt,
the aunt may be prompted to apologize, and so forth).

Fifth, it is interesting that there are ambiguous and divergent feelings
about what is going on. One may feel the possibility, as Frédéric did, that
all this fuss about the neighbors sending *zonbi* could actually turn out to
be nothing more than a product of the old woman's anxiety and fear of
others, her paranoia. It is as if Frédéric also sensed the potential danger
that folktales can become fancies that distract us from the issues at stake
or that relieve us of the responsibility to think and justify ourselves. Indeed, tales are certainly very creative moments in people's ordinary lives
and may help to articulate and make the issues intelligible, but there is a
point at which they can become a seductive fantasy that prevents someone
from recognizing and taking action on a problem (Bubandt 2014; Motta
2023). There exists an internal critique by the Haitians themselves toward
folktales; some see them as decoys that distract us from forms of violence
that ask to be acknowledged.[12] Whereas Bwa Gede and his wife readily
took at face value the accusations of the aunt and somehow fed her rancor,
Frédéric was much more cautious and wary of any hasty, conclusive judgment. He eventually visited the accused neighbors, not to openly talk
about the issues between them and his aunt, but just to have a casual conversation to get a sense of who they had become since he left the valley
more than twenty years ago.

Sixth, if I now draw an analogy with the reality of dreams, a reality
sometimes made of signals possibly announcing or inaugurating different
paths one could take in life, then the symptoms of the presence of *zonbi*
could be perceived as giving a certain quality, a particular color, a certain
inflection to a situation, and thus trigger certain kinds of responses rather
than others. But signs become alive only through our reaction to them
(Wittgenstein 1986, §432). Hence, their liveliness is brought about in one's
highlighting of aspects, which leads to developments of real-life events that
fit, or not, the interests of the persons involved. This is where a certain
amount of tension arises. Thus, the question of the intelligibility of such a
reality is indeed to some extent an epistemological question, but it is more
precisely an aesthetical question in that it asks what the quality is of what is

perceived (and not so much whether the "thing" is there or not, present or absent); and it is unescapably also an ethical problem in that it involves a response.

Seventh, being responsive implies a work of interpretation of what a life with zombies is, which the Haitians themselves are doing all the time. I mean interpretation in Wittgenstein's sense, namely, as seeing an aspect of something, seeing something *as* something (Wittgenstein 1986, 2:xi). Such work is one of perceiving details, analogies, and differences; capturing ambiance; picking up the indications therein; and being disposed to receiving signals. The work is one of adapting modes of perceiving aspects according to the context in which they are inserted. In that sense, it is not a problem of applying a grid or passing reality through a sieve. The interpretation does not consist of an act of decoding a riddle, "but of finding for its aspects the right context, the backdrop that is the ground on which the perplexity will dissolve" (Chauviré 2016, 44). Indeed, all these features—the fact that the zombies enter the scene in the midst of a dispute (of very earthly and human affairs); the fact that they are not merely seen but heard, that they actually needn't be met or directly faced; and the fact that their acoustic presence incites the aunt and the family to take some positive steps toward a resolution of the conflict—give the concept of the zombie a certain physiognomy (or shall I say musicality?) that is quite different from, say, the zombies seen as disfigured cannibals brainlessly and relentlessly creeping toward their victims.[13] If one fails to see the relation between the aunt's claim that there were zombies in her backyard and the fact that the conflicts with the neighbors hints at the small deaths at the core of her quotidian life (forms of baseness, meanness, cowardliness, exclusion, abandonment, and so on), then one might miss the alienating nature of these conflicts. One might also miss what the aunt's claim of noticing zombies roaming around at night in her private garden may tell us about the mode in which she perceived the conflicts (i.e., the mode of intrusion and predation), and how they can slowly corrode a home, pervade one's intimacy, and haunt one's nights. One would be to some extent aspect-blind or tone-deaf to the aunt's problems in life if one could not experience the meaning of the word *zonbi* (Wittgenstein 1986, II:xi)—that is, one would fail to perceive "something as a *zonbi*." What if one were incapable of experiencing the meaning of the word in such a way that one would not perceive how it reveals the decaying of one's home (it has already been infected by deadly forces), or how it is announcing or warning of a possible worsening of the situation and a deterioration of what one loves (one's garden, home, and relationships)? "Could there be human beings lacking in the capacity to see something as something—and what would that be like? What sort of consequences would it have?" (ibid., II:xi).

Finally, this means that the question of how we experience a word (and thus how we live with the concept) becomes a question of the spirit in which words are meant. When Frédéric asked me if I heard anything strange and then added that his aunt had zombies in her compound, I might not have understood what he meant if I did not comprehend the relation between his expression and the kinds of issues at stake. His was an expression of someone very concerned about a loved one, someone worried for a relative but at the same time clearheaded; he was very well aware of how fast things can worsen in such a context. At stake is our own "spirit in which we imagine these words said and meant" (Cavell 1999, 380). It may be that we, non-Haitians, were held captive of a certain picture of the zombie, and more generally a certain picture of knowledge. Hence, it is not only experience that is called for in order to broaden our conception of what a *zonbi* is for Frédéric, his aunt, and his family, as well as in the Haitian context; our imagination of the possible uses of words in new contexts is also needed in order for the concept to be modified (ibid., 345). We can call this our learning to broaden our form of life.

NUANCES IN THE CONCEPTUAL LANDSCAPE

What is called a *zonbi*, and when, can vary considerably. One can call a *zonbi* a respectable woman in a church, members of the government, or the signs of an imminent threat. One can also call *zonbi* the prisoners broken by their languishing in jails (Danticat 2002; Penier 2013); cloistered dissident intellectuals totally paralyzed by their fear of capture by the state police[14]; subjugated young domestic servants whose lives peter out before adulthood[15] (Frankétienne 2018; Glover 2005; 2010); abused women secluded in their silence (Chancy 1997; Danticat 2015a; Jean-Charles 2014; Sanon 2001); or people whose dreams, imagination, and thoughts have been bottled up (Depestre 2017). Cyclones, for instance, are also said to have zombifying effects when, after having destroyed the plantations and demolished all material goods, they leave behind a crowd of hungry homeless (Fignolé 2012; Lucas 2004). In all sorts of contexts, *zonbi* can be used to insult, accuse, critique an oppressive system, describe a condition, spread rumors, refer to fate, produce stereotypes, free oneself from stereotypes, raise consciousness,[16] create wealth, predate, or do harm.

For example, take Elizabeth McAlister's account (2012). During fieldwork in Port-au-Prince, she found herself in an odd situation, accidentally buying from a *bòkò* a colorfully decorated rum bottle containing two captive *zonbi*—a charm housing "fragments of human soul" (ibid., 462) that were extracted from some dead people in order "to enhance luck, wealth and health" (ibid., 463). Or, consider Haitian-born novelist Edwidge Danticat (2002, 69–70), who recalled the day her Tante Denise woke her up one morning "to listen to the radio as an announcer reported that a few dozen zombies had been found wandering the northern hills of the country in a semicomatose state and that their loved ones should come to claim them and take them home" (ibid., 69). But "like many people, Tante Denise had concluded that these found zombies were actually former political prisoners . . . who were so mentally damaged by dictatorship-sponsored torture that they had become either crazy or slow. Tante Denise, like many others, had doubted that any relatives would go and get them, for fear of being locked up themselves" (ibid., 70).

Here we are confronted with very different scenarios. The difference matters between, say, a Western scholar recounting her unplanned purchase of *zonbi* spirits entrapped in a receptacle, and a Haitian writer recalling the peculiar feeling she experienced as a child that something was not quite right with adults who, having to deal with the reintegration into the civil society of former political prisoners destroyed by the Duvalier regime, would abandon them to their own fate. These are not occurrences of the same thing; neither are they different examples illustrating the same problem. And yet, in both cases we speak of zombies.

The fact that a word keeps occurring in many different contexts does not give us reasons to assume that there is a common feature to all these cases (or one would have to answer on what ground one has this assumption). As Wittgenstein warns us: "Don't say: 'there must be anything common' . . . but look and see" (1986, §66). He appeals to our attentiveness to what is there before us. When we go from one situation to another, "much that is common is retained, but much is lost . . . similarities crop up and disappear. And the result of the examination is: we see a complicated network of similarities overlapping and crisscrossing: sometimes overall similarities, sometimes similarities of detail" (ibid., §66). Hence, "in order to see more clearly, here as in countless similar cases, we must focus on the details of what goes on; must look at them from close to" (ibid., §51).

Being attentive to the details and the nuances means notably being sensitive to our conceptual life. When Frédéric asked me if I had heard anything strange, or when he told me he tried to stay up late to hear the *zonbi*, he drew my attention to something out there in the world that mattered to him: a cracking noise from the ceiling, a swoosh of air, stealthy footsteps on the rooftop, a rustling in the bush, a breath on one's back, a hoot behind the window, a remote and hushed drumming, a rumor circulating in the village. Frédéric was somehow telling me that there might be a moment when these signs became signs of something that was not quite right, the signal of a kind of threat that would trigger a response. This howl or that bellow, in such and such circumstances, is not exactly a usual howl or bellow, and it will make one act differently. Hence, one realizes (in the double sense of "becoming aware" and of "making it happen") an internal conceptual possibility of a form of life: This crunching sound of the gravel could indeed be made by a wandering dog, a goat, or someone crossing the garden to reach home, yet something indicates that it could also be something of another nature—this peculiar inflection of the sound, at that very moment, could be heralding a threat, a *zonbi*.

Frédéric, Bwa Gede, and the others, forge from within their lives concepts such as "*zonbi*," "human wickedness," or "neighbor." Then, it is not only my perception as a foreigner that is modified, or say, educated, by what they draw my attention toward, but also my very understanding of what is going on, how things and events are related, and "what I am to expect when" an event arises; all that is an understanding of how concepts relate to each other in this context. To be able to perceive and reflect upon resemblances and differences between various aspects of something, between the various situations and circumstances of its occurrence, is as much an experiential problem as it is a conceptual one. But "the extension of the concept is not closed by a frontier," Wittgenstein says (1986, §68). "We do not know the boundaries because none have been drawn" (ibid., §69); even though "we can draw a boundary—for a special purpose."

The law is an example of a domain where conceptual boundaries are drawn indeed, and for a special purpose. For instance, the new Penal Code disclosed on June 24, 2020, writes in art. 281:

> The administration to a person of substances likely to induce a momentary or prolonged state of lethargy, or to cause lasting impairment of mental or psychic faculties, is punishable by fifteen (15) to twenty (20) years' imprisonment.
>
> The offence is punishable by twenty (20) to thirty (30) years' imprisonment where the death of the person has been declared to a civil registrar and that person, after burial, has been identified and recognized as a person [subsequently found alive] occasionally present or living in the home of a person with whom he or she may or may not be related (my translation).

In an article published in *Le Nouvelliste* on January 14, 2019, Haitian anthropologist Laënnec Hurbon cites a passage of an earlier draft of the text, where witchcraft is supposedly mentioned and defined as follows: "Witchcraft is, among other things, 'the act of shedding one's human skin and adopting any other form of one's choice, most often that of a flying or crawling animal or the act of drinking human blood, eating human flesh or transforming human beings into the form of an animal.'" He says he has discussed it with Jean Rénel Sénatus, the author of the law in question (as well as a member of the commission sent to Benin), and cautioned him: "I told him that if I were him, I'd be very careful: a penal code article on witchcraft would require further research and would have unexpected effects." Whether or not his advice had been taken into account, this part was finally removed from art. 281, which ends up sticking to a more rationalist formulation of the norm. Interestingly, what remains is really the reference to zombification, and leaves aside what could have been associated with the *lougawou*.

If one goes back a bit, the law of 1935 against *les pratiques supersticieuses*, abrogated by the new Haitian Constitution of March 1987 (coinciding with the fall of the Duvalier dictatorship), had defined a particular conception of superstition. If the ordinary concept of *zonbi* is a blurred concept embedded in the daily life of Haitians, serving at times to describe relational distortions between neighbors or kin, address forms of madness, make sense of an unsolved murder, or distance oneself from loathsome people, it is also a normative concept partly shaped by the Penal Code.[17] There are various legislative sections that throughout Haiti's legal history tie the (unnamed) concept of "zombie" to other concepts such as "fines" and "penalties," which also means that there are politically justified and judicially approved sanctions against the creation of zombies; the state thereby shows its mode of governance and the kind of nation it strives for, one in which certain kinds of zombies have no place. These laws also show how concepts can be restricted, for instance when they reduce zombification to poisoning. In the 1883 version of *Les codes haïtiens annotés*, art. 249 of the "Law on Crimes, Offense and their Punishment," entitled "Murder, Assassination, Parricide, Infanticide, and Poisoning," reads: "is also considered attempt on life by poisoning the use made against a person of substances which, without giving death, will cause a more or less prolonged state of lethargy, regardless of the manner in which these substances were used and regardless of the consequences." Additionally, "If the person was buried as a consequence of this state of lethargy, the attempt will be considered a murder." This excerpt about the illegality of burying someone alive can be read as going along with art. 306, which forbids and punishes the profanation of tombs. Yet, a problem arises when people are unaware of when they do bury a person still alive, a situation that is at the heart of Depestre's novel, *Hadriana in All My Dreams* (2017).

The Penal Code does not, for instance, take into account the zombie as a descriptive category of a particular health state that is due not to poisoning, but, say, incest or rape (which I will discuss at the end of this chapter). One could have imagined a subparagraph on these matters in the section of the Penal Code devoted to sexual harassment and domestic violence. There is also a very interesting legal problem that has been debated in the commission charged with revising the criminal law (the group that visited Benin): A person cannot die twice. The problem with people who were legally declared dead and buried and who returned to their families is not only that of their legal status, but that, at some point, they will die a second time; and it is legally inconceivable to produce a second death record for someone who is already dead in the regard of the law. Not to mention the cascading problems that arise from this: How do you deal with a "zombie" who commits a crime? Can someone who has died and returned marry? And what about inheritance rights once the deceased has come back to claim her due?

It seems that our whole conception of law is starting to tatter; or is it rather its premises that need to be revised?

THE VAGUENESS OF CONCEPTS, THE VAGUENESS OF LAW

By stitching the concept of zombie to other concepts, the law reshapes and normalizes the landscape through which one thinks of such issues. In that sense, it can be said to draw clear boundaries of concepts. Yet, law is also necessarily vague. Even more so, vagueness is as intrinsic to law as it is to concepts (law being itself a concept). It is important to say, at this stage, that a widespread tradition of thinking, however heterogeneous, has bequeathed us a certain view of what concepts are and how they work, and which has ended up dominating our epistemologies.[18] Roughly, this view goes as follows: Concepts are abstractions which allow, if correctly applied, the construction of precise and meaningful statements about reality. In other words, concepts are seen as abstract representations of objects, or signifiers, under which a certain number of terms can be pooled, and whose rules of application provide a kind of classification of things. Concepts are thought as if they were pigeonholes in which objects can be put according to a certain logic, the idea being that objects await to be put into classes.[19] In that sense, concepts are thought to be names attached to objects, and thus not only represent reality, but also order it by unlocking the hidden meaning behind diverse and disparate objects. And to do so, they need to be precise and unequivocal. Hence, they are considered necessary because they're what renders reality intelligible and organizable in a certain way. They are of particular interest to scholars (since scholasticism) precisely because they enable analysis, which leads to the discovery of truth, and, consequently, gives authority to those who master them—they authorize you to speak the truth and impose a certain vision of the order of things (we can see here just how attractive this concept of the concept is to promoters of the rule of law). Concepts, indeed, are imagined to be noble objects of thought (like God, law, nature, or society), whereas common, everyday terms are considered second-order, low class, unhandsome (like chairs, plowing, or puppets)—they would actually not be concepts at all and thus not worthy of interest.

I have five remarks at this point. According to this perspective, (1) concepts function like names; (2) concepts are predicated on their truth value;

(3) concepts must be defined, and their boundaries delineated, as precisely as possible (otherwise they are not concepts); (4) using concepts correctly leads to a proper, well-constructed and logical language, which implies that; (5) ordinary language is considered improper, ill-constructed, and unsound. It is seen as what comes in the way and gives us false impressions. It is considered imperfect and unclear, which is why it cannot represent reality correctly; it is also what betrays us. Hence, ordinary language is conceived as an obstacle that must be overcome (by the construction of concepts). In sum, there is little room for indeterminacy in this conception of the concept (let alone the fact that such a view despises ordinary language). Even though some contemporary versions, like in legal theory and fuzzy logics, attempt to acknowledge, and reckon with, the vague and indeterminate character of concepts, they nonetheless stick to the idea that concepts are abstractions that hover above reality and are that which give us the means to represent it correctly; and the standard remains truth-value anyway. So, is there room for another way of thinking of what concepts are and what they do?

If one looks back now at how the concept of the zombie moves and changes according to varying uses, how it is projected in so many different contexts (yet not unlimited), we can see that it has not much to do with representation, truth-value, naming, and classification, let alone analysis. Rather, it is what is revealed within our practices. The concept starts becoming an issue precisely when reality puts pressure on us, and something demands to be thought; only then does a concept start to appear. Concepts like "zombie" already have a life, so to say, over which we have very little control, contrariwise to the view that gives full authority to whom arrogates to herself the right to claim a mastery over the formation of concepts (which may be the legislator). We are no more the creators of the concept of "zombie" than we are the creators of the concept of "threat," "doubt," "neighbor," or "patience." We inherit them because we inherit a whole form of life in which they already have a place, and a texture (Das 2020). What we do is learn to live with concepts in particular contexts, which address themselves to us in any number of ways. They do not hover above reality, but are down-to-earth, common, humble, indeed inherent to ordinary language. They are embedded in the people's lives, embodied in what humans say and do. That also means that they are not intermediaries between us and reality; they replace and represent nothing. They are just what they are when they appear. Nothing more, nothing less. If you expect from concepts that they give you a piece of reality, you have misunderstood what a concept is (Benoist 2013). The expectation is misleading because it asks concepts to do what they are not entitled to do. What the examples show is that concepts do not have the sharp edges some would like them to have. No concept has perfectly defined boundaries. Moreover, vagueness and opacity are, more often than not, precisely what a concept needs in order to be what it is and to do what it is meant to do: allow for projections into new contexts, creative uses, play, and experimentation.

Yet, I do not wish to deny that concepts are also to some extent "inflexible," or, let's say, that there is an inner "constancy" in our language that does not tolerate all uses in all contexts. This is the effect of the normativity of our language (Benoist 2013; Cavell 1999; Laugier 2009; Mulhall 2003). But this is precisely what is so much underscored by scholars, whereas my point here is to underlie the "concept's essential flexibility, its capacity to elicit new reaches of significance from itself, from those who use it, and from the contexts it proves capable of inhabiting" (Mulhall 2014, 309). "So the claim is not that law is necessarily obscure or radically indeterminate. The claim is that a legal system necessarily yields a significant range of 'borderline cases'—cases in which the application of the standards of the law is subject to doubt and disagreement" (Endicott 2001, 379). Certain legal norms in particular evade the demand for determination of the rule of law, since they neither apply nor fail to apply to borderline cases such as, say, a person reclaiming her inheritance after her duly recorded death. In fact, "their open texture cannot be sharpened to a univocal statement of what they require: they are indeterminate, leaving borderline cases where judges lack legal resources to resolve a dispute one way or another" (Culver 2004, 109). It therefore leaves it up to the judge's discretion whether or not "to extend or withhold a particular law purported to govern a particular situation" (ibid., 111). That is to say that the laws themselves seem to generate situations in which there is no obvious way to determine if and how a particular law applies or not, and that the key to a possible resolution lies outside law. The common response to this in law is generally to attempt to give fuzzy concepts sharp edges, as if in being clearer and more precise we would get rid of indeterminacy. Of course, then, one will have to reckon with the fact that each new determination produces its own indeterminacies. Try to define, and more vagueness will follow. This is unsettling for the defenders of the rule of law, who are "disrupted by the suggestion that judges reach to something other than the particular law at hand to decide a borderline case" (ibid., 111). The requirements of an ideal of rule of law make it hard to imagine what lies outside of its grasp.

The question of the boundary of the concept of zombie can be remodeled from many other corners. In 1950, in a response to Depestre and Louis Aragon, who appealed to the use of traditional forms to feed their poetic thrust, Aimé Césaire invented a neologism, the verb *"marronner,"* "to maroon" (Césaire 2000; N. Roberts 2015, 5–6). This verb is nowadays very commonly used in the Artibonite Valley. For Césaire, it meant flight from the plantations and escape from the alienation induced by slavery, to gain a capacity to act upon one's own will, to resist foreign domination, to reclaim agency and rights over one's body and community, and, thereby, avoid being "thingified." In his *Discourse on Colonialism*, Césaire famously counterattacked: "My turn to state an equation: colonization = 'thingification.'" Now, as one can sense, marooning means something like "to avoid being 'zombified.'" We could reverse all the features above and have this possible definition of zombification: to lose one's capacity for action, to lose one's will, to be unable to escape or to flee, to surrender, to become the property of someone else, to become a "thing" half alive and half dead.

So, one can draw boundaries, blur them, and redraw others over them. For that matter, they are drawn for the purpose of law enforcement and state governance, as much as for the purpose of anti-colonial struggles. But that boundaries can be drawn under certain circumstances does not imply that the concept is bounded. The legal definition has no grasp over the reach of the concept of "zombie," no more than Césaire's sharp reformulation. It is therefore not dependent on its definitions but has, one may say, a life of its own; and the life of the zombie is very different if one looks at law, a Vodou healing ceremony aiming at bringing a madman back to normal life, imagines the particular weight of the slave history on contemporary feelings of dispossession, or reads women novelists describing their condition as silenced beings.

HAVING A HUMAN LIFE TO LEAD

To end this chapter, I would like to turn to a short story written by Barbara Sanon (2001), who depicts a region of human experience not usually associated with zombification: rape.[20] There is something we expect, something almost obvious, in the forms of death suddenly brought to light when, for instance, political prisoners who were rotting in the torture chambers of Fort Dimanche[21] are released or escape, or when under labor exploitation people become so exhausted that their hypertrophied fatigue turns them into apathetic beings. There is something to point at, wounds one can see, and grand political causes to defend or fight against that unleash speech and give legitimacy to indignation. But there is also a less spectacular, more silent form of death lodged at the heart of many homes. There are generations of women and children who have been abused by loved ones, relatives, or neighbors.

Sanon opens a window into the world of these countless girls who would have their head down and their eyes lowered, who decided that they were dead without the adults around them realizing it. These are stories "that could only be told through silences too horrific to disturb" (2001, 45). In the story these girls call themselves zombies without saying the word aloud, "who in the midst of the endless political discussions on right or wrong [were] not allowed to disclose the bad things [they] swallowed" (ibid., 45). They "were dumped deeper in their coffins by adults who were supposed to have been safeguarding them" (ibid., 46). And in some cases, the zombie state is passed on from one generation to another: "a matriarchal line of silence" (ibid., 47), ending "with [the] mothers washing, bleaching, even boiling [the] panties in order to make their husbands, their cousins, their lovers, their own judges, their military officers, seem clear" (ibid., 47). These little girls told themselves tales where they "were taken by evil spirits and never seen again until they returned as skeletons, walking, tiptoeing, dancing with their families' lies" (ibid., 47).

Sanon's story, along with Danticat's (2015a), depicts how the slow and sinister progression of silence passed on from generation to generation can become life-threatening, but also seen as a force, a mode of enduring a life dispossessed from oneself, a life subjugated to others' desires. It shows the moment when a form of life becomes toxic, and when the ordinary is equated with repression, squeezing, and impairment.

Now, returning to our initial inquiry, how different does this question of giving a realistic account of these matters sound? As I hope to have shown, the depth of such a question lies not so much in the epistemological endeavor it arouses, or the methodological reflections it gives birth to, as in the texture of our responses to how people live or destroy their lives.

In closing, I would like to suggest, following Cora Diamond, that the issue of realism is tied to something about being sensitive to our "having a human life to lead" (1991a, 48). Indeed, when the Haitian senators sought advice from the Beninese on how to reform the criminal law bequeathed by the French colonizers so that it addresses indigenous issues for which the law was not originally written; when the peasants, who are despised by the ruling class, return the accusation against them; when some communities bury the dead body of a loved one upside down; when women insult each other for peanuts; when disillusioned and worried young men debate about counterintuitive ways of knowing; when children scare each other in the dark alleys and run for their lives; or when writers give shape to the forms of death women have to endure—we are dealing with what it means to be human. But what kind of human life does one lead, and in what kind of world? To what extent do our ways of living depend on what we expect from life, what we imagine possible, and how serious we consider our dreams or nightmares to be? Correlatively, how does all that which we do not know, expect, want, imagine, or long for still make its way into our lives?

If we anthropologists are sensitive to and feel concerned about the issue of rightness of our accounts, then we may want to find a way of being capable of imagining differently the lives we encounter in our fields. What, then, are our responses to having to lead such lives, "to what we find strange or dark or marvelous in [them]"? (Diamond 1991c, 48). In a way, the question of realism is related to "the awakened sense of one's own humanity" (ibid., 50) as well as to "the sense of one's own mortality" (ibid., 51). If one thinks of how people describe some sorts of *zonbi* as "being barely human," it seems to me that, in some of its occurrences, "*zonbi*" could be understood as the name given to what is left from a human being—or from a human life—after it has been crushed and torn to pieces by violence; and by extension, it would also name what is left from a society after its mutilation. Yet, in other circumstances, "*zonbi*" is just a very ordinary way to insult someone perceived as a fool.

I hope to have shown how anthropological practice is at the same time an experience and a conceptual investigation. Let me finish by emphasizing the ethical dimension of our work. If in this chapter I emphasized the importance of thinking of the kind of realism at stake in our accounts, it was in response to my sense that we still strive for a language that would reckon with our imaginative sensibility to "what is mysterious in human life" (Diamond 1991c, 40). And, in Diamond's words, "the sense of mystery surrounding our lives, the feeling of solidarity in mysterious origin and uncertain fate: this binds us to each other, and the binding meant includes the dead and the unborn, and those who bear on their fates 'a look of blank idiocy,' those who lack all power of speech, those behind whose vacant eyes there lurks a 'soul of mute eclipse'" (ibid., 56).

During Mardi Gras, one can come across Chaloska, a character who mimics Charles Oscar Etienne, a former military commander in charge of the police in Jacmel. He is known to have slaughtered around five hundred political prisoners in 1915. Soon after, President Vilbrun Guillaume Sam fell, and the Americans invaded Haiti. To confront their fear of this threatening character marching down the roads with a huge red mouth and protruding teeth, Haitian kids utter a mantra: "Chaloska, *m pa pè w, se moun w ye*" ("Chaloska, I'm not afraid of you. I know you're a human being").

Zombies are sometimes political prisoners, the likes of which had once been locked up and then killed by Charles Oscar Etienne. They are also sometimes just carnival characters. And if one is afraid, one may just want, as Edwidge Danticat did, to put one's hand on the zombie's back and learn to whisper: "Zombie, I'm not afraid of you. I know you're a human being."

6

THE MURMURING STREAM OF LIFE

"But this presence of death in life,
this non-life of a people fighting for its future,
can we finally talk about it?"

—LYONEL TROUILLOT[1]

"Where do we find ourselves?"

—RALPH WALDO EMERSON

"How should we have found ourselves
when we have never looked for ourselves?"

—FRIEDRICH NIETZSCHE

"A philosophical problem has the form:
'I don't know my way about.'"

—LUDWIG WITTGENSTEIN

Shortly before the crack of dawn, I appear on the front porch. The stars are still peeking over the mountains. The roosters' crows, which lasted through the night, are now competing with the barks of the stray dogs and the chirps of the many birds that have found a home in this fertile valley. These will later be joined by the crackling of the fires that will soon burn in the hearths, the clattering of the dishes that the mothers will begin to wash, the loud cries of the hordes of children running to school, and the distant bustle emanating from the central market. For now, however, most humans are still asleep.

I was planning to go and train as I usually do in the morning, but the air is brisk—too brisk. January is almost over; winter has settled in, even in Haiti. I get back into bed as fast as I got out of it.

It's early afternoon when I finally get to the gym. There is nobody there. The gate is locked. It is January indeed, but the Caribbean sun is warm; it's hot enough during these hours for Haitians to avoid the open-air gym on which the sun hits hard. I take the gate key hidden in a slot in the mud hut on which the gate is affixed. I assume the gym-goers won't mind if I take it.

The gym is located under a couple of trees with scattered foliage, nestled between two family compounds (*lakou*) and a wasteland. A few rusty machines have been brought back from the United States, but most of the devices are homemade. These are chiefly composed of recycled gear-wheels, heavy bolts, iron bars, building blocks, and concrete moldings. One of the *lakou* is a Vodou compound (*oumfò*), composed of houses for the family members (*kay*) and houses for the spirits (*badji*). The small portion of land on which the gym was built is adjacent to one of the *badji*. A young man of the *vodouizan* family opened the gym as his little business after he came back from North America; he charges 250 *goud*—about $3.20 at the time—for one year of membership.

Some neighbors are relaxing in the shade at the back of the mud hut. A woman is braiding the hair of a young girl; a couple of men are boozing up with *tafia* (local rum). The drunkard who always hangs around is there, too. I come across the man almost every time I go to the gym. At best, he tugs his swaying body here and there, but never too far, or else he strains to contain its turmoil when he sits chatting, or lays in the shade, navigating his inner swells. His sweating, puffy face harbors a foolish smile from which a hoarse and greasy voice emerges. I hardly understand his words, constantly on the brink of drowning in his mouth. When I do, it ticks me off; he cannot but say stupid things and insult me, as if he were given the mission to harass me. He doesn't like me; I don't like him either. I avoid him as much as I can. However, there is no need for that today; he did not notice me. He seems quite alive, but inattentive to his surroundings, intermittently joking and swearing loudly between moments of alcoholic absorption.

I do my exercises. At some point, something changes. The drunken man leaves the small group and lurches slowly toward a coffin resting just on the other side of the fence. The wasteland serves as an outdoor workshop for carpenters who craft wood and manufacture all kinds of objects, among them funerary boxes.

I watch the man from close by, but he still does not notice me. He is casting a vacant look upon his steps. Withdrawn into himself, he saunters with a somnambulant pace toward his resting place. When he stood up, he did so unexpectedly and left at once without his bottle; his mood appeared to have changed in an instant, as if something important inside of him had suddenly bobbed to the surface. As he moves, it seems as though he has suddenly been called upon to follow a route only he is aware of. The neighbors just let him roam; so there he trudges, hesitantly—no doubt because of his heavy inebriation—but still with an odd conviction I cannot fathom. After several unsuccessful and laborious attempts, he finally creeps up into the casket and lies down quietly.

The unfinished box is a simple four-sided trapezoid, almost a rectangle. It lies on trestles, so that the craftsmen can work properly while standing. There is a slight slope, which makes the structure not quite level and a little unsteady. It so happens that on this day the larger base (for the shoulders of the future corpse) is facing down.

The man lies silently confined between the panels. Sometimes an elbow or a leg protrudes when he feels the need to put a hand on his face or bend a knee. At some point, the woman braiding the girl's hair goes lazily to have a quick look inside the casket. The men shout that she should just let him be. She returns to the group.

Several times the man moans, and says unconvincingly, in a muffled and resigned tone, as if to himself, "help me." It looks like he wants to sleep, but is restless, struggling with something that stirs in him. He is constantly interrupted by weak jolts. He repeatedly starts by saying, "hel . . ." but then his words end up mired in his soaked throat. The agitation grows. I can barely see him in the box but can hear his voice emerging as an echo of despair. I guess that he didn't anticipate that in such a position, the liquid in his stomach would flow back, and his blood would quickly accumulate in his brain. In his current state, he will not withstand this very long. Still, the moaning ends. He finally falls asleep. After a short while though, he wakes up and painstakingly straightens his back, but cannot get out of the coffin. He calls for help again. Nobody responds to his call. I am about to go over and give him a hand when a young lady passes by and very naturally stops; she gently scolds him as she would scold a child who climbed up a tree from which he can't get down on his own, asking kindheartedly why he had put himself in such a position. She helps him out and leaves; he joins the drinking men again.

A DEATH-DEALING VISION

This image of terrifying and surrealist beauty haunted me for months. Yet, this image is not fixed; it's moving. The cinematic quality of its movement— let's say, of the memory I have of it, as if memory were less in pictures than in scenes—shows quite naturally that ephemeral gestures, fleeting attitudes, and the postures of human bodies have their own expressiveness, say their own poetry. And that this poetry, this human expressivity, however fleeting, is worth studying is precisely a matter of aesthetics, of an *ordinary* aesthetics that is, after all, the anthropologist's daily bread—except that we do not always have a sense of the importance of such a study. In such cases, nothing can show us the value of such observation unless we discover it through our own experience, in the tenacious exercise of our taste and, therefore, in the way our current tastes are put to the test, including our disgust by or aversion to what appears at first glance to be morally deplorable, even contemptible. On the contrary, it's in our encounters with the minute details of other people's lives that we cultivate our interest in the world and a certain taste for intellectual adventure.

The scene kept bubbling up and stuck around my mind as something that stood in need of a response. This text is just that—my response—which took the form of a meditation on what it is to live up to one's finitude in a world that may already seem dead. This landscape of dwindled vitality that bears countless traces of combats slowly became the backdrop against which the aspects of the other stories I recount in this book become salient.

As readers will have noticed, each chapter is marked in one way or another by the theme of death. My reflections on law and justice themselves can be said to stem from reflections on what it is to be alive, to be a living human being within a community or society. And for good reason: It's only humans with language who can ask the questions they have about the rules of conduct, social organization, or how to settle a conflict and imagine what it's like to follow a rule, break it, subvert it, bend it, or invent new ones. But can they imagine what life would be like without organization, without rules, without law, without justice? Wouldn't that be like imagining death?

Is that imaginable? What's for sure, the questions raised by what it means and takes to be alive in a community is pressured by the vicinity of death. In Chapter 1, a massacre, and the echoes of countless others, prompt people to react to their reverberation in their ordinary lives. In Chapter 2, the partly improvised and cautious search for a settlement is stimulated by a certain vision of the catastrophic consequences of a murder. In Chapter 3, it's war whose duplicitous face prompts local communities to find other ways of responding to its devastating effects. In Chapter 4, the fact that law is embodied in our practices makes it subject to as much violence and mortal impulse as we, as humans, display. And in Chapter 5, concerns about the adequacy of state law to local realities are rooted in the sharp perception that life-within-death is not only possible, but must be thought of from a legal point of view. Hence, law and justice can only be seriously thought of in close relation to thinking about death.

That's why I'd like to end this book with a chapter that makes way for a meditation on the mortal condition of human beings. Haitians educated my gaze and sharpened my capacity to listen more carefully to these matters. I was taught, not only how to listen to "stories, songs, and specific styles of talk and recollection" (Ochoa 2010, 13), but also how to apprehend more viscerally the contiguousness and immanence of the dead in the world of the living. And so did philosophical and literary texts. Those I read emphasize the proliferation of modes by which the dead make themselves present and address us, the multiplicity of stories and speech that coexist and contradict each other. Vinciane Despret (2021), for instance, has played a decisive role in the way I allow myself to be instructed by what others say and do, particularly when it comes to caring for the dead, or, for that matter, for the living. Her method of philosophical inquiry, which consists in committing "to following things as they present themselves, hoping, in an experimental mode, to learn about their complicities and frictions" (ibid., 26), while paying close attention to the effects of the events prompted by her encounters, has inspired my anthropological approach. But to begin, let me take a cue from Stanley Cavell instead. He speaks of "the tragic character of human experience" (2022, 119), which induces "philosophy's requirement, hence I suppose that of any serious writing, to incorporate death (you might, more decorously, say finitude) into its reflections" (ibid., 119). Retrieving and reformulating an old philosophical theme, Cavell describes "philosophy as learning how to die" (ibid., 115), as learning my separateness from others, my isolation, as it were.[2] And the scene of this apprenticeship, "the scene of the recognition of one's own death" (ibid., 115), is not the philosopher's library, the salon or the academy, nor the moment of an extraordinary event, but the ordinary: The scene is in fact composed of the never-ending, repetitive, and always different scenes of the quotidian life. Faced with this man, with the vision of his death, his death in me, I was in a way contemplating the possibility of my own, perhaps my death in him. Indeed, "there is no possibility of human relationship that has not been enacted. The worst has befallen, befalls everyday. It has merely, so far as I know, not befallen me" (Cavell 1999, 432).

It appeared to me that this scene also revealed some kind of stubbornness of reality, an unstoppable murmuring stream of life that flows in the interstices between the small deaths of the ordinary. And it puts pressure on thinking.[3] Something was echoed in the repeated reappearance of this scene in my mind, or, say, in the rehearsal of its reality; something which acquired a different kind of force once I got the sense that its disgrace as much as its splendor said something about the ways that forms of death are lodged at the core of forms of life. It equally said something about how life sparks again and goes on.

When it dawned on me that this scene did not only exhibit a man's—*this* man's—death, but Haiti's death as a whole, I was reminded of Manuel's words, Greg Beckett's friend in Port-au-Prince: "'Haiti is dead,'" he said. "'There is no more Haiti'" (2019, 6). These words stuck with Beckett, and gave the title to his book. Similarly, Marvin Victor (2011, 33) wrote, "*Le pays est mort!*" "The country is dead!" On the field, I have heard many times people say things like "*Ayiti kraze!*" "Haiti has been crushed!" or "*Ayiti fini*" "Haiti is finished." Some even said, "*Yo te touye l*" "They killed it!"—as if the world had died at our hands from a violent shock. Sometimes these expressions were cynical jokes, others were expressions of people's chagrin and anger and powerlessness in the face of an excruciating situation. Out of the vision of a whole nation about to be buried grew in me an ominous sentiment of having witnessed something of great importance; and from there grew the need to investigate how my shifting sense of importance would raise something like an anthropological thinking. I described in Chapter 2 the troubling feeling that people sometimes deliberately seemed to be taking the path that would lead them toward a catastrophe already in motion, as if something in them was willfully and implacably heading toward death.

Perhaps such a vision is not unrelated to the "death-dealing vision" Cavell identifies in Poe, the "horrified vision of ordinariness, of the unremarkable other seen as just the unremarkable other" (1994, 158), a vision that becomes the subject of an investigation "of what it is to have an interest in your own experience" (1981, 7).[4] But there may however be something else; such a vision circulates within my knowledge that Haiti houses among the most lively and blazing thrusts of life I have ever witnessed. It may well be that they know something I don't about the relation between death and rebirth.

The image of that man in the grip of death also has a poetic beauty that lies in the way life insists on continuing and making its way regardless. He *is* alive; and I who am watching realize how much I am, too. Despite his declining force, he stands up once again and goes back to his life; it is not yet over. And the sudden gesture of care given by that passing girl, her evanescent gentleness, amazed me all the more when I became aware how much such a fleeting moment of attention mattered in a Haitian world on the brink of collapsing. Yet, my sense of the beauty is also captured by the fact that, if we consider that the world consists "of endlessly fragmented, messy encounters" (Puett 2017, 25), to which human beings tend to respond by creating patterned reactions, this man actually disrupts, even for a brief moment, his own patterns (his complacency in alcohol, the sepulchral repetition of his behavior, the deadening redundancy of his words). Moreover, as I take it, his act could even be seen as a refined response to the ordinary messiness, a response whose refinement, in line with Michael Puett's view, is notably realized through ritualized behavior. My sense, here, is that the man does indeed accomplish, or rehearse, something like a fine-tuned ritual act he may have seen or done on other occasions (like, for instance, in certain Vodou ceremonies where rebirth is played out by literally being laid in a coffin), and certainly witnessed many times (in funerals). The act doubtlessly was improvised on the spot, yet still ritualized. In that way, it was beautiful. "Even the corpse has its own beauty," writes Ralph Waldo Emerson (2000 [1836], 9). But perhaps, beauty is also wounding and bitter.

Now, my impression is that there is something else in this scene, which speaks to the comical register: Perhaps it was just an accident—not fate— that this man was drunk at that very moment, in that spot, and luck that there was an unfinished casket perfectly fitting his body just there. I am unsure how tragic, solemn, or somber, the act of this man is, for it seems to me that there is nonetheless also a hint of derision in his act. This aspect did not strike me at first sight, but appeared progressively only months later as I was writing and reading and making connections with other moments I experienced in Haiti. The fact that this possibility is offered to my imagination matters; I mean, that I can actually imagine this man conveying the sense that all this may just be absurd, a farce—"all this" being perhaps the natural history of the human, the "human comedy"—and that what remains for human beings in the face of death is, sometimes, perhaps, only playfulness. Indeed, "imagination is called for, faced with the other, when I have to take the facts in, realize the significance of what is going on, make the behavior real for myself, make a connection" (Cavell 1999, 354). "Taking the facts in," here, amounts to seeing this man's behavior *in a certain way*, a way that makes us see his genuine gait as a possible joke. Isn't the inattentiveness of the neighbors—as if they were bored by his schemes—telling us something about the man's tendency to act out his foolishness, and how, once again, his goofy behavior made him do silly things? We may want to be reminded here of the self-derision of which Haitians are capable, when they enact an earnest mockery in the face of death (like, for example, during the Feast of the Dead). Part of the beauty of this scene is also that it is equivocal in *that* way, as if he theatricalized himself so as to play out his dissatisfaction with the responses of others to him; which is also the unsatisfiability of the responses he provides to himself. And yet, this does not mean he is foolish nor intentionally making a joke.

This poor man is at the dusk of his earthly life. No doubt he was knocked over and broken under the duress of his times; his whole being bears the traces of all the wars he has fought. People say he won't last long; who knows? I met him again in February 2020. He seemed in better shape, even though dented by the harsh conditions of his path. There is not much one can do. This is the ordinary drama of life, and there is no consolation for our powerlessness. Now, my sense is that beyond the particularity of that moment and of that man, something broader is conveyed by his waning, dying voice, as if it spoke not only his own extinction—his proper condition of being already half way between worlds, his slow and painful drift out of mundane matters—but also made audible a more general condition of human life alongside death, perhaps the condition of a life of death among the living.[5] Being attentive to the details of that moment may tell us something about what we, human beings, do and do not endure and go through; it says something about *us*.

If we take that man seriously; if we pay attention to his way of being in the world and let him teach us the way we should look at him; if we are committed "to being guided by our experience but not dictated to by it" (Cavell 1981, 10); then we allow ourselves to be educated on matters of the world that could have eluded us. This man is all but exemplary; he may be not much more than a passerby in this earthly life, and even appear to some as an incarnation of failure. But to what extent are we ready to receive what this anonymous man has to teach us?

A MATTER OF DETAIL

I began this chapter with epigraphs that echo each other. Cavell takes Emerson's question—"Where do we find ourselves?"—to be "emblematic of a perfectionist quest for orientation" (2005a, 392). I do not quite know how the philosophical investigation triggered by such a momentum is to be translated into anthropology, but what I do know is that, as anthropologists, we have something to learn from the way in which these particular philosophers recognize their own loss. My hunch is that an anthropological problem has a comparable shape; or, let's say, its formulation has a similar sound or hue. From then on, we could say that the anthropological investigation of our forms of life begins when we lose our footing in the world and have to find our bearings again.[6] And that begins in the midst of messy details.

I tried to take Emerson's (2000 [1837]) exhortation seriously to embrace the common, explore and sit at the feet of the familiar and the low, and thus de-sublimize thought precisely there where we are inclined to feed unsatisfiable cravings, and thus disable our intelligence. I also tried to incorporate Ludwig Wittgenstein's idea of a (re)turn to the ordinary lives we live with each other, as the really important difficulty from which all other difficulties derive, and to which philosophy is liable to respond. And we may not know exactly where the common and the familiar and the low lie, nor what our ordinary lives look like exactly—indeed, Wittgenstein asks, "does what is ordinary always make the *impression* of ordinariness?" (1986, § 600).

These are the sorts of questions I believe anthropology to be concerned with. Hence, the practice of anthropology is exploratory and not merely given; it is indeed an experience, an experiment, an adventure of sorts, that may "be understood as a matter of directedness, of being on the road, on the way" (Cavell 1981, 29), through which one changes ways of seeing the world, and hence changes oneself. We search for something (don't we?), and at times it happens that we find something worthwhile; but it might just as well be that what we think we have found actually found us, as if something out there was looking for us too. The details of the stories or dreams or scenes that haunt us, then, not only shift our interests, and thus educate us about what counts for us now, but also make us take a certain path rather than another; they *direct* us.

On our paths, we move from one point to another, but we change as we move.[7] It is precisely through the transformative process implied by one's taking a direction that one may become able to make space for the small events and minor characters, and allow them to have a form, a gait, a face, a voice; say, a life. The men drinking loudly; the women braiding as usual; a certain look between them; the pace of the drunkard; a waning whine; a passerby; a gentle rebuke; a helping hand; a hearty laughter; all these details convey a certain sense of the directedness of life, of what blocks or prompts the advancement, where the vitality transpires. This is how I understand Cavell's notion of a "physiognomy of the ordinary" (1992). It is at once an ethics and aesthetics of everyday life. And "our attitude to what is alive and to what is dead is not the same" (Wittgenstein 1986, § 284). Hence, details play an essential role in finding one's footing again among the living, and thus among the dying and the dead, perhaps among the living-dead.

Now, in what way do details signal something important? I'd like to put forward the idea that details are not so much signs as signals. They are not signs in the sense that they indicate something hidden (of which the sign would be the symptom), as if they were simply the visible face of a reality not immediately accessible to us. Rather, they are signals in the sense that they "beckon," that they draw our attention to an aspect of reality not previously considered. In this sense, details alert us, and sometimes foreshadow something. The kind of anthropological realism I'm trying to put forward here (Brandel and Motta 2021; Motta 2019b), is the sharpening of our attention to what's there in front of us—and not an investigation designed to decipher clues. What's more, it is also a cultivation of a certain spirit by which we dispose ourselves to be receptive to these signals, or signal details, and to what is signaled to us through them. The world hints at certain aspects; we take cues. What then is revealed, or announced, for example, by an inflection of the voice, a gesture, an attitude?

It is characteristic of a signal that it draws attention to, marks, suggests, indicates; a signal may also arouse (interest), trigger (a reaction), motivate (change), prompt (a response), and/or spur (a turn in thinking). I am specifically interested in seeing signals as beacons for orientation. It may be that the details of the scene of that drunkard announce something that has already happened, perhaps herald something to come, and, in that movement, incite one to be responsive to reality. Yet, more importantly, these (signal) details mark a landscape in such a way that one can find orientation within it. However, there is no guarantee whatsoever that we will indeed find our way; nothing ensures us that we won't end up like Amasa Delano in Herman Melville's short story *Benito Cereno*, for despite his acute attentiveness to a remarkable amount of minute details, he does not manage to, or perhaps refuses to, see what is there just before him. Captain Delano is struck by many subtle and uncanny details and shifting moments in his encounter with Captain Cereno and the crew on board his slave ship called the *San Dominick*[8]; he notices an abundance of clues, knots, locks, keys, masks, and shadows, and continuously senses the insinuations, innuendos, undertones, allusions, and conspiring whispers behind his back, yet he remains blind to that which happened on the ship before its anchorage in the misty Santa Maria bay, part of a deserted and uninhabited island at the southern extremity of the Chilean coast. "Shadows present, foreshadowing deeper shadows to come," announces Melville in the beginning (2016, 54). Delano registers everything but does not see what is important. He is bewildered because he denies what he sees, not because he misses the relevant details. In fact, he misses nothing, but beguiles himself; he clings on to a preconceived version, and this makes him misinterpret the details that signal what is really happening on board. In other words, he is not yet ready to receive what he sees; he is not in a position of letting himself be educated by what he sees. He cannot yet allow change.

Such a risk is ours too. It is mine when I wander in Haiti's rugged landscapes. Yet, I guess there is not much more that I can do than to follow the furrows dug by previous deaths as the grounds in which people move and speak and live, and out of which they grow.

HUMAN FINITUDE AND LAUGHTER

Many details strike us and mark our knowledge of a place, a person, or a situation. Equally, many details escape us. Most will remain in the dark.

Others will start to appear progressively only later, as if their manifestation for some reason had to be delayed. For example, many details of the scene of the man lying in the coffin stuck with me and, so to say, accompanied me, without me being aware of them. Some details seem to have a life of their own, and shadow us until there is some kind of opportunity for them to come to light. Andrew Brandel (2025) speaks of the quality of details, their animacy, their vividness; there is indeed something like a vitality of certain details (not all) that does not leave us unmoved. They are thus not given once and for all. My feeling is that there is something like a teeming life of details that demands acknowledgment, and thus incentivizes an exploration of the means by which we allow these very details to come into the light.

In my case, I wasn't aware of details such as the inclination of the coffin and its effects on the man until I started to write about it, but they were there somewhere; I had recorded them in spite of myself, so to say. As Sandra Laugier puts it (2025), the appearance of significance appears "only afterwards, after words. *Little Did I Know . . .*"[9] Moreover, it feels like it was meant to be that way, as if details had waited for my readiness (my maturation?) to fully materialize. I was probably not yet ready to see, for instance, what that detail about the coffin reveals, that is, that it is no coincidence that the downward slope would not let the man rest for eternity just yet. There is a natural inclination of life, a tendency, against which one cannot go, as if there were a particular tilt, or curve, or turn of existence. One cannot go against gravity, nor against life's insistence. This is perhaps part of our natural history. This man wanted to rest; but he had to go back to his life.

One would also have to reckon with the fact that others draw our attention to something, make us notice aspects, and thus make things matter. We learn from each other to hone our perceptions. A friend and fellow anthropologist, Grégoire Hervouet-Zeiber, pointed out that there was also something absurdly comical, almost burlesque and clownish, about this drunken man lying upside down, until he almost regurgitates; something I had not seen. My friend's own experiences of inebriation during his fieldwork with war veterans in Russia (Hervouet-Zeiber 2023), and his noticing the particular way alcohol makes broken men laugh in the face of death, informed his reading of this passage in a way that actually informed my own. Indeed, my friend's remark could be added to what I've previously said, about this scene not being quite as tragic as it first appeared.

Other sorts of details dawned upon me only much later, like the peculiar pace and silence of the man as he was trudging toward the coffin. No doubt I did absorb something of it at the time, but I was not quite awake to what was happening. It made a deep impression on me; suddenly this man looked different. However, I could not relate to it or make anything explicit about it until I started this text. Only then did details like his change of attitude, the discrepancy between his general unhandsome being in this world (his grossness), and the dignity, barely perceptible, conveyed by his gait when he headed toward the casket, become relevant, for a spark was lit in this man's dead life. Hence, writing too may be a way to sharpen our sense of what matters (although it may also warp our perception).

Moreover, the fact that someone checked on the man's condition, kept track of him, is very important. And it is remarkable that it was a woman, whereas the men were roughly unconcerned. There is also the beautiful reaction of that young lady who helped the man to get back on track. These improvised acts of daily care, not really meant to be especially caring, but just carrying the sense that this is what humans do, were ungraspable moments of deep humanity. They tell us something about what buds in the interstices of devastated lives.

The man walking dumbly toward his coffin is also reminiscent of the zombie. It is a well-known fact that the Haitian landscapes and the lives of its inhabitants are imbued with powerful "mystical forces" (*fòs mistik*) and populated with creatures such as zombies (*zonbi*), werewolves (*lougawou*), and spirits of the realm of death (*gede*) (Deren 1953; Herskovits 1937; Hurbon 1979; Jordan 2016; Métraux 1972; K. Smith 2012). Haiti is also a place where unnatural deaths of many kinds occur, and thus has long been an object of fascination and contempt, as much in anthropology as elsewhere. Yet, much of the dread and the excitement has to do with our inability to pause and pay attention to the details that actually really matter; we are often too quick, and too easily give into the eerie feeling those stories raise in us. What if we stopped and looked closer?

There's no doubt that there's something of an imagery or cultural repertoire at work in our recognition of such an analogy. The image echoes other images, or, say, the scene rehearses previous scenes. Details repeat themselves, like the pattern in the weave of life. So, there's a temporality to the emergence of details. These "same" details are never quite the same, revealing a context that begins to carry a certain weight. Yet, its thickness, something of its texture, will elude us if we fail to see the way in which figures such as the *zonbi* or the *gede* make up the context. We need to see these internal relations within the form of life to understand certain things. What's important, then, is that by seeing such connections, we are actually paying attention to an important aspect of our human condition: our vulnerability to death, and our sense of finitude. And the coffin materializes this connection.

OF COFFINS

The coffin is indeed an important motif in Haitians' lifestyle—something that did not appear to me right away. I had at first been blind to the fact that, in the numerous *badji* I visited and the many Vodou *sèvis* I attended, caskets are painted on the walls, and wooden or cupboard coffins are used as ritual devices. The signature (*vèvè*) of the patron of the *gede*, Bawon Sanmdi, is itself a tomb with a cross. Some initiations even require that the initiate be laid to rest in a coffin (with the lid closed) and then reborn, brought back as another person. It often happens during a funeral procession that the men and the spirits of death share the duty of dragging the casket together, and at some point, they dance back and forth in order to mislead the dead person's soul, so that it can leave once and for all.

In René Depestre's famous novel *Hadriana in All My Dreams* (2017), the funeral of Nana Siloé first resembles a revelry where humans and spirits of the realm of death commune in a frenzy:

> their musical fury carried each of us back and forth between death and birth, between anguished screams and triumphant orgasmic cries. The musical volcano reduced the legendary obstacles between Thanatos and Eros to ashes. . . . The explosion of guédé spirits, enlivened by our seething blood, placed our bodies and souls, our frenzied penises and vaginas, into a space of cosmic harmony, fueled by the crazy hope that we might somehow snatch Nana Siloé back from death so that the radiance of her earthly being might shine in our lives once again (ibid., 84).[10]

Then, during the procession, the *gede* spirits take the lead and start their dance:

> The convoy marched off at a good pace behind the crucifer, in a tide of flowers. From the temple to the cemetery, there was not more than a mile

to walk. About a hundred yards from the entry gate there was a little hill to climb. It was well known to frequent funeral-goers by the name of "Melpomène Saint Amant's pubis." It was there that the convoy suddenly reared up like a spooked horse. A man who looked a lot like Baron-Samedi invited some of the guédés present to take the coffin from the hands of its apostolic bearers. These Vodou gods of death immediately began to sing and dance. They staggered forward then back with the coffin, making a series of shifts and sudden about-turns, such that the whole of the funeral procession was obliged to do the same. They repeated this exercise three times around the perimeter of that erotic hill before deciding to run across it at top speed.

"What are they doing?" I asked my uncle Féfé.

"The gods are trying to disorient Nana's innermost self—her *petit bon ange*. Should it ever get the idea to head back home, it won't be able to find its way" (ibid., 95–96).[11]

After the dazzling ballet of U-turns, humans take over for the *gede*—but for what fate? The *gede* are the conveyors of dead souls, escorting them from this realm into the other. They also make people think, and live.[12] I would recall the question: "What were those guédés up to? Whose path were they trying to confuse?" (ibid., 185). The child-narrator asks, "What are they doing?"

Many years later, the adult narrator confides: These questions will ultimately remain unanswered. What humans and spirits do, has its share of mystery. Indeed, there are no riddles to decipher here. I am nevertheless amazed that, in order for the living to orient themselves and continue on their way, they sometimes have to undergo a certain amount of confusion, a confusion deliberately brought about by them, cocreated by the spirits, as if out of this chaos were to emerge a certain order, out of the darkness a light. Is the act of disorienting the souls of the dead also an act of orienting the souls of the living? When death mocks itself with crude jokes, luscious dance steps, and bursts of laughter, isn't it celebrating the power of the living?

A living man lying in a coffin is also the image in the first scene of Charles Najman's film (2011), *A Strange Cathedral in the Viscous Darkness* [*Une étrange cathédrale dans la graisse des ténèbres*]. It starts with a still shot of poet, writer, painter, and performer Frankétienne, half naked, eyes closed, in a casket laid vertically against the falling roots of an enormous tree which I assume to be the home of some spirit (*lwa*). Over the sound of buzzing insects, his voice—in voice-over narration—says, "I, Jean-Pierre Basilique d'Antor Frank Étienne d'Argent, I speak for those who are dead. For those who had no burial. Thousands of them. Tens of thousands of them. I hear their cries. I hear death's call.[13] We are in the realm of death, and nobody wants to see it." He refers here to the thousands that were crushed by the earthquake on January 12, 2010. The film is shot among the ruins of the Cathedral of Our Lady of the Assumption, built in downtown Port-au-Prince between 1884 and 1914, which collapsed that day.

Frankétienne is known to be one of the founders of spiralism, a literary movement born in the 1960s from within the debris and the madness produced by the Duvalier dictatorship. "I'm suffocating," he writes. "In wanting so desperately to speak, I've become no more than a screaming mouth" (Frankétienne 2014)—yet, a screaming mouth that is clairvoyant about what it is meant to do: "[Re-create] wholes from mere details and secondary materials," as a way of reconciling art and life, something he calls "re-cognition"[14] (ibid., 7). Maybe something similar is at stake in anthropology.

LEARNING TO DIE

Allow me now to depart from Haiti for a moment and make a detour. In Cora Diamond's (2003) reflections on John Coetzee's Tanner Lectures on Human Values,[15] she invites us "to think of what it would be not to be 'deflected' as an inhabiting of a body (one's own, or an imagined other's) in the appreciation of a difficulty of reality" (ibid., 13). She asks the reader to do something that conventional philosophy does not know how to do, that is, "to inhabit a body" (ibid., 13), for it seems that our bodies stand in the way of our knowledge of each other's minds.[16] This is precisely what Elizabeth Costello, the heroine of Coetzee's lectures and his later novel (2003), asks us to imagine when she invokes Ted Hughes's poems "The Jaguar" and "Second Glance at a Jaguar": "Hughes is feeling his way towards a different kind of being-in-the-world, one which is not entirely foreign to us. . . . In these poems we know the jaguar not from the way he seems but from the way he moves. The body is as the body moves, or as the currents of life move

202 *The Murmuring Stream of Life*

within it. The poems ask us to imagine our way into that way of moving, to inhabit that body" (Coetzee 2003, 173–74).

Diamond's diagnosis underscores philosophy's inclination to deflect from the very pressure reality puts on bodies, thus on thinking. According to her, professional philosophy characteristically deviates by avoiding allowing thought to be, or by refusing to admit that it is, in fact, sometimes defeated by something difficult in reality—something inexplicable, overwhelming, and wounding. Part of the problem is precisely our inability "to imagine our way into *that* way of moving, to inhabit *that* body," that is, *another* body. If we imagine inhabiting the body of the broken man lurching toward the coffin, what sorts of currents of life would we feel moving within it? And how would the sound of death resonate within these currents? To envision some kind of answer to these questions, one would have to think of certain details, as I did in the opening of this chapter. Indeed, details are inescapable if we are to appreciate the scene of this man lying in a casket, precisely because they are what gives us a sense of these movements and currents and impetuses. Someone unable to imagine the details from which such movements emerge, or blind to these details if one were to witness the scene, wouldn't see much of the matters currently under discussion. That person, Wittgenstein would say, would be aspect-blind, "lacking in the capacity to see something *as something*" (1986, 213). An additional important feature of Coetzee's novel is that, in asking us to imagine another's life, it asks us to imagine our own death, our "having a genuinely embodied knowledge of being extinguished"[17] (Diamond 2003, 13). What would it change if we looked at the scene of this drunken man against the backdrop of our own subjection to death?

Do we see a man withering and rotting, or a man in a moment of change, ripening for something still to come? With some intellectual scrupulousness,[18] there is a way to look at this scene as one picturing a man who, for all his faults, livens up for even a fleeting moment. He may be in a position in which he proves himself of the intuition that he has come to a point of maturity in his earthly life, a point at which he may now accept something about his knowledge of death, and may be ready to agree to a new departure. So, to say that these are undecidable matters is perhaps neither as true nor as just as it sounds, for it might be too easy an escape before the obligation to bear, or take, or find, or disclaim, responsibility for our words; it would indeed "strip ourselves from the responsibility we have in meaning (or in failing to mean) one thing, or one way, rather than another" (Cavell 1994, 135). But of course, this scene might appear to some as utterly trivial, showing nothing more than a drunkard seizing the occasion for a nap, as it were, in a wooden box. I have no further justification here (and certainly no proof) of the possibility that appeared to me; either one sees it or does not. But if one does, then it matters to imagine that this particular man shows us something more general about human endings. What he reveals is something of ourselves, of our human finitude and our vulnerability to different forms of deaths; but then, it equally shows us something about new beginnings and, perhaps, also human laughter.

How does one learn to die? This question was Henry David Thoreau's when, in February 1862, at the age of forty-four, shortly before his death, he gave a last lecture entitled *October, or Autumnal Tints* (2012). In it, he describes how the hues and shades and behavior of the falling leaves of October constitute cues for his own ending. On the threshold of death, he saw a deep connection between the color and the conduct of foliage and bodily extinction—the leaves "teach us how to die," he writes. There are things out there like leaves and colors and seasons that enabled him to find his way; they were like benchmarks for his orientation in a moment of life when loss and winter loomed on the horizon. "One wonders if the time will ever come when men, with their boasted faith in immortality, will lie down as gracefully and as ripe" as the leaves "painted in a thousand hues," fluttering "beautifully," soaring "so loftily" "before they rest quietly," going "to their graves," trooping "to their last resting-place, light and frisky," "contentedly," to "return to dust again" (ibid., 118–19).

The least I can say is that the man I saw was not painted with the vibrant colors of autumn, and did not flutter light and loftily, content to return to dust. He seemed to me more like an emanation of slough, or a joker. Yet, something grew out of the humus. He did stand up and go on "selecting the spot, choosing the lot . . . whispering all through the woods" (ibid., 118). He did allow himself to want to rest quietly in a casket, maybe his to come. But the time was not yet his, although he may have started to die a while before. He *did* do *some*thing, and not *any*thing. "Human beings: you've never fathomed them," writes Henri Michaux (1997, 25). "Nor have you truly observed them, nor fully loved or hated. You've leafed through them.

So accept that being likewise leafed by them you too are no more than leaves, a few leaves."[19]

LIFE AT A THRESHOLD

Let's leave this anonymous man aside for a moment. Before concluding this chapter, I'd like to take up the question from another angle and leaf through another story of how humans grapple with themselves as mortals. I'd like to tell, in a very different style, a few fragments of Rodny's story as he told it to me. Rodny is a young man I've come to know relatively well over the years. I thought it appropriate to contrast the very small and fleeting scene of the anonymous man at the beginning of this chapter with a piece of life history, which makes us change scale and register of narration and thought. In keeping with my desire to engage with the question of our own finitude, I will address two issues relating, on the one hand, to the ordinary tragedies that humans endure and, on the other hand, to the human's wish to escape the human condition. The two questions come together in that they raise the problem of what it means to live in a certain intimacy with death. This is not merely a question of knowledge. Here, "what is at stake is, even before the idea of knowledge, the sense of how human experience is to be called to account" (Cavell 2005, 2).

Although the story that follows is a rewrite in indirect discourse, and therefore a fictionalization, of Rodny's oral account, I want to keep it sober. One will immediately notice the change of tone with respect to my previous accounts in this chapter. We had several long, in-depth exchanges in the dark of the evenings. I suppose this is not entirely coincidental, as Rodny's stories had a philosophical tinge that couldn't be expressed in plain daylight, say at the zenith, as if a certain philosophical consciousness could only emerge in a nocturnal wake. This is perhaps because, as Cavell saw it, the "great responsibility of philosophy is responsiveness—to be awake after all the others have fallen asleep" (2012, 240).

Our meetings happened in my host family's courtyard or in Basile's. Rodny not only agreed to recording these meetings, but wished that they be recorded. He wanted to tell us his story, but without insistence or eagerness. And so he did. I also cross-referenced the story emerging from these nocturnal sessions with the long conversations we had in our spare time in the street or on our way from one point to another.

I've tried to stay as close as possible to Rodny's words and storyline, without qualifying or adjectivizing any more than he did himself. Nor did I try to aestheticize it; I tried to keep both the very soft, slow, and calm character of his voice, and the asperities, roughness, and violence of the content. There are also some inconsistencies here and there that I haven't tried to resolve, but rather to keep alive, as they are not only part of his narrative, but are constitutive of his world, of his understanding of it. They also reveal the difficulty of making oneself intelligible to the other. As pointed out by Cavell in his discussion of *Macbeth*, "the question of human intelligibility takes the form . . . of a question of the intelligibility of human history, a question whether we can see what we make happen and tell its difference from what happens to us, as in the differences between human action and human suffering" (2012, 223). The small incongruities also betray the difficulty of reading a world that appears in many ways incoherent, baffling, stupefying. What is striking in Rodny's voice is the contrast between his gentleness—an immediately perceptible kindness—and the brutality of the story. I thus hope this story will shed a different light on human dramatizations of the difficulty of living. For it happens that one's very existence can cause harm, injury, or offend others, as much as oneself, the spirits, or the world. What does it take, then, to live up to this awareness, to make sense of the fact that one exists, and exists as a human being, a being born and fated to death, and that this existence to some extent eludes us and has consequences beyond our reach, that life pushes on regardless? How attuned are we to the task of living, and how fenced off from our experiences of the world? How do contingencies shape our lives? What is it to embrace our fate? And how difficult is the task of being willing "to accept responsibility for another whom fate has placed in our vicinity?" (Das 2014, 491). My way of accepting responsibility for Rodny's proximity is to tell snippets of his story, snippets that show what improvisation in the face of contingency can teach us about our own human finitude. Rodny's story makes us see, in some ways, the fantastic vibrancy of a form of life whose incompleteness allows "individual improvisations, inventions, creativity, contestation and second chances" (Das 2023).

Let's get the story started on Friday, January 15, 2016. Rodny was twenty-six. It was Market Day in Bwa-Mapou, and he was going about his business in the bustling crowd when, suddenly, he got hit by Diego's motorbike. Diego used to persecute Rodny for no apparent reason whenever he came in the former's way. There had been small clashes now and then, but Diego's harassments seemed to have evolved into an open tyranny. "In my life, there are nice things, and there are hard things," Rodny confides with no bitterness, no regret, no anger.

Later, as Rodny was heading home, he crossed paths with Diego again. Diego punched Rodny several times in the face. Rodny tried to leave but was forced to the ground and got hit again ten to twelve times in the head. "I thought a lot about whether I had a problem with him, but I never found an answer. I believe it's resentment in his heart," Rodny reflects calmly. He eventually managed to extricate himself and escape. He went home and came back with a gun under his belt and a machete in his hands. "Angry, I spent two hours looking for Diego," he says with a peculiar neutrality, as if he were speaking of someone else. When he found him, he landed one blow with the sharp edge of the machete in Diego's shoulder, and another blow with the flat of the blade in his back. The slash was deep. Diego cried out in horror for help. A nervous crowd started to gather. Others ran in panic. The tension was quickly amplifying, and the spiral could easily get out of control. Some might have been ready to join the fight; machetes, knives, and sticks are many on the market, if not guns. Rodny fled and took refuge in his mother Lily's shack, a well-known merchant. He closed himself in and asked her to call the police. He says with a slightly quivering voice: "this was the scariest moment of my life." He believed that if the police did not come quickly—which they often don't, if at all—he would be lynched and most probably killed. The crowd had already gathered in front of the closed but flimsy door, and his mother could do nothing to cool their anger. Thankfully, police and MINUSTAH soldiers arrived, as it happened that a troop was patrolling in the zone. "They fired more than twenty times to get me out," he specifies. In the meantime, his mother had brought the JP judge, Enock Saintil, who happened to live nearby. He was the one who finally convinced Rodny to surrender.

Rodny was first brought to the precinct of Bouquet-Duvoisin, where he was locked up in a cell with no mattress and no food. After twenty days, he was transferred to the Civil Prison of Saint-Marc without trial. "That's because in Haiti there are no laws. Normally, I shouldn't spend more than three days in custody," he says assuredly. In fact, indefinite preventive detention is a huge problem in Haiti. Some people spend years on remand in atrocious conditions. In some cases, the movements of those detained without trial are lost, and they disappear into the limbo of overcrowded prisons, mainly due to a failing bureaucracy, poor management, and lack of resources. Many end up dying there. According to the joint report of the BINUH and the OHCHR (2021), the proportion of pretrial detainees in Haitian prisons continues to grow and reached 82 percent of the overall prison population in May 2021.

That spring, Rodny spent three months in pretrial detention in a prison of about six hundred detainees.[20] His cell had four beds and thirty-two inmates, no windows, and no light. He was incarcerated with men serving time (or awaiting trial) for murder, drug trafficking, kidnapping, or arson. Others had not done anything but had simply been in the wrong place at the wrong moment. Some were minors, waiting to turn eighteen to be judged. A whole hierarchy was already in place. Rodny was allocated a tiny space on the concrete floor, so tiny that he couldn't stretch out. At night, he couldn't lie down with his whole body, as he was surrounded by other bodies trying to occupy every available space. Under these conditions, he obviously couldn't sleep. "I couldn't dream," he said.

The day he arrived he was searched by the prisoners. They took everything he had on him, including his 1,350 HTG (which was, at the time, the equivalent of a little more than $27). They also took the Adidas sneakers he was wearing, for which he paid 1,500 HTG ($23), he recalls. The next morning, in the courtyard, a guard called out to him: "*Eh! Blan!*" (in prison, a newcomer is a foreigner and therefore called "*blan*," "whitey"). "Come!" he said with a wink. Although he was scared, Rodny went anyway. The guard asked him what was taken from him the previous day, and by whom. Rodny, under pressure, pointed to the inmate who racketeered him, whereupon the guard lined up the prisoners and hit them with a stick "very hard," says Rodny. After that, he was obviously terrified at the thought of returning to the cell with the others, although the guard told him not to worry, that he'd be protected. As it turned out, he did not get in trouble. He later learned that the chief guard took a share of the stolen money from Rodny and made sure the inmates wouldn't retaliate.

From the very beginning, his mother came once a week, but he had visitors almost every day. They brought money, essential to one's survival in these conditions. He shared with other prisoners; this bought him friendships. He could then also complement the repulsive meals by buying milk, for instance. "I need milk," he says, "because sometimes my heart hurts because of high blood pressure." Indeed, there are dealers selling everything: cigarettes, razor blades (only the "chief" of the cell can sell these), bread, sugar, water, milk, matches, and so on. In the cell, he tried to pass the time playing dominoes, reading the Bible, or trying to sleep.

The conditions described by Rodny, with particular emphasis on detail, are atrocious. One can get an idea by imagining the problems posed by the simple fact of having to relieve oneself. When they needed, the prisoners did it in plastic bags in the cell, in full view of everyone. They only had access to the latrines during their daily outing, and then only for five minutes. Otherwise, they had to fend for themselves inside the cell. All they had was a little water in a tub with Clorox and hand disinfectant (which, by the way, had to be bought on the underground prison market). And yet, Rodny didn't add any emotion or excitement to his tale, but he wasn't indifferent. He simply recounted, plainly.

His talk with the first commissioner and his relations with Judge Saintil[21] helped him out. In fact, Saintil pleaded for his cause behind the scenes. The commissioner took this into account and weighed his indictment. It was in March, after three months, that the public prosecutor finally called him in for trial. It happened without Diego's presence. Rodny had two lawyers, hired by his mother. His lawyers were able to get the court to admit a document Rodny calls a "disclaimer paper" (*papier de désistement*) seemingly accredited by the notary. The document attested to the rumor about him but disavowed it. As it was, it indeed said that Rodny was involved in such and such, but the document stated that this was not the case and could not be considered as fact.[22] The competent authority sanctioned this version, which exonerated Rodny from the charges brought against him by the opposing party, who accused him of being a thief.

While the judge wanted to send him back to prison, the lawyers argued that he had already served his sentence and that, with this document, he was entitled to a provisional release. The judge was finally convinced. Rodny returned to prison only to retrieve his belongings, but the prisoners had stolen everything. "It's all right," he says without fatalism or regret, "I've earned my freedom, that's enough."

Upon his return to Bwa-Mapou, he fell sick. He stopped eating and only drank rum. He confides, "my life became really complicated. Every day I just wanted to drink." This lasted awhile before he was hospitalized. A nurse (who became his girlfriend for a time) took great care of him. She also treated him for diseases he got in prison, known as the vector of many infectious diseases. He was quite affected by the sodium bicarbonate the prison cooks used to put in the food.[23] He claims that he came out of prison all "swollen," although he didn't eat his fill. Clearly, the prison's deplorable hygiene had taken its toll on him.

"My head also was not quite right when I got out," he said. At first, he couldn't open his eyes, for being so blinded. "I've spent three months in a dark cell. Oh! It was so difficult to open my eyes after that, you can't imagine! It took four to five days to open them up!" And still, as we were speaking in October, he said he had not yet fully recovered. Eventually he'd pull through but something had changed, inexorably. His eyes had been opened to a transfigured reality.

As he got better, he went back to prison to visit his friends, those who protected him, who washed his clothes (who, unlike him, had access to water and buckets), and who threw away his excrement (because they could circulate within the space).

Although he was of course relieved to be out, he found himself heavily indebted. All this had had a cost: 20,000 HTG (~$300) for the lawyers; 30,000 HTG (~$500) as compensation to the injured party; 5,000 HTG (~$80) each for the judge, the first commissioner, the second commissioner, and the notary who issued the "disclaimer"; and 2,500 HTG (~$40) for the court clerk, for a total of more than 72,000 HTG, or $1,200. His mother had had some savings, but it had all gone into the financial support she'd given her son while he was in prison and the fees she'd paid for him.

Back in Bwa-Mapou, he was nonetheless able to build a wooden hut with a tin roof, which became his small stationery shop where he sold memory cards, USB sticks, notebooks, paper, pens, and so on. He also had a printer and a computer. He was remaking a life, patiently. Two months later however, his business was looted. He lost it all.

It ensued nonetheless that Diego got out of the way. He didn't plan to retaliate and many in the village now perceive Rodny as half crazy, perhaps ill, or at least potentially violent. Since he got out of jail, he admits, "I don't walk without my Glock anymore."

These shared moments of intimacy with Rodny, when he patiently recounted in detail his story, gave birth to some kind of friendship. We liked each other. He was indeed a bit offbeat, but very caring and very bright. I cherished his company. So, we hung out together. As we sat down one night, he told me another piece of his story. I wish to say a few words about this first part, before getting to the rest.

One remarkable thing, as I said, is the pitch and the pace of Rodny's voice when he recounted this piece of story. We were sitting in the darkness, sipping coffee. The air was still. Insects were swarming all around us in the muggy heat of the late day, while the stars were beginning to appear. On the recording, you can sometimes hear the distant voices of passersby or the exclamations of children. Village life went on all around, while Rodny, Basile, Mesac, and I entered a moment of rare intimacy. But the further the evening advanced, the calmer the environment and the thicker the atmosphere. Passersby and children gradually disappeared. The insects of the day, much more numerous, gave way to the less noisy, more subtle insects of the night. Rodny told his story very calmly, with almost no gestures or body movements. He was as if fixed in his chair, impassive. His eyes stared at us in the dark, clairvoyant. There was no rush, no fuss, as if this were the perfectly adequate moment for what he had to say. He exuded a great serenity and distance from himself. You could feel him thinking about what he was saying as he said it. His pauses, the blanks he sometimes left between sentences and words, marked reflective rather than emotional pauses. A thought was unfolding before our eyes, or rather in our ears; an incarnate, vibrant, living thought. It felt like he was really trying to mean what he was saying. And what he meant has a philosophical breadth.

I suppose he meant something like this: "Listen, I am where I am now, I am who I am now, at that precise moment of my life when you meet me. And this is not so much because I wanted it (what have I really decided in my life?), but because it befell me. And while I can't do anything about it, any more than you can, I can sharpen my sense of response to what's happening to me. What's more, as it happens, my fate is a violent one. Yet, this does not relieve me from my responsibilities. On the contrary, it intensifies them, for if I do not awaken myself to what is happening to me, I could, or would, yield to the sort of violence that befell me; and that's anything but desirable."

Of course, one could argue that this is my projection, an empathic projection perhaps, mere speculation or overinterpretation. I will not counterargue. Suffice it to say that anyone who fails to see the possibility that Rodny might have meant something of the kind is missing the point of this chapter, which is to emphasize the extent to which humans live their ordinary lives as tragedies, and that sometimes this awakens spirits ready to dream of other horizons.

The tragic character of the human is precisely that human action is ever open to contingencies, not merely accidents like in comedy: the human is subject to fate (Cavell 2012; 1999; Dufourmantelle 2007; Romilly 2014; Vernant 2004). Humans are thus vulnerable to failure. And since the consequences of our actions are uncertain, they are also ever open to violence. It's a tragic fact that human beings set in motion a course of events that they can neither calculate nor control, but also that they are set in motion by obscure forces one cannot fathom. Something began long before Rodny's story began, something that led him to where he is today. He was pushed to the limit. He was hurt, not only by Diego, but by the world, one that puts *that* kind of pressure on people, a world in which men like Diego exist, where these kinds of prisons and inmates and judges and mothers exist, a world in which that kind of tyranny, threat, cruelty, love, and redemption exist. It's a fact that Rodny reacted to something that happened to him, viscerally. On impulse, he hurt others. At the same time, he hurt himself. The consequences were unpredictable and irreparable; yet, if it is true that our actions have consequences we cannot foresee and imply wider effects than we can actually be answerable for the question of our responsiveness remains.

Such an uncertain life, made up of twists and turns, demands a great deal of adaptation and improvisation. It demands the art of seizing opportunities as they arise; but it also exposes us to a high risk of slipping into situations that can be hurtful or fatal to ourselves and others. Cavell characterized *Macbeth* as taking up "the question of responsiveness, the question, we might say, of the truth of response, of whether an action or a reaction is— or can be—sensually or emotionally adequate to its cause, neither withholding nor excessive. More than any other Shakespearean tragedy," he writes, "*Macbeth* thematically shows melodramatic responsiveness as a contest over interpretations, hence whether an understanding is—or can be— intellectually adequate to its question, neither denying what is there, nor affirming what is not there (a deed, a dagger). As if what is at stake is the intelligibility of the human itself" (2012, 223). By telling his story the way he did, by posing the problem of the undecidability of human actions, I believe Rodny expressed a concern about the very intelligibility of his story, of himself, and therefore of the human.

The other snippet I'm about to tell delves even deeper into these concerns, but shifts from the question of what it's like to be subjected to a violent fate to that of being at once bewitched and the actor of one's own escape.

SLIPS IN UNCERTAIN BORDERLANDS

It was 2011. Rodny was twenty-one. It was a Friday again. He met an elder man in his sixties or seventies as both were waiting in the morning sun for a bus, in the city of Saint-Marc. When they arrived in Pont-Sondé, they both got off, but the man had no money to pay for his way. The driver started to get angry, but Rodny intervened and paid for the man. Rodny continued his journey to Bwa-Mapou, and it turned out that the elder man was also heading in that direction. He got off in Bouquet-Duvoisin, just before Bwa-Mapou, and again, he got in trouble with the driver. And Rodny again intervened and paid for the man who then said, "Come down and follow me!"

They walked near a field. There, the man asked Rodny to kneel. He gave him a bag and invoked a spirit: "Master, open Rodny's mind. He will continue the battle on my behalf." Rodny says that he had a strange feeling then; something in the air was odd.

The man told him to go home and open the bag, that inside he'd find a book entitled *The Red Dragon*. The book in question is better known as the *Grand Grimoire*, a European black magic manual whose date and author are uncertain, but most probably of medieval origin. In any case, it contains instructions for summoning demons and for the construction of tools with which to force a demon to do one's bidding. It also contains riskier ritual instructions to make a deal with a demon and command the spirit. The man instructed Rodny to go to page 65, rip it out, and place it under his pillow.

Back home, Rodny read a passage that explained how to call upon a dead being. "I said to myself, 'I'd like to try it.' I want to know what this means." So, he went to buy all the material he needed, closed himself in his room, hung a white sheet in the middle of the room, and started what he calls his "meditation." He summoned the dead and prayed. After a little while, he recounts, the dead appeared behind the sheet. A conversation started[24]:

The Dead (TD): "Why do you call me here?"

Rodny (R): "I think you can help me. There are many problems here with which I need help."

TD: "What problems?"

R: "Economical and social problems. I want you to help me. My parents are poor. I need money to help them."

TD: "But what do you want?"

R: "I told you already. I need money."

TD: "I'm not here for this. I'm here to cure diseases, to heal, but not to give money or influence one's fate."

The spirit then gave him the reference of another book better suited for his needs. Rodny incidentally also found that book in the bag the old man gave him. As he started reading, tears fell down his cheeks like "waterfalls." "The book was very powerful," he recalls.

At 3 p.m. that day, he went as usual to see his mother so that she might give him money to buy food at the market for the family. This time however, he told her that he had other work to do, very important to him, and would not be able to buy the things needed. His mother took the money back and said, "In that case, you'll be hungry, kid." He didn't care; he was totally obsessed with what he calls his "work" (*travay* is a term used in the *mistik*). Alone, he started a complex ritual where he drew kabbalistic circles on the floor in which he invoked another demon. The spirit appeared bit by bit, he explains: first an ear, then a foot, then an arm, until it all fell into the circle, and then assembled itself in a sort of vortex:

The demon (D) then said, "What for do you summon me here?"

Rodny (R) answered, "You're part of me, just as I'm part of you. You can help me solve my problems."

D: "Of course I can. But after I've solved your problems, what are you going to do for me?"

R: "I'll set a table for you."

D: "And what will you be putting on it?"

R: "Whatever you want."

D: "I want bread, wine, and pieces of fried pork."

But Rodny had read not to yield to the spirit's wish, "for that would be to give your soul to it." The whole point was to resist the demon tempting you.

The issue, as he framed it, is about who has the power to define who gives what to whom. So, Rodney refused. But the demon did not let up. The negotiations failed, after which the demon angrily asked to be sent back to his realm. As Rodny did just that, he inadvertently stepped back out of the circle. He calls this his "error."

The most dangerous thing in the manipulation of magic, Rodny said, are "errors." If you commit an error in the procedures, problems begin. He called it the "choc in return." This retroactive loop will harm you; you'll then be prompted to "correct" your error by redoing what must be done for the performance to work out well, but in doing that correction you may be doing exactly the reverse, that is, confirming your error.

As he exited the circle, he fainted, and only woke up hours later.

As he came to his senses a little, he realized that he was far from home, on the central public square in Saint-Marc (about a three- to four-hour drive away from home). He wanted to call his mother but had no money and no phone. As he often developed photos in a laboratory in Saint-Marc, he headed there to explain the situation and to ask the owner, whom he knew, to help him. Before he reached the lab, however, he lost control again. Some force made him go back to the park from where he had come. He was then conscious enough to ask someone what time it was: 8 p.m. He stayed in the park and spent the night there. Early in the morning, more awake, he managed to take a bus back to Pont-Sondé, but there he lost control once again and woke up only much later, this time even further away from home, in Arcahaie, on the Arcadian Coast. He tried to return home once more, but again lost control, regaining consciousness in yet another town, Cabaret (getting always closer to the capital city, despite himself). He was aware then, he says, that he was very much at risk, being far from home with no resources, and even more so in such a vulnerable mental state, with no control over himself. He asked to use someone's phone to call his mother, but realized that he had forgotten her number. The situation had become very critical. Finally, he arrived in Port-au-Prince against his will, at the bus station in the slum of Cité Soleil. He wandered the streets of the capital half-conscious until Monday, in a zombie-like state. He remembers almost nothing of that period, only that he had a chat with a policeman and that he didn't eat in all that time. He also remembers having slept in the street in front of a precinct.

On Monday, Rodny crossed paths with Eugene, a cousin who also lived in Bwa-Mapou but had business to attend to in the capital. Eugene immediately stopped him: "Hey, Rodny, where have you been for God's sake, your Mom is looking for you everywhere!" Because Rodny was struggling, Eugene tied him up tightly with a rope and put him on a bus to Bwa-Mapou, whose driver Eugene knew.

At home, Rodny's mother, distressed, bathed him and put him to bed. A few relatives were by his side as he was falling asleep. Rodny recounts that at that moment, an angel appeared to him and said, "Make the people go out, I need to talk to you." Rodny did as he was told, and the angel said, "Take a white tub, a white towel, and portion of 'tranquil' oil [a special oil used in *mistik*]. Go also to a source nearby, take a gallon of water and pay the source. Back home, put the water in the tub, baptize it with basil leaves, three grains of salt, and a prayer, and take a bath and meditate."

He followed these instructions. As he bathed, the angel appeared again and instructed him to read page 33 of the book by Abbé Giglio, "an important doctor." He was told that in this book he would find healing prayers and recipes for medicine. He again followed the angel's instructions. As he read and meditated, he began to feel better, he says. Slowly, he recovered.

From there on, he decided he'd use the books only to do good, and for no other purpose. Indeed, he had since made use of various magic tools and techniques, notably to seduce women or to employ *"ti zonbi"* (little zombies) in order to make them work for him. But he said that he'd made no use of the *Petit Albert* anymore (a European grimoire from the late Renaissance that includes a chapter on "Sexual Magic" and others on recipes for practical living), since it is "very wicked." He said that he'd stop. After that, his skills in "white magic" were recognized by Odlon, his grandfather and an important *oungan* in the zone. They even collaborated in their work. As his first grandson, Rodny was supposed to inherit his grandfather's *oumfò* and take up his work. This did not happen.

All this was told to me during the autumn of 2016. When I returned in 2017, things had changed. According to rumors and hearsay, Rodny had gotten involved in some shady dealings. His close cousin Mesac had fallen out with him after Rodny was implicated in the theft of a high-quality camera from his other cousin, Rosalvo. They hadn't spoken since. Rodny himself told me that he had gotten angry with his mother Lily, after which he'd left home. Lily herself confirmed that she was no longer speaking to her son. When we met again, something had indeed changed. Rodny had hardened. His attitude was tougher, his gaze fearless. He had perfected a slight sneer, the kind you sometimes see on the faces of stiff-necked criminals. He had become used to hanging out with guys from the *baz*, cliques of young men who, in the neighborhood, are for the most part young deportees from the United States (having known prison there) or disillusioned young men who have been disinherited, looking for a little dough in the business of petty crime. Above all, he had become downright muscular. Whereas he'd been small and frail the year before, he now had a wrestler's build and the shoulders of a boxer.

We are nevertheless happy to see each other again. When we do meet again, we sit down in the street and catch up on missed time. The first thing he tells me, as if we were picking up the thread of the conversation broken the previous year, is that after the looting of his shop, he was recruited by a special anti-gang police unit. At some point (but the timeline is confusing) he began working as a secret agent for a fee. He is said to be a kind of informal informer who helps the police in special operations aimed at capturing convicts, escapees, drug traffickers, and high-ranking criminals. In recent years, he has learned enough about these underground affairs to be considered an expert. He can probably see from my face that I'm having a little trouble believing him, so he pulls a card out of his pocket, a sort of pass issued by the HNP for if he gets arrested by officers who aren't aware of his mission. I nod in understanding, although I don't entirely buy his story: The pass could well be fabricated. He then tells me that his future project is to open a beauty salon for men and women, because his current job is too dangerous. He won't live long if he keeps doing it. As he says this, he lifts his shirt to show me a bullet wound.

Over the years, it happened that our relationship became more distant, and we would not meet up as frequently, nor as intimately as before. His life took the kind of turn that would incite many people to avoid him, including his close ties, who have often repeated that Rodny is not quite on the right path, or that he's into some obscure business that one wants to avoid having anything to do. Otherwise, people would just not comment and keep their silence, but everything in their behavior showed that they were not nourishing their relationships with him anymore, although they were kind and sometimes friendly when they occasionally met him. I also sensed that a general ambiance was pushing against our initial friendship; my enthusiasm (probably naïve) when I saw him was becoming embarrassing to others, for whatever reason. I don't know what Rodny was really up to, but more than once I saw a police car pull up on the high street and Rodny approach it to exchange a few words at the window, or commissioners greet him when they were in the area on one case or another. It was obvious that Rodny had a special relationship with the police, about which little was known. And his long, unexplained absences added to the mystery. He would tell me in bits and pieces that he'd been to the Dominican border or to the capital to help arrest a big bandit, that it'd been very dangerous and that he'd almost died. His current stories, unlike his earlier ones, became more hyperbolic, more extravagant, more heroic. Our relationship thus quite naturally faded, although I was always happy to hear, hailing out of the pitch-black night, his rallying cry: "*Mako bloda modafoka!*"—before we spent a moment on the side of the street chitchatting and making jokes.

There is obviously much more to say about all this than what I can possibly offer here. For the purposes of this chapter, and before moving on to the conclusion, let me just raise three points that shed a different light on what has been said. First, one way to interpret Rodny's life as he recounts it, is to interpret it as a life at once of resistance and surrender to fate. What stands out is the constant play between the passive and the active, sleepwalking and watchfulness. On the one hand, Rodny is subject to different kinds of slips, risks, and mistakes—he is in the grip of a force, but also of a certain kind of thinking that goes with it.[25] A chain of events over which he's had no control ended up having unpredictable and irreversible consequences on his life. On the other hand, at every stage, he acts, reacts, and responds to what is happening to him. He is not totally powerless, even if that may seem to be the case at times. In fact, while there's no doubt that he is under the influence of some power, that he is acted upon by that power, whatever it might be, he also theatricalizes himself in various ways. His penchant for experimentation, his pleasure in improvising, and his propensity to try something that could change his life all at once open up certain possibilities for him, while subjecting him to specific risks. They make him prone to mistakes and vulnerable to failure. Yet, all this is not to be considered as an anomaly as such, but rather as an inherent aspect of what it is to be human—it is "part of what we conceive human life to be" (Cavell 1994, 52). Importantly, Rodny's tendency to be seduced by magic, to allow himself to be captivated by practices whose power is unfathomable, does mean that things easily get out of hand and put him in danger; but giving in to such seduction has also opened up a new path in life, and with it a whole new horizon of possibilities.

Second, if Rodny's trials didn't destroy him, it's because he was able to learn something from trying, failing, and trying again. Rodny conducted an experiment at once self-conscious and accidental, haphazard, and careless: He wanted to explore and learn something about the mysteries of his human condition, but his acts betray a certain wish to escape it. As it were, he ends up learning something about himself (cf. "I said to myself . . . I want to know what this means"). Think of it as a kind of grammatical exploration of his form of life. And the spirits, to a certain extent, helped (and still help) him in his quest: One of them gave him additional references, more suitable for his quest, and advised him on what he should do (see also Motta 2022). So he learned from his experiences something about himself as much as about the world he lives in: He educated himself on matters pertaining to his particular milieu. It is true that he has taken huge risks—nobody in Haiti wants to mess around with these powerful mystical forces (*fòs mistik*). But as it happened, what he did empowered him, although it didn't come without damage. He has learned a certain use of secrecy as well as the art of creating mysteries, both of which make him attractive and fearsome at the same time. And he was later able to make good strategic and political use of such power and to leverage his position. What's more, after this experience of closeness to death, Rodny's reanimated body/mind came back reinforced and with new knowledge about where and what home is for him. In his crisis, he was always pushed farther away from home. He wanted to return, but a force prevented him from doing so. Eventually, he was taken back home violently (not by himself). And somehow, he found a home again: his mother, a bath of warm water, care, and tenderness (a kind of intrauterine life?); but also, I suppose, reproaches and reprimands (isn't that also part of home?). At the end of his crisis, it's as if he's returned to childhood, to the warmth of home, to maternal love. But he's not back where he started: Everything has changed. He's changed, of course, but so have other people's perceptions of him. His return home is not a return to the point of origin, but is rather growth. And growth can be synonymous with violent separation, as was later the case with his mother Lily. Rodny's experimentation with his condition of mortality, and therefore with his condition of natality, enabled him to come to terms not only with his birth as a human (and not, say, as a spirit or a god), but also with the birth of a world, his world. Something is reborn in and for him. The issues here touch upon what Veena Das has called "the opacity of one's own reactions to the powerful experiences of grief" (Das 2020, 134). Such opacity prompts, I suppose, one's examination of one's own life. That Rodny is drawn into such an examination is no accident, but no destiny either.

Lastly, I'd like to underscore the strong indeterminacy of context. One can be born in the Artibonite Valley and master the local language, codes, and behavior, and yet fail to grasp certain subtleties of this way of life. Rodny wasn't quite aware of certain eventualities, although he did have a sense that the practice of *mistik* had the potential to change his life, for better or for worse. His haste, his youthful arrogance perhaps—in other words, the fact that he gave in a little too easily to the temptation of manipulating certain powers alone and unaccompanied—all led him into obscure recesses from which he had to return. In the end, he came back with the help of others, transformed by his drift. What's interesting is that Rodny has learned to embody and play with this indeterminacy of context. His experience put him in touch with reality in such a way that he could thereafter appear to his fellow citizens as the embodiment of a certain ambivalence of reality itself; and such enactment also serves his purposes. To what extent is he collaborating with the police? What do we know about that? Is he also involved in illegal activities? If he is, of what kind? How powerful is he? And what exactly are his intentions? Nobody around me really knows, and most don't want to know, because it would lead them to take too close an interest in dangerous matters. Over the years, Rodny has become very good at raising doubts and creating mystery around facts, at least those that concern him. He knows well how to play on people's doubts and fears. These uncertainties have become part of his character, part of his theatricality. But it's not just a game: What's at stake here is undoubtedly tragic.

THE LIGHT OF SHADOWS

There can be no closing to this meditation. I can however lay down a few more words, all of which, I hope, could be seen as tags for a further path in thinking about human life.

In a workshop on concepts and realism, held at Harvard in spring 2018, in which I presented a paper that became Chapter 5 of this book, Jocelyn Benoist asked me, "What is it exactly to depict a form of life?" I would like to take up again the challenge posed to me by his question, and relate it to another question Veena Das asked in the same workshop: "How is thinking tied to death?" It seems to me that there is a path worth following if we take the question of the depiction of our forms of life to be related as much to the question of our attention to the details that matter, as to what prevents us from looking at those details; and our seeing (or not) such a relation seems to be a function of our being (or not) disposed to receive what dawns and dies and dawns again, what grows and withers and grows again; what passes and transforms. Then, such attentiveness seems to me to already contain a notion of thinking (and a tempo of thinking) that bears indeed some relation to death, or, say, to the dying forms of our lives. In that case, this text is something like a sketch of my sense of the worth of such a connection.

At the center of the grand cemetery of Port-au-Prince, there is a tree on which certain objects—puppets, miniature chairs, wrapped bottles—are nailed or pinned or attached. These spells and counterspells serve either to thwart deadly attacks by mooring the enemy with what in Creole one calls "mystical" strings, preventing the attacks from reaching someone, or to carry out such attacks. It is an interesting locus of ambiguous and indeterminate actions, where no one really knows what exactly the other is doing. It seems to me that this tree is the embodiment of the indefinite character of death's intentionality. In the end, whatever human beings want, plan, or intend to do, death has its own life. Bawon Sanmdi, or his henchmen the gede, will make it happen or not (others would say it is God). Despite the strong desire that these amulets will inflect death's itinerary, it may be that weak ropes tie us to frail hopes. But, what else is there to do?

For anthropologists, and philosophers alike I assume, the depiction of our forms of life and death has a worth inasmuch as it enables us to orient ourselves in the world we live in. Orientation is not so much given to us by the explicit and clear-cut language of signposts than by the subtler light of beacons placed here and there as we go along. It feels like there is something minor that emerges from the rumble and hubbub of a form of life, something like a tint of details that comes to have a certain relevance. At times, like in music, minor keys have a particular color of quietness, intimacy, and sorrow. This is often my sense of the color of the details that are singled out in the experiences I describe. However, it may also turn out that, much like in painting, *chiaroscuro* brings out the light emanating from the prevalence of low-key black, dark brown, and blue. Something is brought into the light and made visible, not because one illuminates it directly—one may be dazzled by the lighting—but by a work in contrasts; something becomes remarkable, say, in an oblique way. So, would we, anthropologists and philosophers, instead of shedding light on the world, be able to let the light arise from shadows? How different, then, would our work and the people and the world look?

■ ■ ■

The journey I've undertaken in this chapter began before daybreak. And it does not end at dusk. The concluding lines of Thoreau's *Walden* (2004, 333) state, "The light which puts out our eyes is darkness to us. Only that day dawns to which we are awake. There is more day to dawn. The sun is but a morning star."

During my stay in the Artibonite Valley, I would usually rise to attend the purplish opening of the new day offered by the dawn. Like Emerson (2000, 9), I too "dilate and conspire with the morning wind," before the kids and the rest of the family wake up. Emerson's admiration for nature was more than philosophical interest. My own admiration for Haiti is more than wonder—it is a way, I suppose, of bowing before the murmuring stream of its life.

I said earlier that the drunkard might know something I do not about the relation between death and rebirth. So, what if Emerson and Thoreau were right, that every end is a beginning, and that the morning star is as well a mourning star? Then it could be said that Rodny found a form of freedom in a cell, and learned something about peace through the violence of fate. And the man who opened this chapter has found his cradle, not yet his grave.

"S'il faut mourir demain
Je vivrai."

"If I have to die tomorrow
I will live."

—KERMONDE LOVELY FIFI

ACKNOWLEDGMENTS

On October 19, 2022, in a WhatsApp group, Alix wrote (in French) a poetic tribute to Frédéric's bakery: "Haiti is between the worse and the worst. A defective life of suffering and fear where hunger triumphs since dawn. Since dawn, my Lady, I think of you. Since dawn, the wind seeks the color pink under the nocturnal influence. From time to time, the house of bread denounces its worst ordeal, its sleepless nights, its locked doors. It's a wave inflicted by pain. A one-eyed hand caresses the anticipated grief. Despite everything, my Lady, I still resist, for the love of my clients."

Frédéric replied to Alix's message the next day: "The house of bread resists! The house of bread persists!"

My deepest gratitude goes to all those in Haiti who, in one way or another, resist the powers of annihilation and persist in trying to imagine a possible future. I dedicate this book to my dear friends whose real names I wish to avoid divulging. I don't have words strong enough to express my indebtedness. Special thanks go to Basile Despland, who took me to Haiti for the first time and opened wide the doors to the world of Bwa-Mapou. His love for Haiti, its people, its literature, and its theater are so contagious that I didn't hesitate for a second when he asked me to accompany him. Without him, I'd never have set foot there.

My heartfelt thanks also go to the children and teenagers who have constantly surrounded me, teaching me invaluable things about how life goes on in the cracks of an ordinary one that is fissured by violence. My gratitude, of course, also goes to all the other family members I've known, to friends of friends, to neighbors, to those I've met only sporadically or sometimes only once, but who have left a lasting mark. This includes those who have passed away (RIP) and the anonymous people whose paths I crossed in a vodou service, in the streets of Port-au-Prince, at a crossroads, or in the tap-taps, which make up the background to this vibrant and resourceful Haitian form of life.

Thanks to the three consecutive postdocs awarded to me by the Swiss National Science Foundation, who placed its trust in me—the Early Postdoc Grant, the Advanced Postdoc Grant, and the Return Grant—I was lucky to have been affiliated with the Departments of Anthropology at Johns Hopkins University, the University of Toronto, and the University of Bern, and to be able to travel so much. It has been such an incredibly rich and stimulating intellectual adventure. I've never read, written, or developed my thinking as much as I have during these years, thanks to all the inspiring people whose paths I've crossed, some of whom have become indispensable companions in thought. I've learned so much from Veena and Ranen Das, Clara Han, Naveeda Khan, Debbie Poole, Jane Guyer, Alessandro Angelini, Tom and Canay Özden-Schilling, Paola Marrati, Michael Lambek, Michael Jackson, Andrew Brandel, Bhrigu Singh, Michael Puett, Sandra Laugier, Jocelyn Benoist, Estelle Ferrarese, Perig Pitrou, Anne Lovell, Richard Rechtman, Piergiorgio Donatelli, Nayanika Mookherjee, Diana Allan, Anne Meneley, Alejandro Paz, Donna Young, Julia Eckert, Michaela Schäuble, and Sabine Strasser. I would like to extend my warmest thanks to all those who were graduate students or postdocs at the time, and with whom, over the years, I have exchanged ideas, often passionately, sometimes just in passing, on one or other of the issues raised in this book, and who have contributed to making the process of thinking so radiant: Grégoire Hervouet-Zeiber, Megha Sedhev (†), Victor Kumar, Miki Chase, Fouad Halbouni, Ghazal Asif, Maya Ratnam, Bican Polat, Benita Menezes, Arpan Roy, Bürge Abiral, Sumin Myung, Nathaniel Adams, Audrey Fastuca, Marios Falaris, Mariam Banahi, Anna Whery, Elmira Alihosseini, Kunal Joshi, Sarah Roth, Letha Victor, Alonso Gamarra, Alessandro Corso, Mathilde Heslon, Marianne Tøraasen, Pascale Schild, Kiri Santer, Lucien Schönenberg, Nora Trenkel, Johanna Mugler, David Loher, Laura Affolter, and Gerhild Perl. A special thought goes to Loumia Ferhat, whose luminous company was so precious at a pivotal moment.

When it came to writing the chunks of text that would make up this book, I was extremely fortunate to benefit, over the years, from the generous, incisive, and always frank remarks of friends and colleagues who read the first versions, sometimes in French, of one or other of the chapters: Marie-Célie Agnant, Grégoire Hervouet-Zeiber, Lotte Buch Segal, Andrew Brandel, Veena Das, Bhrigu Singh, Clara Han, Michael Jackson, Loumia Ferhat, Basile Despland, Claude Welscher, Michaël Cordey, Sophie and Benoît Kaelin, Chelsey Kivland, Claire Payton, Chip Carrey, Ellen Hertz, and Judith Beyer. I am immensely grateful to them for having accepted to engage genuinely with some of the thoughts I was trying to put together. I must add the incredibly encouraging, critical, and constructive feedback from the two reviewers, Greg Beckett and an unnamed reviewer. I owe so much to Danielle Robert, who read more of my stuff than anyone did and copyedited the texts while I was writing them, that words fail me. She was able to hear my voice which, coming from French, was somehow distorted, or muffled, in English. And not only did she hear it, but she was able to help me reveal it in a language that was not my own, and which, thanks to her, has partly become mine. She was so meticulous, detecting as if it were my own tone, that she succeeded in making this text a text in which I recognize myself. That's no mean feat. Thank you from the bottom of my heart, Danielle.

I would also like to thank the following people for having inspired one or another of the lines in this book, sometimes during long and repeated conversations, sometimes just like that, in a corridor, during an online meeting or a coffee break: Edouard Duval-Carrié, Sharon M. Bell, Anthony Balzano, Régine Michelle Jean-Charles, Jennifer Greenburg, Mario LaMothe, Kasia Mika, Oliver Kusimano, Anne Aronsson, James Noël, Pascale Monnin, Lyonel Trouillot, Mehdi Chalmers, Laura Beaubrun, Arnaud Robert, Hans-Peter Znoj, Tobias Haller, Zainabu Jallo, Dora Imhof, and U5. As every researcher knows, there are those informal spaces where you converse with this or that person and which you leave sometimes with just an idea, or with a desire to express yourself better after having been misunderstood, or with just something a little different in posture, but that are so decisive. These are the most important moments, I suppose. Nevertheless, the more formal spaces also move us forward. I have had the chance to brainstorm ideas and present preliminary versions of the chapters of this book on several occasions, including at Johns Hopkins University's Department of Anthropology, Humanities Center, and Center for Africana Studies; Harvard University's Committee on Degrees in Social Studies; Yale University's Department of Anthropology; Cornell University's School of Criticism and Theory; the University of Edinburgh's Social Anthropology Department; the

University of Bern's Institute of Social Anthropology; the University of Lausanne's Laboratory of Social and Cultural Anthropology; Konstanz University's Social and Cultural Anthropology Department; the Sapienza University's Philosophy Department; and at the Collège de France; as well as during the meetings of the American Anthropological Association in Washington, D.C., in Baltimore, and at Princeton; the American Ethnological Society in Philadelphia; the Haitian Studies Association in Gainesville, FL, and in Washington, D.C.; the Swiss Anthropological Association in Neuchâtel and online during the COVID-19 pandemic; and the German Anthropological Association in München. I am very thankful to the participants for their provocations, suggestions, and precious feedback.

I am also deeply indebted to the editors of the "Thinking from Elsewhere" series—Clara Han, Bhrigu Singh, and Andrew Brandel—as well as Tom Lay, Fordham University Press's senior acquisitions editor, for their enthusiasm and unfailing support of the book project.

This book would not have seen the light of day without the profound care of my close and long-standing thinking partners in Lausanne: Basile Despland, Claude Welscher, Yves Erard, Joséphine Stebler, Michaël Busset, Line Rochat, Michaël Cordey, Raphaël Rapin, Serkan Camyurdu, Jean-François Meuwly, Kevin Melchior, Julien Nussbaum, and Giuseppe Merrone. Nor would it have been possible without the unconditional love of my mother, who kept me on my feet when the ground sometimes gave way, or without Sophie, who listened to me with such patience, soothing the voices that haunted me and giving me the confidence to carry on. On October 14, 2022, Naïm appeared like a new light in my life, giving me the courage and the strength I needed to finish a project I'd almost given up on many times.

Earlier versions of some chapters have been published elsewhere. I thank the presses and publishers for allowing me to reuse some of the material. Chapter 1 is a translation of an article published in French in *A Contrario* 32, published by BSN Press in 2021. Chapter 2 is a modified and updated version of an article published in vol. 52, no. 2 of *Journal of Legal Pluralism and Unofficial Law,* published by Taylor & Francis in 2020. Chapter 3 reproduces with substantial changes and additions an article published in vol. 11, no. 2 of the *Journal of International Organizations Studies,* published by UNSA Global Networks in 2020, and includes a partial and modified translation of an article published in French in vol. 5 of *Condition humaine / Condition politique*, published by the EHESS in 2023. Chapter 5 includes substantial changes and additions to a chapter published in the collective book *Living with Concepts: Anthropology in the Grip of Reality*, published by Fordham University Press in 2021. Chapter 6 reproduces, with substantial changes and additions, a chapter published in the collective book *A Matter of Detail: Anthropology, Philosophy, and Aesthetics*, published by University of Toronto Press in 2025.

ACRONYMS

ADR   Alternative Dispute Resolution
ANAMAH   Association nationale des magistrats haïtiens (National
                    Association of Magistrates)
APENA   Administration pénitentiaire nationale (National Pen-
                    itentiary Administration)
APM   Association professionnelle des magistrats (Profes-
                    sional Association of Magistrates)
BINUH   Bureau international des Nations Unies en Haïti (The
                    United Nations Integrated Office in Haiti)
BOID   Brigade d'opération et d'intervention départementale
                    (Departmental Operations and Intervention Brigade)
CASEC   Conseil d'administration de la section communale
                    (The Board of Directors of the Communal Section)
CARDH   Centre d'analyse et de recherche en droits humains
                    (Center for Analysis and Research in Human Rights)
CBO   Community-Based Organization
CC   Civil Code
CEH   Conférence épiscopale d'Haïti (The Episcopal Confer-
                    ence of Haiti)
CSCCA   Cour supérieure des comptes et du contentieux admi-
                    nistratif (Superior Court of Accounts and Administra-
                    tive Disputes)
CSPJ   Conseil supérieur du pouvoir judiciaire (Superior
                    Council of the Judiciary Power)

CVR	Community Violence Reduction
DAP	Département d'administration pénitentiaire (Prison Administration Department)
DDR	UN Disarmament, Demobilization and Reintegration Programme
DGI	Direction générale des impôts (General Directorate of Taxation)
FAO	Food and Agriculture Organization of the United Nations
FJKL	Fondasyon Jè Klere (Clear-Sighted Eyes Foundation)
FPH	Fédération protestante d'Haïti (The Protestant Federation of Haiti)
HNP	Haitian National Police (also PNH)
HTG	Haitian gourde (national currency)
ICE	US Immigration and Customs Enforcement
ICTR	UN International Criminal Tribunal for Rwanda
IJS	Informal Justice System
INARA	Institut national de réforme agraire (National Institute for Agrarian Reform)
IOM	International Organization for Migration
IPC	Integrated Food Security Phase Classification
JP	Justice of the Peace
MANUH	Mission d'appui des Nations unies en Haïti (United Nations Support Mission in Haiti)
MICAH	Mission civile internationale d'appui en Haïti (International Civilian Support Mission in Haiti)
MICIVIH	Mission civile internationale en Haïti (International Civilian Support Mission in Haiti)
MINUAH	Mission des Nations Unies en Haïti (United Nations Mission in Haiti)
MINUJUSTH	Mission des Nations Unies pour l'appui à la justice en Haïti (The United Nations Mission for Justice Support in Haiti)
MINUSTAH	Mission des Nations Unies pour la stabilisation en Haïti (United Nations Stabilization Mission in Haiti)
MIPONUH	Mission de police civile des Nations Unies en Haïti (United Nations Civilian Police Mission in Haiti)

MITNUH	Mission de transition des Nations Unies en Haïti (United Nations Transition Mission in Haiti)
NSV	National Security Volunteers (also VSN)
ODVA	Organisation pour le développement de la vallée de l'Artibonite (Organization for the Development of the Artibonite Valley)
OHCHR	Office of the High Commissioner for Human Rights
ONACA	Office national du cadastre (National Cadastral Office)
ONUVEH	Groupe d'observateurs des Nations Unies pour la vérification des élections en Haïti (United Nations Observer Group for the Verification of Elections in Haiti)
PHTK	Parti haïtien tèt kale (Haitian Tèt Kale Party)
PC	Penal Code
PNH	Police nationale haïtienne (Haitian National Police, also HNP)
RC	Rural Code
RNDDH	Réseau national de défense des droits humains (National Human Rights Defense Network)
UNDP	United Nations Development Programme
UNODC	United Nations Office on Drugs and Crime
USAID	United States Agency for International Development
USIP	United States Institute of Peace
VSN	Volontaires de la sécurité nationale (National Security Volunteers, also NSV)
WFP	World Food Programme
WPJ	World Justice Project

GLOSSARY

Badji: house of the spirits

Bal mawon: stray bullet

Balèn: type of candle used in Vodou services

Bayonèt: bayonet; rifle

Bòkò: person with mystical and secret powers; ambivalent figure, close to the secret societies

Baz: base; street corner; clique of young men; gang

Blan: foreigner; white

Chachè lavi: to search for life; to survive

Chèf: chief; boss

Chimè: young men from the slums used as henchmen and contract killers

Chwal: horse; person mounted by a spirit

Ekspedisyon: expedition; spell; curse

Ensekirite: insecurity

Envite: to invite; to summon someone to court

Gede: spirits; conveyors of the souls of the dead

Fèt gede: gede revelry, All Saints' Day

Goud: national currency, the Haitian gourdes (HTG)

Jij de pè: judge of peace

Jistis: justice

Kay: house

Kay lwa: house of the spirits

Kleren: homemade rum

Konbit (peyizan): mutual aid group between farmers, based on rotational labor

Kout poud: "blow of powder," spell

Kout lè: "blow of air," spell

Kovè: corvée; forced labor; chore

Kraze: to destroy

Lakou: home; household; courtyard

Lalo: kind of spinach

Lanmò: death

Lapè: peace

Lave tèt: "to wash the head," first step into a Vodou initiation

Lavi: life

Lougawou: from the French "*loup-garou*"; werewolf; mystical, vampire-like creature

Lwa: spirit

Malfèktè: wrongdoer; criminal

Manba: peanut paste

Manbo: female Vodou master of ceremony, expert in the work with spirits; doctor and community mediator

Mèt: master

Mèt bitasyon: master (spirit) of a family compound

Mèt tèt: master (spirit) of an initiate

Mistik: mystic; mystical

Atak mistik: mystical attack; spell; curse

Fòs mistik: mystical force; power

Moun: person; human being

Moun andeyò: outsider; peasant

Nèg: man; male person; acquaintance; friend

Nèg mawon: runaway slave; maroon; fugitive

Oumfò: family compound that is also a Vodou sanctuary

Oungan: male Vodou master of ceremony, expert in the work with spirits; a doctor and community mediator

Ounsi: initiate; server of a mystical congregation

Peristil: centerpiece of a Vodou sanctuary where most rituals take place

Pèp: the people; the popular masses

Poto-mitan: central pole of the *peristil;* pillar; mothers

Remèd: remedy; cure; solution

Règleman: rule; regulation; settlement; spell; curse

Restavèk: child servant; adopted child; slave

Sèvis: service for the spirits; ritual; ceremony

Sosyete sekrè: secret societies

Sanpwèl: powerful secret society, literally "those without hair"

Tafia: locally made, artisanal rum

Tap-tap: local transportation; buses; pickup trucks

Tounen: tour; Vodou march through the village or the neighborhood, praying, singing, and dancing

Travay: work; labor; mystical transaction

Vèvè: symbols and signature of the spirits

Vodouizan: Vodou practitioners

Wanga: trap; spell; curse; harmful potion

Zonbi: living dead; zombie

NOTES

INTRODUCTION

1. In French, the verse is: "*Le pays galérien tristement rame sur l'étang noir/des petits drames quotidiens*" (Phelps 2023, 67).

2. As communes are often large territories, each commune is divided into several sections, usually numbered (section 1, 2, etc.). This is the smallest administrative entity.

3. CASEC members are elected for a four-year term by the local population and may be reelected indefinitely.

4. An *oungan* is a Vodou ritual expert, a doctor, a community mediator. A *manbo* is the female equivalent.

5. An important number of these young people are deportees. This was during Donald Trump's first mandate when he had decided to send back to Haiti thousands of migrants who had made it into the United States, often after years of very tough exile throughout South and Central America. It is reasonable to estimate that in 2016 there were up to twenty-five young deportees in Bwa-Mapou. Many had left Haiti at an early age and traveled to Brazil or Chile, then gone along the migrant trails in Colombia, Panama, Nicaragua, Honduras, Guatemala, and Mexico until the United States, where they sometimes stayed for a while illegally before getting caught and jailed. Some had spent up to two or three years in prison in the United States before being sent back. Others had traveled through the Bahamas and Florida, and ended up in Miami, New York, or Boston.

6. Hear: Bruce Lee. He named his son after the famous kung fu actor because, he said, he would have to fight hard in this world to survive.

7. See the subchapter "The Vagueness of Concepts, The Vagueness of Law" in Chapter 5.

8. Yet, in times of extreme violence, things may appear differently. Since 2021, Bwa-Mapou's neighboring communes have been heavily attacked by armed

groups, leaving hundreds dead and wounded and tens of thousands displaced, many of whom have found refuge in Bouquet-Duvoisin, the commune to which Bwa-Mapou belongs. Against this backdrop, CASEC and local residents have come together to create vigilante brigades: They have armed themselves, set up checkpoints, and established curfews to keep assailants at bay. Depending on the circumstances, the CASEC help to provide intelligence, arm the population, and develop guerrilla tactics. In other cases, however, they side with the gangs. CASEC are, in a way, the changing and versatile face of the state.

9. I am not unaware of Walter Benjamin's (2021) critical thesis on the relationship between violence, law, and justice, nor of Jacques Derrida's (1992) subsequent developments. Although it would be interesting to follow some of the avenues opened up by these authors, particularly on the aspects of the conservative violence of law, this is beyond the scope of the present work. For reasons that will become clear as one reads on, I have chosen instead to place my empirical material in dialogue with approaches inspired by Foucault, Wittgenstein, and Cavell.

10. More recent examples show how, while the focus on the connection with everyday life remains present, objects of investigation and problematizations have diversified: Patricia Ewick and Susan Silbey's *The Common Place of Law* (1998); Michael Taussig's *Law in a Lawless Land* (2003); Laura Nader's *The Life of The Law* (2005); Judith Beyer's *The Force of Custom* (2016); Sameena Mulla's *The Violence of Care* (2018); Susan H. Ellison's *Domesticating Democracy* (2018); and Veena Das's *Slum Acts* (2022). One can also look at these three books that have attempted to cover the issues with which legal anthropology is concerned: Sally Falk Moore's *Law and Anthropology* (2005); Michael Freeman and David Napier's *Law and Anthropology* (2009); and Mark Goodale's *Anthropology and Law* (2017).

11. The anxiety that accompanies this skepticism can be such that it leads to complete madness. What happened in the shantytown of Wharf Jérémie in the first two weeks of December 2024 is a case in point. The son of the local gang leader, Micanor, had died. The father attributed the death of his son to the witchcraft of an old local. He then set up an extrajudicial tribunal where he forced the neighborhood's residents to march. After an ultra-expeditious inquisitorial process, he slaughtered at least 184 people in two days, most of them elderly, whom he judged to be malevolent manipulators of occult forces.

12. Of course, one cannot but think of James Scott's (1985; 1990; 2009) influential interventions in the human sciences, and, before him, Pierre Clastres (1990) and many others.

13. Compare, for example, the case of Jamaica. Deborah Thomas's (2011; 2019) detailed accounts show how forms of violence in the wake of the plantation are specific to the type of legacy left by the colonial system.

14. Malick Ghachem's (2012) in-depth analysis of the tensions inherent in the application of the Code Noir in Haiti shows just how complex things were.

Contrary to a simplistic vision, he shows that the Code Noir was not only a tool of oppression and legitimization of a brutality difficult to imagine, but also a tool for regulating the authoritarian power of the masters and their excesses of violence. It was therefore at the heart of the issues at stake, and the object of debate and conflict between administrators, planters, jurists, free people of color, and the enslaved. The interests of some planters converged with those of some free folks, while others did not. So, there were both conflicts and collaborations between individuals and heterogeneous groups with multiple interests. Importantly, the law and therefore the relations were modified by these debates and conflicts. For instance, the idea that the relationship between master and slave was autonomous and self-regulating outside the law—an idea inherited from the Roman law doctrine of *patria protestas*, which postulates the supreme authority of the father and husband over the household—invoked by the masters of sugar and coffee plantations to deny accusations of breaking legal or moral rules when they mistreated the enslaved (to say that the way they treated them was a domestic, private affair), gave way to another idea and use of the law. A contrario, the Code Noir was used to criticize that kind of sovereignty of masters, invoking the idea that slaves should instead be governed by civil law rather than the law of the master of the house.

15. As early as April 4, 1792 (barely thirteen months after the mass revolt of August 1791), the French Legislative Assembly in Paris granted full citizenship to all free people of color, but it also decided to send a fully empowered civil commission, comprising Sonthonax, Polverel, and Ailhaud, with the mission of imposing this controversial law, reestablishing French authority and encouraging slaves to return to the plantations. Both leaders of the insurrection in North Haiti, Jean-François and Georges Biassou negotiated the legal terms of an agreement with the commission (Ghachem 2012, ch. 6).

16. Boyer also annexed the Spanish side of the island in 1822 until his overthrow in 1843, which precipitated the Dominican War of Independence (Dubois 2012; Théodat 2003).

17. The Rural Code has since been revised. In the latest versions of 1962 and 1984, there is no longer any question of repressing cooperatives, but on the contrary of promoting them. Indeed, art. 81 states, "In each rural section, the Board of Directors shall encourage the formation of agricultural cooperatives." And art. 82, "Agricultural cooperatives, duly constituted, will benefit from the technical and financial assistance of the State and will enjoy certain privileges."

18. This authorization prolongs Toussaint Louverture's attempt to establish and generalize, back in 1801, the *carte de sûreté* (security card), whose model was France's Revolutionaries' national identity cards established during the Reign of Terror (Gonzales 2019, 114–20; Spieler 2021). Of course, the repression of vagrants is not new and would require more attention than I can give here. Interesting

reflections on this subject can be found in Robert Castel (2003) and Michel Foucault (2018).

19. The ban was even reinforced after the French-dominated Roman Catholic Church signed the 1860 Concordat. In fact, the Church contributed to putting in place and running two big persecution campaigns against Vodou, famously called the "anti-superstition campaigns." Another such campaign was conducted by the US military during its occupation of Haiti between 1915 and 1934 (Clorméus 2012; Delisle 2003; Ramsey 2011).

20. In his analysis of the birth of the modern penal institutions, Foucault (2019) notes that one of the scopes of the use of the Penal Code in its early days was to criminalize practices that were associated with insurrection. It was meant to show that the acts committed (say pillage, contraband, arson, and killing) were illegitimate, acts of undue power incompatible with the idea of a peaceful nation-state, while at the same time it had to show that its own use of violence was legitimate and acceptable. This was not self-evident. It had to define that these acts were in fact misdemeanors, felonies, crimes, and that they therefore were reason for punishment, whereas the forced levying of money (tax), fines, imprisonment, and death sentence were legitimized.

21. This clash is reminiscent of the way Foucault interprets the popular revolt of the Nus-pieds in 1639, the point of departure of his lectures on the birth of the penal institutions and theories. An undue tax increase jeopardized the possibilities of survival for the poorest classes. The peasants and workers thus rebelled against increased tax pressure that had crossed the threshold of tolerance of the poorest populations. Their refusal to accept the law and struggles against the public power took many forms: smuggling, burglary, assault, arson, public execution, riot. In the face of it, the power in place had to constitute a specific armed force, which would have to exert pressure on the poor, and some of the privileged along with them, essentially to keep them in check and force them to pay up. This is why, for Foucault, there is a congenital link between one of the mainsprings of capitalism, i.e., fiscal taxation, and the modern penal system.

22. I owe much to my conversations with Lotte B. Segal and my reading of her very sensitive and tactful book, *No Place for Grief* (2016), on "what it means to live with violence at your front door as a permanent feature of life rather than as an occasional, discrete occurrence" (ibid., 10). I owe as much to Bhrigupati Singh's very inspiring *Poverty and the Quest for Life* (2015), where his alternative picture of sovereignty has definitely changed the way I perceive what the quest for a better life can mean for the most disadvantaged.

23. "*Baz*" translates as "base," and refers to "a complex network of affiliated, social cliques that have no centralized leadership structure" but are more something like a "core network of leaders" (Kivland 2020, 5; Neiburg 2017). The *baz* "emerged following the collapse of the Duvalier family dictatorship in 1986

and alongside the democratization and the neoliberalization of the political economy" (Kivland 2020, 6). They embody a veritable politics of the street, imagining themselves as replacements for absent or dysfunctional state institutions. "*Nou fè leta*," "We make the State," they say, as they profile themselves as intermediaries or brokers between government agents, politicians, or NGO workers, in order to secure an income and resources for the neighborhood. This is how they manage to supply residents with electricity or clean up the streets of their mountains of garbage. Yet, as Chelsey Kivland's compelling ethnography shows, the aspirations of these young men for peace, development, and democracy must be understood against a backdrop of high insecurity produced in large part by a structured economy of terror, as well as their competitive spirit, their ways of reproducing hierarchies, and their use of violence. By seeking to protect local residents, and by acting as spokesmen for their needs and desires, the *baz* are caught up in contradictory injunctions. In the name of the neighborhood's residents, they sometimes act against their own interests and well-being, and the violence often backfires. Their efforts often undermine their own intentions: They end up brokering with corrupt politicians and wage war against one another, thus making neighborhoods even more precarious.

24. According to a 1996 analysis by the Fondation haïtienne des écoles privées (FONHEP), public schools accounted for just 17 percent of schools, compared with 83 percent for private schools. That same year, the same report estimated that only 53 percent of children attended school (Joint 2008, 19–20; Erard 2021). There is every reason to believe that, in the current situation, there are probably even fewer public schools and fewer children in school overall.

25. Anaïca turned eighteen in 2023 and decided to leave Haiti. She set off alone along the Central American migration trail. She eventually entered the United States under Biden's Temporary Protection Status (TPS) program and joined a cousin in the Boston area. But her future is more than uncertain, since in 2025 Donald Trump revoked the TPS and threatened half a million Haitians with deportation. In this chaos, where no one really knows what will happen, she has applied for asylum and waits for an answer. Apart from that, she continues to study English (which she does not yet speak) and does small jobs to earn her daily bread.

26. "PetroCaribe" refers to an energy cooperation agreement signed in 2005 between Venezuela, who was trying to bypass the American hegemony on the oil business, and the Caribbean countries, which provides for the purchase of oil on preferential payment terms. Haiti joined the agreement in 2007, and as early as 2008, the country's top officials began planning the biggest embezzlement scandal in the country's history. In 2019 the scandal broke out when the first report of the Superior Court of Accounts and Administrative Disputes (CSCCA) was published: Haiti was facing a colossal squandering of at least $3.8 billion, involving

four presidents and six governments over a period of more than ten years. Presidents Jovenel Moïse and Michel Martelly (both from the PHTK party), were indicted by the Office of the Public Prosecutor. *"Kòt kob PetwoKaribe a,"* "Where is the PetroCaribe money?" is a question that has been on everyone's lips since. It also became a slogan printed on T-shirts, painted on cupboards, and sprayed on walls, bringing huge crowds of protesters, dubbed "Petrochallengers" by the media, onto the streets. These massive and regular protests since 2018, often involving hundreds of thousands, regularly more than a million, people, have become an organized resistance movement known as *peyi lòk*, "locked country," named after the blockage of all roads and the functioning of state institutions. See Mélissa Béralus et al. (2021); Gustav Cederlöf and Donald Kingsbury (2019); Mamyrah Dougé-Prosper and Mark Schuller (2021); Bret Gustavson (2017); and Claire Payton (2019).

27. According to the World Food Programme's April 2023 briefing, "Haiti ranks 170 out of 189 countries on the 2020 Human Development Index. The country has one of the highest levels of chronic food insecurity in the world with more than half of its total population chronically food insecure and 22 percent of children chronically malnourished. The latest Integrated Food Security Phase Classification (IPC) results of March 2023 show that almost half the population in Haiti, or 4.9 million people, are food insecure (IPC3+), an increase of 200,000 people compared to the previous analysis of September 2022. In addition, 1.8 million people are in Emergency phase or IPC 4 (Emergency)."

28. Kidnapping has been a political tool in the past to put pressure on the opposition; it's nothing new, but it reached a peak with Moïse, who, it seems, used it recklessly. Having reached an all-time high in the country, the situation has been out of control for several years, with two hundred or more armed groups using it to finance war as much as to put pressure on opposing parties. In fact, after Jovenel Moïse's assassination, Jimmy Cherizier, aka Barbecue, an ex-policeman employed by the HNP and trained by UN and bilateral agencies, had brought together, a year earlier, nine (then eleven) of Port-au-Prince's main armed groups (or gangs) and created a coalition called *G9 an Fanmi e Alye* (the G9 Family and Allies). It would appear, from evidence provided by a host of local NGOs and my own informants, that Cherizier had close links with President Moïse and the ruling PHTK party. It's no coincidence that the neighborhoods and rival groups he systematically attacked were hotbeds of the opposition, notably Jean-Bertrand Aristide's Lavalas party. Upon Moïse's death, the G9 stepped into the breach of power and took possession and control of most of the capital's territory, including the port of Varreux (Haiti's main import port), the markets, the north and south axes, as well as the national archives, the court of first instance, and several ministries (foreign affairs, defense, economy and trade, taxes, etc.). Massacres of civilians, arson attacks, and assaults on state institutions

(notably police stations and courts) became relentless. In the war with the other major coalition, the G-Pèp, with whom the G9 disputes the territory, as well as with the interim government represented by Ariel Henry, there have been thousands of casualties. On February 29, 2024, however, an agreement between the G9 and the G-Pèp was reached and a new coalition called *Viv Ansanm*, "Living Together," was formed with Cherizier at its head. Yet, the violence has not ended. As recently as November 15, 2024, the IOM announced the displacement of 20,000 people in Port-au-Prince in just four days and a total of more than 700,000 displaced in the whole country since the war began. Kidnappings are on the rise again. And it's clear to many Haitians I know that the understaffed and underarmed contingent of Kenyan police and military personnel sent under the latest UN Security Council resolution (no. 2699, adopted on October 2, 2023) to support the Haitian police appears to be a farce.

29. The fact that, on July 18, 2019, twenty-two officers of the Correctional Unit of the United Nations Mission in Support of Justice in Haiti (MINUJUSTH) received the United Nations Medal, with the inscription "In the service of peace" on the back, says a lot about the motivations of the United Nations and the place that prisons occupy in the imagination of peace. I will come back to this in Chapter 3. See also the issues around Rodny's incarceration in the subchapter entitled "Life at a Threshold" in Chapter 6.

30. By way of comparison, the promotion of the broad, foreign-funded alternative dispute resolution (ADR) programs in Bolivia have also deeply reshaped inner conflicts and the politics of the country. Susan Ellison shows minutely how the macro-politics of the promotion of ADR programs—heavily influenced by USAID, accused by Morales of political meddling—were in keeping with the more general promotion of democracy in Latin America, which sees itself as the favorable "conditions under which private enterprise might flourish" (Ellison 2018, 6). Her book shows "what happens when foreign aid programs hit the ground," programs that "seek to transform democratic institutions and influence political behavior" (ibid., 7).

31. The Core Group comprises the ambassadors of Brazil, Canada, France, Germany, the European Union, Spain, and the United States, as well as the special representative of the Organization of American States and the special representative of the secretary-general of the United Nations. It's an informal influence group within the United Nations itself with an unclear mandate, acting as a catalyst by proposing "solutions," coordinating international efforts, facilitating negotiations, and targeting leadership. Many critics, including Daniel L. Foote, American diplomat and former special envoy to Haiti, denounce the Core Group's interference in Haiti's domestic affairs.

32. The Montana Accord is an agreement signed on August 30, 2021 by several Haitian civil parties and political formations to set up a new provisional

government following the assassination of President Moïse. The members of the agreement oppose the government of Prime Minister Ariel Henry, who exercises de facto presidential powers. The agreement led to the organization on January 30, 2022 of an unofficial ballot by the parliamentary members of the agreement to choose by indirect suffrage a provisional president to lead a transitional period. Fritz Jean's election was not recognized by Ariel Henry's government, which remained in power.

33. According to the letter dated October 8, 2022 from the UN secretary-general addressed to the president of the UN Security Council, the ratio of police officers to the population is at 1.06 per 1,000 inhabitants, which is well below the United Nations-suggested international ratio of 2.2 per 1,000. Moreover, of all the officers involved in law enforcement, only a third are believed to be operational. The high rate of attrition in the HNP is due primarily to increasing attacks on the police. The letter states that some twenty-eight police stations were vandalized or destroyed from January to August 2022 alone, reducing, and in some cases eliminating totally, police and state authority in vast areas and leaving them under the control of gangs. Thirteen police officers had been killed before August the same year. And the situation has since worsened. According to the United Nations, in 2024, at least 5,600 people were killed in gang violence. These deaths represent an increase of over 1,000 on the total killings for 2023. The United Nations further reports 2,212 people injured and 1,494 kidnapped, and documents 315 lynchings of gang members and people allegedly associated with gangs, which on some occasions were facilitated by Haitian police officers. Additionally, 281 cases of alleged summary executions involving specialized police units occurred during 2024. This results in growing rates of post abandonment, absenteeism, resignation, desertion, dismissal, retirement, and exile.

34. As I complete the final version of this book manuscript, in January 2025, Haiti still does not have a functioning Parliament. The National Assembly—made up of two chambers: the upper chamber (the Senate of the Republic) and the lower chamber (the Chamber of Deputies)—is at a complete standstill. Since January 13, 2020, the term of office of all deputies and two-thirds of senators has come to an end. The last ten senators still in office saw their term of office end in early January 2023 without being replaced, leaving the country without parliamentary representation. Following the resignation of Prime Minister Ariel Henry in April 2024, Michel Patrick Boisvert acted as interim prime minister until the appointment of Garry Conille in June 2024. Conille, who had previously served as prime minister in 2011, was appointed by the Presidential Transitional Council to lead the country pending elections scheduled for February 2026. However, in November 2024, Conille was removed from office, and Alix Didier Fils-Aimé, a businessman and former leader of the Chamber of Commerce, was appointed interim prime minister.

1. "WE'RE HOLDING ON!": A CHRONICLE

1. René Char's verse goes, "*Nous sommes écartelés entre l'avidité de connaître et le désespoir d'avoir connu*" (1995, 184). In Kermonde Lovely Fifi, the original goes, "*Les mots pleurent ce soir*" (2013, 13). Georges Castera's is, "*mais comment raconteur/les mots sont fous*" (2006, 23). And Lyonel Trouillot's (in Béralus et al. 2021, 10), "*Écrire est fragile comme vivre.*"

2. See the detailed investigation reports on: https://web.rnddh.org/; https://www.fjkl.org.ht/; https://cardh.org/; and https://hrp.law.harvard.edu/. The reports of the United Nations Integrated Office (https://binuh.unmissions.org/en) are, on the contrary, very ambiguous and opaque. The BINUH does not clearly establish the nature of the links between the state and the so-called "gangs," even though evidence of their complicity exists and is known.

3. The *kay* refers to a house, a home, in the conventional sense, but also a house for the *lwa*, the spirits. It is then referred to as a *kay lwa* or a *badji*. As an *oungan* (Vodou master of ceremonies) and therapist, Ariel has a family compound called *oumfò* (or *lakou*); it is a Vodou sanctuary. In his compound, there are the *kay* where the members of his family sleep and the *kay* that house the *lwa*.

4. Mesac went into exile in 2021. He used to live in Mattapan (South Boston), MA, close to kin and other members the Bwa-Mapou community who live there; he now lives in Lynn, MA.

5. In Haiti, "notables" are people of a certain rank who have authority in local affairs, such as municipal officials, retired police officers, school principals, priests or pastors, *manbo* or *ougan* (Vodou ceremony masters).

6. A Vodou ritual is usually called a "service" (*sèvis*) that is offered to the *lwa*, the spirits.

7. The novels of Emmelie Prophète (2020) and Jean d'Amérique (2021) set their stories in this area. See also Chelsey Kivland's excellent book (2020) on the lives of young men from the *baz* in the *geto* of Bel-Air.

8. A "mystical attack" can be understood as a "spell" or "hex."

9. *Bòkò* generally refers to a person whose mystical powers come from *lwa achte*, purchased spirits, as opposed to *manbo* and *oungan*, who (normally) practice only with *lwa ginen*, ancestral spirits from Africa (mythical Guinea), which they have inherited or have chosen themselves. However, Vodou practitioners often trade with both, which blurs the distinction between *bòkò* and *oungan* or *manbo*. The main difference is that an *oungan* or *manbo* makes it a point of honor to be exemplary of a certain ethic of the Vodou tradition, whereas the *bòkò* have a darker reputation that they do not necessarily seek to restore, and they sometimes even willingly accept, in exchange for payment, to undertake actions of a more dubious and troubled nature, or even downright illicit and criminal. *Wanga* are considered magical objects a *bòkò* uses.

10. On the magic of guns, see Kivland 2018.

11. The reports are available here: https://www.cscca.gouv.ht/rapports_petro
_caribe.php. See note 26 in the Introduction for more details about the agreement
and the embezzlement.

12. A person who is "possessed" by a spirit is said to be "ridden" because the
body is conceived as a *chwal*, a horse, which is ridden by a guiding power.

13. An *ounsi* (pl. *ounsi*) is an initiate and server in mystical congregations.

14. A *balèn bouji* is a candle used in Vodou ceremonies and in the cemetery
during the Feast of the Dead.

15. The *peristil* is the centerpiece of an *oumfò* (a Vodou shrine) where most
rituals take place. In the center of the *peristil* is the *poto-mitan*, the central pole
around which people dance and through which the *lwa* arrive.

16. The "tour" (*tounen*) consists of a march through the village or neighborhood singing and dancing. At the head of the procession, there is the ox that will
be sacrificed and presented to the community.

2. THE SILENT WARS OF THE ORDINARY

1. Bawon and the *gede* are figures heavily loaded with a memory of violence.
The Duvalier dictatorship (1957–1986) had erected itself as the incarnation of these
spirits. "Papa Doc" (François Duvalier) used to dress like Bawon Sanmdi, wearing
a black suit and dark sunglasses; his private militia, the *tonton makout* (the name
recalls the popular figure of the bogeyman who is said to kidnap children and
make them disappear in his sack), were ambiguously assimilated to the henchmen of Bawon, the *gede* (Johnson 2006). Thus, Bawon is reminiscent of the
political institutionalization of a pervasive terror economy (James 2010, 57–58;
Trouillot 1990). See Alfred Métraux (1972) for a detailed account of the role these
kinds of spirits play in the ritual economy.

2. On the secret *sanpwèl* society, see Chapter 1 and Chapter 5.

3. Chelsey Kivland (2014, 679) mentions in her description of the complex
organization of the "base" (*baz*)—a clique dwelling on a corner of an urban
block—the association between the activities of these groups and the *sanpwèl*.
Other authors also point to the specific history of these societies, which must be
taken into account: These groups were born in a context of marronage as
organizations resisting the hegemony of nation-states. The latter, of course,
criminalized them by fighting them and forcing them underground. These
organizations were sometimes perceived as parallel societies or sects, sometimes
as guerrillas, paramilitary organizations, or seditious occult orders (Gonzales
2019; Hurston 2009; Ramsey 2011).

4. I obtained much information from the commissioner of the government
living in the village and working as a lawyer at one of the two special land

tribunals in the country, located in Saint-Marc and Gonaïves. They were created specifically to arbitrate disputes of the sort in other parts of the country. A team of scholars from Columbia University conducting a survey for a report called "Options for Land Tenure Dispute Management in Rural Haiti" (2012) reported that, unlike the litigations they have recorded in the South, those that take place in Artibonite are more frequent, intensive, and violent.

5. See Métraux (1951) for an early account of rotational work in rural Haiti, and Scott Freeman (2017), who critically addressed the issue of contour canals within a history of collective labor in rural Haiti.

6. Anthropology has long demonstrated that the boundaries between official and unofficial law, formal (state) law and informal (nonstate) law, a criminal and a civil case, and order and lawlessness are uncertain and never clear-cut (Brandel and Randeria 2018; Comaroff and Comaroff 2009; Das and Poole 2004; Nader 2003). These dichotomies have often eclipsed the empirical realities that ethnographers have attempted to bring to light. In the Haitian context, Kivland (2014; 2017) has revealed how, for instance, in the troubled neighborhood of Bel-Air, in Port-au-Prince, the enactment of street sovereignty by members of cliques of young men is both legal and illegal, thereby constantly shifting the boundaries between state and street law as it conflicts with, or serves, the particular interests of state officials. Others, like the researchers of the Interuniversity Institute for Research and Development (INURED) (Marcelin 2015; Marcelin and Cela 2020), have for years surveyed entire shantytowns in Port-au-Prince, in order to demonstrate how unclear the boundaries are between crime and official politics. The generalized economy of violence, the dynamics of "production and reproduction of marginalization and social indifference" (Marcelin 2015, 240) fueled by the ruling class, and the ways in which the normalization of violence throughout a community erodes the possibilities of taking collective action against it, show us how important it is to reconsider the standard angles from which we consider the problem at hand.

7. Interestingly, there is a similarity in structure with the problem posed by Michel Foucault in the moment of constitution, at the end of the Middle Ages, of the modern judiciary. "Those who judge also take a risk: of being in turn involved in a private war . . . [and] of not being obeyed, of seeing their power weakened and compromised" (2019, 119).

8. These matters were later taken up by André Cabanis and Louis Martin (1996), who reflected on the appropriation of the Napoleonic Civil Code by the Haitian state, which gave birth to what they called a "judicial modulated creolization." For his part, Pierre-Louis Naud (2007) has thought of the limits and the issues at stake in the judicialization of the sociopolitical and economic life of Haiti, and Gélin Collot (2007) reflected on the historical genesis of the Haitian Civil Code. See Michel Hector and Laënnec Hurbon (2009) for an account of the genesis of the Haitian state.

9. It is not unlikely that the concept of "notable" in Haiti is strongly influenced by the history of the concept in France, where it was used after the French, and therefore Haitian, Revolution to characterize certain nineteenth-century ruling elites, understood as a restricted group of individuals and family lines who combined economic wealth (mainly land), social prestige, and political power. These were those who had a monopoly on access to elective office and administrative functions, whether de jure or de facto. The notabiliary class was thus defined by its qualities, its prerogatives (wealth, active citizenship, the exercise of public functions), and its lifestyle (sociability, leisure activities, involvement in community life, etc.) and practices (clientelism, constitution and maintenance of a personalized and territorialized political patrimony, mediation between local space and political-administrative authorities, etc.).

10. One should note how much playfulness and seriousness are porous categories. Other examples can be found in Chapters 4 and 6.

11. See note 28 in the Introduction for more details on this moment of unrest.

12. Jean and John Comaroff (2016) and Laura Nader (2003) have demonstrated, in other contexts, how the transformations of global capital lead state justice, police, and crime to be ever more complicit.

13. It is not fortuitous that Joseph's clique established in the zone, since it's a jurisdiction heavily influenced by senator, singer, songwriter, and actor Garcia Delva. He has been accused by Jean Renel Senatus, the Senate's Justice, Public Security and National Defense Commission leader, as well as by the judicial police, of being in cahoots with Joseph, and of criminal association, kidnapping, and sequestration for ransom, after which the lifting of his parliamentary immunity was debated. It turns out that Delva was born and grew up in Marchand Dessalines, of which he was a deputy before becoming senator of the Artibonite.

14. According to the Center for Analysis and Research in Human Rights (CARDH), "A Report from the Departmental Intelligence Service"—Fiche: DDA/SDR -00345 (1/28/2023)—concluded that the attack causing the killing of the police officers was planned by three high-ranking police officers (two inspectors general and a divisional commissioner) in order to 'cause chaos in Artibonite.'" https://cardh.org/archives/4304.

15. See the 2022 FAO, WFP, and BINUH reports: https://www.fao.org/newsroom/detail/catastrophic-hunger-levels-recorded-for-the-first-time-in-haiti/en; https://www.wfp.org; and https://binuh.unmissions.org/en/reports. According to the UNDP 2018 statistics, the working poor at Purchasing Power Parity (PPP) \$3.10 a day constitute 50.7 percent (of 58.8 percent employment ratio) of the population, and those living below the income poverty line, PPP \$1.90 a day, accounted for 23.4 percent. Moreover, 87.5 percent of total employment is considered "vulnerable" by the UNDP. In short, for a total population of around

eleven million whose median age is twenty-three, the UNDP considers that there are more or less three million working poor, 1.5 million living below the poverty line, and 5.2 million unemployed (but says nothing about the informal sector). See also Catherine Maternowska's (2006) study of life conditions in the slums of Cité Soleil in the early 2000s, as well as Greg Beckett's (2019) portrait of the daily struggles of Port-au-Prince residents during the de facto period.

3. THE MANY FACES OF PEACE

1. Laura Ring's (2006) account of the micro-mechanisms of coexistence in Karachi's apartment blocks is an example of similar concerns. By examining the daily work of peacekeeping amid civic strife, she more specifically highlights the difficult, domestic, and creative work of women. Although women's work is not the main focus of my survey, I'd like to emphasize just how important their work is in Haiti—holding households, kinship ties, and neighboring communities together. With a different inflection, Pascale Schild's (2023) work on "civilian peace-building"—initiatives taken for and by ordinary Kashmiris to overcome the social divisions imposed by the Kashmir conflict and enable intergroup relations and collaboration—shows how these civilians carefully avoid politics while operating across one of the world's most politicized and militarized borders. The contradictions, dangers, and opportunities inherent in these "non-political" initiatives and civilian peace-building aspirations in Kashmir are instructive in the case of Haiti. Although the context and problems are obviously very different, the question also arises in Haiti as to what (non)political form peace-building efforts from below take.

2. See https://peacekeeping.un.org/en/mission/minustah.

3. Michel Foucault evoked "the old struggle against paper and writing," (2019, 7) in his first lecture, on November 7, 1971, referring to the anti-fiscal riots of the sixteenth century and the birth of modern penal institutions.

4. The question of summoning the defendant or witnesses is a serious and delicate matter since the very first developments of formal legal proceedings, because the charges are generally filed independently by the plaintiff or else by the state (Olivelle et al. 2024, 327–32). Different systems then developed varying and often complex rules and technicalities, as is the case today, in order to ensure, for example, that the plaint is plausible, that it falls under the titles of law, or that it is not specious, otherwise it would be dismissed. The burden of enforcing the summons can befall the plaintiff or the courts. And there were, and still are, provisions to avoid unreasonable demands, like summoning a farmer during harvest or a woman who just gave birth. In her ethnography, Susan Ellison (2018) shows in detail the tensions inherent to the processes of alternative dispute resolution (ADR) programs in Bolivia in which "inviting" someone to

conciliation, even though it presents itself as a friendly act, is all but a trivial gesture that can trigger animosities.

5. According to a large survey conducted in 2001, supervised by Gélin Collot (in Paisant 2003), dean of the Faculty of Law and Economical Sciences of the State University of Haiti, more than 70 percent of the interviewees do not hesitate to slaughter an animal that has trespassed and caused damage to their fields.

6. This is an illustration of the ordinary resistance against alien rule. Most people in the valley would say it doesn't matter if it's illegal, that's the way they do it, period. This underlies the fact that the people who wrote these laws are not peasants and what's more, they wrote them to take away the peasants' way of life.

7. Bossou Twa Kòn is a well-known *lwa* in the Artibonite, inventor of magic and mirror of justice, associated in Catholicism with Saint Nicholas of Myra. Among other things, he's the saint of children and unmarried people. The story goes that, one day, St. Nicholas saved three children from the hands of a horrible butcher who had put them in a salt cellar and was about to chop them up. The saint is also said to have saved three young girls from an indebted father who wanted to sell them. Bossou, like St. Nicholas, is therefore considered a child protector. "Twa kòn" means "three horns." They hint at the holy trinity; the three kings Gaspard, Melchior, and Balthazar; the three apostles Paul, Jude, and Peter; as well as life, death, and judgment.

8. Danbala is the primordial creator of life, water sources, and rivers. He helps humans to take the right directions and orient themselves toward the good. In Catholicism, he is associated with Saint Patrick, known for driving the bad snakes out of Ireland and into the sea (a hagiographic theme probably taken from the passage in Exodus where Moses and Aaron fight Pharaoh's sorcerers, who turn into snakes).

9. See https://www.nobelprize.org/prizes/peace/2001/summary/.

10. My analysis coincides with Laura Zanotti's who concludes her book on UN peace operations "that in Haiti the importation of Western political models has fostered disorder, eroded the capacity of the state to govern, and reinforced international regulatory power" (2011, 10). My perspective is also consistent with the one developed by Ugo Mattei (2010).

11. See the developments on the notion of "*lakou*" in the Introduction, as well as in the Glossary.

12. The emergence of JP courts in France coincides with the beginning of the systematic uprisings of slaves and runaways that would lead to Haitian independence. It is also telling that at exactly the same time, municipal police were created in New Orleans to reply to rising misdemeanors, crimes, and slave revolts.

13. Many factors contribute to hindering the functioning of the CASEC system. In particular, the combined effects of the political nonrecognition of their competence and responsibility, and the systematic back wages (often of several

months) not only preclude the CASEC from engaging fully in their task, but also prompt them to avoid doing their jobs (such as collecting taxes or taking care of the estate), if not squarely encouraging them to accept bribes. On January 18, 2018, President Moïse created a media spectacle by welcoming the CASEC at the presidential palace (in front of journalists) and promised to give them 570 motorbikes to facilitate their work; take care of the four-month payment backlog; make available the funds for the implementation of rural police in areas where there were none; build social housing; and distribute 171,000 food kits to the needy. Needless to say, most of these promises have not been kept, except the distribution of Chinese motorbikes, which had already been bought at the time of the promise.

14. For more details on the Frédéric's bakery, see the subchapter "Of Valley, Mountains, and Cities" in the Introduction.

15. There is an interesting question here concerning the specific space (or scene) in which the law is exercised, a question that I will address in more detail in Chapter 4. Nevertheless, it should be noted at this stage that anthropologists, like historians of ancient societies (Olivette et al. 2024), emphasize that in the vast majority of cases studied, spaces devoted to the adjudication of disputes are generally public and do not constitute separate structures such as courthouses. These include temples, city gates, public squares, and communal buildings. In this respect, courthouses, designed specifically and solely for judicial proceedings, seem to be more the exception than the rule.

16. A point perhaps better understood if one imagines that the canonical Roman Law conceived the state as that which reflects the pontifical council; that is, as a legislator state (Supiot 2009, 28).

17. The organization of the *lakou* is probably the most compelling example of a way of living that is at the same time a way of resisting the attempts on part of the centralized power to control them.

18. See the definitions on the official website: http://www.cspj.ht/index.php/les -cours-et-les-tribunaux/cspj-haiti-mnu-tribunaux-et-cours-personnel. The name *hoqueton* in French (*acton* in medieval English) was originally for a padded vest or jacket made of cloth or leather and worn under armor during the Middle Ages. It then became the name of a function and a profession: the caretaker of the court, who is also the doorman, or the guardian.

19. See https://home.treasury.gov/news/press-releases/jy1080.

20. Resolution 1542 adopted by the Security Council at its 4961st meeting, on April 30, 2004.

21. Resolution 1908 adopted by the Security Council at its 6261st meeting, on January 19, 2010.

22. Resolution 2350 adopted by the Security Council at its 7924th meeting, on April 13, 2017.

23. As, for instance, works by James D. Wilets, associate dean of International Programs and professor of law at the Shepard Broad College of Law at NSU and chair of the Inter-American Center for Human Rights; works by Hans-Jörg Albrecht, director emeritus at the Max Planck Institute for the Study of Crime, Security and Law in Freiburg, as well as honorary professor and faculty member at the law faculty of the University of Freiburg; works by Louis Aucoin, United Nations secretary-general deputy special representative (rule of law) for Liberia and academic director of the Master of Laws program in international law at The Fletcher School of Law and Diplomacy at Tufts University; and works by Louis-Alexandre Berg, assistant professor in the Global Studies Institute and Political Science Department, Center for Human Rights & Democracy, at Georgia State University.

24. Their main reference is the Working Paper no. 37 (2006) of the network of the Conflict Prevention and Reconstruction Unit in the Social Development Department of the Sustainable Development Network of the World Bank, as well as the United Nations' official position on the promotion of the rule of law. This is not surprising, given that the World Bank was "the prime sponsor of this vocabulary from 1989, [and] placed it at the center of a new vision of wealth creation" (Humphreys 2010, xvi).

25. Another component of American and international interventionism I cannot discuss here, but which is of utmost importance, is humanitarian aid. See especially Jonathan Katz (2013) and Mark Schuller (2012).

26. A telling example is Bill Clinton's farm bill—the Federal Agricultural Improvement and Reform Act of 1996 (the FAIR Act)—that stipulated the shift from subsidies to direct payment programs, notably for rice crops. Among the effects was an increase of export to Haiti, where the rice coming mostly from Arkansas (Clinton's home state) was underpriced and took over the local rice market (Edmond 2019; Kivland 2020): "Since 1995, when [Haiti] dropped its import tariffs on rice from 50 to three percent as part of the structural adjustment program run by the International Monetary Fund (IMF) and the World Bank [and under the influence of the US], Haiti has steadily increased its imports of rice from the north. Today, it is the fifth-largest importer of American rice in the world . . . Haiti today imports over 80 percent of its rice from the U.S." (O'Connor 2013); in 1980, by contrast, Haiti was still self-sufficient. The adjustment plan was called *plan lanmò* (death plan) by Haitian farmers. Another example of America's profitable trade provision is the "Haitian Hemispheric Opportunity Through Partnership Encouragement Act of 2008" or the "HOPE II Act," subtitle D, part 1, titled "Extension of Certain Trade Benefits," of the Public Law 110–246 enacted on June 18, 2008, by the 110th Congress. See Schuller's (2012) detailed description of the history, structure, functioning, and effects of America's corporatist model of governance.

27. For instance, see the works by Max G. Manwaring, a retired US Army colonel and retired professor of military strategy at the Strategic Studies Institute of the US Army War College; works by Walter Kemp, director of global strategy against TOC, Global Initiative Against Transnational Organized Crime, formerly head of the Strategic Policy Support Unit at the Organization for Security and Cooperation in Europe (OSCE), as well as formerly leader of the "Peace Without Crime" project at the International Peace Institute (IPI); works by Mark Shaw, the director of the Global Initiative Against Transnational Organized Crime, previously National Research Foundation Professor of Justice and Security at the University of Cape Town (Department of Criminology), and as well worked for ten years at the United Nations Office on Drugs and Crime (UNODC), including as interregional advisor, chief of the Criminal Justice Reform Unit and with the Global Programme Against Transnational Organised Crime, with extensive field work; and works by Michael J. Dziedzic, a retired colonel with over twenty years of experience in the international civil/military and stabilization field, senior fellow at The Terrorism, Transnational Crime and Corruption Center (TraCCC) of the Schar School of Policy and Government at George Mason University, as well as senior program officer at the International Institute for Strategic Studies, the Institute for National Strategic Studies, and US Institute of Peace. See Stephen Humphreys (2010) for a literature review and briefing on the numerous parallels and continuities between European colonialism in Africa and the contemporary promotion of the rule of law.

28. See, for example, the particularly eloquent remarks on the reform of the Penal Code made by US Ambassador Michele J. Sison at the event "Toward the Modernization of Haitian Criminal Justice," on September 28, 2018: "The adoption of these new penal and criminal procedure codes will help strengthen the rule of law in Haiti, which in turn will foster investment and economic growth, and prosperity. Countries with effective legal systems and sound legislative frameworks will attract domestic and foreign direct investment: strengthening the rule of law stimulates economic growth by attracting investors who value the protections offered by transparent and fair systems. Promoting stability and economic development in Haiti is a top U.S. priority in our partnership with the Haitian people" (my translation from the French). https://ht .usembassy.gov/fr/remarques-de-lambassadeur-michele-j-sison-lors-de -levenement-vers-la-modernisation-de-la-justice-penale-haitienne/.

29. Besides the numerous documents and reports produced by grassroots organizations, associations, journalists, NGOs, and different agencies, evidence can be found in Greg Beckett 2019; Dan Coughlin 2006; Coughlin and Kim Ives 2011; Ralph Frerichs 2020; Katz 2013a; 2013b; Sabine Lee and Susan Bartels 2019; Nicolas Lemay-Hébert 2014; Reed 2007; Claire Payton 2017; 2019; Schuller 2012.

30. See https://www.usip.org/guiding-principles-stabilization-and-reconstruction -the-web-version/rule-law.

31. A symptom of this situation is the definitive closure, in 2005, of the "Investigation and Anti-Gang Service," composed mainly of former FAD'H soldiers and other mercenaries. It was known for using torture and carrying out arbitrary arrests and executions. Their methods were those of the mercenaries of the Duvalier dictatorship. Their function was surveillance, intimidation, and executions and the targets mainly members of the Lavalas party (Aristide).

32. Since I wrote this chapter, things have changed. After the fierce war between the G9 and the G-Pèp (the other armed coalition that controlled a large part of Port-au-Prince's territory), an agreement was reached and a new coalition called *Viv Ansanm*, "Living Together," was formed on February 29, 2024, with Cherizier at its head.

33. It would be interesting to compare these policies regarding IJS and CVR with those that concern alternative dispute resolution (ADR) programs. In fact, ADR is seen as a tool designed, not only to foster the rule of law in other contexts, but also "systematically favors stronger economic and political interests against the weaker ones while at the same time effectively taming social dissent and silencing the demand for justice" (Mattei 2010, 90; Nader 1999; Sternlight 2007). See Ellison (2018) for a detailed ethnographic account of the politics of ADR in Bolivia.

34. The CVR was then applied by the MINUSMA in Mali, by the MONUSCO in the Democratic Republic of Congo, by the MINUSCA in Central African Republic, and by the UNAMID in North and South Soudan. Interestingly, the CVR was applied only in African countries; but this would require further analysis.

4. THEATRICALIZING THE LAW

1. It is interesting to note that "the double meaning of the word 'court' (*curia*)—both royal court and law court—reminds us how hard it may be to disentangle law from political power" (Peters 2022, 21).

2. See, for instance, the mutual interest between anthropologists, philosophers, scholars of law, and specialists of theater (Ball 1975; Biet 2011; Huizinga 1980; Leiboff 2018; Meyer-Plantureux 2015; Nield 2019; A. Reed 2015; Y. Robert 2019; Rogers 2008; Schwarte 2006; C. Smith 2013; Soulier 1991). Some authors, following Hannah Arendt's contempt of the theatrical disruption in the judicial process, coined the term "theaters of justice" to emphasize the spectacularity of some trials, that is, when trials become smokescreens as well as popular entertainment (Bachmann 2010; Felman 2002; Horsman 2010). They are right, of course, to highlight the problematic excitement raised by these mediatized and sensational mega-trials. But the sort of theatricality I endeavor to emphasize is of a different kind.

3. For the purposes of this chapter, I will limit my discussion to the legal tradition that emerged with the dawn of the modern era. I cannot, of course, take

into account other known legal traditions that would however constitute interesting points of contrast. That said, I would nevertheless like to mention, by way of example and comparison, that in the legal tradition of the Dharmaśāstra (धर्मशास्त्र), the conduct of judges is described in an interesting way. Judges were required to possess certain qualities that are reminiscent of those I mention in professional ethics: impartiality, honesty, kindness, calmness, and selflessness (Olivelle et al. 2024, 312). It should also be noted that the practice of judicial oaths was not new and is not specific to modern legal practice. For instance, in ancient Athens, all judges took an oath comprising four clauses, the purpose of which was: to swear to judge in accordance with the laws; to hear both parties impartially; to vote with the utmost discernment, that is, with honesty and sincerity; and to limit the vote to the charges contained in the indictment.

4. I chose this example arbitrarily simply because I was in Vancouver when I wrote this section. I could have taken any other example, for that matter.

5. See https://www.lawsociety.bc.ca/.

6. International Bar Association, *International Principles on the Conduct of the Legal Profession*, adopted on May 28, 2011.

7. See the subsection "The Vagueness of Concepts, The Vagueness of Law" in Chapter 5.

8. In summer 2023, the UNDP reported that over 90 percent of Haitians have recourse to informal means of justice, outside of any state intervention.

9. Compare, for example, the difference between the uses of the courts in my cases and those cases studied by Sally Engle Merry (1990) among the native-born white American working class in the 1980s, or by Mindie Lazarus-Black (2007) among the survivors of domestic violence in Trinidad. What happens not only in the courts, but also around them, is highly instructive for understanding how different forms of legality are made and unmade. Their study of legal consciousness shows how different the uses, but also the expectations, of the law can be.

10. I cannot expand this point here but let me just remind the reader of Haiti's particular history and its role in redefining legal concepts of property (including the human as movable asset, as the 1685 Code Noir states), in reshaping boundaries and territories (when, for instance, it won its independence), and in inventing new modes of living based on new forms of inhabitation (the system of the *lakou*) (Dubois 2012; Fischer 2004; C. James 2023; Maguire and Freeman 2017; Sala-Molins 2018).

11. In their study of Congolese's JP courts outside Lubumbashi, Benjamin Rubbers and Emilie Gallez (2012) at some point describe a similar ambiance: proceedings are not respected; people talk when they're not supposed to, or stand up and move; the police smoke and drink alcohol in the forbidden areas; a curious and noisy crowd agglutinates in the street and peeps through the windows, and comments upon the hearings.

12. Likewise, Caleb Smith (2013) shows how in seventeenth- and eighteenth-century American legal practice, the orality of the voice is what gives existence to the sermon and the curse, but also what gives them efficiency.

13. Lauren Benton (2002) also shows how, during colonial rule, intermediaries (litigants or legal practitioners) not only took part in legal proceedings, but also had an immediate and apparent interest in altering the rules. They maneuvered in all kinds of ways, eventually benefiting narrow groups of interests.

14. See the subsection "Slips in Uncertain Borderlands" in Chapter 6 where I transcribe the testimony of a friend who was in pretrial detention for three months. This is a very short time considering the number of cases where custody on remand lasts for years, sometimes without end.

5. INNER FORMS OF CORROSION

1. The petition was entitled "*Revoke legalizasyon pwostitisyon timoun, moun ak bèt, fanm ak fanm, gason ak gason,*" and was signed online by a little less than 200,000 people.

2. The question of incorporating customary law into formal law is a major concern for Haitian jurists, and a fundamental problem in the "philosophy" of Penal Code reform.

3. To glean information about this trip, I have primarily relied on these media sources: *Bénin To, Daily Mail, L'Express, La Nouvelle Tribune, Le Nouvelliste, Alterpresse, Loop, Nation Bénin, Rezo Nòdwès,* and *Le Point.*

4. See Giselle Anatol (2015), Wilson Chen (2011), and Alissa Jordan (2016) for other accounts of these figures in the Caribbean context.

5. I have shown in another context (Zanzibar) the way in which the dwindling of the life force is understood as an act of witchcraft or sorcery that creates zombies (Motta 2019a; see also Comaroff and Comaroff 2002).

6. I remind the reader of that moment described in the subchapter "The Play of Law Outside the Courts" in Chapter 4 when students at the back of the classroom were debating about legal issues related precisely to the zombie's (lack of) agency.

7. For instance, in 2012, a "zombie apocalypse" was announced by some American media after thirty-one-year-old Rudy Eugene, a Black man of Haitian descent, was shot dead by police as he was, according to police, eating the face of a homeless man on a deserted Miami causeway; he is known as the "Miami zombie" and the "Causeway cannibal." Lin Linnemann, Tyler Wall, and Edward Green (2014) show how stereotyping can be a way to conceal the normalization of state violence. It should also be noted that in the northern countries, zombies are generally depicted as predators, whereas in Haiti, zombies are primarily victims.

8. One should know that a *zonbi* can be sent by a *bòkò*, an expert in the manipulation of Vodou's evil forces, to steal the harvests.

9. And a desirable woman, often the mistress, is called a *femme-jardin*, "garden-woman."

10. This is shown, for instance, by the oversized erect phallus and the smiling human skulls of the sculptures of these spirits made by the artists of the collective Atis Rezistans. See also the excessively sexualized behavior of the butterfly spirit Baltazar Grandchiré in René Depestre (2017).

11. The *lwa* are said "to mount" a person's body, which becomes a *"chwal,"* a "horse" for them. One should hear the sexual undertone of the verb here.

12. For examples of such critique, see the novels of Yanick Lahens (2013) and Edwidge Danticat (2015a), as well as Mireille Rosello's commentary (2010).

13. An account of the concept of cannibalism in the Caribbean women's writings can be found in Njeri Githire (2014).

14. Censorship and repression of voice during the Duvalier's dictatorship were perceived as modes of zombification, especially by the authors of the spiralist movement, Frankétienne and Jean-Claude Fignolé.

15. These girls are called *"restavèk,"* meaning "staying with." They are children mostly born in poor rural areas and sent to wealthier families, often in towns, who are supposed to sponsor their education and provide food, in exchange for domestic duties. In reality, what happens is that they are often not sent to school and have to endure 24/7 hard work, regular beatings, and quite often sexual harassment. After a few years, if they do not escape, or have the chance to be unleashed, from their slave-like condition, the state of these girls quickly deteriorates; they decline and may turn into living dead beings.

16. For instance, in Frankétienne (2018) and Depestre (1990), the realization that the civil society (under the Duvaliers) is a zombified mass, a society plagued by its collective immobility (a mass frozen by fear), is at once realizing its profound desire for change. So here, against the common view, the zombies are depicted as being endowed with desire, potentially awakening, and capable of taking action. The figure of the zombie thus becomes the cornerstone of the emancipation of the people from the alienating state power (Glover 2005; 2010; 2012).

17. See Kate Ramsey's (2011) genealogy of the legal ban of popular ritual practices and its consequences on the law itself. One should also think of how, at different moments of history, legal definitions of personhood in the Afro-Atlantic world forged the concept of the zombie, notably in relation to the figure of the slave (slave is a legal category). See Angela Naimou (2017) for a particular insight into these matters.

18. It would be out of place here to go into the details of the various philosophical debates concerning the concept of "concept." For what is in question in this chapter, I have been particularly interested in the disagreement between Gottlob Frege (1951; 1952; 1979) and Ludwig Wittgenstein (1986) on this point, and in the subsequent analyses of it proposed by Cora Diamond (1981; 1984; 1988a; 1988b;

2012; 2013; 2014). Stanley Cavell's masterful developments on concepts in *The Claim of Reason* (1979) are obviously central to my argument, as well as Jocelyn Benoist's take on these matters (2013). For a more general account of how concepts work in anthropology, see the collection *Living with Concepts* (Brandel and Motta 2021).

19. The paradigm of this mode of thinking is probably the Linnean and the derived phylogenetic classification where each organism is assigned a series of names that more and more specifically locate it within a nested hierarchy (like a series of boxes within boxes). Take the (concept of) beetle: It is part of the order of coleoptera, itself part of the clade of Neuropteridal, which is part of the superorder of Endopterygota, belonging to the class of insects.

20. Danticat (2015a) also shows how a particular history of violence is inscribed in the female body and how children, in particular the female, have to bear the wound that has been inflicted on them. This history is political (several generations of Haitian women had to endure the Tonton Macoute's daily harassments and tortures), yet it is also a domestic, more intimate history of the relationships between mothers and daughters, where girls reaching puberty are "tested" by their forebears to make sure they are "whole" (see also Clitandre 2014; Francis 2004; 2010; Marouan 2013; Rosello 2010; Sarthou 2010; Watkins 2016). And if a virgin dies, the corpse-washer may be asked to deflower the cadaver to prevent her from being raped by the lascivious Bawon Sanmdi, who is known to be particularly fond of virgins.

21. Fort Dimanche was built by the French before the 1804 revolution and is today located between the slums of La Saline and Cité Soleil. It was annexed by US military forces during the first American occupation (1915–1934). Thereafter, over the period of twenty-nine years—from François Duvalier's rise to power in 1956 to the end of the reign of the son Jean-Claude in 1986—it became the Fò Lanmò, the Fort of Death, where tens of thousands were tortured and killed. The fort was abandoned in 1991 by the Aristide administration and has since become an open landfill, the locus of sewage discharge, and an overpopulated settlement.

6. THE MURMURING STREAM OF LIFE

1. Touillot's original French phrase is, *"Mais cette présence de la mort dans la vie, cette non-vie d'un peuple luttant pour son avenir, peut-on en parler enfin?"* (in Béralus et al. 2021, 10)

2. This theme is as old as philosophy itself. In continental philosophy, Plato was inspired by the meditations on death, transformation, and immortality of pre-Socratics. Plato himself (in his *Phaedo*, he asks, "What is the philosopher's attitude to death?") inspired the Stoics of the Hellenistic and Roman periods. Plutarch, Lucretius, and Seneca (especially his *Moral Epistles to Lucilius*) became

sources of inspiration for Montaigne. Significantly, the twentieth chapter of book 1 of his *Essays* is entitled: "To Philosophize Is to Learn How to Die." And after him, this aphorism has had multiple derivations in Emerson, Thoreau, and Nietzsche as well as in Michel Foucault, who was primarily interested in the tremor of the question "how will we die." They have of course reached Stanley Cavell, and therefore us. However, to understand the genealogy of these questions, it would be advisable not to restrict ourselves to so-called "continental philosophy," but to trace the considerable, but still under-recognized, influence of Middle Eastern and Indian subcontinent philosophies on the thinking of Greek-Roman antiquity, the Renaissance, and European modernity. However, such a perspective would still rely (too much) on historically valued, written traditions, to the detriment of traditions of thought inscribed in gestures, words, and bodies that leave no written trace as such. What I'm trying to do in this chapter is to shed some light on a philosophy that is rooted in the ordinary, an ordinary philosophy preoccupied with death and remarkably in tune with it, and whose importance we very rarely recognize.

3. In their introduction to *Formes de vie* (2018, 15), Estelle Ferrarese and Sandra Laugier write: "To think a form of life is to describe the persistence of a form, of a 'how,' whose obstinacy is to be accounted for." Andrew Brandel and I have elsewhere (2021) also raised the question about the ways in which anthropology is to be conceived as a response to the pressure that reality puts on us.

4. Cavell, in one of his texts primarily concerned with gothic and romantic tales of horror, further qualifies such an investigation "specifically as a spiritual task, one demanding a willingness for the experience of horror, and as a datable event in the unfolding of philosophical skepticism in the West" (1994, 158). I am unsure how and whether this applies in my case, and more generally in (Western) anthropology put to the test through its confrontation with other forms of life. Raphael Hoermann (2016) develops an account of the "Gothicisation of the Haitian Revolution" as the major modality of the transatlantic hegemonic discourse. Such issues have to be thought through much more carefully than what I can possibly do here.

5. From fall 1975, to spring 1976, Jacques Derrida gave a seminar at the École Normale Supérieure entitled "La vie la mort"—"Life Death"—whose typescript has been published in French (2019). By suppressing the expected "and," replacing it (but is it replacing?) by a space, a blank, he wanted to bring into question the traditional dialectical relation between life "and" death (ibid., 19–21). His explicit aim was to bring under scrutiny the oppositional, or contradictory, "relation between life and death," by asking if it is adequate at all to think of a life/death limit through (op)positional logics. He immediately cautions his students that the blank he introduced is not to be thought of as an identification of life with death (life *is* death) (ibid., 22). I wanted to mention specifically this point to underscore

that my own remarks, although not concerned with dialectics, are nonetheless concerned with the common assumption about the oppositional nature of life and death. Moreover, I too wish not to be misunderstood, and would like to emphasize that I do not consider life and death as permutable and symmetric terms.

6. I developed this question of the loss of a footing in relation to the loss of balance and a loss of rhythm in my book on the companionships between humans and spirits in Zanzibar (2019a). In a different vein but with a similar sort of impetus, Vinciane Despret (2019; 2021) also asks us to take seriously the dead and their creative demands (also commentaries by Lambek 2019; Noret 2019).

7. The sort of path life takes along the trajectory of death are many. One can take the measure of the variety, for example, by reading Robert Desjarlais (2016), Clara Han (2012), Andrew Irving (2017), or Heonik Kwon (2008).

8. Herman Melville's short story takes place in 1799, and undoubtedly evokes the slave revolts that have started around 1791 in Saint-Domingue (which is also the name of the ship), and which led to the independence of the western part of the island, baptized "Haiti" on January 2, 1804 (Beecher 2007; Ciarcia 2004).

9. This refers to the title of Cavell's memoirs (2010).

10. I use the Creole spelling "*gede*," instead of the French transliteration "guédé."

11. This novel adds another dimension—the erotic—to the beauty, the horrific, and the comical I had mentioned earlier.

12. In Leah Gordon's documentary "Atis Rezistans: The Scupltors of Grande Rue," part of the collection of her films entitled *Iron In the Soul* (2015), an artist of Port-au-Prince says to the camera: "The *gede* make me think, they make me live. . . . You're speaking to a *gede*. Because I'm dead already, but I haven't been buried yet. I'm a *gede*" ("*Gede yo fèm panse, yo fèm viv . . . Se yon gede kap pale ave nou. Paske m mouri deja mwen menm. Entere m poko entere. Se yon gede m ye*"). The title of Gordon's collection is taken from Sartre's third novel of his *Roads To Freedom* series, originally published in French as *La mort dans l'âme* (1949)—literally "death in the soul"—first translated by Gerard Hopkins as *Iron In The Soul*, then later as *Troubled Sleep*. There's an interesting connection here between living, dying, thinking, and freedom.

13. The French goes, "J'entends *le souffle* de la mort," which would be closer to "I hear the breath of death."

14. In French, the word he uses is "reconnaissance," which does indeed mean "recognition," or "acknowledgment," but plays out more explicitly the sense of "re-knowing," or "knowing again."

15. The lectures were delivered on October 15 and 16, 1997, at Princeton University, and were first published with commentaries by Amy Gutmann, Marjorie Garber, Peter Singer, Wendy Doniger, and Barbara Smuts, as *The Lives of Animals* (1999). In 2003—the year John Coetzee received the Nobel Prize—a novel entitled *Elizabeth Costello* (2003) grew out of the lectures.

16. In his own Tanner Lectures on Human Values given nine years earlier, Cavell writes that it is not merely that we underestimate the role of the body, "but that we falsify it . . . in philosophizing we turn the body into as it were an impenetrable integument" (1994, 163).

17. Coetzee and Cora Diamond take a strong and provocative stance against the more conventional philosophical view (epitomized by Martin Heidegger and Derrida) that holds onto the metaphysical argument that it is impossible to experience one's own death.

18. I borrow the idea from Cavell for whom intellectual scrupulousness is the "sense of what one is or could be in a position to say, to claim authority for imparting, in our common finitude, to a fellow human being" (1994, 162).

19. Henri Michaux's passage is reminiscent of *Walden*, in which Thoreau "interprets reading . . . as a process of *being read*" (Cavell 1994, 16).

20. Four inmates died in the civil prison of Saint-Marc, in May 2023 alone, due to overcrowding and malnutrition, notably anemia. According to BINUH's briefing of August 10, 2022, Haiti's prison system is saturated. The occupancy rate in the country's four main prisons is 401 percent. As a result, in some prisons inmates have only 0.24m2 per person. The Saint-Marc civil prison was rehabilitated with funding from the government of Norway, under an agreement with the UNDP signed on December 4, 2007. One of the main priorities of the strategic plan of the Haitian Prison Administration (DAP) was to improve prison infrastructure and conditions. The inauguration took place in October 2012 in the presence of the HNP and UNDP authorities. And yet, things have gotten worse. According to the World Prison Brief, Haiti ranks second in terms of occupancy level (based on official capacity) after the DRC, with an overall 454.4 percent. Comparatively, the neighboring Dominican Republic is at 162.3 percent, Brazil 143.8 percent, and Jamaica 87 percent.

21. Rodny used to work for him for free (in exchange for what favor, I don't know), although he's not trained in any of the legal professions: He used to draw up court reports and issue certificates of good conduct; he also did copies for him, drafted letters, and prepared extracts from the registries.

22. I couldn't find any reference to this document in the law, and haven't had a chance to investigate it further, but from what I understand, it's a document designed to counter the deleterious effects of rumors.

23. Sodium bicarbonate is used in prisons to improve digestion and relieve bloating, flatulence, itching, and gastralgia. It is also used to relieve various pathologies and lesions in the gums, mouth, and teeth. It acts as an antibacterial and antifungal agent, and has a buffering function, notably in the blood, where it helps maintain the hydrogen potential, known in this case as homeostasis. Additionally, it is used for its antacid properties, and thus helps relieve pyrosis (heartburn). Bicarbonate deficiency leads to muscle wasting and osteoporosis.

However, daily consumption is not recommended. Sodium bicarbonate often causes belching and abdominal discomfort. Due to excessive sodium intake, prolonged use can lead to ankle edema and nausea. For the same reason, it is contraindicated in cases of cardiac or renal insufficiency (risk of edema).

24. This is the translation of a transcript of a taped interview conducted with Rodny in French and Creole. At some point, he replayed the dialogues he had with the spirits.

25. For a detailed account of what it's like to be in the grip of a certain kind of thinking that leads to slippage, see my article on how skepticism emerges in anthropology (Motta 2023).

REFERENCES

Abi-Habib, Maria, and Andre Paultre. 2021a. "Why Has Haiti's President Been Assassinated?" *New York Times*, December 14.
———. 2021b. "Gangs Advance on the Seat of Haitian Government Power: 'Haitians are Hostages.'" *New York Times*, July 30.
Abu-Lughod, Lila. 1990. "The Romance of Resistance: Tracing Transformation of Power Through Bedouin Women." *American Ethnologist* 17 (1): 41–55.
Agamben, Giorgio. 2005 (2003). *State of Exception*. Translated by K Attell. Chicago: The University of Chicago Press.
Albrecht, Hans Joerg, Louis Aucoin, and Vivienne O'Connor. 2009. "Building the Rule of Law in Haiti: New Laws for a New Era." *United States Institute of Peace Briefing* (August).
Alphonse, Roberson. 2021. "Insécurité: le problème est de nature militaire, selon Mario Andrésol." *Le Nouvelliste*, October 1.
Amérique, Jean d'. 2021. *Soleil à coudre*. Paris: Actes Sud.
Anatol, Giselle L. 2015. *The Things That Fly in the Night: Female Vampires in Literature of the Circum-Caribbean and African Diaspora*. New Brunswick, NJ: Rutgers University Press.
Armstrong, Kimberly. 2014. "Justice Without Peace? International Justice and Conflict Resolution in Northern Uganda." *Development and Change* 45 (3): 589–607.
Asad, Talal. 2000. "Agency and Pain: An Exploration." *Culture and Religion: An Interdisciplinary Journal* 1 (1): 29–60.
Asgeirsson, Hrafn. 2015. "On the Instrumental Value of Vagueness in the Law." *Ethics* 125 (2): 425–48.
Asselin, Charles. 2002. "Haitian Exceptionalism and Caribbean Consciousness." *Journal of Caribbean Literatures* 3 (2): 115–30.

Bachmann, Michael. 2010. "Theater and the Drama of Law: A 'Theatrical History' of the Eichmann Trial." *Law Text Culture* 14: 94–116.

Ball, Milner S. 1975. "The Play's the Thing: An Unscientific Reflection on Courts Under the Rubric of Theater." *Stanford Law Review* 28 (1): 81–115.

Barthélemy, Gérard. 1990. *L'univers rural haïtien. Le pays en dehors.* Paris: L'Harmattan.

Beckett, Greg. 2013a. "Thinking with Others: Savage Thoughts About Anthropology and the West." *Small Axe* 42: 166–81.

———. 2013b. "Rethinking the Haitian Crisis." In *The Idea of Haiti: History, Development and the Creation of New Narratives*, edited by Millery Polyné, 27–49. Minneapolis: University of Minnesota Press.

———. 2014. "The Art of Not Governing Port-au-Prince." *Social and Economic Studies* 63 (2): 31–57.

———. 2019. *There Is No More Haiti: Between Life and Death in Port-au-Prince.* Berkeley: University of California Press.

———. 2020. "Unlivable Life: Ordinary Disaster and the Atmosphere of Crisis in Haiti." *Small Axe* 24 (2): 78–95.

———. 2021. "The Specificity of the Ordinary." *Small Axe* 25 (3): 210–19.

Beecher, Jonathan. 2007. "Echoes of Toussaint Louverture and the Haitian Revolution in Melville's 'Benito Cereno.'" *Leviathan* 9 (2): 43–58.

Bell, Beverly. 2013. *Fault Lines: Views Across Haiti's Divide.* Ithaca, NY: Cornell University Press.

Benda-Beckmann, Frantz von. 2002. "Who's Afraid of Legal Pluralism?" *Journal of Legal Pluralism and Unofficial Law* 34 (47): 37–82.

Benda-Beckmann, Keebet von, ed. 2007. *Order and Disorder: Anthropological Perspectives.* Oxford: Berghahn Books.

Benjamin, Walter. 2021 (1921). *Towards the Critique of Violence: A Critical Edition.* Edited by Peter Fenves and Julia Ng. Stanford: Stanford University Press.

Benoist, Jocelyn. 2013. *Concepts. Une introduction à la philosophie.* Paris: Flammarion.

———. 2019. "Judgment and Beyond." *Critical Inquiry* 45 (2): 260–79.

———. 2021a. "How Social Are Our Concepts?" In *Living with Concepts: Anthropology in the Grip of Reality*, edited by Andrew Brandel and Marco Motta, 140–54. New York: Fordham University Press.

———. 2021b. *Towards a Contextual Realism.* Cambridge, MA: Harvard University Press.

Benton, Lauren. 2004 (2002). *Law and Colonial Cultures: Legal Regimes in World History, 1400–1900.* Cambridge: Cambridge University Press.

Béralus, Mélissa, Chanral Kénol, Litainé Laguerre, Marie-Bénédicte Loze, Hélène Mauduit, Evelyne Trouillot, Lyonel Trouillot, and Gary Victor. 2021. *Nouvelles du peyi lòk. Témoignages littéraires sur le crise politiques en Haïti*, préface de Lyonel Trouillot. Selles-sur-Cher: Atlantiques déchaînés.

Besnier, Christiane. 2017. *La verité côté cour. Une ethnologue aux assises*. Paris: La Découverte.

Bettini, Maurizio. 2022. *Roma, città della parola. Oralità, memoria, diritto, religione, poesia*. Torino: Giulio Einaudi Editore.

Beushausen, Wiebke, Miriam Brandel, Joseph Farquhason, Maruis Littschwager, Annika McPherson, and Julia Roth, eds. 2018. *Practices of Resistance in the Caribbean: Narratives, Aesthetics, and Politics*. London: Routledge.

Beyer, Judith. 2016. *The Force of Custom: Law and Ordering of Everyday Life in Kyrgyzstan*. Pittsburgh, PA: University of Pittsburgh Press.

Biagioli, Mario. 2019. "Justice out of Balance." *Critical Inquiry* 45 (2): 280–306.

Biet, Christian. 2011. "Law, Literature, Theater: The Fiction of Common Judgment." *Law and Humanities* 5 (2): 281–92.

Bohannan, Paul. 1957. *Justice and Judgment Among the Tiv*. London: Oxford University Press.

Bonilla, Yarimar. 2013. "Ordinary Sovereignty." *Small Axe* 42: 153–65.

———. 2015. *Non-Sovereign Futures: French Caribbean Politics in the Wake of Disenchantment*. Chicago: The University of Chicago Press.

Bouchet, André du. 2011. *Aveuglante ou banale. Essais sur la poésie: 1949–1959*. Edited by Clément Layet and François Tison. Preface and notes by C. Layet. Gouville-sur-Mer: Le Bruit du Temps.

Bourdieu, Pierre. 1987 (1986). "The Force of Law: Toward a Sociology of the Judicial Field." Translated by R. Terdiman. *Hastings Law Journal* 38 (5): 814–53.

———. 2000 (1997). *Pascalian Meditations*. Translated by R. Nice. Stanford, CA: Stanford University Press.

Branch, Adam. 2014. "The Violence of Peace: Ethnojustice in Northern Uganda." *Development and Change* 45 (3): 608–30.

Brandel, Andrew. 2025. "Forgetting Quotation: Detail in the Dreams of Borges and Le Guin." In *A Matter of Details: Anthropology, Aesthetics, and Philosophy*. Edited by Andrew Brandel, Veena Das, Sandra Laugier, and Perig Pitrou. Toronto: University of Toronto Press.

Brandel, Andrew, and Marco Motta, eds. 2021. *Living with Concepts: Anthropology in the Grip of Reality*. New York: Fordham University Press.

Brandel, Andrew, and Shalini Randeria. 2018. "Anthropological Perspectives on the Limits of the State." In *The Oxford Handbook on Governance and Limited Statehood*, edited by Anke Draude, Tanjy A. Börzel, and Thomas Risse, 68–88. Oxford: Oxford University Press.

Brooks, Peter. 1976. *The Melodramatic Imagination: Balzac, Henry James, Melodrama and the Mode of Excess*. New Haven, CT: Yale University Press.

Brundage, James A. 2008. *The Medieval Origins of the Legal Profession: Canonists, Civilians, and Courts*. Chicago: The University of Chicago Press.

Brunnegger, Sandra, ed. 2019. *Everyday Justice: Law, Ethnography, Injustice*. Cambridge: Cambridge University Press.

Bubandt, Nils. 2014. *The Empty Seashell: Witchcraft and Doubt on an Indonesian Island*. Ithaca, NY: Cornell University Press.

Cabanis, André G., and Michel Louis Martin. 1996. "Un exemple de créolisation modulée: le code civil haïtien et le code Napoléon." *Revue Internationale de Droit Comparé* 48 (2): 443–56.

Carey, Henry. 2001. "'Women and Peace and Security': The Politics of Implementing Gender Sensitivity Norms in Peacekeeping." *International Peacekeeping* 8 (2): 49–68.

———. 2005. "Militarization Without Civil War: The Security Dilemma and Regime Consolidation in Haiti." *Civil Wars* 7 (4): 330–56.

———. 2012. *Privatizing the Democratic Peace: Policy Dilemmas of NGO Peacebuilding*. London: Palgrave MacMillan.

Carpentier, Alejo. 1989 (1949). *The Kingdom of This World*. Translated by H. de Onís. New York: Noonday Press, Farrar, Straus and Giroux.

Casimir, Jean. 2020. *The Haitians: A Decolonial History*. Translated by Laurent Dubois. Foreword by Walter D. Mignolo. Chapel Hill: The University of North Carolina Press.

Cassin, Barbara. 2014 (1995). *Sophistical Practice: Towards a Consistent Relativism*. New York: Fordham University Press.

Castel, Robert. 2003 (1995). *From Manual Workers to Wage Laborers: Transformations of the Social Question*. Edited and translated by Richard Boyd. New Brunswick, NJ: Transaction Publishers.

Castera, Georges. 2006. *L'encre est ma demeure*. Anthology established and prefaced by Lyonel Trouillot. Arles: Actes Sud.

———. 2012. *Gout pa gout*. Preface by Rodney Saint-Éloi. Montreal: Mémoire d'Encrier.

Cavell, Stanley. 1981. *Pursuits of Happiness: The Hollywood Comedy of Remarriage*. Cambridge, MA: Harvard University Press.

———. 1992 (1972). *Senses of Walden*, expanded edition. Chicago: The University of Chicago Press.

———. 1994 (1988). *In Quest of The Ordinary. Lines of Skepticism and Romanticism*. Chicago: The University of Chicago Press.

———. 1996. *Contesting Tears: The Hollywood Melodrama of the Unknown Woman*. Chicago: The University of Chicago Press.

———. 1999 (1979). *The Claim of Reason. Wittgenstein, Skepticism, Morality, And Tragedy*. New York: Oxford University Press.

———. 2005a. *Cities of Words: Pedagogical Letters on a Register of the Moral Life.* Cambridge, MA: Harvard University Press.

———. 2005b. *Philosophy the Day After Tomorrow.* Cambridge, MA: Harvard University Press.

———.2007 "Preface." In *Life and Words: Violence and the Descent into the Ordinary* by Veena Das, xi–xiv. Berkeley: University of California Press.

———. 2010. *Little Did I Know . . . Excerpts from Memory.* Stanford, CA: Stanford University Press.

———. 2012 (1987). *Disowning Knowledge in Seven Plays of Shakespeare,* 2nd edition. Cambridge, MA: Harvard University Press.

———. 2015 (1969). *Must We Mean What We Say?* Updated edition. Cambridge: Cambridge University Press.

———. 2022. *Here and There.* Edited by Nancy Bauer, Alice Crary, and Sandra Laugier, Cambridge, MA: Harvard University Press.

Cavender, Gray. 1988. "A Note on Vodou as Alternative Mechanism for Addressing Legal Problems." *Journal of Legal Pluralism and Unofficial Law* 27 (1): 1–17.

Cederlöf, Gustav, and Donald V. Kingsbury. 2019. "On PetroCaribe: Petropolitics, Energypower, and Post-neoliberal Development in the Caribbean Energy Region." *Political Geography* 72: 124–33.

Césaire, Aimé. 2000 (1950). *Discourse on Colonialism.* Translated by Joan Pinkham. New York: Monthly Review Press.

Chalmers, Mehdi, Chantal Kénol, Jean-Laurent Lhérisson, and Lyonel Trouillot. 2015. *Anthologie bilingue de la poésie créole haïtienne de 1986 à nos jours.* Arles: Actes Sud.

Chancy, Myriam J. A. 1997. *Framing Silence: Revolutionary Novels by Haitian Women.* New Brunswick, NJ: Rutgers University Press.

Chanock, Martin. 1985. *Law, Custom, and Social Order: The Colonial Experience in Malawi and Zambia.* Cambridge: Cambridge University Press.

Char, René. 1995 (1943–1944). "Feuillets d'Hypnos." In *Œuvres complètes,* edited by René Char, 171–233. Introduction by Jean Roudaut. Paris: Gallimard (Bibliothèque de la Pléiade).

Charlier-Doucet, Rachelle. 2005. "Anthropologie, politique et engagement social." *Gradhiva* 1: 109–25.

Chauviré, Christiane. 2004. *Le moment anthropologique de Wittgenstein.* Paris: Kimé

———. 2016. *Comprendre l'art: L'esthétique de Wittgenstein.* Paris: Kimé.

Chen, Wilson C. 2011. "Figures of Flight and Entrapment in Edwidge Danticat's *Krik? Krak!*" *Rocky Mountain Review* 65 (1): 36–55.

Ciarcia, Gaetano. 2004. "L'objet invisible, ou le gambit du capitaine." *L'Homme* 170: 181–98.

Clastres, Pierre. 1990 (1974). *Society Against the State*. Princeton, NJ: Zone Books.

Clitandre, Nadège. 2011. "Haitian Exceptionalism in the Caribbean and the Project of Rebuilding Haiti." *Journal of Haitian Studies* 17 (2): 46–53.

———. 2014. "Mapping the Echo Chamber: Edwidge Danticat and the Thematic Trilogy of Birth, Separation, and Death." *Palimpsest: A Journal on Women, Gender, and the Black International* 3 (2): 170–90.

———. 2021. "Notes on Radical Hope; Or, The Ethical Turn in Anthropology." *Small Axe* 25 (3): 186–98.

Clorméus, Lewis A. 2012. "À propos de la seconde campagne anti-superstitieuse en Haïti (1911–1912). Contribution à une historiographie." *Histoire, Monde et Cultures Religieuses* 24 (4): 105–30.

Coetzee, John M. 1999. *The Lives of Animals*. Edited and introduced by Amy Gutman. Contributions by Marjorie Garber, Peter Singer, Wendy Doniger, Barbara Smuts. Princeton, NJ: Princeton University Press.

———. 2003. *Elizabeth Costello*. New York: Viking.

Collot, Gélin. 2007. "Le code civil haïtien est son histoire." *Bulletin de la Société d'Histoire de la Guadeloupe* 146/47: 167–85.

Colson, Elizabeth. 1953. "Social Control and Vengeance in Plateau Tonga Society." *Africa* 2 (33): 199–212.

Comaroff, Jean. 1985. *Bodies of Power, Spirit of Resistance: The Culture and History of a South African People*. Chicago: The University of Chicago Press.

Comaroff, Jean, and John Comaroff, eds. 2002. "Alien-Nation: Zombies, Immigrants, and Millennial Capitalism." *South Atlantic Quarterly* 101 (4): 779–805.

———. 2006. *Law and Disorder in the Postcolony*. Chicago: The University of Chicago Press.

———. 2009. "Reflections on the Anthropology of Law, Governance and Sovereignty." In *Rules of Law and Law of Rulings: On the Governance of Law*, edited by Frantz von Benda-Beckmann, Kabeet von Benda-Beckmann, and Julia Eckert, 31–59. Surrey: Ashgate.

———. 2016. *The Truth About Crime. Sovereignty, Knowledge, Social Order*. Chicago: The University of Chicago Press.

Conley, John M., and William M. O'Barr. 1988. "Fundamentals of Jurisprudence: An Ethnography of Judicial Decision Making in Informal Courts." *North Carolina Law Review* 66: 467–507.

Corrin, Jennifer. 2019. "Plurality and Punishment: Competition Between State and Customary Authorities in Salomon Islands." *The Journal of Legal Pluralism and Unofficial Law* 51 (1): 29–47.

Coughlin, Dan. 2006. "WikiLeaks Haiti: US Cables Paint Portrait of Brutal, Ineffectual and Polluting UN Force." *The Nation*, October 11.

Coughlin, Dan, and Kim Ives. 2011. "WikiLeaks Cables Reveal 'Secret History' of U.S. Bullying in Haiti at Oil Companies Behest." *Democracy Now!* June 2003.

Culver, Keith C. 2004. "Varieties of Vagueness: Review of *Vagueness in Law*, by Timothy A. O. Endicott." *The University of Toronto Law Journal* 54 (1): 109–27.

Curtis, Jennifer. 2014. *Human Rights as War by Other Means: Peace Politics in Northern Ireland*. Philadelphia: University of Pennsylvania Press.

Danticat, Edwidge. 2002. *After the Dance: A Walk Through Carnival in Jacmel, Haiti*. New York: Crown Journeys.

———. 2015a (1994). *Breath, Eyes, Memory*. New York: Soho.

———. 2015b (1996). *Krik? Krak!* New York: Vintage Books.

Das, Veena. 2007. *Life and Words: Violence and the Descent into the Ordinary*. Preface by Stanley Cavell. Berkeley: University of California Press.

———. 2013. "Neighbors and Acts of Silent Kindness." *HAU: Journal of Ethnographic Theory* 3 (1): 217–20.

———. 2014. "Ethics, the Householder's Dilemma, and the Difficulty of Reality." *HAU: Journal of Ethnographic Theory* 4 (1): 487–95.

———. 2020. *Textures of the Ordinary: Doing Anthropology After Wittgenstein*. New York: Fordham University Press.

———. 2021. *Voix de l'ordinaire. L'anthropologue face à la violence*. Edited and translated by Marco Motta and Yves Erard. Preface by Sandra Laugier. Lausanne: BSN Press.

———. 2022. *Slum Acts*. London: Polity Press.

———. 2023. "Hanna Pitkin on Conceptual Puzzlement." *Polity* 55 (3): 461–69.

Das, Veena, and Clara Han, eds., 2016. *Living and Dying in the Contemporary World: A Compendium*. Berkeley: University of California Press.

Das, Veena, and Deborah Poole, eds. 2004. *Anthropology in the Margins of the State*. New Delhi: Oxford University Press.

Dash, Michael J. 1997 (1988). *Haiti and the United States: National Stereotypes and the Literary Imagination*. Basingstoke: Macmillan.

———. 2010. "Haiti: Seismic Shock or Paradigm Shift." *Social Text*, January 26.

———. 2013. "Neither Magical nor Exceptional: The Idea of the Ordinary in Caribbean Studies." *The Journal of Haitian Studies* 19 (2): 24–32.

Davis, Wade. 1997 (1985). *The Serpent and the Rainbow: A Harvard Scientist's Astonishing Journey into the Secret Societies of Haitian Voodoo, Zombie, and Magic*. New York: Simon & Schuster.

Dayan, Colin. 2004. "A Few Stories About Haiti, or, Stigma Revisited." *Research in African Literatures* 35 (2): 157–72.

Degoul, Franck. 2006. "Du passé faisons table d'hôte: Le mode d'entretien des zombis dans l'imaginaire haïtien et ses filiations historiques." *Ethnologies* 28 (1): 241–78.

Delisle, Philippe. 2003. *Le Catholicisme en Haïti au XIXᵉ siècle. Le rêve d'une "Bretagne noire" (1860–1915)*. Paris: Karthala.

Depestre, René. 1977 (1967). *A Rainbow for the Christian West*. Translated by J. Dayan. Amherst: University of Massachusetts Press.

———. 2017 (1988). *Hadriana in All My Dreams: A Novel*. Translated by K. L. Glover. Foreword by E. Danticat. New York: Akashic Books.

Deren, Maya. 1953. *Divine Horsemen: The Living Gods of Haiti*. London: Thames & Hudson.

Derrida, Jacques. 1992. "Force of Law: 'The Mystical Foundation of Authority.'" In *Deconstruction and the Possibility of Justice*, edited by Drucilla Cornell, Michel Rosenfield, and David Gray Carlson, 3–67. New York; London: Routledge.

———. 2019. *La vie la mort. Séminaire (1975–1976)*. Paris: Seuil.

Desjarlais, Robert. 2016. *Subject to Death: Life and Loss in a Buddhist World*. Chicago: The University of Chicago Press.

Despland, Basile. 2021. "Au creux d'une calebasse." *A Contrario* 32: 171–96.

Despret, Vinciane. 2019. "Inquiries Raised by the Dead." Translated by Catherine V. Howard. *HAU: Journal of Ethnographic Theory* 9 (2): 236–48.

———. 2021 (2015). *Our Grateful Dead: Stories of Those Left Behind*. Translated by Stephen Muecke. Minneapolis: University of Minnesota Press.

De Waal, Alex. 2015. *The Real Politics of the Horn in Africa: Money, War, and the Business of Power*. Cambridge: Polity Press.

Diamond, Cora. 1981. "What Nonsense Might Be." *Philosophy* 56 (215): 5–22.

———. 1984. "What Does a Concept Script Do?" *The Philosophical Quarterly* 34 (136): 343–68.

———. 1988a. "Losing Your Concepts." *Ethics* 98 (2): 255–77

———. 1988b. "Throwing Away the Ladder." *Philosophy* 63 (243): 5–27

———. 1991a. *The Realistic Spirit: Wittgenstein, Philosophy, and the Mind*. Cambridge, MA: MIT Press.

———. 1991b. "Knowing Tornadoes and Other Things." *New Literary History* 22 (4): 1001–15.

———. 1991c. "The Importance of Being Human." In *Human Beings*, edited by David Cockburn, 35–63. Cambridge: Cambridge University Press.

———. 1997. "Moral Differences and Distances: Some Questions." In *Commonality and Particularity in Ethics*, edited by Lilli Alanen, Sara Heinämaa, and Thomas Wallgren, 197–223. New York: St. Martin's Press.

———. 2003. "The Difficulty of Reality and the Difficulty of Philosophy." *Partial Answers: Journal of Literature and the History of Ideas* 1 (2): 1–26.

———. 2012. "The Skies of Dante and Our Skies: A Response to Ilham Dilman." *Philosophical Investigations* 35 (3–4): 187–204.

———. 2013. "Criticising from Outside." *Philosophical Investigations* 36 (2): 114–32.

———. 2014. "Wittgenstein and What Can Only Be True." *Nordic Wittgenstein Review* 3 (2): 9–40.

Dillard, Annie. 1974. *Pilgrim at Tinker Creek*. New York: Harper Perennial.

Donais, Timothy. 2015. "Bringing the Local Back in: Haiti, Local Governance and the Dynamics of Verticality Integrated Peacebuilding." *Journal of Peacebuilding & Development* 10 (1): 40–55

Donatelli, Piergiorgio. 2015. "Forms of Life, Forms of Reality." *Nordic Wittgenstein Review*, special issue "Wittgenstein and Forms of Life": 43–62.

Dorigny, Marcel. 2014. "Préface à l'édition française." In *Haïti. Naissance d'une nation*, by Carolyn Fick, 5–22. Translated by Frantz Voltaire. Rennes: Les Perséides.

Dorigny, Marcel, Jean Marie Théodat, Gusti-Klara Gaillard, and Jean Claude Bruffaerts. 2021. *Haïti-France. Le rapport Machau (1825)*. Preface by Thomas Piketty. Introduction by Fritz Alphonse Jean. Paris: Hémisphères Éditions.

Dougé-Prosper, Mamyrah, and Schuller Mark. 2021. "After Moïse Assassination, Popular Sectors Must Lead the Way." *NACLA: Reporting on the Americas*, July 8.

Dubois, Laurent. 2004. *Avengers of the New World: The Story of the Haitian Revolution*. Cambridge, MA: The Belknap Press of the Harvard University Press.

———. 2012. *Haiti: The Aftershocks of History*. New York: Picador.

Dufourmantelle, Anne. 2007. *La Femme et le sacrifice. D'Antigone à la femme d'à côté*. Paris: Denoël.

Eckert, Julia. 2006. "From Subjects to Citizens: Legalism from Below and the Homogenization of the Legal Sphere." *The Journal of Legal Pluralism and Unofficial Law* 38 (53–54): 45–76.

Eckert, Julia, Brian Danahoe, Christian Strümpell, and Zerrin Ö. Biner, eds. 2012. *Law Against the State: Ethnographic Forays into Law's Transformations*. Cambridge: Cambridge University Press.

Edmonds, Kevin. 2010. "Empty Promises and Empty Bellies: Bill Clinton's Double Talk on Haitian Agriculture." *NACLA: Report on the Americas*, May 17.

Ellison, Susan H. 2018. *Domesticating Democracy: The Politics of Conflict Resolution in Bolivia*. Durham, NC: Duke University Press.

Emerson, Ralph Waldo. 2000 (1836). "Nature." In *The Essential Writings of Ralph Waldo Emerson*, edited by Brooks Atkinson, 3–42. Introduction by Mary Oliver. New York: The Modern Library.

———. 2000 (1837). "The American Scholar." In *The Essential Writings of Raph Waldo Emerson*, edited by Brooks Atkinson, 43–62. Introduction by Mary Oliver. New York: The Modern Library.

———. 2000 (1844). "Experience." In *The Essential Writings of Raph Waldo Emerson*, edited by Brooks Atkinson, 307–26. Introduction by Mary Oliver. New York: The Modern Library.

Endicott, Timothy A. O. 2001. "Law Is Necessarily Vague." *Legal Theory* 7 (4): 379–85.

———. 2014. "Interpretation and Indeterminacy: Concepts of Andrei Marmor's Philosophy of Law." *Jerusalem Review of Legal Studies* 10 (1): 46–56.

————. 2021. "Law and Language." In *The Stanford Encyclopedia of Philosophy*, edited by Edward N. Zalta, Department of Philosophy, Stanford University (online open source, https://plato.stanford.edu/entries/law-language/).

————. 2022. "Legal Misinterpretation." *Jurisprudence: An International Journal of Legal and Political Thought* 13 (1): 99–106.

Engler, Yves. 2021. "Racial Capitalism and the Betrayal of Haiti." *Canadian Dimension*, February 26.

Epstein, Arnold L. 2017 (1967). "The Case Method in the Field of Law." In *The Craft of Social Anthropology*, edited by A. L. Epstein, 205–30. Introduction by Max Gluckman. London: Routledge.

Erard, Yves. 2021. "Éthiquette éclair, un éclat de lumière sur l'école haïtienne." *A Contrario* 32: 131–70.

Esteban, Claude. 1984 (1968). "A Season of Devastation." Translated by S. Cavell and K. Cavell. *Pequod: A Journal of Contemporary Literature and Literary Criticism* 16/17: 240–41.

————. 2006. *Le jour à peine écrit (1967–1992)*. Paris: Gallimard.

Evans-Pritchard, Edward E. 1940. *The Nuer.* Oxford: Oxford University Press.

Ewick, Patricia, and Susan Silbey. 1998. *The Common Place of Law: Stories from Everyday Life.* Chicago: The University of Chicago Press.

Famin, Victoria. 2017. "*Les Griots*, entre indigénisme et négritude." *Revue de Littérature Comparée* 364 (4): 422–32.

Farmer, Paul. 2001 (1999). *Infections and Inequalities: The Modern Plague.* With a new preface by the author. Berkeley: University of California Press.

————. 2004. *Pathologies of Power: Health, Human Rights, and the New War on the Poor.* Foreword by Amartya Sen. Berkeley: University of California Press.

Fassin, Didier, and Mariella Pandolfi, eds. 2010. *Contemporary States of Emergency: The Politics of Military and Humanitarian Interventions.* New York: Zone Books.

Fatton, Robert. 1999. "The Impairment of Democratization: Haiti in Comparative Perspective." *Comparative Politics* 31 (2): 209–29.

————. 2017. "Haiti and the Limits of Sovereignty: Trapped in the Outer Periphery." In *Who Owns Haiti? People, Power, and Sovereignty,* edited by Robert Maguire and Scott Freeman, 29–49. Gainesville: University Press of Florida.

————. 2021. *The Guise of Exceptionalism: Unmasking the National Narratives of Haiti and the United States.* New Brunswick, NJ: Rutgers University Press.

Felman, Shoshana. 2002. *The Judicial Unconscious: Trials and Trauma in the Twentieth Century.* Cambridge, MA: Harvard University Press.

Ferrarese, Estelle, and Sandra Laugier, eds. 2018. *Formes de vie.* Paris: CNRS Éditions.

Fick, Carolyn. 2004 (1990). *The Making of Haiti: The Saint-Domingue Revolution from Below.* Knoxville: University of Tennessee Press.

Fifi, Kermonde Lovely. 2013. *Cassés*. Léogâne: Éditions Ruptures.

———. 2015. "Ma soif." In *Anthologie de la poésie haïtienne contemporaine*, edited by James Noël, 519. Paris: Seuil.

Fignolé, Jean-Claude. 2012 (1987). *Les possédés de la pleine lune*. La Roque d'Anthéron: Vents D'ailleurs.

Fischer, Sibylle. 2004. *Modernity Disavowed: Haiti and the Cultures of Slavery in the Age of Revolution*. Durham, NC: Duke University Press.

———. 2007. "Haiti: Fantasies of Bare Life." *Small Axe* 23: 1–15.

———. 2010. "Beyond Comprehension." *Social Text*, January 26.

Follain, Antoine. 2003. "De la justice seigneuriale à la justice de paix," In *Une justice de proximité, la justice de paix (1790–1958)*, edited by Jacques-Guy Petit, 19–33. Paris: PUF.

Foucault, Michel. 2001. *Dits et écrits I, 1954–75*. Paris: Gallimard.

———. 2009. *Security, Territory, Population: Lectures at the Collège de France, 1977–1978*. Edited by Michael Senellart. Translated by Graham Burchell. New York: Palgrave MacMillan.

———. 2018. *Punitive Society: Lectures at the Collège de France, 1972–1973*. Edited by Bernard E. Harcourt. Translated by Graham Burchell. General Editors: François Ewald and Alessandro Fontana. English Series Editor: Arnold I. Davidson. New York: Palgrave MacMillan.

———. 2019. *Penal Theories and Institutions: Lectures at the Collège de France, 1971–1972*. Edited by Bernard E. Harcourt. Translated by Graham Burchell with Elisabetta Basso, Claude-Olivier Doron, and the assistance of Daniel Defert. General Editors: François Ewald and Alessandro Fontana. English Series Editor: Arnold I. Davidson. New York: Palgrave MacMillan.

Francis, Donette A. 2004. "'Silences Too Horrific to Disturb': Writing Sexual Histories in Edwidge Danticat's *Breath, Eyes, Memory*." *Research in African Literatures* 35 (2): 75–90.

———. 2010. *Fictions of Feminine Citizenship. Sexuality and the Nation in Contemporary Caribbean Literature*. New York: Palgrave Macmillan.

Frankétienne. 2014 (2004). *Ready to Burst*. Translated by K. L. Glover. New York: Archipelago Books.

———. 2018 (1975). *Dezafi*. Translated by Asselin Charles. Charlottesville: University of Virginia Press.

Freedman, Rosa, Nicolas Lemay-Hébert, and Siobhán Wills. 2021. *The Law and Practice of Peacekeeping: Foregrounding Human Rights*. Cambridge: Cambridge University Press.

Freeman, Michael F. B. A., and David Napier, eds. 2007. *Law and Anthropology*. New York: Oxford University Press.

Freeman, Scott. 2017. "Sovereignty and Soil: Collective and Wage Labor in Rural Haiti." In *Who Owns Haiti? People, Power, and Sovereignty*, edited by

Robert Maguire and Scott Freeman, 125–39. Gainesville: University of Florida Press.

Frege, Gottlob. 1951 (1892). "On Concept and Object." Translated by Peter T. Geach. Revised by M. Black. *Mind* 60 (238): 168–80.

———. 1952 (1891). "Function and Concept." In *Translations from the Philosophical Writings of Gottlob Frege.* Edited and translated by Peter T. Geach and Max Black. Oxford: Basil Blackwell.

———. 1979. *Posthumous Writings.* Translated by Peter Long and R. White. Chicago: The University of Chicago Press.

Frerichs, Ralph R. 2020. *Deadly River: Cholera and Cover-Up in Post-Earthquake Haiti.* Ithaca, NY: Cornell University Press.

Ghachem, Malick W. 2012. *The Old Regime and the Haitian Revolution.* Cambridge: Cambridge University Press.

Githire, Njeri. 2014. *Cannibal Writers: Eating Others in Caribbean and Indian Ocean Women's Writings.* Urbana: University of Illinois Press.

Glover, Kaiama L. 2005. "Exploiting the Undead: The Usefulness of the Zombie in Haitian Literature." *Journal of Haitian Studies* 11 (2): 105–21.

———. 2010. *Haiti Unbound: A Spiralist Challenge to the Postcolonial Canon.* Liverpool: Liverpool University Press.

———. 2012. "New Narratives of Haiti; or, How to Empathize with a Zombie." *Small Axe* 16 (3): 199–207.

Gluckman, Max. 1955. *The Judicial Process Among the Barotse of Northern Rhodesia.* Manchester: Manchester University Press.

Gonzales, Johnhenry. 2019. *Maroon Nation: A History of Revolutionary Haiti.* New Haven, CT: Yale University Press.

Goodale, Mark. 2017. *Anthropology and Law: A Critical Introduction.* Foreword by Sally Engle Merry. New York: New York University Press.

Gordon, Leah. 2010. *Kanaval: Vodou, Politics and Revolution in the Streets of Haiti.* London: Soul Jazz Books.

———. 2015. *Iron In the Soul.* London: Soul Jazz Records/Films.

Greenburg, Jennifer. 2013. "The 'Strong Arm' and the 'Friendly Hand': Military Humanitarianism in Post-Earthquake Haiti." *Journal of Haitian Studies* 19 (1): 95–122.

———. 2017. "Selling Stabilization: Anxious Practices of Militarized Development Contracting." *Development and Change* 48 (6): 1262–86.

Gustavson, Bret. 2017. "The New Energy Imperialism in the Caribbean." *NACLA: Report on the Americas* 49 (4): 421–28.

Hadfield, Gillian K. 2017. "The Problem of Social Order: What Should Count as Law?" *Law & Social Inquiry* 42 (01): 16–27.

Han, Clara. 2012. *Life in Debt: Times of Care and Violence in Neoliberal Chile.* Berkeley: University of California Press.

———. 2018. "Precarity, Precariousness, and Vulnerability." *Annual Review of Anthropology* 47 (1): 331–43.

———. 2020. *Seeing Like a Child.* New York: Fordham University Press.

Harrington, John, Lucy Series, and Alexander Ruck-Keene. 2019. "Law and Rhetoric: Critical Possibilities." *Journal of Law and Society* 46 (2): 302–27.

Hartman, Saidiya. 2008. "Venus in Two Acts." *Small Axe* 26 (2): 1–14.

———. 2022 (1997). *Scenes of Subjection: Terror, Slavery, and Self-Making in Nineteenth Century America*, revised and updated edition. New York: W. W. Norton.

Hauge, Wenche, Rachelle Doucet, and Alain Gilles. 2015. "Building Peace from Below—the Potential of Local Models of Conflict Prevention in Haiti." *Conflict, Security & Development* 15 (3): 259–82.

Hector, Michel, and Laënnec Hurbon, eds. 2009. *La genèse de l'État Haïtien (1805–1859).* Paris: Éditions de la Maison des Sciences de l'Homme.

Herskovits, Melville J. 1937. *Life in a Haitian Valley.* New York: Alfred A. Knopf.

Hervouet-Zeiber, Grégoire. 2023. "The 'Salt' of Life: Of Wars and Domesticities in Contemporary Russia." *American Ethnologist* 50 (1): 43–53.

Hoermann, Raphael. 2016. "'A Very Hell of Horrors?' The Haitian Revolution and the Early Transatlantic Haitian Gothic." *Slavery and Abolition* 37 (1): 183–205.

Horsman, Yasco. 2010. *Theaters of Justice: Judging, Staging, and Working Through in Arendt, Brecht and Delbo.* Stanford, CA: Stanford University Press.

Huizinga, Johan. 1980 (1938). *Homo Ludens: Study of the Play Element in Culture.* London: Routledge & Kegan Paul.

Humphreys, Stephen. 2010. *Theater of the Rule of Law: Transnational Legal Intervention in Theory and Practice.* Cambridge: Cambridge University Press.

Hurbon, Laënnec. 1979. "Sorcellerie et pouvoir en Haïti." *Archive de Sciences Sociales des Religions* 48 (1): 43–52.

———. 1988. *Le barbare imaginaire.* Paris: Cerf.

———. 2005. "Le statut du vodou et l'histoire de l'anthropologie." *Gradhiva* 1: 153–63.

———. 2019. "Le nouveau code pénal haïtien et la sorcellerie: un examen critique." *Le Nouvelliste*, January 14.

Hurston, Zora N. 2009 (1938). *Tell My Horse: Voodoo and Life in Haiti and Jamaica.* New York: HarperCollins

International Bar Association. 2011. *International Principles on the Conduct of the Legal Profession*, adopted on May 28.

Irving, Andrew. 2017. *The Art of Life and Death. Radical Aesthetics and Ethnographic Practice.* Chicago: HAU Books.

Jaffe, Rivke. 2015. "From Maroons to Dons: Sovereignty, Violence and Law in Jamaica." *Critique of Anthropology* 35 (1): 47–63.

James, Cyril L. R. 2023 (1938). *The Black Jacobins: Toussaint Louverture and the San Domingo Revolution*, 2nd edition. Introduction by David Scott. New York: Vintage Books.

James, Erica C. 2010. *Democratic Insecurities: Violence, Trauma, and Intervention in Haiti*. Berkeley: University of California Press.

Jarayam, Kiran C. 2018. "Fruits of Colonialism: The Production of Mangoes as Commodities in Northern Haiti." *Critique of Anthropology* 38 (4): 461–82.

Jean-Charles, Régine M. 2014. *Conflicting Bodies: The Politics of Rape Representation in the Francophone Imaginary*. Columbus: Ohio State University.

Johnson, Paul C. 2006. "Secretism and the Apotheosis of Duvalier." *Journal of the American Academy of Religion* 74 (2): 420–45.

Johnston, Jake. 2024. *Aid State: Elite Panic, Disaster Capitalism, and the Battle to Control Haiti*. New York: MacMillan.

Joint, Louis-Auguste. 2008. "Système éducatif et inégalités sociales en Haïti. Le cas des écoles catholiques." *Recherches et ressources en éducation et formation* 2: 17–24.

Jordan Alissa. 2016. *Atlas of Skins: A Sensual Map of Becoming Persons, Becoming Werewomen, and Becoming Zonbi in a Haitian Vodou Courtyard*. PhD Dissertation, University of Florida.

Jullien, François. 2011 (2009). *Silent Transformations*. Translated by K. Fijalkowski and M. Richardson. Chicago: The University of Chicago Press.

Katz, Jonathan. 2013a. *The Big Truck That Went By: How the World Came to Save Haiti and Left Behind a Disaster*. New York: St Martin's Press.

———. 2013b. "In the Time of Cholera: How the U.N. Created an Epidemic—Then Covered It Up." *Foreign Policy*, January 10.

Kelly, Tobias. 2006. *Law, Violence and Sovereignty Among West Bank Palestinians*. Cambridge: Cambridge University Press.

Kivland, Chelsey L. 2014. "Becoming a Force in the Zone: Hedonopolitics, Masculinity, and the Quest for Respect on Haiti's Streets." *Cultural Anthropology* 29 (4): 672–98.

———. 2017. "Street Sovereignty: Power, Violence, and Respect Among Haitian Baz." In *Who Owns Haiti? People, Power, and Sovereignty*, edited by Robert Maguire and Scott Freeman, 140–65. Gainesville: University of Florida Press.

———. 2018. "The Magic of Guns: Scriptive Technology and Violence in Haiti." *American Ethnologist* 45 (3): 354–66.

———. 2020. *Street Sovereigns: Young Men and the Makeshift State in Urban Haiti*. Ithaca, NY: Cornell University Press.

Krever, Tor. 2011. "The Legal Turn in Late Development Theory: The Rule of Law and the World Bank's Development Model." *Harvard International Law Journal* 52 (1): 288–319.

———. 2017. "Law, Development and Political Closure Under Neoliberalism." In *Neoliberal Legality: Understanding the Role of Law in the Neoliberal Project*, edited by Honor Brabazon, 22–42. Abingdon: Routledge.

Kwon, Heonik. 2008. *Ghosts of War in Vietnam*. Cambridge: Cambridge University Press.

Lahens, Yanick. 2013 (2008). *The Color of Dawn*. Translated by A. Layland. Bridgend: Seren.

———. 2016 (2008). *La couleur de l'aube*. Paris: Sabine Wespieser Éditeur.

———. 2019. "La petite corruption." In *L'oiseau Parker dans la nuit, et autres nouvelles*. Paris: Sabine Wespieser Éditeur.

Lambek, Michael. 2019. "The Ends of the Dead." *HAU: Journal of Ethnographic Theory* 9 (2): 253–56.

Latour, Bruno. 2010 (2002). *The Making of Law: An Ethnography of the Conseil d'État*. Translated by M. Brilman and A. Pottage. Cambridge, MA: Polity Press.

Laugier, Sandra. 2009. *Wittgenstein. Les sens de l'usage*. Paris: Vrin.

———. 2010. "Aspect, Sense, and Perception." In *Seeing Wittgenstein Anew: New Essays on Aspect-Seeing*. Edited by William Day and Victor Krebs. Cambridge: Cambridge University Press.

———. 2025. "The Matter of Description: Detailing, Telling, Collecting." In *A Matter of Details: Anthropology, Aesthetics, and Philosophy*. Edited by Andrew Brandel, Veena Das, Sandra Laugier, and Perig Pitrou. Toronto: University of Toronto Press.

Lazarus-Black, Mindie. 2007. *Everyday Harm: Domestic Violence, Court Rites, and Cultures in Reconciliation*. Urbana: University of Illinois Press.

Lee, Sabine, and Susan Bartels. 2019. "'They Put Few Coins in Your Hands to Drop a Baby in You'—265 stories of Haitian Children Abandoned by UN Fathers." *The Conversation*, December 17.

Leiboff, Marett. 2018. "Theatricalizing Law." *Law & Literature* 30 (2): 351–67.

Lemay-Hébert, Nicolas. 2014. "Resistance in the Time of Cholera: The Limits of Stabilization Through Securitization in Haiti." *International Peacekeeping* 21 (2): 198–213.

Levy, Michel. 2001. "Conflits terriens et réformes agraires dans la plaine de l'Artibonite (Haïti)." *Cahiers des Amériques Latines* 36: 183–206.

Linnemann, Lin, Tyler Wall, and Edward Green. 2014. "The Walking Dead and Killing State: Zombification and the Normalization of Police Violence." *Theoretical Criminology* 18 (4): 506–27.

Lipset, David. 2004. "'The Trial': A Parody of Law Amid the Mockery of Men in Post-Colonial Papua New Guinea." *The Journal of the Royal Anthropological Institute* 10 (1): 63–89.

Llewellyn, Karl N., and E. Adamson Hoebel. 1941. *The Cheyenne Way*. Norman: The University of Oklahoma Press.

Lombard, Louisa. 2016. *State of Rebellion: Violence and Intervention in the Central African Republic*. New York: Bloomsbury Publishing.

Lucas, Rafaël. 2004. "The Aesthetics of Degradation in Haitian Literature." *Research in African Literatures* 35 (2): 54–74.

Maguire, Robert, and Scott Freeman, eds. 2017. *Who Owns Haiti? People, Power, and Sovereignty*. Gainesville: University Press of Florida.

Malinowski, Bronislaw. 2014 (1926). *Crime and Custom in Savage Society*. Mansfield Center: Martino Publishing.

Marcelin, Louis L. 2015. "Violence, Human Insecurity, and the Challenge of Rebuilding Haiti: A Study of a Shantytown in Port-au-Prince." *Current Anthropology* 56 (2): 230–55.

Marcelin, Louis L., and Toni Cela. 2020. "Justice and Rule of Law Failure in Haiti: A View From the Shanties." *Journal of Community Psychology* 48 (2): 267–82.

Marouan, Maha. 2013. "In the Spirit of Erzulie: Vodou and the Reimagining of Haitian Womanhood in Edwidge Danticat's *Breath, Eyes, Memory*." In *Witches, Goddesses, and Angry Spirits: The Politics of Spiritual Liberation in African Diaspora Women's Fiction*, 37–70. Columbus: Ohio State University Press

Maternowska, Catherine M. 2006. *Reproducing Inequalities: Poverty and the Politics of Population in Haiti*. Foreword by Paul Farmer. New Brunswick, NJ: Rutgers University Press.

Mattei, Ugo. 2010. "Emergency-Based Predatory Capitalism: The Rule of Law, Alternative Dispute Resolution, and Development." In *Contemporary States of Emergency: The Politics of Military and Humanitarian Interventions*. Edited by Didier Fassin and Mariella Pandolfi. New York: Zone Books.

Mattei, Ugo, and Laura Nader. 2008. *Plunder: When the Rule of Law is Illegal*. Malden, MA: Blackwell Publishing

McAlister, Elizabeth. 2012. "Slaves, Cannibals, and Infected Hyper-Whites: The Race and Religion of Zombies." *Anthropological Quarterly* 85 (2): 457–86.

McPherson, Alan. 2012. "The Irony of Legal Pluralism under U.S. Occupations." *The American Historical Review* 117 (4): 1149–72.

Melville, Herman. 2016. "Benito Cereno." In *Billy Budd, Bartleby, and Other Stories*. Edited by Peter Coviello. New York: Penguin Books.

Merry, Sally Engle. 1988. "Legal Pluralism." *Law and Society Review* 22 (5): 869–96.
———. 1990. *Getting Justice and Getting Even: Legal Consciousness Among Working-Class Americans*. Chicago: The University of Chicago Press.

Métraux Alfred. 1951. "Les Paysans Haïtiens." *Présence Africaine* 12 (3): 88–111.
———. 1953. "Croyances et pratiques religieuses dans la vallée de Maribal, Haïti." *Journal de la Société des Américanistes* 42: 135–98.

———. 1955. "Dramatic Elements in Ritual Possession." Translated by J. H. Labadie. *Diogenes* 3 (11): 18–36.

———. 1972 (1958). *Voodoo in Haiti* Translated by Hugo Charteris. Introduction by Sidney W. Mintz. New York: Schocken Books.

Meudec, Marie. 2007. *Maladie, Vodou et Gestion des Conflits en Haïti: Le cas du kout poud*. Paris: Karthala.

Meyer-Plantureux, Chantal. 2015. "Théâtre et justice d'Eschyle à Jean Vilar." *Les Cahiers de la Justice* 1 (1): 37–58.

Mézié, Nadège. 2019. "Être Haïtien en Haïti: protestation et appartenance dans les débats sur le Champ de Mars à Port-au-Prince." *L'Espace Politique* [online], 38 (2), consulted November 9, 2020.

Michaux, Henri. 1997 (1978). *Tent Posts*. Translated by Lynn Hoggard. København: Green Integer.

———. 2016 (1949). *Life in the Folds*. Translated by Darren Jackson. Adelaïde: Wakefield Press.

Milcé, Jean-Euphèle. 2004. *L'Alphabet des nuits*, Orbe: Bernard Campiche Éditeur.

Mintz, Sydney. 1959. "Internal Market Systems as Mechanisms of Social Articulation." In *Proceedings of the American Ethnological Society*, edited by Verne F. Ray, 20–30. Seattle: University of Washington Press.

———. 1971. "Men, Women, and Trade." *Comparative Studies in Society and History* 13 (3): 247–69.

———. 2011 (1961). "*Pratik*: Haitian Personal Economic Relationships." *Open Anthropology Cooperative Press* (Interventions Series #2): 1–15.

Mobekk, Eirin. 2017. *UN Peace Operations: Lessons from Haiti, 1994–2016*, New York: Routledge.

Montalvo-Despeignes, Jaquelin. 1976. *Le Droit Informel Haïtien. Approche Socio-Ethnographique*. Paris: PUF.

Moore, Sally Falk, ed. 2005. *Law and Anthropology: A Reader*. Malden, MA: Blackwell Publishing.

Motta, Marco. 2019a. *Esprits fragiles. Réparer les liens ordinaires à Zanzibar*. Foreword by Michael Lambek. Lausanne: BSN Press.

———. 2019b. "Ordinary Realism: A Difficulty for Anthropology." *Anthropological Theory* 19 (3): 341–61.

———. 2021. "The Signal Gait of the Human." *A Contrario* 31 (1): 165–86.

———. 2022. "The Fragility of Voice: Hosting Spirits in Urban Zanzibar." *Current Anthropology* 63 (3): 270–88.

———. 2023. "The Bewitchment of Our Intelligence: Scepticism About Other Minds in Anthropology." *Anthropological Theory* 23 (2): 125–46.

Mulhall, Stephen. 2003. "Stanley Cavell's Vision of the Normativity of Language: Grammar, Criteria, and Rules." In *Stanley Cavell*, edited by Richard Eldrige, 79–106. Cambridge: Cambridge University Press.

———. 2014. "Inner Constancy, Outer Variation: Stanley Cavell on Grammar, Criteria, and Rules." In *Varieties of Skepticism: Essays After Kant, Wittgenstein, and Cavell*, edited by James Conant and Andrea Kern, 291–310. Boston: De Gruyter.

Mulla, Sameena. 2018. *The Violence of Care: Rape Victims, Forensic Nurses, and Sexual Assault Intervention*. New York: New York University Press.

Müller, Frank, and Andrea Steinke. 2018. "Criminalizing Encounters: MINUS- TAH as a Laboratory for Armed Humanitarian Pacification." *Global Crime* 19 (3–4): 228–49.

Nader, Laura. 1999. "The Globalization of Law: ADR as 'Soft' Technology." *Proceedings of the Annual Meeting of the American Society of International Law*, March 24–27, Vol. 93: 304–11.

———. 2003. "Crime as a Category—Domestic and Globalized." In *Crime's Power: Anthropologists and the Ethnography of Crime*, edited by Philip C. Parnell and Stephanie C. Kane, 55–76. New York: Palgrave MacMillan.

———. 2005. *The Life of The Law: Anthropological Projects*. Berkeley: University of California Press.

Nader, Laura, ed. 1969. *Law in Culture and Society*. Berkeley: University of California Press.

Nader, Laura, and Harry F. Todd. Jr. 1978. "Introduction." In *The Disputing Process–Law in Ten Societies*, edited by Laura Nader and Harry F. Todd Jr., 1–40. New York: Columbia University Press.

Naimou, Angela. 2017. *Salvage Work: U.S. and Caribbean Literatures Amid the Debris of Legal Personhood*. New York: Fordham University Press.

Najman, Charles. 2011. *Une étrange cathédrale dans la graisse des ténèbres*. France; Haiti: La Huit / Les Productions Finales / Trace TV.

Naud, Pierre-Louis. 2007. "La judicisation de la vie sociopolitique et économique en Haïti. Enjeux et limites." *Droit et Société* 65 (1): 123–51.

Neiburg, Federico. 2017. "Serendipitous Involvement: Making Peace in the Geto." In *If Truth Be Told: The Politics of Public Ethnography*, edited by Didier Fassin, 119–37. Durham, NC: Duke University Press.

Nield, Sophie. 2019. "How Does Theatricality Legitimize the Law?" In *Thinking Through Theatre and Performance*, edited by Maaike Bleeker, 284–95. London: Methuen Drama/Bloomsbury Publishing.

Noret, Joël. 2019. "Inquiries Raised by the Living." *HAU: Journal of Ethnographic Theory* 9 (2): 249–52.

Ochoa, Todd R. 2010. *Society of the Dead: Quita Manaquita and Palo Praise in Cuba*. Berkeley: University of California Press.

O'Connor, Maura R. 2013. "Subsidizing Starvation." *Foreign Policy*, January 11.

O'Connor, Vivienne. 2015. "The Rule of Law in Haiti After the Earthquake." *United States Institute of Peace Brief*, 18.

Olivelle, Patrick, Michael Gagarin, Caroline Humfress, Geoffrey MacCormack, Joseph G. Manning, and Bruce Wells. 2024. "Legal Procedure." In *The Cambridge Comparative History of Ancient Law,* edited by Caroline Humfress, David Ibbetson, and Patrick Olivelle, 303–75. Cambridge: Cambridge University Press.

Orcel, Makenzy. 2021. *L'Empereur.* Paris: Rivages.

Paisant, Gilles, ed. 2003. *De la place de la coutume dans l'ordre juridique haïtien. Bilan et perspectives à la lumière du droit comparé.* Grenoble: Presses Universitaires de Grenoble.

Payton, Claire A. 2017. "In Moral Debt to Haiti." *NACLA: Report on the Americas* 49 (1): 64–70.

———. 2018. *The City and The State: Construction and the Politics of Dictatorship in Haiti (1957–86).* PhD Dissertation. Duke University.

———. 2019. "Building Corruption in Haiti." *NACLA: Report on the Americas* 51 (2): 182–87.

Penier, Izabella. 2013. "The Black Atlantic Zombie: National Schisms and Utopian Diasporas in Edwidge Danticat's *The Dew Breaker.*" *International and Political Studies Faculty.* http://dspace.uni.lodz.pl:8080/xmlui/handle/11089/3275.

Peters, Julie S. 2022. *Law as Performance: Theatricality, Spectatorship, and the Making of Law in Ancient, Medieval, and Early Modern Europe.* Oxford: Oxford University Press.

Petit, Jacques-Guy, ed. 2003. "Introduction." In *Une justice de proximité, la justice de paix (1790–1958),* 9–16, Paris: PUF.

Pepe, Laura. 2020. *La voce delle sirene: I Greci e l'arte della persuasione.* Bari: Laterza.

Phelps, Anthony. 2023 (1968). *Mon Pays que voici.* Paris: Éditions Bruno Doucey.

Pierre, Jemima. 2023. "Haiti as Empire's Laboratory." *NACLA: Reporting on the Americas* 55 (3): 244–50.

Pingeot, Lou. 2018. "United Nations Peace Operations as International Practices: Revisiting the UN Mission's Armed Raids Against Gangs in Haiti." *European Journal of International Security* 3 (3): 364–81.

Podur, Justin. 2012. *Haiti's New Dictatorship: The Coup, the Earthquake and the UN Occupation.* London: Pluto Press.

Polat, Necati. 2010. "Peace as War." *Alternatives: Global, Local, Political* 35 (4): 317–45.

Pluchon, Pierre. 1987. *Vaudou, sorciers, empoisonneurs. De Saint-Domingue à Haïti.* Paris: Karthala.

Price, Richard, ed. 1996 (1973). *Maroon Societies: Rebel Slave Communities in the America's.* Baltimore, MD: Johns Hopkins University Press.

Prophète, Emmelie. 2020. *Les villages de Dieu.* Montréal: Mémoire d'Encrier.

Puett, Michael. 2017. *The Path.* New York: Simon & Schuster.

Ramsey, Kate. 2011. *The Spirits and the Law: Vodou and Power in Haiti*. Chicago: The University of Chicago Press.

Reed, Alan. 2015. *Theater and Law*. New York: Macmillan International.

Reed, Lindsay. 2007. "Peace Despite Peacekeepers in Haiti." *NACLA: Report on the Americas*, September 25.

Ring, Laura. 2006. *Zenana: Everyday Peace in a Karachi Apartment Building*. Bloomington: Indiana University Press.

Robert, Arnaud. 2018. "Mario Andrésol: 'Michel Martelly transportait de la drogue pour les Colombiens.'" *Ayibopost*, July 5.

———. 2021. "La logique du pire." *Le Temps*, July 8.

Robert, Yann. 2019. *Dramatic Justice: Trial by Theater in the Age of the French Revolution*. Philadelphia: University of Pennsylvania Press.

Roberts, Neil. 2015. *Freedom as Marronage*. Chicago: The University of Chicago Press.

Roberts, Simon A. 1998. "Against Legal Pluralism: Some Reflections on the Contemporary Enlargement of the Legal Domain." *The Journal of Legal Pluralism and Unofficial Law* 30 (42): 95–106.

Rogers, Nicole. 2008. "The Play of Law: Comparing Performances in Law and Theater." *Queensland University of Technology Law and Justice Journal* 8 (2): 429–43.

Romilly, Jacqueline de. 2014 (1970). *La Tragédie grecque*. Paris: PUF.

Rosello, Mireille. 2010. "Marassa with a Difference: Danticat's *Eyes, Breath, Memory*." In *Edwidge Danticat: A Reader's Guide*, edited by Martin Munro, 117–29. Charlottesville: University of Virginia Press.

Rubbers, Benjamin, and Emilie Gallez. 2012. "Why Do Congolese People Go to Court? A Qualitative Study of Litigants' Experiences in Two Justice of the Peace Courts in Lubumbashi." *The Journal of Legal Pluralism and Unofficial Law* 44 (66): 79–108.

Sala-Molins, Louis. 2018 (1987). *Le Code Noir ou le calvaire de Canaan*. Paris: PUF.

Sanon, Barbara. 2001. "Black Crows and Zombie Girls." In *The Butterfly's Way: Voices from the Haitian Diaspora in the United States*, edited by Edwige Danticat, 43–48. New York: Soho.

Sarat, Austin, Lawrence Douglas, and Martha Merrill Umphrey, eds. 2006. *The Place of Law*. Ann Arbor: The University of Michigan Press.

Sarat, Austin, and Thomas R. Kearns, eds. 1993. *Law in Everyday Life*. Ann Arbor: The University of Michigan Press.

Sarthou, Sharròn Eve. 2010. "Unsilencing Défilé's Daughters: Overcoming Silence in Edwidge Danticat's *Breath, Eyes, Memory* and *Krik? Krak!*" *The Global South* 4 (2): 99–123.

Schneider, Winter Rae. 2018. "Between Sovereignty and Belonging: Women's Legal Testimonies in Nineteenth-Century Haiti." *The Journal of Caribbean History* 52 (2): 117–34.

Schuller, Mark. 2012. *Killing with Kindness: Haiti, International Aid, and NGOs.* New Brunswick, NJ: Rutgers University Press.

———. 2021. "The Foreign Roots of Haiti's 'Constitutional Crisis.'" *NACLA: Reporting on the Americas*, February 6.

Schwarte, Ludger. 2006. "La mise en scène du droit. Le corps inconnu dans la décision démocratique." *Labyrinthe* 23 (1): 31–40.

Scott, James. 1985. *The Weapons of the Weak: Everyday Forms of Peasant Resistance.* New Haven, CT: Yale University Press.

———. 1990. *Domination and the Arts of Resistance: Hidden Transcripts.* New Haven, CT: Yale University Press.

———. 2009. *The Art of Not Begin Governed: An Anarchist History of Upland Southeast Asia.* New Haven, CT: Yale University Press.

Segal, Lotte Buch. 2016. *No Place for Grief: Martyrs, Prisoners, and Mourning in Contemporary Palestine.* Philadelphia: University of Pennsylvania Press.

Singh, Bhrigupati. 2015. *Poverty and the Quest for Life: Spiritual and Material Striving in Rural India.* Chicago: The University of Chicago Press.

Smith, Caleb. 2013. *The Oracle and the Curse: A Poetics of Justice from the Revolution to the Civil War.* Cambridge, MA: Harvard University Press.

Smith, Jennie Marcelle. 2001. *When the Hands Are Many: Community Organization and Social Change in Rural Haiti.* Ithaca, NY: Cornell University Press.

Smith, Katherine. 2012. "Genealogies of the *Gede*." In *In Extremis: Life and Death in the 21st Century Haitian Art.* Los Angeles: Fowler Museum of Cultural History.

Soulier, Gérard. 1991. "Le théâtre et le procès." *Droit et Société* 17–18: 9–24.

Spieler, Miranda Frances. 2021. "Peasant Resistance in Post-Revolutionary Haiti." *Reviews in American History* 49 (3): 413–21.

Sprague, Jeb. 2012. *Paramilitarism and the Assault on Democracy in Haiti.* New York: Monthly Review Press.

Sternlight, Jean R. 2007. "Is Alternative Dispute Resolution Consistent with the Rule of Law? Lessons from Abroad." *DePaul Law Review* 56 (2): 569–92.

Supiot, Alain. 2009 (2005). *Homo juridicus. Essai sur la fonction anthropologique du droit.* Paris: Seuil.

Suresh, Mayur R. 2023. *Terror Trials: Life and Law in Delhi's Courts.* New York: Fordham University Press.

Taussig, Michael. 2003. *Law in a Lawless Land: Diary of a Limpieza in Colombia.* Chicago: The University of Chicago Press.

The Earth Institute and the School of International and Public Affairs at Columbia University. 2012. "Options for Land Tenure Dispute Management in Rural Haiti: Challenges and Opportunities in the Côte Sud." Report presented to the United Nations Environment Program, May 9, 2012.

Théodat, Jean-Marie. 2003. *Haïti, République Dominicaine. Une île pour deux (1804–1916)*. Paris: Karthala.

Thomas, Deborah A. 2011. *Exceptional Violence: Embodied Citizenship in Transnational Jamaica*. Durham, NC: Duke University Press.

———. 2019. *Political Life in the Wake of the Plantation: Sovereignty, Witnessing, Repair*. Durham, NC: Duke University Press.

Thoreau, Henry D. 2004. *Walden*. Edited by J. Lyndon Shanley. Princeton, NJ: Princeton University Press.

———. 2012. *October, or Autumnal Tints*. Edited by Robert D. Richardson. New York: W. W. Norton.

Tøraasen, Marianne. 2022. "Women's Judicial Representation in Haiti: Unintended Gains of State-Building Efforts." *Politics and Gender* 19 (1): 34–45.

Trouillot, Lyonel. 2015. *C'est avec mains qu'on fait chansons*, Montreuil: Le Temps des cerises.

Trouillot, Michel-Rolph. 1990. "The Odd and the Ordinary: Haiti, the Caribbean, and the World." *Cimmaròn: New Perspectives on the Caribbean* 2 (3): 3–12.

———. 1991. "Anthropology and the Savage Slot: The Poetics and Politics of Otherness." In *Recapturing Anthropology: Working in the Present*, edited by Richard G. Fox, 17–44. Santa Fe: School of American Research Press.

———. 1992. "The Caribbean Region: An Open Frontier in Anthropological Theory." *Annual Review of Anthropology* 21: 19–42.

———. 1998. "Culture on the Edge: Creolization in a Plantation Context." *Plantation Society in the Americas* 5 (1): 8–28.

———. 2003. *Global Transformations: Anthropology and the Modern World*. New York: Palgrave MacMillan.

———. 2015. (1995). *Silencing the Past: Power and the Production of History*, 20th anniversary edition. Preface by H. V. Carby. New York: Penguin Random House.

Ulysse, Gina Athena. 2015. *Why Haiti Needs New Narratives: A Post-Quake Chronicle*, trilingual edition. Foreword by Robin D. G. Kelly. Middletown, CT: Wesleyan University Press.

UN Development Programme (UNDP), UN Women, and UNICEF. 2015. "Informal Justice Systems: Charting a Course for Human Rights-Based Engagement."

UN Development Programme (UNDP). 2023. "Justice Programme—Fact Sheet," February.

UN Department of Peace Operations (UNDPO). n.d. "DDR—Community Violence Reduction: Creating Space for Peace."

UN Department of Peace Operations (UNDPO). 2004. "Year in Review 2004."

UN Office on Drugs and Crime (UNODC). 2011. Report developed jointly with the United States Institute of Peace, "Criminal Justice Reform in Post-Conflict States: A Guide for Practitioners."

Verna, Chantalle F. 2017. *Haiti and the Uses of America: Post-U.S. Occupation Promises.* New Brunswick, NJ: Rutgers University Press.

Vernant, Jean-Pierre. 2004 (1974). *Mythes et société en Grèce ancienne.* Paris: La Découverte.

Victor, Marvin. 2011. *Corps mêlés.* Paris: Gallimard

Watkins, Angela. 2016. "Restoring Haitian Women's Voices and Verbalizing Sexual Trauma in *Breath, Eyes, Memory.*" *Journal of Haitian Studies* 22 (1): 106–27.

Whitman, James Q. 2008. *The Origins of Reasonable Doubt: Theological Roots of Criminal Trial.* New Haven, CT: Yale University Press.

Wilets, James D., and Camilo Espinosa. 2011. "Rule of Law in Haiti Before and After the 2010 Earthquake." *Intercultural Human Rights Law Review* 6: 181–206.

Wittgenstein, Ludwig. 1986 (1953). *Philosophical Investigations.* Translated G. E. M. Anscombe. Oxford: Basil Blackwell.

Zanotti, Laura. 2011. *Governing Disorder: UN Peace Operations, International Security, and Democratization in the Post-Cold War Era.* University Park: The Pennsylvania State University Press.

INDEX

accord, 149–50, 172

accusation, 31, 96, 185; accused, 49, 85, 95–97, 99–101, 108, 134, 138, 141, 166, 173, 209, 243n30, 248n13

acknowledgment, 11, 198, 250n14; acknowledge, 60, 77, 80, 88, 127, 142, 181

adjudication, 5, 9, 167, 251n15; adjudicate, 80, 105, 135

aesthetic(s), 83, 132, 141, 153, 163–64, 196, 229

agency, xvi, 5, 90, 151–52, 159, 164, 170, 256n6

agreement, 98, 143, 239n15, 241n26, 243n28, 243–44n32, 246n11, 254n32, 261n20

America(n), 25, 50–51, 104, 157, 165, 186, 228, 241n26, 243n31, 252n23, 252n25, 252n26, 255n9, 256n12, 256n7, 258n21; Central, 237n5, 241n25; Latin, 243n30; North, xvii, 188

apparatus, 96, 128, 144; state, 32, 78, 84, 110; terror, 85

arbitrate, xv, 15, 25, 52, 167, 247n4; arbitrariness, 121; arbitrary, xv, 136, 157, 254n31; arbitration, 2, 23, 155; arbitrator, 110

Aristide, Jean-Bertrand, 63, 69, 115–16, 157, 242n28, 254n32, 258n21

armed groups, 28, 30, 33, 41–42, 56, 61, 85–88, 113, 123–24, 242n28

army, 25, 32, 40, 106, 115; Cannibal Army, 113; US Army, 252n27

arrest, 2, 7, 8, 43, 46–47, 96, 100, 108, 120, 154, 217–18, 254n31

arson, 120, 208, 240n20, 240n21, 242n28

Artibonite, xi, 24–25, 43, 47, 67, 86–87, 94, 112, 120, 133, 183, 220, 222, 247n4, 248n13, 248n14, 250n7

aspect, xxi, 8, 14, 16, 35, 37, 39, 88, 96, 100, 131, 142, 144, 149, 151, 164, 170–74, 177, 190, 193, 196, 198, 200, 203, 218, 238n9

assassin, 169; assassinated, 40, 65, 79, 114; assassination, 28, 32, 68, 79, 87, 116, 169, 179, 242n28, 244n32

attentiveness, 176, 197, 221

attorney, 78, 95, 97, 111, 133–34, 139, 141

bailiff, xiii, 79, 94, 107, 114, 146, 154

Barbecue, 40, 124, 242n28. *See also* Cherizier, Jimmy

Barthélemy, Gérard, 18, 23

battle, xx, 15, 26, 40, 72, 75, 84, 87, 106, 124, 144–45, 213. *See also* war

baz, 27, 46, 47, 58, 217, 235, 240–241n23, 245n7, 246n3

Beckett, Greg, 14, 23, 25, 33, 192, 227, 249n15

behavior, xv, 12, 23, 76, 82, 89, 100, 134, 137, 146, 161, 168, 193–94, 204, 217, 220, 243n30; illegal, 127; ritualized, 193; sexualized, 257n10

Bel-Air, 57, 104, 126, 245n7, 247n6

Bicentenaire, 47, 79, 86

BINUH (United Nations Integrated Office in Haiti), 32, 116, 120, 208, 231

Board of Directors of the Communal Section. *See* CASEC (Board of Directors of the Communal Section)

body, 3, 34, 50, 63, 67, 97, 101, 151, 160, 183, 188, 193, 202–3, 208, 211, 219, 246n12, 257n11, 258n20, 261n16; dead, 185; embody, xxi, 145, 149, 153, 220, 241n23; language, 141. *See also* corpse

border, 24, 26, 46, 64–65, 71, 151, 166, 218, 249n1; borderlands, 213, 256n14; borderline, 182–83

Bossou, 51, 101–2, 250n7

Boyer, Jean-Pierre, 20–22, 105, 110, 239n16

bureaucracy, 60, 96, 208; bureaucratic, 32, 80, 96, 124, 140

Canada, 113, 123, 243n31

carceral, xx; incarcerated, 47, 154, 208; incarceration, 8, 243n29

care, xviii, xix–xx, 3, 15–17, 26, 30, 34, 46, 48, 55–56, 68, 75, 91, 104, 122, 145, 165, 169, 173, 193, 199, 209, 214, 219, 228, 238n10, 251n13; -ful, 16, 27, 49, 113, 142, 178; -fully, xx, 68, 139, 191, 249n1, 259n4; -less, 219; -lessness, 49; -taker, 251n18; child-, 17

Caribbean, 14, 18, 24, 188, 241n26, 256n4, 257n13

CASEC (Board of Directors of the Communal Section), viii, 2, 7–8, 43–44, 48, 61, 86, 95–100, 107–8, 231, 237n3, 238n8, 250–51n13

Casimir, Jean, 17–18, 20

Catholic, 53, 160, 240n19; Catholicism, 250n7, 250n8

Cavell, Stanley, 131, 145, 163, 165, 171, 175, 182, 191–96, 204–6, 212, 218, 238, 258n18, 259n2, 259n4, 260n9, 261n16, 261n18, 261n19

Charles X, 21, 105

Cherizier, Jimmy, 40, 124, 242n28. *See also* Barbecue

church, vii, 44, 48, 109, 145, 150, 160, 175, 240n19

Cité Soleil, 26, 53, 57, 116, 123, 215, 249n15, 258n21

clandestine, 19, 33, 151; clandestinity, 19, 22

clerk, xiii, 73, 76, 78, 94, 95, 97, 107–9, 112–14, 125–26, 131, 133, 141–42, 146, 148–49, 154, 210

Clinton, Bill, 252n26

code, xvi, 21–22, 32, 37, 105, 111, 122, 127, 137, 139, 141, 149, 152, 157–58, 179, 220, 253n28; civil, 22, 82, 105, 160, 231, 247n8; Code Noir, 18, 20, 238–39n14, 255n10; criminal, 32; Napoleonic, 105, 247n8; penal, 22, 37, 122, 157–58, 178–79, 233, 240n20, 253n28, 256n2; rural, 22, 72, 100, 105, 140, 233, 239n17

Colombia, 19, 114, 123, 237n5

colonial, 18, 20–21, 105, 183, 238n14, 253n27, 256n13; colonialism, 183; postcolonial, xi, 34, 85, 147, 150, 159

comedy, 84, 154, 194, 212; comical, 153, 193, 198, 260n11

community, vii, viii, xviii, 3, 5, 7–8, 28, 32, 34, 44, 48, 68, 70, 82, 93, 103–5,

107–10, 112, 115, 118–20, 126–27, 132, 148, 151, 157, 183, 190–91, 231–32, 235–36, 237n4, 245n4, 246n16, 247n6, 248n9; communal, 2, 4, 7–8, 23, 28, 37, 86, 90, 94, 95–96, 98, 107–8, 113, 163, 232, 251n15; commune, vi, 8, 44, 52, 69, 79–80, 86–88, 95, 107–8, 200, 237n2, 237–38n8

conciliation, xvi, 35, 74, 133, 135–36, 143–45, 150, 250n4; conciliatory, 83, 89; reconciliation, 141

conflict, viii, xi, xiv, 1, 3, 5, 7, 12–14, 17, 27, 35, 41, 44, 47, 53–54, 66–67, 70, 73, 76–77, 80–81, 84, 91–94, 96, 100, 102, 104–6, 109–10, 116, 118, 121–22, 125, 126, 128, 142, 166–67, 174, 190, 239n14, 243n30, 247n6, 249n1, 252n24; conflicting, xv, 20, 90, 95, 126

constitution, 14, 20, 25, 118, 122, 131, 157–58, 178, 247n7, 248n9; constitutional, 117; constitutionally, 90; unconstitutional, 41

contract, 69, 80, 96, 140, 167, 235

convention, xv, 10, 81–82, 157–58; conventional, 10, 17, 90, 120, 126, 150, 202, 245n3, 261n17; conventionally, 135

corpse, 43, 50, 97, 156, 162, 189, 193, 258n20

corrupt, 33, 43, 89, 114, 137, 138, 142, 241n23; corruption, 34, 54, 64, 79, 85, 119–20, 124, 138, 154, 158, 253n27

Creole, 17, 29, 49, 78, 100, 111, 134, 139, 149, 168, 221, 260n10, 262n24; Creolization, 247n8

crime, 8, 34, 49, 119–20, 152, 159, 179, 217, 233, 240n20, 247n6, 248n12, 250n12, 252n23, 252n27; criminal, ix, 2, 8, 32, 34, 41, 69, 81, 84, 91, 100, 105, 113, 116, 118–19, 122, 124–25, 135–38,

150–52, 157–59, 167, 179, 185, 217, 232, 235, 245n9, 247n6, 248n13, 253n27, 253n28; criminally 120; criminalize, 22, 116, 119, 150, 240n20, 246n3; decriminalize, 158

crisis, 14–15, 69, 76, 116–17, 219

criticism, 128, 227; criticize, 239n14; critique, 147, 173, 176, 257n12

custom, xvi, 21–22, 42, 96, 158, 232, 238n10, 256n2; customary, 82, 127, 133

Danbala, 101–2, 250n8

Danticat, Edwidge, 157, 161, 169, 175–76, 184, 186, 257n12, 258n20

Das, Veena, 6, 41, 84, 125, 135, 142, 181, 206, 219–20, 226–27, 238n10, 247n6

decision, 5, 21, 31, 42, 44, 113, 148; -making, xiii, 117, 135

defense, 40, 98, 118, 160, 233, 242n28, 248n13; defend, xi, xiv, 2, 69, 126, 152, 158, 184; defendant, 141, 150, 249n4; defender, 136, 182; self-, 18, 125

deliberation, xiii, xvi, 5, 9, 74, 84, 136, 146

Delmas, 57, 62, 63, 124

democracy, xvii, 33, 35, 40, 85, 89, 90–91, 94, 102, 104, 109, 114, 125–27, 155, 238n10, 241n23, 243n30, 252n23; democratic, xvii, 14, 35, 89, 90, 103, 118–20, 124, 157, 243n30, 254n34; democratization, 241n23; undemocratic, 158

Depestre, René, 156, 161–62, 169, 171, 175, 179, 183, 200, 257n10, 257n16

Dessalines, Jean-Jacques, 18–19, 24, 40, 65, 86, 248n13

detention, 7, 120, 154, 157, 207–8, 256n14

Diamond, Cora, 6, 41, 164, 185–86, 202–3, 257n18, 261n17

diaspora, 25, 31, 50

disagreement, 11, 24, 172, 182, 257n18
dispute, 1, 3, 5, 9, 12, 24–25, 34, 52, 54,
    66, 79–81, 83–84, 92, 96, 105, 107–8,
    110, 112, 115, 120, 121, 135, 141, 145–46,
    148, 150–52, 166–67, 174, 182, 241n26,
    243n28, 247n4, 251n15; alternative
    dispute resolution, xvi, 231, 243n30,
    249n4, 254n33; settlement, 92, 141
domestic, 94, 175, 239n14, 243n31,
    249n1, 253n28, 257n15, 258n20;
    domesticity, 18; violence, 179, 255n9
Dominican, 4, 24, 42, 46, 68, 86, 218,
    239n16, 261n20
drama, 1, 10, 84, 138, 194; dramatic, 106,
    116, 134, 144, 146, 153–54; dramati-
    cally, 93; dramatization, 206; melo-
    dramatic, 145, 212; undramatic, 10
dream, 36–37, 40, 42, 53, 104, 114, 161,
    164, 169, 170, 173, 175, 179, 185, 196,
    200, 208, 212; dreaming, 163
drug, 85, 113–14, 217, 233, 253n27;
    trafficking, 114, 119–20, 208
Dubois, Laurent, 20, 22, 25, 239n16,
    255n10
Duvalier, 40, 122, 157, 176, 240n23,
    257n16; dictatorship, xiv, 33, 48, 115,
    178, 202, 246n1, 254n31, 257n14;
    François, 157, 246n1, 258n21;
    Jean-Claude, 32, 107, 157

economic(s), 7, 17, 34, 82, 85, 108, 117,
    125, 214, 247n8, 248n9, 250n5,
    253n28, 254n33; economy, 17, 18, 20,
    70–71, 84, 86, 140, 241n23, 242n28,
    246n1, 247n6; socio-, 20, 117
emancipation, 19–21, 125, 257n16
ethic(s), xvi, 138, 153, 153, 165, 196,
    245n9, 255n3; ethical, 6, 137, 174,
    185
evidence, xx, 36, 94, 96–97, 100, 111, 113,
    124, 242n28, 245n2, 253n29

execution, 120, 157, 169, 240n21, 244n33,
    254n31
experience, xvi, 10–12, 19, 37, 40, 59, 80,
    127, 130–32, 142, 162, 164, 174–76, 183,
    185, 190–91, 193–95, 198, 205–6,
    219–21, 252n27, 259n4, 261n17
expression, 35, 49, 92, 109, 139, 142,
    144–45, 148–49, 171, 175, 192;
    expressive, 149; expressiveness, 190;
    expressivity, 190

Fick, Carolyn, 18–19
fiction, 121; fictionalization, 205
finitude, 37, 190–91, 197, 200, 204–6,
    261n18
firearms, 7, 26, 53, 63,69, 82, 120–21. See
    also gun; weapon
folly, 136. See also madness
Foucault, Michel, 77–78, 106, 110, 128,
    132–33, 135, 238n9, 240n18, 240n20,
    240n21, 247n7, 249n3, 259n2
France, 21, 105, 123, 137, 228, 239n18,
    243n31, 248n9, 250n12
Frankétienne, 175, 201–2, 257n14,
    257n16
freedom, xv, 18, 33, 209, 222, 260n12

gang, 8, 47, 56, 58, 63–64, 68, 85–87, 116,
    119–20, 123, 127, 167, 169, 217, 235,
    238n8, 238n11, 242n28, 244n33,
    245n2, 254n31; gangsterize, 116
gede, vii, 53–55, 58–59, 67, 168–70, 173, 179,
    199–221, 235, 246n1, 260n10, 260n12
Ghachem, Malick W., 20, 238n14,
    239n15
Gonaïves, 24, 30, 42, 46, 141, 149, 151,
    247n4
Gonzales, Johnhenry, 20, 239n18, 246n3
government, viii, 18, 20–23, 32, 33,
    52–54, 74, 85, 89, 113–14, 116, 118–19,
    123–24, 128, 154, 156, 159–60, 175,

241n23, 243n28, 244n32, 246n4, 253n27, 261n20; governance, xiv, xvii, 9, 32, 79, 91, 118, 178, 183, 252n26

gun, 34, 53, 69, 74, 207, 246n10; -fire, xviii, 47, 54; -powder, 20; -shot, 47, 53; hand-, 69

Hartman, Saidiya, 162–63
homicide, 34. *See also* kill
household, xxi, 26–27, 30, 70–71, 75, 86, 236, 239n14, 249n1. See also *lakou*
humanitarian, xix, 103, 252n25; humanitarianism, 119
Hurbon, Laënnec, 18, 178, 199, 247n8
Hurston, Zora Neale, 162, 246n3

imagination, 23, 51, 161, 163, 175, 194, 243n29; imagine, xv, 15, 28, 33, 38, 84, 91, 102, 121, 125, 130, 135, 137, 143, 146–47, 161, 163–64, 170, 175, 179, 180, 183, 185, 190, 194, 202, 203–4, 210, 225,239n14, 251n16
imperialism, 118; imperial, 17
improvisation, 15, 36, 136, 148, 152–53, 206, 212; improvise, xiii, 11, 30, 31, 54, 55, 128, 136, 139, 146–48, 152–53, 163, 191, 193, 199, 218
indeterminate, xvi, 164, 181–82, 221; indeterminacy, 5, 181–82, 220
inequality, xvi, 35, 93, 121, 122, 125
informal, 10–11, 34, 62, 77, 80–82, 96, 104, 125, 127–28, 133, 149, 152, 157, 217, 227, 232, 243n31, 247n6, 249n15, 255n8; informality, 23, 108; informally, 98, 155
insurgent, 18, 20–21, 24, 119; counterinsurgency, 115, 123
international, 5, 20, 38, 32, 40, 90, 92–93, 103, 114–15, 117, 118–19, 124–27, 132, 150, 154, 231–33, 243n31,

244n33, 250n10, 252n23, 252n25, 252n26, 253n27, 255n6; community, 32, 118, 132, 157; conventions, 158; diplomacy, 34, 104; force, 117, 125; internationally, 169; organizations, 28, 33, 118, 228, 232; trade, 119
interpretation, 20, 119, 145, 163, 174, 212; over-, 211

James, Erica C., 84, 246n1
judge, viii, xiii, xviii, 2, 6–8, 52, 54, 61, 62, 70, 72–74, 77–81, 94–100, 106–9, 111–15, 121, 125–26, 128, 133–36, 138–41, 144–46, 148–49, 154, 182, 184, 207–10, 212, 235, 238n11, 247n7, 235n3; judgment, xiii, xiv, 5–6, 84, 89, 106, 113, 112–21, 135–36, 138, 142, 148, 153, 161, 250n7
judiciary, xiv, 12, 21–22, 32, 35–36, 78, 79, 90, 104, 106–9, 111, 114, 118–20, 124, 132–33, 142, 150, 154, 156–57, 231, 247n7; extrajudicial, xi, xiv, 34, 90, 128, 157, 238n11; judicial, xv, 7, 12, 21, 31, 32, 60, 79, 85, 89–90, 96, 105–6, 124, 129, 133, 135–36, 142, 157, 167, 247n8, 248n13, 251n15, 254n2, 255n3; juridical, xv, 21, 82, 133, 144, 159
justice, xiii, 6, 8, 11–12, 14, 22, 33, 34, 42, 48, 50, 59, 62, 73, 75–79, 81, 85, 89–92, 94, 103, 105–7, 109–11, 114, 115–17, 119–20, 122, 125, 127–28, 133, 135–37, 141–42, 148, 150–51, 153–57, 160, 190–91, 232–33, 235, 238n9, 243n29, 248n13, 250n7, 253n27, 253n28, 254n33, 254n2, 255n8; criminal, 157, 253n27, 253n28; customary, 127; democratic, 90; everyday, 10–11; extrajudicial, xiv; informal, 62, 127, 323; injustice, 110, 142, 144; local, 133; nonstate, xi; popular, 78; state, xi, 70, 154, 248n12; transitional, xvi

Kalfou, xxi, 51, 58, 68, 167
kidnapping, 23, 28, 31, 52, 85, 113, 123, 208, 242–43n28, 244n33, 248n13
kill, 1, 36, 40, 43, 45, 47, 49, 50–52, 56, 68–70, 79, 86–88, 98–99, 101, 114, 116, 120, 123, 136, 138, 144, 153–54, 169, 172, 186, 192, 207, 216, 135, 240n20, 248n14, 258n21; killer, 69, 167, 169, 172, 235; killings, 40, 56, 70, 85, 244n33. *See also* homicide
Kivland, Chelsey L., 9, 125–26, 147, 154, 227, 240–41n23, 245n7, 246n10, 246n3, 247n6, 252n26
knowledge, 16, 18, 48, 60, 77, 80, 88, 108–10, 127, 131–32, 144, 152, 160, 161, 171, 175, 193, 197, 202–3, 205, 219
Kriminel, 51, 55, 167

La Saline, 40, 56, 63, 124, 258n21
Lahens, Yanick, 15, 40, 257n12
lakou, 17–18, 20, 59, 67, 69, 103–4, 109, 139, 188, 135, 245n3, 250n11, 251n17, 255n10. *See also* household
lawless, xv, 118, 238n10, 247n6; lawlessness, xv, 23, 103
lawsuit, 35, 89, 133, 136
lawyer, vii, xiii, 36, 52, 59, 65, 70, 76, 79, 97, 109, 111, 113–14, 125–26, 134–35, 137–38, 142, 144–46, 148, 149–50, 152–54, 209–10, 246n4
Legba, 51, 167
legitimacy, 79–80, 117, 124, 135, 137, 143, 184; illegitimate, 240n20; illegitimately, 139; legitimate, 11, 106, 125, 139, 240n20; legitimately, 132
liberal, xviii, 90, 104, 117–18, 122, 135; neoliberalization, 241n23
litigant, 35, 76, 80, 107, 109, 121, 128, 144, 150, 256n13; litigation, xiii, xvi, 25, 106, 109, 120, 135, 247n4

lougawou, 48–49, 57, 160–61, 178, 199, 236
Louverture, Toussaint, 18–19, 47, 239n18
lwa, 41, 53–55, 58, 101, 109, 151–52, 166–67, 202, 235, 245n3, 245n6, 245n9, 246n15, 250n7, 257n11. *See also* spirits

madness, 42, 154, 179, 202, 238n11. *See also* folly
magic, 53, 213, 215–16, 218, 245n9, 246n10, 250n7
magistrate, 11, 32, 53, 79–80, 94, 107, 110–11, 113, 122, 150, 231
marronage, 16, 19, 246n3; maroon, 19, 23–24, 183, 236; *mawon*, 24, 18, 65, 235; *mawonaj*, 19
Martelly, Michel, 123, 157, 242n26
Martissant, 47, 68, 104, 168, 170
massacre, xvii, 23, 40, 42, 56, 63, 67, 124, 191, 242n28
method, 13, 30–31, 116, 163, 191, 254n31; methodological, 31, 184; methodology, 158
Métraux Alfred, 84, 162, 168, 199, 246n1, 247n5
military, xvii, 19–21, 32–33, 35, 105, 107, 115–16, 119, 123, 184, 186, 240n19, 243n28, 253n27, 258n2; militarization, 119; militarized, 249n1; para-, 123, 157, 167, 246n3
MINUJUSTH (United Nations Mission for Justice Support in Haiti), 32, 116, 122, 232, 243n29
MINUSTAH (United Nations Stabilization Mission in Haiti), 94, 102, 107, 115–16, 120, 122–23, 207, 232, 249n2
mistik, 3, 48, 53, 59, 110, 112, 162, 169, 199, 214, 216, 219, 220, 236

modern, 18, 106, 122, 128, 135–37, 150, 240n20, 240n21, 247n7, 249n3; modernity, 33, 136, 138, 147, 254–55n3, 259n2; modernization, 94, 253n28

Moïse, Jovenel, xi, 31–34, 40, 58, 60, 84, 116, 123–24, 158, 242n26, 242n28, 244n32, 251n13

Montalvo-Despeignes, Jaquelin, 82, 142

Montana Accord, 33, 243n32

moral, 158, 164, 190, 239n14, 258n2; morality, 145

murder, 63, 66, 72, 75–76, 81, 84, 92, 98, 113, 124, 138, 171, 179, 191, 208; murderer, 99; murderous, 42

myth, 121; mythical, 164, 245n9

Nader, Laura, 9, 118–19, 225, 238n10, 247n6, 248n12, 254n33

Napoleon, 53, 65

NGO, 63, 103–4, 241n23, 242n28, 253n29

norm, 10, 34, 127, 137, 145, 178, 182; normal, 78, 100, 163, 183; normalize, 168, 180; normalization, 247n6, 256n7; normative, xi, 12, 14, 35, 121, 136, 161, 179; normatively, 5; normativity, 164, 182

notable, 7, 23, 43, 70, 80, 82–83, 96, 107, 109, 245n5, 248n9

notary, 209, 210; notarial, 96; nota- rized, 96

offense, 82–83, 97, 114, 179

Ogou, xxi, 58

order, 8–10, 12, 21–23, 26, 41, 97, 105–6, 110, 118–20, 127, 136, 157, 180, 201, 247n6; disorder, 9, 17, 103, 121, 250n10; legal, 127, 167; occult, 246n3; ordered, 89, 122, 146; orderly, xvii;

public, 106; social, 110, 126; world, 119

ordinary, xiii–xiv, xvi–xix, 6, 9–11, 14–15, 19, 23–24, 30, 34–37, 41, 67, 75–76, 82, 91, 93, 98, 103, 106, 125–26, 128–30, 132, 138–39, 142–42, 147, 154, 149, 159, 163, 171–73, 178, 184–85, 190–96, 205, 211, 225, 249n1, 250n6, 259n2; language, 111, 143, 181; ordinarily, 84, 163; ordinariness, 193, 195

paper, 59, 60, 64–65, 88, 90, 96, 108, 111, 126, 209–10, 220, 249n3, 252n24; news 160; paperwork, 78, 115; *papye*, 96

passion, 9, 138, 142; dispassionate, 91, 144; passionate, 35, 44, 139, 144; passionately, 67, 226

Payton, Claire A., 110, 227, 242n26, 253n29

peace, 9, 28, 33, 40, 48, 88–89, 92–94, 102–7, 110–12, 114–22, 124–32, 135, 154, 222, 233, 235, 241n23, 243n29, 250n9, 250n10, 253n27; courts of, 15, 79–88; justice of the, 7, 22, 48, 94, 105, 133, 232; *lapè*, 103–5, 235; -building, 35, 90, 93, 102–4, 249n1; -ful, 12, 28, 58, 67, 77, 93, 102, 104, 109–10, 115, 128, 171, 240n20; -keeping, 90, 102, 115–17, 119, 132, 249n1, 249n2

peasant, 18, 21–23, 25, 44, 45, 70, 71, 73, 75, 79, 87, 96, 98–99, 110, 112, 126, 133, 141, 185, 236, 240n21, 250n6; peasantry, 18, 20, 24, 25

performance, 36, 83–84, 134–35, 137–39, 143–44, 146–47, 149, 152–54, 215; perform, 7, 53, 167; performative, 138, 153; performatively, 143

Pétion-ville, 26, 58, 79

PetroCaribe, 28, 54, 241–42n26

philosophy, 115, 158, 191, 195, 202–3, 205, 228, 229, 256n2, 258–59n2; philosopher, 195, 221–22, 254n2; philosophical, 37, 187, 191, 195, 205, 211, 222, 257–58n18, 259n4, 261n17

plaintiff, 9, 80, 95, 141, 144, 249n4

plantation, 18–20, 98, 176, 183, 238n13, 239n14, 239n15; counterplantation, 18

playfulness, 36, 84, 111, 139, 194, 248n10; playfully, 25

poetry, xii, xx, 190; poem, xii, xix–xx, 60, 61, 171, 202–3; poet, xx, 172, 201; poetic, xvi, 164, 183, 193

police, vii, xiv, 2, 7–8, 12, 24, 33, 41–44, 47, 49, 52, 63, 68, 70–72, 74, 76, 79, 81, 85, 87, 95–97, 99–100, 102, 105–10, 112, 115–16, 119–24, 132, 138, 151, 154, 157–58, 167, 175, 186, 207, 217–18, 220, 232, 242–43n28, 244n33, 245n5, 248n12, 248n13, 248n14, 250n12, 251n13, 255n11, 256n7; Haitian National Police, 32, 47, 120, 122, 232–33, 242n8, 242–43n28, 244n33; policeman, 68, 79, 87, 95, 123, 215, 242–43n28

political, 4, 6, 16, 19–20, 23, 34, 40, 65, 69, 76–77, 84–86, 89, 94, 103, 108, 113, 116–19, 124–26, 132, 154, 159, 184, 219, 241n23, 242n28, 243n30, 243n32, 246n1, 249n1, 250n10, 250n13, 252n23, 254n33, 258n20; micro-, xix; politically, 28, 179; politics, xiv, xviii, 16–17, 34, 44, 50, 64, 103, 126, 132, 153–54, 241n23, 242n30, 247n6, 249n1, 254n33; power, 33, 52, 132, 248n9, 254n1; prisoners, 176, 184, 186; sociopolitical, 247n8

Port-au-Prince, viii, xxi, 23, 25–26, 30, 33, 41, 44, 47, 51, 53–55, 58–60, 62–63, 68–69, 76, 79, 85–86, 88, 114, 122–24, 127, 168, 176, 192, 202, 215, 221, 226,

242–43n28, 247n6, 249n15, 254n15, 260n12

prison, xvi, 1, 8, 37, 43, 47, 74, 78, 138, 153, 161, 207–10, 212, 217, 232, 237n5, 243n29, 261n20, 261n23; imprisoned, 49; imprisonment, 178, 240n20; prisoner, 47, 175–76, 184, 186, 208–9; system, 32, 156

procedure, xvi, 6, 12, 66, 78, 98, 100, 106, 125, 127, 133, 135, 138, 140–42, 152, 215; arrest, 2, 154; conciliatory, 89; criminal, 32, 122, 137, 151–52, 157–58, 253n28; legal, 5, 7, 95

proceedings, 135, 249n4, 251n15, 255n11, 256n13

proof, xix, 82, 96, 100, 146, 149, 204

prosecutor, xiii, 76, 209, 242n26

Protestant, 62, 158, 232

punishment, xiv, 81, 115, 121, 126, 150, 179, 240n20; punish, 21; punishable, 137, 178

quotidian, 37, 66, 146, 162, 163, 172, 174, 192

Ramsey, Kate, 22, 165, 167, 240n19, 246n3, 257n17

rape, 63, 85, 120, 159, 179, 183, 258n20

rational, 12, 35, 84, 139; rationale, 111, 129, 134–35, 142; rationalist, 178; rationality, 135; rationalization, 110; rationalize, 105

realism, 37, 162, 165, 185, 196, 220

realistic, 162, 165, 184; unrealistic, 12

reason, xv–xvi, xviii, xxi, 2, 4, 8–9, 12, 19, 44, 66, 73, 78, 83–84, 89–90, 112, 128, 132, 136, 138, 143–44, 146–47, 152, 161, 165, 176, 190, 198, 206, 217, 237n5, 238n9, 240n20, 241n24; reasonable, 8, 135, 138, 140, 142, 165; reasonableness, 145; reasonably, 81; reasoned, 146;

reasoning, 35, 133, 136, 139; unreasonable, xv, 8, 249n4, 258n18, 262n23

reform, xiv, 31–32, 37, 87, 94, 122, 125, 157–60, 185, 232, 252n26, 253n27, 253n28, 256n2

representation, 132, 144, 147, 165, 180–81, 244n34

resilience, xviii; resilient, xviii, 17

resistance, xviii–xxi, 2, 16–19, 22–23, 25, 29, 31, 34, 41, 105, 110, 150, 159, 218, 242n26, 250n6; resist, xviii, xx, 2, 16, 25, 36, 41, 90, 183, 214; resistant, xviii

resolution, xvi, 9, 12–13, 92, 100, 115, 120, 125, 174, 182, 231, 242n28, 242n30, 249n4, 251n20, 251n21, 251n22, 254n33

responsibility, 58, 76, 104, 137, 145, 151, 164, 173, 203–6, 250n13; responsible, xii, 32, 51, 152

responsiveness, 82, 205, 212; responsive, 174, 197

revolution, 20, 40, 258n21; French Revolution, 248n9; Haitian Revolution, 17–18, 53, 248n9, 259n4; postrevolutionary, 19; revolutionary, 24, 65, 239n18

rhetoric, 35, 102, 114, 117–18, 125, 136, 149, 152; rhetorical, xvii, 101; rhetorically, 1

rightness, 76, 89, 164–65, 185; righteous, 137; rightly, 14

rights, 2, 7, 20, 25, 29, 32, 35–36, 76, 79–81, 89, 105–6, 114, 123, 125–26, 134, 140, 142–44, 146, 152, 179, 181, 183–84; human, xvi, 32, 40, 103, 124, 127, 151, 157–58, 231, 248n14, 252n23; divine, 136; women's, 122

ritual, xi, xiv, 22, 55, 84, 107, 109, 159, 161, 167, 170, 193, 200, 213–14, 236, 237n4, 245n6, 246n15, 246n1, 257n17, 259n4; ritualize, 138, 193; ritually, xxi, 52

rule of law, xiv–xv, xvii, 12, 35, 79, 90, 93, 102, 104, 114, 116–21, 125–28, 156–57, 180, 182–83, 252n23, 252n24, 253n27, 253n28, 254n33

Saint-Marc, 42, 46, 62, 73, 77, 100, 141, 207, 213, 215, 247n4, 261n20

sanpwèl, viii, 51–52, 57, 67–68, 167, 170, 236, 246n2, 246n3. See also secret society

Schuller, Mark, 33, 103, 242n26, 252n25, 252n26, 253n29

secret society, viii, 20, 23, 51, 57, 67–68, 167, 235–36, 246n2. See also sanpwèl

settlement, xvi, 19, 72, 77, 92, 98, 109, 110, 115, 117, 120, 141, 191, 236, 258n21

sex, 59, 95, 168; homosexuality, 158; sexual, 120, 158–59, 168, 179, 216, 257n11, 257n15; sexualized, 257n10

shooting, 47, 85

skepticism, 15, 161, 168, 238n11, 259n4, 262n25; skeptical, xx

slave, xvii, 18–19, 21, 53, 183, 197, 236, 239n14, 239n15, 250n12, 257n15, 257n17, 260n8; enslaved, 19, 239n14; slavery, 17–18, 20, 65, 85, 162–63, 183

sorcery, 256n5; sorcerer, 250n8

soul, 17, 53, 138, 162, 171, 176, 186, 200–1, 214, 235, 260n12

sovereignty, 14–15, 85, 110, 117, 239n14, 240n22, 247n6; sovereign, xv, 17

spell, 3, 22, 80, 112, 152, 121, 235–236, 245n8; counter-, 121

spirit(s), xiv, xxi, 17, 25, 42, 53, 67–68, 101, 109, 150–52, 162, 166–68, 170, 175–76, 184, 188, 196, 199–202, 206, 212–14, 219, 235–36, 241n23, 245n3, 245n6, 245n9, 246n12, 246n1, 257n10, 260n6, 262n24; spiritual, 259n4; spiritually, 55. See also lwa stabilization, 35, 94, 102, 115, 117, 232, 253n27, 253n30

standard, 110–11, 117, 127, 134–35, 137, 150, 181–82, 247n6; standardize, 32, 106

structure, xi, xv, xx, 5, 12–13, 18, 21, 23–24, 29, 82, 103, 127, 131, 189, 240–41n23, 247n7, 251n15, 252n26; infra-, 4, 33, 36, 75, 94, 261n20; structural, 18, 104, 119, 252n26; structuration, 63; super-, 23

suffering, xiii, 59, 84, 128, 206, 225

summon, 99, 213–14, 235, 249n4; summons, 97, 147, 249n4

terror, 84–85, 119, 150, 163, 239n18, 241n23, 246n1; terrorism, 253n27; terrorist, xvi

testimony, 96, 109, 120, 146, 256n14; testify, 82, 114; testimonial, 96, 113

texture, xvii, 6, 81, 102, 181–82, 184, 200

theatre, vii, xi, 105, 113, 136–38, 142, 153–54, 225, 254n2; theatrical, xi, 35, 83–84, 133, 136, 138, 146–47, 149, 153, 254n2; theatricality, xiv, 135, 137, 147, 153, 220, 254n2; theatricalize, 130; theatrics, 145

theft, 28, 84, 92, 98, 112–13, 121, 166; thief, 43, 48, 85, 88, 209

theory, 90, 93, 121, 132, 137, 181, 227, 240n21; theoretical, xv

tonton makout, 124, 157, 246n1, 258n20

torture, 84, 100, 120, 157, 176, 184, 254n31, 258n20, 258n21

trade, 106, 118–19, 125, 242n28, 245n9, 252n26,

tragedy, 66, 171, 205, 212; tragic, 191, 193, 198, 212, 220

trial, xx, 31, 131, 136, 138, 146, 148, 150, 153–54, 207–9, 219, 254n2; pretrial, 208, 256n14

tribunal, viii, xvi, 25, 73–74, 78, 83, 100, 107–8, 139, 141, 143, 150, 152, 232, 238n11, 247n4

Trouillot, Lyonel, 39, 60, 188, 227, 245n1

Trouillot, Michel-Rolph, 9, 94, 162, 246n1

Trump, Donald, 237n5, 241n25

truth, 48, 106, 135–36, 168, 180–81, 212; truthfulness, 137

uncertain, 15, 24, 143, 161, 186, 212–13, 241n25, 247n6, 256n14; uncertainty, 6, 28, 119, 144, 148, 164, 220

UNDP (United Nations Development Programme), 156–57, 233, 248–49n15, 255n8, 261n20

United Nations, xvii, 32, 87, 93–95, 102, 104, 115–18, 120, 122, 125, 127–28, 156, 231–33, 243n29, 243n31, 244n33, 245n2, 252n23, 252n24, 253n27

United Nations Integrated Office in Haiti. *See* BINUH (United Nations Integrated Office in Haiti)

United Nations Mission for Justice Support in Haiti. *See* MINUJUSTH (United Nations Mission for Justice Support in Haiti)

United Nations Stabilization Mission in Haiti. *See* MINUSTAH (United Nations Stabilization Mission in Haiti)

United States, 42, 50, 67–68, 117–19, 123, 146, 150, 165, 188, 217, 233, 237n5, 241n25, 243n31

vague, 47, 159, 180–81; vaguely, 19, 82; vagueness, 5, 76, 139, 180, 182, 237n7, 255n7

value, 5–6, 111, 118, 150, 152, 158, 166, 180, 190, 202, 253n28, 259n2, 261n16; truth-, 181

Venezuela, 241n26

violence, xi, xiii, xv–xviii, 3, 5, 9, 11–16, 18, 20, 23–24, 28, 35–37, 40–43, 45, 64, 66–68, 76, 80, 86, 88, 92–94, 98, 100, 102–5, 109–10, 112, 117, 120–21, 125–27, 132, 138–39, 142, 150, 153, 155, 159, 173, 179, 185, 191, 206, 211, 212, 222, 225, 232, 237n8, 238n9, 238n10, 238n13, 239n14, 240n20, 240n22, 241n23, 243n28, 244n33, 246n1, 247n6, 255n9, 256n7, 258n20

Vodou, viii, xi, 17, 20, 22–23, 25, 31, 48, 51, 53–54, 62–63, 67, 84, 107, 109, 150, 158–61, 166–68, 183, 188, 193, 200, 201, 226, 235–36, 237n4, 240n19, 245n3, 245n5, 245n6, 245n9, 246n14, 246n15, 256n8; *vodouizan*, viii, 23, 55, 59, 101, 166, 188, 236

vulnerable, 4, 15, 28, 52, 91, 114, 153–54, 166, 212, 215, 218, 248n15; vulnerability, xviii, 200, 204

war, xii, xv, xx, xxi, 15, 30, 35, 47, 58, 65, 67–68, 75–76, 78, 92, 94, 102, 106, 110–11, 115–17, 120–21, 125, 191, 194, 198, 239n16, 241n23, 241n28, 243n28, 247n7, 253n27, 254n32; post-, 117; -fare, 23, 106, 119

weapon, 20, 33, 53, 56–57, 68, 71, 88, 106, 113, 128, 169

witchcraft, 22, 159, 178, 238n11, 256n5; bewitchment, 37, 213

witness, 2, 10, 28, 32, 45, 53, 59, 80, 82, 95–99, 102, 109, 111, 126, 132, 138, 149, 169, 192–93, 203, 249n4

Wittgenstein, Ludwig, 163, 171, 173–74, 176–77, 186, 195–96, 203, 238n9, 257n18

wrong, 43, 58, 68, 70, 76, 98, 165, 184, 208; -doer, 235; -ful, 7

zombie, 37, 41, 89, 152, 156, 159–67, 170–72, 174–76, 179–81, 183–84, 186, 199, 215, 216, 136, 256n5, 256n6, 256n7, 257n16, 257n17; *zonbi*, 37, 152, 160, 162, 164, 166–70, 173–78, 185, 199–200, 216, 236, 256n8

Marco Motta is SNF Assistant Professor of Anthropology at the Institute of Social Sciences, University of Lausanne. He is coeditor of *Living with Concepts: Anthropology in the Grip of Reality* (2021).

THINKING FROM ELSEWHERE

Robert Desjarlais, *The Blind Man: A Phantasmography*

Sarah Pinto, *The Doctor and Mrs. A.: Ethics and Counter-Ethics in an Indian Dream Analysis*

Veena Das, *Textures of the Ordinary: Doing Anthropology after Wittgenstein*

Clara Han, *Seeing Like a Child: Inheriting the Korean War*

Vaibhav Saria, *Hijras, Lovers, Brothers: Surviving Sex and Poverty in Rural India*

Richard Rechtman, *Living in Death: Genocide and Its Functionaries.* Translated by Lindsay Turner, Foreword by Veena Das

Jérôme Tournadre, *The Politics of the Near: On the Edges of Protest in South Africa.* Translated by Andrew Brown

Cheryl Mattingly and Lone Grøn, *Imagistic Care: Growing Old in a Precarious World*

Heonik Kwon and Jun Hwan Park, *Spirit Power: Politics and Religion in Korea's American Century*

Mayur R. Suresh, *Terror Trials: Life and Law in Delhi's Courts*

Thomas Cousins, *The Work of Repair: Capacity after Colonialism in the Timber Plantations of South Africa*

Hélène Dumas, *Beyond Despair: The Rwanda Genocide against the Tutsi through the Eyes of Children.* Translated by Catherine Porter. Foreword by Louisa Lombard

Elizabeth Anne Davis, *The Time of the Cannibals: On Conspiracy Theory and Context*

Basit Kareem Iqbal, *The Dread Heights: Tribulation and Refuge after the Syrian Revolution*

Marco Motta, *Life in the Cracks: Law, Violence, and Resistance in Haiti*

www.ingramcontent.com/pod-product-compliance
Lightning Source LLC
Chambersburg PA
CBHW031140020426
42333CB00013B/459